Pittsburgh Series in Social and Labor History

The Andrew Carnegie Reader

Edited and with an Introduction by
Joseph Frazier Wall

University of Pittsburgh Press
Pittsburgh and London

Published by the University of Pittsburgh Press, Pittsburgh, Pa., 15260
Copyright © 1992, University of Pittsburgh Press

All rights reserved
Eurospan, London

Library of Congress Cataloging-in-Publication Data

Carnegie, Andrew, 1835–1919.
    The Andrew Carnegie reader / edited with an introduction by Joseph Frazier Wall.
    p.   cm.
    ISBN 0-8229-3700-X. — ISBN 0-8229-5464-8 (pbk.)
    1. Carnegie, Andrew, 1835–1919.   2. United States—Biography.   3. Philanthropists—United States—Biography.   4. Industrialists—United States—Biography.   5. Steel industry and trade—United States—History.   I. Wall, Joseph Frazier.   II. Title.
CT275.C3A25   1992
338.7'672'092—dc20
[B]
                                                                  91-32718
                                                                    CIP

A CIP catalogue record for this book is available
from the British Library.

Frontispiece photo: Andrew Carnegie on the terrace at Skibo.
Courtesy of Carnegie Library, Pittsburgh.

For my three children
APRIL ANE, JOEL, AND JULIA
who have grown up with Andrew Carnegie
as the family icon

Contents

Introduction / ix

I. Prelude: The Making of the "Self-Made Man" / 1
   1. Parents and Childhood / 3
   2. Dunfermline and America / 16
   3. Letters to George "Dod" Lauder / 25

II. Carnegie at Work, Making Money / 29
   4. How I Served My Apprenticeship / 31
   5. Memorandum of 1868 / 40
   6. The Road to Business Success / 42
   7. The Age of Steel / 51
   8. My Experience with Railway Rates and Rebates / 79
   9. An Employer's View of the Labor Question / 91
   10. Results of the Labor Struggle / 102
   11. The Homestead Strike / 114

III. Carnegie at Work, Giving Away Money / 125
   12. The Gospel of Wealth According to St. Andrew / 129
   13. Carnegie's Report on Spreading the Gospel / 155

IV. Carnegie at Work, Playing / 167
   14. On Books, Theater, Music, and Keeping the Sabbath / 169
   15. Round the World / 175

16. Our Coaching Trip / *188*
17. Letters from Skibo / *202*

v. Carnegie, the Pundit / *205*
18. Democracy: "The Republic" / *207*
19. Capitalism: "The Bugaboo of Trusts" / *221*
20. Populism: "The ABC of Money" / *232*
21. Progressivism: Trusts, the Bane of America / *259*
22. Socialism: "Individualism versus Socialism" / *262*
23. Race Relations: "The Negro in America" / *272*
24. Imperialism: "Distant Possessions: The Parting of the Ways" / *294*
25. Pacifism: "'Honor' and International Arbitration" / *305*

vi. Coda: The Undoing of the Self-Made Pacifist / *317*
26. Meeting the German Emperor / *321*

Introduction

Andrew Carnegie is unique among American entrepreneurs, but not for those accomplishments usually assigned as the reasons for preeminence in the business world. It was not for the dominant position he achieved in a single industry, nor for the great wealth he personally amassed, nor even for the munificence of his philanthropy, spectacular as was his success in all of these areas. It can be cogently argued that such titans as John D. Rockefeller, Henry Ford, Andrew Mellon, and J. P. Morgan were at least his peers in these fields. Andrew Carnegie's claim to uniqueness within the business community is based upon certain roles he energetically assumed for himself and to which his fellow capitalists did not even aspire. In an age when most businessmen scrupulously subscribed to the motto that Silence is Golden, Carnegie was the voluble, self-appointed spokesman for capitalism and democracy. The norm for the businessman was the tight-mouthed railroad magnate Collis P. Huntington, who upon arriving in his office one morning and being asked by his secretary, "How are you, Mr. Huntington?" is reputed to have replied, "Wouldn't you like to know!" Carnegie was always ready to tell his secretary and everybody else, for that matter, not only how he was, but how his business was—and how the world in general was, as well.

Carnegie's volubility and candor on such matters as trusts and labor unions were often a cause for embarrassment and dismay among his partners, but none of them dared to tell him bluntly to keep quiet. Only his cousin George Lauder dared to reprimand Carnegie, and he only through a parable. He told Carnegie the story of a man who was killed by a streetcar. Having no identification on him, he was placed on public view in an undertaker's parlor in the hope that someone would claim the body. A short time later a wealthy woman drove up in her carriage, identified the corpse as her husband, and then ordered the most expensive funeral the establishment offered. As she was leaving, the elated undertaker, in showing her to the door, inadvertently bumped the slab upon which the corpse was displayed. The jolt knocked the dead man's mouth open, revealing a handsome gold tooth. The lady took another look at the corpse and at once canceled the order. She said that she was sorry but she must have made a mistake. Her missing husband had no such gold tooth. As she went out the door, the disappointed undertaker turned angrily on the corpse and cried, "What kind of idiot are you anyway? If you'd only known enough to keep your damned mouth shut—!" Carnegie got the point of his cousin's story and laughed heartily, but neither then nor ever could he keep his mouth shut.

If Carnegie had a busy tongue, he had an equally facile pen. Just as Jefferson, Lincoln, and Wilson are probably the only American presidents who could have achieved fame outside of politics as writers, so most certainly Carnegie is the only American entrepreneur who could have won distinction as an author even if he had never seen a steel mill. At the age of seventeen, Carnegie wrote his first letter-to-the-editor, protesting the policy of providing free library privileges to Colonel James Anderson's Mechanics Library in Allegheny only to bound apprentices, and then had the immense satisfaction of seeing his letter printed in the *Pittsburgh Dispatch*. A journalistic ambition was born which Carnegie would spend the remainder of his life attempting to satisfy.

In the memorandum he wrote to himself in 1868 (see #5), Carnegie promised that he would quit business at age thirty-five in order to "get a thorough education . . . pay especial attention to speaking in public" and then settle "in London & purchase a controlling interest in some newspaper or live review . . . , taking a part in public matters especially those connected with education & improvement of the poorer classes." Because Carnegie did not quit business at age thirty-five and continued "to make more money in the shortest time," it has been generally assumed by historians that he had totally disregarded his self-addressed adjuration. It is more remarkable, however, how much of this promise he did fulfill over the next four decades. Beginning with his first article, "As Others See Us," written in 1882 at the request of John Morley, editor of the prestigious British journal, *Fortnightly Review*, Carnegie produced a bibliography of his own published writings so impressive that it might well be coveted by most university professors. From 1882 until 1916, he wrote sixty-three articles, eight books, and had ten of his major public addresses published in pamphlet form—a remarkable record for someone who had had only four years of formal education.

Almost all of his articles appeared in the most intellectually respectable magazines produced for the general reading public in both Britain and America. Carnegie seldom if ever knew the pain of receiving a rejection slip. Editors were eager for his manuscripts, and Carnegie was in the fortunate position of a writer able to select his own forum. He was generous in dispensing the products of his pen to a broad spectrum of periodicals ranging from the *Youth's Companion* and the *Woman's Home Companion* to the more elitist *Nineteenth Century, Fortnightly Review, Review of Reviews, Century, Forum,* and *Contemporary Review*. His favorite publication, however, was the *North American Review*. One-third of his total production of magazine articles, including four of his most celebrated, "Wealth, Parts I and II," "The Bugaboo of Trusts," "The A B C of Money," and "Distant Possessions," first appeared in that journal. His books carried equally impressive publication imprints: Charles Scribner's Sons; Century; Doubleday, Page; and Houghton Mifflin.

For a brief time in the mid 1880s, he more than fulfilled his memorandum promise to "purchase a controlling interest in some newspaper" by establishing a newspaper syndicate in England that had a "controlling interest" in seven daily and ten weekly newspapers, covering a territory that extended from Portsmouth on the southern coast to Sunderland and Newcastle in the northeast. All of these papers carried the imprimatur of the Carnegie brand of radical Liberalism with the immediate objective of passing the Reform Act of 1884, and the ultimate goal of achieving the Republic of Great Britain. Surprisingly enough, however, there is no evidence that Carnegie himself wrote any of the stirring editorials calling for the abolition of the British monarchy, the disestablishment of the Church of England, and the popular election of the members of the upper chamber of Parliament to replace the hereditary British lords. He left the actual writing to the editors he had carefully selected for each journal. Editorial anonymity had no particular appeal for Carnegie. He preferred the article and book that bore his name.

So prodigious was Carnegie's literary output that inevitably the question of the true authorship of his published works has been raised. Was it possible that anyone so busily engaged as he, first in making money and later in dispensing that wealth in philanthropic projects, could possibly have found the time to write all the books and articles attributed to him? This is a question that has bothered twentieth-century historians more than it did Carnegie's contemporaries, who were more willing to accept his authorship as genuine. Ghost-writers did not haunt the literary scene in the nineteenth century with as great a frequency as they do at present. In those more simple times, even American presidents were expected to, and frequently did, write their own speeches. Even so, there must have been considerable surprise at the volume of Carnegie's writings, if not an outright suspicion that he had contributed little more than his name to someone else's prose. The only writing business leaders were expected to engage in was that correspondence essential to their mundane affairs, dictated to a secretary in a style so devoid of color as to have about as much literary grace as a bill of lading. But here was America's Steel King, year after year, turning out books of impressive size and articles with impressive frequency.

Some present-day historians, including Fritz Redlich, have claimed to have found the anonymous ghost-writer in the person of James H. Bridge, Carnegie's secretary during the 1880s. Bridge did indeed serve as Carnegie's research assistant in compiling data for *Triumphant Democracy*, and Carnegie in the preface to the book wrote that "I acknowledge with great pleasure the almost indispensable aid received in the preparation of this work from my clever secretary, Mr. Bridge." The statistical data was provided by Bridge, but the book is unmistakably Carnegie's own work. For anyone who has ever read any of Carnegie's personal correspondence to friends and business associates there can be no doubt that the same style, the same rhetoric, often precisely the same metaphors pervade all his writings and provide an authentic signature to every page of prose that carries his name. A man as vain as Carnegie and as confident in his ability as a writer would have regarded the services of a ghost-writer with the same scorn as he would look upon resorting to a vanity press to publish his work. If further proof of authenticity is sought, one need only refer to the fragments of manuscripts, handwritten in pencil by Carnegie, still extant in the depositories of the Carnegie papers in Dunfermline, Scotland, and in Washington, D.C.

Carnegie had no difficulty in finding a publisher for the simple reason that his writings sold well. His popularity as a writer can be attributed in great part to style. He wrote in simple, declaratory sentences that caught and held the reader's attention. His early training as a telegraph operator to be chary of words and punctuation marks clearly influenced his style as a writer. There is a staccato abruptness to his writing that has a finger-snapping effect upon the reader. "Bang! click! the desk closes, the key turns . . . ; I'm off for a holiday!" So begin both of his travel books, and the reader is immediately ready to join him. "The old nations of the earth creep on at a snail's pace; the Republic thunders past with the rush of the express," the opening line of *Triumphant Democracy*, has as much punch as "A spectre is haunting Europe—the spectre of Communism," the first sentence of the *Communist Manifesto*.

Introduction   xiii

Not a profound thinker himself, Carnegie never became mired in a profundity so deep as to hinder the clear expression of his views. He had a remarkable talent for taking a subject as complicated as bimetallism and making it appear as simple and as easily understood as an A B C primer. Carnegie was ready to pronounce judgment on any subject no matter how complex it might be, and whatever he may have lost in the depth of respect from the expert he more than gained in the breadth of readership from the general public.

Carnegie was read because of the controversy most of his articles and even his travel books provoked. He seldom pulled his punches. He wrote bluntly what he thought, and whether he was loved or hated for his attacks on Bryan's Populism or his strictures against Protestant missionaries in China, he was nevertheless read by supporters and critics alike. He could purr sweet words of honey with shameless sycophancy when it suited his purpose, but he could also recklessly slash with naked knife. Often the same person, Bryan or Theodore Roosevelt, would in a relatively short period of time receive both treatments.

Carnegie was a Carlylean in subscribing to the Great Man theory of history. He was always looking for and always finding a new Hero of the People. Few of his heroes, however, remained heroes for long. Blaine, Harrison, McKinley, Roosevelt, Taft, and Kaiser Wilhelm all failed him and were knocked off the pedestal where he had placed them. Only Lincoln, Booker T. Washington, William Gladstone, and interestingly, Grover Cleveland (whom Carnegie had at first considered so uncouth as to be unmentionable) remained safely ensconced as Immortals in Carnegie's very exclusive Hall of Fame.

Carnegie's effectiveness as a writer can also be attributed to his personalizing even the most abstract concepts, of making specific the broadest of generalizations. He gave immediate reality to such ideals as peace, democracy, the rights of labor, and conflict resolution by anecdotal illustrations drawn from his personal experiences. He was a master of the pungent aphorism: "Take what the gods offer"; "Put all your eggs in one basket, and then watch that basket"; "Pioneering don't pay"; "Don't do in public what should be done behind closed doors—that's what doors are for"; "Thou shalt not take thy neighbor's job"; "Don't shoot the millionaire, he is the bee that makes the honey"; "The man who dies rich, dies disgraced"; "Things grow ever better. Onward and upward forever." His adages passed into common parlance and remained fresh long after most of his moralizing had been forgotten.

There is a great deal of sentimentality in Carnegie's writings. In an age of macho taciturnity, Carnegie flaunted his emotions proudly, never ashamed to weep openly, never hesitant to laugh uproariously. The hearts-and-flowers sentiment he displayed in expressing his love for his mother, his flag, and his native land frequently trembled on the brink but fortunately seldom fell into pure bathos.

It was more than style or content, however, that gave Carnegie's writings their great appeal. It was the spirit of optimism coloring all his writings that the general public found particularly attractive. Carnegie never wanted for targets at which to aim his literary arrows, never lacked leaders to criticize, but no situation was ever so dire that he could not find some illuminating hope, no problem so severe that he did not see a solution. Optimism is part of the American credo, and Carnegie was that credo's unrelenting, untiring booster. He told Americans what they wanted to hear. They were a great people, their opportunities were unlimited, and perfection, if not just around the corner, was most certainly just up the hill they were all climbing. As Ronald Reagan would to his profit discover a century later, the public above anything else wants to be massaged by words into feeling good, no matter how bad things may really be. Both Carnegie and Reagan were the master masseurs of their respective times. One got lots of readers, the other got lots of votes.

Carnegie could never decide which gave him the greater satisfaction—seeing his words in print or delivering his words aloud from the public platform. There was a great comfort in knowing that books endure, but there was a more immediate gratification in actually hearing the applause of an audience. He frequently managed to have it both ways by publishing in pamphlet form his major addresses.

Carnegie was not a silver-tongued orator. His voice was too high-pitched to be pleasant to the ear, his speech too heavily laded with Scottish dialect to be easily comprehended by his American audiences, too Americanized in idiom to be acceptable to his Scottish auditors. But what Carnegie lacked in mellifluous tone he more than compensated for in body language. His style of delivery was very similar to that of his one-time hero, Theodore Roosevelt. Both men had enough of the actor's vanity to make them highly dramatic figures on the public platform. Both used the same vigorous chopping motions of their arms to give emphasis to their words. Because of his short stature and his desire to get close to his audience, Carnegie would frequently step away from the lectern and, rising on tiptoes, would pump his short arms so vigorously that to his audience he must have looked like a bantam rooster ready to crow. Crow he did. The audience loved it, and he loved the audience. There were frequent interruptions by cheers and laughter, and in those moments Carnegie was sure that here was the best possible conveyance for spreading the word.

Most of Carnegie's articles and formal speeches have been reprinted in various collections, most comprehensively in the ten-volume series, *The Books of Andrew Carnegie*, edited by Burton J. Hendrick (Garden City: Doubleday, Doran & Co., 1933). The anthology presented here, however, is the first to bring together in a single volume a representative selection of Carnegie's writings. Included in this work are some of the most important and controversial of Carnegie's articles. Here also are reprinted two of his major lectures, "The Negro in America" and "'Honor' and International Arbitration."

The articles and public addresses chosen for inclusion are reprinted in their entirety. It has been necessary, of course, to give only a selection of chapters and passages from the four books included in this anthology, but the pages chosen are illustrative in both style and content of the complete texts. No anthology of Carnegie's writings would be complete without a sampling of his personal letters, for he was a tireless letter writer to his family, his business associates, and to a host of friends on two continents.

The material in this collection covers a time period of over sixty years, from his letters to his cousin George Lauder, written in 1853, until the final chapter of his autobiography completed in 1914 just as the Great War he had so desperately tried to prevent tore the world apart. Although many of the selections were written a century or more ago, they have a remarkable freshness and pertinence to our own age. Carnegie's hopes for world peace, his views on "the Labor Question," his concern for better race relations in America, his sensitivity to and appreciation of a multicultural world are apparently timeless in their continuing applicability to human society.

The writings are arranged topically in six sections, covering the major facets of his long and energetic life. Several chapters from his autobiography provide some chronological order to the organization of these selected writings. Footnotes, with the exception of those initialed JFW, are reprinted from the original editions.

A complete bibliography of Carnegie's writings can be found in Burton J. Hendrick's *The Life of Andrew Carnegie* (Garden City: Doubleday, Doran, 1932), vol. 2, pp. 389–92. Readers may also wish to consult, in addition to Hendrick's two-volume biography of Carnegie, the following works: Harold C. Livesay, *Andrew Carnegie and the Rise of Big Business* (Boston: Little, Brown, 1975), a short but excellent evaluation of Carnegie's business career; George Swetnam, *Andrew Carnegie*, Twayne's United States Authors Series (Boston: G. K. Hall & Co., 1980), a very useful and comprehensive study of Carnegie as writer and orator; and Joseph Frazier Wall, *Andrew Carnegie* (1970; rpt. Pittsburgh: University of Pittsburgh Press, 1989), a full biography dealing with all aspects of Carnegie's life.

Grinnell, Iowa   J. F. W.
4 April 1991

Part I

Prelude: The Making of the "Self-Made Man"

Although Andrew Carnegie frequently made reference to his own experiences in his many writings and speeches on current issues, it was not until after he had retired from business in 1901 that he gave serious attention to the writing of a formal autobiography. Beginning in 1904, the Carnegie family at the insistence of Louise Carnegie had begun the practice of going for three weeks into retreat from the hectic social life at their castle in Scotland to a small cottage high up on the moors of their estate, first at Auchindinagh and later at Aultnagar. It was here that Carnegie did most of the writing of his autobiography as well as finishing the writing of a biography of James Watt.

On the flyleaf of the manuscript of his autobiography, which was not completed until 1914, Carnegie wrote: "It is probable that material for a small volume might be collected from these memoirs which the public would care to read.... Much I have written from time to time may, I think, wisely be omitted. Whoever arranges these notes should be careful not to burden the public with too much."

The man who did the "arranging" of Carnegie's memoirs was Professor John C. Van Dyke of Rutgers University, the brother of the poet Henry Van Dyke and a close friend of the Carnegie family. It was to him that Mrs. Carnegie gave the manuscript for editing and publishing in 1920, one year after Carnegie's death.

What the critic George William Curtis had said of Carnegie's magnum opus, Triumphant Democracy – "It's all sunshine, sunshine, sunshine. Where are the shadows?" – could with equal pertinency be said of Carnegie's autobiography. There are few shadows here. It is the self-portrait of a self-satisfied man, with much of the turmoil of his life and all the aggressiveness that might have been included carefully expunged.

The autobiography follows a rough chronological order. The first two chapters given below deal with Carnegie's ancestry, his birth and early childhood in the ancient town of Dunfermline across the Firth of Forth from Edinburgh, and the family's emigration to the United States in 1848 to establish a home in Allegheny, Pennsylvania.

Carnegie in these introductory chapters makes explicit his relationship with his parents, especially his extraordinary devotion to his mother, the strong-willed and ambitious Margaret Morrison Carnegie. The father remains a somewhat shadowy figure, respected by his son for his gentleness and for his dedication to the high ideals of social equality and justice as expressed by the Scottish Chartists; but the dominating figure, the leader and mover of the family, is quite clearly Carnegie's mother.

I
Parents and Childhood

Chapter 1 of the Autobiography of Andrew Carnegie, *ed. John Van Dyke (Boston: Houghton Mifflin, 1920).*

If the story of any man's life, truly told, must be interesting, as some sage avers, those of my relatives and immediate friends who have insisted upon having an account of mine may not be unduly disappointed with this result. I may console myself with the assurance that such a story must interest at least a certain number of people who have known me, and that knowledge will encourage me to proceed.

A book of this kind, written years ago by my friend, Judge Mellon, of Pittsburgh, gave me so much pleasure that I am inclined to agree with the wise one whose opinion I have given before; for, certainly, the story which the Judge told has proved a source of infinite satisfaction to his friends, and must continue to influence succeeding generations of his family to live life well. And not only this; to some beyond his immediate circle it holds rank with their favorite authors. The book contains one essential feature of value—it reveals the man. It was written without any intention of attracting public notice, being designed only for his family. In like manner I intend to tell my story, not as one posturing before the public, but as in the midst of my own people and friends, tried and true, to whom I can speak with the utmost freedom, feeling that even trifling incidents may not be wholly destitute of interest for them.

To begin, then, I was born in Dunfermline, in the attic of the small one-story house, corner of Moodie Street and Priory Lane, on the 25th of November, 1835, and, as the saying is, "of poor but honest parents, of good kith and kin." Dunfermline had long been noted as the center of the damask trade in Scotland.[1]

---

[1]. The eighteenth-century Carnegies lived at the picturesque hamlet of Patiemuir, two miles south of Dunfermline. The growing importance of the linen industry in Dunfermline finally led the Carnegies to move to that town.

My father, William Carnegie, was a damask weaver, the son of Andrew Carnegie after whom I was named.

My Grandfather Carnegie was well known throughout the district for his wit and humor, his genial nature and irrepressible spirits. He was head of the lively ones of his day, and known far and near as the chief of their joyous club—"Patiemuir College." Upon my return to Dunfermline, after an absence of fourteen years, I remember being approached by an old man who had been told that I was the grandson of the "Professor," my grandfather's title among his cronies. He was the very picture of palsied eld;

> His nose and chin they threatened ither.

As he tottered across the room toward me and laid his trembling hand upon my head he said: "And ye are the grandson o' Andra Carnegie! Eh, mon, I ha'e seen the day when your grandfaither and I could ha'e hallooed ony reasonable man oot o' his jidgment."

Several other old people of Dunfermline told me stories of my grandfather. Here is one of them:

One Hogmanay night[2] an old wifey, quite a character in the village, being surprised by a disguised face suddenly thrust in at the window, looked up and after a moment's pause exclaimed, "Oh, it's jist that daft callant Andra Carnegie." She was right; my grandfather at seventy-five was out frightening his old lady friends, disguised like other frolicking youngsters.

I think my optimistic nature, my ability to shed trouble and to laugh through life, making "all my ducks swans," as friends say I do, must have been inherited from this delightful old masquerading grandfather whose name I am proud to bear.[3] A sunny disposition is worth more than fortune. Young people should know that it can be cultivated; that the mind like the body can be moved from the shade into sunshine. Let us move it then. Laugh trouble away if possible, and one usually can if he be anything of a philosopher, provided that self-reproach comes not from his own wrongdoing. That always remains. There is no washing out of these "damnèd spots." The judge within sits in the su-

---

2. The 31st of December.

3. "There is no sign that Andrew, though he prospered in his wooing, was specially successful in acquisition of worldly gear. Otherwise, however, he became an outstanding character not only in the village, but in the adjoining the city and district. A 'brainy' man who read and thought for himself he became associated with the radical weavers of Dunfermline, who in Patiemuir formed a meeting-place which they named a college (Andrew was the 'Professor' of it)." (*Andrew Carnegie: His Dunfermline Ties and Benefactions*, by J. B. Mackie, F. J. I.)

preme court and can never be cheated. Hence the grand rule of life which Burns gives: Thine own reproach alone do fear.

This motto adopted early in life has been more to me than all the sermons I ever heard, and I have heard not a few, although I may admit resemblance to my old friend Baillie Walker in my mature years. He was asked by his doctor about his sleep and replied that it was far from satisfactory, he was very wakeful, adding with a twinkle in his eye: "But I get a bit fine doze i' the kirk noo and then."

On my mother's side the grandfather was even more marked, for my grandfather Thomas Morrison was a friend of William Cobbett, a contributor to his "Register," and in constant correspondence with him. Even as I write, in Dunfermline old men who knew Grandfather Morrison speak of him as one of the finest orators and ablest men they have known. He was publisher of "The Precursor," a small edition it might be said of Cobbett's "Register," and thought to have been the first radical paper in Scotland. I have read some of his writings, and in view of the importance now given to technical education, I think the most remarkable of them is a pamphlet which he published seventy-odd years ago entitled "Head-ication versus Hand-ication." It insists upon the importance of the latter in a manner that would reflect credit upon the strongest advocate of technical education to-day. It ends with these words, "I thank God that in my youth I learned to make and mend shoes." Cobbett published it in the "Register" in 1833, remarking editorially, "One of the most valuable communications ever published in the 'Register' upon the subject, is that of our esteemed friend and correspondent in Scotland, Thomas Morrison, which appears in this issue." So it seems I come by my scribbling propensities by inheritance—from both sides, for the Carnegies were also readers and thinkers.

My Grandfather Morrison was a born orator, a keen politician, and the head of the advanced wing of the radical party in the district—a position which his son, my Uncle Bailie Morrison, occupied as his successor. More than one well-known Scotsman in America has called upon me, to shake hands with "the grandson of Thomas Morrison." Mr. Farmer, president of the Cleveland and Pittsburgh Railroad Company, once said to me, "I owe all that I have of learning and culture to the influence of your grandfather"; and Ebenezer Henderson, author of the remarkable history of Dunfermline, stated that he largely owed his advancement in life to the fortunate fact that while a boy he entered my grandfather's service.

I have not passed so far through life without receiving some compliments, but I think nothing of a complimentary character has ever pleased me so much as this from a writer in a Glasgow newspaper, who had been a listener to a speech on Home Rule in America which I delivered in Saint Andrew's Hall. The correspondent wrote that much was then being said in Scotland with regard to myself and family and especially my grandfather Thomas Morrison, and he went on to say, "Judge my surprise when I found in the grandson on the platform, in manner, gesture and appearance, a perfect *facsimile* of the Thomas Morrison of old."

My surprising likeness to my grandfather, whom I do not remember to have ever seen, cannot be doubted, because I remember well upon my first return to Dunfermline in my twenty-seventh year, while sitting upon a sofa with my Uncle Bailie Morrison, that his big black eyes filled with tears. He could not speak and rushed out of the room overcome. Returning after a time he explained that something in me now and then flashed before him his father, who would instantly vanish but come back at intervals. Some gesture it was, but what precisely he could not make out. My mother continually noticed in me some of my grandfather's peculiarities. The doctrine of inherited tendencies is proved every day and hour, but how subtle is the law which transmits gesture, something as it were beyond the material body. I was deeply impressed.

My Grandfather Morrison married Miss Hodge, of Edinburgh, a lady in education, manners, and position, who died while the family was still young. At this time he was in good circumstances, a leather merchant conducting the tanning business in Dunfermline; but the peace after the Battle of Waterloo involved him in ruin, as it did thousands; so that while my Uncle Bailie, the eldest son, had been brought up in what might be termed luxury, for he had a pony to ride, the younger members of the family encountered other and harder days.

The second daughter, Margaret, was my mother, about whom I cannot trust myself to speak at length. She inherited from her mother the dignity, refinement, and air of the cultivated lady. Perhaps some day I may be able to tell the world something of this heroine, but I doubt it. I feel her to be sacred to myself and not for others to know. None could ever really know her—I alone did that. After my father's early death she was all my own. The dedication of my first book[4] tells the story. It was: "To my favorite Heroine My Mother."

---

4. *An American Four-in-Hand in Great Britain* (New York, 1888).

Fortunate in my ancestors I was supremely so in my birthplace. Where one is born is very important, for different surroundings and traditions appeal to and stimulate different latent tendencies in the child. Ruskin truly observes that every bright boy in Edinburgh is influenced by the sight of the Castle. So is the child of Dunfermline, by its noble Abbey, the Westminster of Scotland, founded early in the eleventh century (1070) by Malcolm Canmore and his Queen Margaret, Scotland's patron saint. The ruins of the great monastery and of the Palace where kings were born still stand, and there, too, is Pittencrieff Glen, embracing Queen Margaret's shrine and the ruins of King Malcolm's Tower, with which the old ballad of "Sir Patrick Spens" begins:

> The King sits in Dunfermline *tower*,[5]
> Drinking the bluid red wine.

The tomb of The Bruce is in the center of the Abbey, Saint Margaret's tomb is near, and many of the "royal folk" lie sleeping close around. Fortunate, indeed, the child who first sees the light in that romantic town, which occupies high ground three miles north of the Firth of Forth, overlooking the sea, with Edinburgh in sight to the south, and to the north the peaks of the Ochils clearly in view. All is still redolent of the mighty past when Dunfermline was both nationally and religiously the capital of Scotland.

The child privileged to develop amid such surroundings absorbs poetry and romance with the air he breathes, assimilates history and tradition as he gazes around. These become to him his real world in childhood—the ideal is the ever-present real. The actual has yet to come when, later in life, he is launched into the workaday world of stern reality. Even then, and till his last day, the early impressions remain, sometimes for short seasons disappearing perchance, but only apparently driven away or suppressed. They are always rising and coming again to the front to exert their influence, to elevate his thought and color his life. No bright child of Dunfermline can escape the influence of the Abbey, Palace, and Glen. These touch him and set fire to the latent spark within, making him something different and beyond what, less happily born, he would have become. Under these inspiring conditions my parents had also been born, and hence came, I doubt not, the potency of the romantic and poetic strain which pervaded both.

As my father succeeded in the weaving business we removed from Moodie

---

5. *The Percy Reliques* and *The Oxford Book of Ballads* give "town" instead of "tower"; but Mr. Carnegie insisted that it should be "tower."

Street to a much more commodious house in Reid's Park. My father's four or five looms occupied the lower story; we resided in the upper, which was reached, after a fashion common in the older Scottish houses, by outside stairs from the pavement. It is here that my earliest recollections begin, and, strangely enough, the first trace of memory takes me back to a day when I saw a small map of America. It was upon rollers and about two feet square. Upon this my father, mother, Uncle William, and Aunt Aitken were looking for Pittsburgh and pointing out Lake Erie and Niagara. Soon after my uncle and Aunt Aitken sailed for the land of promise.

At this time I remember my cousin-brother, George Lauder ("Dod"), and myself were deeply impressed with the great danger overhanging us because a lawless flag was secreted in the garret. It had been painted to be carried, and I believe was carried by my father, or uncle, or some other good radical of our family, in a procession during the Corn Law agitation. There had been riots in the town and a troop of cavalry was quartered in the Guildhall. My grandfathers and uncles on both sides, and my father, had been foremost in addressing meetings, and the whole family circle was in a ferment.

I remember as if it were yesterday being awakened during the night by a tap at the back window by men who had come to inform my parents that my uncle, Bailie Morrison, had been thrown into jail because he had dared to hold a meeting which had been forbidden. The sheriff with the aid of the soldiers had arrested him a few miles from the town where the meeting had been held, and brought him into the town during the night, followed by an immense throng of people.[6]

Serious trouble was feared, for the populace threatened to rescue him, and, as we learned afterwards, he had been induced by the provost of the town to step forward to a window overlooking the High Street and beg the people to retire. This he did, saying: "If there be a friend of the good cause here tonight, let him fold his arms." They did so. And then, after a pause, he said, "Now depart in peace!"[7] My uncle, like all our family, was a moral-force man

---

6. At the opening of the Lauder Technical School in October, 1880, nearly half a century after the disquieting scenes of 1842, Mr. Carnegie thus recalled the shock which was given to his boy mind: "One of my earliest recollections is that of being wakened in the darkness to be told that my Uncle Morrison was in jail. Well, it is one of the proudest boasts I can make to-day to be able to say that I had an uncle who was in jail. But, ladies and gentlemen, my uncle went to jail to vindicate the rights of public assembly." (Mackie.)

7. "The Crown agents wisely let the proceedings lapse.... Mr. Morrison was given a gratifying assurance of the appreciation of his fellow citizens by his election to the Council and his elevation to the Magisterial Bench, followed shortly after by his appointment to the office of Burgh Chamberlain.

and strong for obedience to law, but radical to the core and an intense admirer of the American Republic.

One may imagine when all this was going on in public how bitter were the words that passed from one to the other in private. The denunciations of monarchical and aristocratic government, of privilege in all its forms, the grandeur of the republican system, the superiority of America, a land peopled by our own race, a home for freemen in which every citizen's privilege was every man's right—these were the exciting themes upon which I was nurtured. As a child I could have slain king, duke, or lord, and considered their deaths a service to the state and hence an heroic act.

Such is the influence of childhood's earliest associations that it was long before I could trust myself to speak respectfully of any privileged class or person who had not distinguished himself in some good way and therefore earned the right to public respect. There was still the sneer behind for mere pedigree—"he is nothing, has done nothing, only an accident, a fraud strutting in borrowed plumes; all he has to his account is the accident of birth; the most fruitful part of his family, as with the potato, lies underground." I wondered that intelligent men could live where another human being was born to a privilege which was not also their birthright. I was never tired of quoting the only words which gave proper vent to my indignation:

> There was a Brutus once that would have brooked
> Th' eternal devil to keep his state in Rome
> As easily as a king.

But then kings were kings, not mere shadows. All this was inherited, of course. I only echoed what I heard at home.

Dunfermline has long been renowned as perhaps the most radical town in the Kingdom, although I know Paisley has claims. This is all the more creditable to the cause of radicalism because in the days of which I speak the population of Dunfermline was in large part composed of men who were small manufacturers, each owning his own loom or looms. They were not tied down to regular hours, their labors being piece work. They got webs from the larger manufacturers and the weaving was done at home.

These were times of intense political excitement, and there was frequently

---

The patriotic reformer whom the criminal authorities endeavored to convict as a law-breaker became by the choice of his fellow citizens a Magistrate, and was further given a certificate for trustworthiness and integrity." (Mackie.)

seen throughout the entire town, for a short time after the midday meal, small groups of men with their aprons girt about them discussing affairs of state. The names of Hume, Cobden, and Bright were upon every one's tongue. I was often attracted, small as I was, to these circles and was an earnest listener to the conversation, which was wholly one-sided. The generally accepted conclusion was that there must be a change. Clubs were formed among the townsfolk, and the London newspapers were subscribed for. The leading editorials were read every evening to the people, strangely enough, from one of the pulpits of the town. My uncle, Bailie Morrison, was often the reader, and, as the articles were commented upon by him and others after being read, the meetings were quite exciting.

These political meetings were of frequent occurrence, and, as might be expected, I was as deeply interested as any of the family and attended many. One of my uncles or my father was generally to be heard. I remember one evening my father addressed a large outdoor meeting in the Pends. I had wedged my way in under the legs of the hearers, and at one cheer louder than all the rest I could not restrain my enthusiasm. Looking up to the man under whose legs I had found protection I informed him that was my father speaking. He lifted me on his shoulder and kept me there.

To another meeting I was taken by my father to hear John Bright, who spoke in favor of J. B. Smith as the Liberal candidate for the Stirling Burghs. I made the criticism at home that Mr. Bright did not speak correctly, as he said "men" when he meant "maan." He did not give the broad *a* we were accustomed to in Scotland. It is not to be wondered at that, nursed amid such surroundings, I developed into a violent young Republican whose motto was "death to privilege." At that time I did not know what privilege meant, but my father did.

One of my Uncle Lauder's best stories was about this same J. B. Smith, the friend of John Bright, who was standing for Parliament in Dunfermline. Uncle was a member of his Committee and all went well until it was proclaimed that Smith was a "Unitawrian." The district was placarded with the enquiry: Would you vote for a "Unitawrian"? It was serious. The Chairman of Smith's Committee in the village of Cairney Hill, a blacksmith, was reported as having declared he never would. Uncle drove over to remonstrate with him. They met in the village tavern over a gill:

"Man, I canna vote for a Unitawrian," said the Chairman.

"But," said my uncle, "Maitland [the opposing candidate] is a Trinitawrian."

"Damn; that's waur," was the response.

And the blacksmith voted right. Smith won by a small majority.

The change from hand-loom to steam-loom weaving was disastrous to our family. My father did not recognize the impending revolution, and was struggling under the old system. His looms sank greatly in value, and it became necessary for that power which never failed in any emergency—my mother—to step forward and endeavor to repair the family fortune. She opened a small shop in Moodie Street and contributed to the revenues which, though slender, nevertheless at that time sufficed to keep us in comfort and "respectable."

I remember that shortly after this I began to learn what poverty meant. Dreadful days came when my father took the last of his webs to the great manufacturer, and I saw my mother anxiously awaiting his return to know whether a new web was to be obtained or that a period of idleness was upon us. It was burnt into my heart then that my father, though neither "abject, mean, nor vile," as Burns has it, had nevertheless to

> Beg a brother of the earth
> To give him leave to toil.

And then and there came the resolve that I would cure that when I got to be a man. We were not, however, reduced to anything like poverty compared with many of our neighbors. I do not know to what lengths of privation my mother would not have gone that she might see her two boys wearing large white collars, and trimly dressed.

In an incautious moment my parents had promised that I should never be sent to school until I asked leave to go. This promise I afterward learned began to give them considerable uneasiness because as I grew up I showed no disposition to ask. The schoolmaster, Mr. Robert Martin, was applied to and induced to take some notice of me. He took me upon an excursion one day with some of my companions who attended school, and great relief was experienced by my parents when one day soon afterward I came and asked for permission to go to Mr. Martin's school.[8] I need not say the permission was duly granted. I had then entered upon my eighth year, which subsequent experience leads me to say is quite early enough for any child to begin attending school.

The school was a perfect delight to me, and if anything occurred which prevented my attendance I was unhappy. This happened every now and then

---

8. It was known as Rolland School.

because my morning duty was to bring water from the well at the head of Moodie Street. The supply was scanty and irregular. Sometimes it was not allowed to run until late in the morning and a score of old wives were sitting around, the turn of each having been previously secured through the night by placing a worthless can in the line. This, as might be expected, led to numerous contentions in which I would not be put down even by these venerable old dames. I earned the reputation of being "an awfu' laddie." In this way I probably developed the strain of argumentativeness, or perhaps combativeness, which has always remained with me.

In the performance of these duties I was often late for school, but the master, knowing the cause, forgave the lapses. In the same connection I may mention that I had often the shop errands to run after school, so that in looking back upon my life I have the satisfaction of feeling that I became useful to my parents even at the early age of ten. Soon after that the accounts of the various people who dealt with the shop were entrusted to my keeping so that I became acquainted, in a small way, with business affairs even in childhood.

One cause of misery there was, however, in my school experience. The boys nicknamed me "Martin's pet," and sometimes called out that dreadful epithet to me as I passed along the street. I did not know all that it meant, but it seemed to me a term of the utmost opprobrium, and I know that it kept me from responding as freely as I should otherwise have done to that excellent teacher, my only schoolmaster, to whom I owe a debt of gratitude which I regret I never had opportunity to do more than acknowledge before he died.

I may mention here a man whose influence over me cannot be overestimated, my Uncle Lauder, George Lauder's father.[9] My father was necessarily constantly at work in the loom shop and had little leisure to bestow upon me through the day. My uncle being a shopkeeper in the High Street was not thus tied down. Note the location, for this was among the shopkeeping aristocracy, and high and varied degrees of aristocracy there were even among shopkeepers in Dunfermline. Deeply affected by my Aunt Seaton's death, which occurred about the beginning of my school life, he found his chief solace in the companionship of his only son, George, and myself. He possessed an extraordinary gift of dealing with children and taught us many things. Among others I remember how he taught us British history by imagining each of the

---

9. The Lauder Technical College given by Mr. Carnegie to Dunfermline was named in honor of this uncle, George Lauder.

monarchs in a certain place upon the walls of the room performing the act for which he was well known. Thus for me King John sits to this day above the mantelpiece signing the Magna Charta, and Queen Victoria is on the back of the door with her children on her knee.

It may be taken for granted that the omission which, years after, I found in the Chapter House at Westminster Abbey was fully supplied in our list of monarchs. A slab in a small chapel at Westminster says that the body of Oliver Cromwell was removed from there. In the list of the monarchs which I learned at my uncle's knee the grand republican monarch appeared writing his message to the Pope of Rome, informing His Holiness that "if he did not cease persecuting the Protestants the thunder of Great Britain's cannon would be heard in the Vatican." It is needless to say that the estimate we formed of Cromwell was that he was worth them "a' thegither."

It was from my uncle I learned all that I know of the early history of Scotland—of Wallace and Bruce and Burns, of Blind Harry's history, of Scott, Ramsey, Tannahill, Hogg, and Fergusson. I can truly say in the words of Burns that there was then and there created in me a vein of Scottish prejudice (or patriotism) which will cease to exist only with life. Wallace, of course, was our hero. Everything heroic centered in him. Sad was the day when a wicked big boy at school told me that England was far larger than Scotland. I went to the uncle, who had the remedy.

"Not at all, Naig; if Scotland were rolled out flat as England, Scotland would be the larger, but would you have the Highlands rolled down?"

Oh, never! There was balm in Gilead for the wounded young patriot. Later the greater population in England was forced upon me; and again to the uncle I went.

"Yes, Naig, seven to one, but there were more than that odds against us at Bannockburn." And again there was joy in my heart—joy that there were more English men there since the glory was the greater.

This is something of a commentary upon the truth that war breeds war, that every battle sows the seeds of future battles, and that thus nations become traditional enemies. The experience of American boys is that of the Scotch. They grow up to read of Washington and Valley Forge, of Hessians hired to kill Americans, and they come to hate the very name of Englishman. Such was my experience with my American nephews, Scotland was all right, but England that had fought Scotland was the wicked partner. Not till they became men was the prejudice eradicated, and even yet some of it may linger.

Uncle Lauder has told me since that he often brought people into the room assuring them that he could make "Dod" (George Lauder) and me weep, laugh, or close our little fists ready to fight—in short, play upon all our moods through the influence of poetry and song. The betrayal of Wallace was his trump card which never failed to cause our little hearts to sob, a complete breakdown being the invariable result. Often as he told the story it never lost its hold. No doubt it received from time to time new embellishments. My uncle's stories never wanted "the hat and the stick" which Scott gave his. How wonderful is the influence of a hero upon children!

I spent many hours and evenings in the High Street with my uncle and "Dod," and thus began a lifelong brotherly alliance between the latter and myself. "Dod" and "Naig" we always were in the family. I could not say "George" in infancy and he could not get more than "Naig" out of Carnegie, and it has always been "Dod" and "Naig" with us. No other names would mean anything.

There were two roads by which to return from my uncle's house in the High Street to my home in Moodie Street at the foot of the town, one along the eerie churchyard of the Abbey among the dead, where there was no light; and the other along the lighted streets by way of the May Gate. When it became necessary for me to go home, my uncle, with a wicked pleasure, would ask which way I was going. Thinking what Wallace would do, I always replied I was going by the Abbey. I have the satisfaction of believing that never, not even upon one occasion, did I yield to the temptation to take the other turn and follow the lamps at the junction of the May Gate. I often passed along that churchyard and through the dark arch of the Abbey with my heart in my mouth. Trying to whistle and keep up my courage, I would plod through the darkness, falling back in all emergencies upon the thought of what Wallace would have done if he had met with any foe, natural or supernatural.

King Robert the Bruce never got justice from my cousin or myself in childhood. It was enough for us that he was a king while Wallace was the man of the people. Sir John Graham was our second. The intensity of a Scottish boy's patriotism, reared as I was, constitutes a real force in his life to the very end. If the source of my stock of that prime article—courage—were studied, I am sure the final analysis would find it founded upon Wallace, the hero of Scotland. It is a tower of strength for a boy to have a hero.

It gave me a pang to find when I reached America that there was any other country which pretended to have anything to be proud of. What was a country without Wallace, Bruce, and Burns? I find in the untraveled Scotsman of to-day something still of this feeling. It remains for maturer years and wider knowledge to tell us that every nation has its heroes, its romance, its traditions, and its achievements; and while the true Scotsman will not find reason in after years to lower the estimate he has formed of his own country and of its position even among the larger nations of the earth, he will find ample reason to raise his opinion of other nations because they all have much to be proud of—quite enough to stimulate their sons so to act their parts as not to disgrace the land that gave them birth.

It was years before I could feel that the new land could be anything but a temporary abode. My heart was in Scotland. I resembled Principal Peterson's little boy who, when in Canada, in reply to a question, said he liked Canada "very well for a visit, but he could never live so far away from the remains of Bruce and Wallace."

2
Dunfermline and America

Chapter 2 of the Autobiography of Andrew Carnegie, *ed. John Van Dyke (Boston: Houghton Mifflin, 1920).*

My good Uncle Lauder justly set great value upon recitation in education, and many were the pennies which Dod and I received for this. In our little frocks or shirts, our sleeves rolled up, paper helmets and blackened faces, with laths for swords, my cousin and myself were kept constantly reciting Norval and Glenalvon, Roderick Dhu and James FitzJames to our schoolmates and often to the older people.

I remember distinctly that in the celebrated dialogue between Norval and Glenalvon we had some qualms about repeating the phrase—"and false as *hell.*" At first we made a slight cough over the objectionable word which always created amusement among the spectators. It was a great day for us when my uncle persuaded us that we could say "hell" without swearing. I am afraid we practiced it very often. I always played the part of Glenalvon and made a great mouthful of the word. It had for me the wonderful fascination attributed to forbidden fruit. I can well understand the story of Marjory Fleming, who being cross one morning when Walter Scott called and asked how she was, answered:

"I am very cross this morning, Mr. Scott. I just want to say 'damn' [with a swing], but I winna."

Thereafter the expression of the one fearful word was a great point. Ministers could say "damnation" in the pulpit without sin, and so we, too, had full range on "hell" in recitation. Another passage made a deep impression. In the fight between Norval and Glenalvon, Norval says, "When we contend again our strife is mortal." Using these words in an article written for the *North American Review* in 1897, my uncle came across them and immediately sat down and wrote me from Dunfermline that he knew where I had found the words. He was the only man living who did.

My power to memorize must have been greatly strengthened by the mode of teaching adopted by my uncle. I cannot name a more important means of benefiting young people than encouraging them to commit favorite pieces to memory and recite them often. Anything which pleased me I could learn with a rapidity which surprised partial friends. I could memorize anything whether it pleased me or not, but if it did not impress me strongly it passed away in a few hours.

One of the trials of my boy's life at school in Dunfermline was committing to memory two double verses of the Psalms which I had to recite daily. My plan was not to look at the psalm until I had started for school. It was not more than five or six minutes' slow walk, but I could readily master the task in that time, and, as the psalm was the first lesson, I was prepared and passed through the ordeal successfully. Had I been asked to repeat the psalm thirty minutes afterwards the attempt would, I fear, have ended in disastrous failure.

The first penny I ever earned or ever received from any person beyond the family circle was one from my school-teacher, Mr. Martin, for repeating before the school Burns's poem, "Man was made to Mourn." In writing this I am reminded that in later years, dining with Mr. John Morley in London, the conversation turned upon the life of Wordsworth, and Mr. Morley said he had been searching his Burns for the poem to "Old Age," so much extolled by him, which he had not been able to find under that title. I had the pleasure of repeating part of it to him. He promptly handed me a second penny. Ah, great as Morley is, he wasn't my school-teacher, Mr. Martin—the first "great" man I ever knew. Truly great was he to me. But a hero surely is "Honest John" Morley.

In religious matters we were not much hampered. While other boys and girls at school were compelled to learn the Shorter Catechism, Dod and I, by some arrangement the details of which I never clearly understood, were absolved. All of our family connections, Morrisons and Lauders, were advanced in their theological as in their political views, and had objections to the catechism, I have no doubt. We had not one orthodox Presbyterian in our family circle. My father, Uncle and Aunt Aitken, Uncle Lauder, and also my Uncle Carnegie, had fallen away from the tenets of Calvinism. At a later day most of them found refuge for a time in the doctrines of Swedenborg. My mother was always reticent upon religious subjects. She never mentioned these to me nor did she attend church, for she had no servant in those early days and did all the housework, including cooking our Sunday dinner. A great reader, always, Channing the Unitarian was in those days her special delight. She was a marvel!

During my childhood the atmosphere around me was in a state of violent disturbance in matters theological as well as political. Along with the most advanced ideas which were being agitated in the political world—the death of privilege, the equality of the citizen, Republicanism—I heard many disputations upon theological subjects which the impressionable child drank in to an extent quite unthought of by his elders. I well remember that the stern doctrines of Calvinism lay as a terrible nightmare upon me, but that state of mind was soon over, owing to the influences of which I have spoken. I grew up treasuring within me the fact that my father had risen and left the Presbyterian Church one day when the minister preached the doctrine of infant damnation. This was shortly after I had made my appearance.

Father could not stand it and said: "If that be your religion and that your God, I seek a better religion and a nobler God." He left the Presbyterian Church never to return, but he did not cease to attend various other churches. I saw him enter the closet every morning to pray and that impressed me. He was indeed a saint and always remained devout. All sects became to him as agencies for good. He had discovered that theologies were many, but religion was one. I was quite satisfied that my father knew better than the minister, who pictured not the Heavenly Father, but the cruel avenger of the Old Testament—an "Eternal Torturer" as Andrew D. White ventures to call him in his autobiography. Fortunately this conception of the Unknown is now largely of the past.

One of the chief enjoyments of my childhood was the keeping of pigeons and rabbits. I am grateful every time I think of the trouble my father took to build a suitable house for these pets. Our home became headquarters for my young companions. My mother was always looking to home influences as the best means of keeping her two boys in the right path. She used to say that the first step in this direction was to make home pleasant; and there was nothing she and my father would not do to please us and the neighbors' children who centered about us.

My first business venture was securing my companions' services for a season as an employer, the compensation being that the young rabbits, when such came, should be named after them. The Saturday holiday was generally spent by my flock in gathering food for the rabbits. My conscience reproves me today, looking back, when I think of the hard bargain I drove with my young playmates, many of whom were content to gather dandelions and clover for a whole season with me, conditioned upon this unique reward—the poorest return ever made to labor. Alas! what else had I to offer them! Not a penny.

I treasure the remembrance of this plan as the earliest evidence of organizing power upon the development of which my material success in life has hung—a success not to be attributed to what I have known or done myself, but to the faculty of knowing and choosing others who did know better than myself. Precious knowledge this for any man to possess. I did not understand steam machinery, but I tried to understand that much more complicated piece of mechanism—man. Stopping at a small Highland inn on our coaching trip in 1898, a gentleman came forward and introduced himself. He was Mr. MacIntosh, the great furniture manufacturer of Scotland—a fine character as I found out afterward. He said he had ventured to make himself known as he was one of the boys who had gathered, and sometimes he feared "conveyed," spoil for the rabbits, and had "one named after him." It may be imagined how glad I was to meet him—the only one of the rabbit boys I have met in after-life. I hope to keep his friendship to the last and see him often. [As I read this manuscript to-day, December 1, 1913, I have a very precious note from him, recalling old times when we were boys together. He has a reply by this time that will warm his heart as his note did mine.]

With the introduction and improvement of steam machinery, trade grew worse and worse in Dunfermline for the small manufacturers, and at last a letter was written to my mother's two sisters in Pittsburgh stating that the idea of our going to them was seriously entertained—not, as I remember hearing my parents say, to benefit their own condition, but for the sake of their two young sons. Satisfactory letters were received in reply. The decision was taken to sell the looms and furniture by auction. And my father's sweet voice sang often to mother, brother, and me:

> To the West, to the West, to the land of the free,
> Where the mighty Missouri rolls down to the sea;
> Where a man is a man even though he must toil
> And the poorest may gather the fruits of the soil.

The proceeds of the sale were most disappointing. The looms brought hardly anything, and the result was that twenty pounds more were needed to enable the family to pay passage to America. Here let me record an act of friendship performed by a lifelong companion of my mother—who always attracted stanch friends because she was so stanch herself—Mrs. Henderson, by birth Ella Ferguson, the name by which she was known in our family. She boldly ventured to advance the needful twenty pounds, my Uncles Lauder and Morrison guaranteeing repayment. Uncle Lauder also lent his aid and advice, managing all the details for us, and on the 17th day of May, 1848, we left Dunfermline. My father's age was then forty-three, my mother's thirty-three. I was in my thirteenth year, my brother Tom in his fifth year—a beautiful white-haired child with lustrous black eyes, who everywhere attracted attention.

I had left school forever, with the exception of one winter's night-schooling in America, and later a French night-teacher for a time, and, strange to say, an elocutionist from whom I learned how to declaim. I could read, write, and cipher, and had begun the study of algebra and of Latin. A letter written to my Uncle Lauder during the voyage, and since returned, shows that I was then a better penman than now. I had wrestled with English grammar, and knew as little of what it was designed to teach as children usually do. I had read little except about Wallace, Bruce, and Burns; but knew many familiar pieces of poetry by heart. I should add to this the fairy tales of childhood, and especially the "Arabian Nights," by which I was carried into a new world. I was in dreamland as I devoured those stories.

On the morning of the day we started from beloved Dunfermline, in the omnibus that ran upon the coal railroad to Charleston, I remember that I stood with tearful eyes looking out of the window until Dunfermline vanished from view, the last structure to fade being the grand and sacred old Abbey. During my first fourteen years of absence my thought was almost daily, as it was that morning, "When shall I see you again?" Few days passed in which I did not see in my mind's eye the talismanic letters on the Abbey tower—"King Robert The Bruce." All my recollections of childhood, all I knew of fairyland, clustered around the old Abbey and its curfew bell, which tolled at eight o'clock every evening and was the signal for me to run to bed before it stopped. I have referred to that bell in my "American Four-in-Hand in Britain"[1] when passing the Abbey and I may as well quote from it now:

As we drove down the Pends I was standing on the front seat of the coach with Provost Walls, when I heard the first toll of the Abbey bell, tolled in honor of my mother and myself. My knees sank from under me, the tears came rushing before I knew it, and I turned round to tell the Provost that I must give in. For a moment I felt as if I were about to faint. Fortunately I saw that there was no crowd before us for a little distance. I had time to regain control, and biting my lips till they actually

---

1. *An American Four-in-Hand in Britain* (New York, 1886).

bled, I murmured to myself, "No matter, keep cool, you must go on"; but never can there come to my ears on earth, nor enter so deep into my soul, a sound that shall haunt and subdue me with its sweet, gracious, melting power as that did.

By that curfew bell I had been laid in my little couch to sleep the sleep of childish innocence. Father and mother, sometimes the one, sometimes the other, had told me as they bent lovingly over me night after night, what that bell said as it tolled. Many good words has that bell spoken to me through their translations. No wrong thing did I do through the day which that voice from all I knew of heaven and the great Father there did not tell me kindly about ere I sank to sleep, speaking the words so plainly that I knew that the power that moved it had seen all and was not angry, never angry, never, but so very, *very* sorry. Nor is that bell dumb to me to-day when I hear its voice. It still has its message, and now it sounded to welcome back the exiled mother and son under its precious care again.

The world has not within its power to devise, much less to bestow upon us, such reward as that which the Abbey bell gave when it tolled in our honor. But my brother Tom should have been there also; this was the thought that came. He, too, was beginning to know the wonders of that bell ere we were away to the newer land.

Rousseau wished to die to the strains of sweet music. Could I choose my accompaniment, I could wish to pass into the dim beyond with the tolling of the Abbey bell sounding in my ears, telling me of the race that had been run, and calling me, as it had called the little white-haired child, for the last time — *to sleep.*

I have had many letters from readers speaking of this passage in my book, some of the writers going so far as to say that tears fell as they read. It came from the heart and perhaps that is why it reached the hearts of others.

We were rowed over in a small boat to the Edinburgh steamer in the Firth of Forth. As I was about to be taken from the small boat to the steamer, I rushed to Uncle Lauder and clung round his neck, crying out: "I cannot leave you! I cannot leave you!" I was torn from him by a kind sailor who lifted me up on the deck of the steamer. Upon my return visit to Dunfermline this dear old fellow, when he came to see me, told me it was the saddest parting he had ever witnessed.

We sailed from the Broomielaw of Glasgow in the 800-ton sailing ship Wiscasset. During the seven weeks of the voyage, I came to know the sailors quite well, learned the names of the ropes, and was able to direct the passengers to answer the call of the boatswain, for the ship being undermanned, the aid of the passengers was urgently required. In consequence I was invited by the sailors to participate on Sundays, in the one delicacy of the sailors' mess, plum duff. I left the ship with sincere regret.

The arrival at New York was bewildering. I had been taken to see the Queen at Edinburgh, but that was the extent of my travels before emigrating. Glasgow we had not time to see before we sailed. New York was the first great hive of human industry among the inhabitants of which I had mingled, and the bustle and excitement of it overwhelmed me. The incident of our stay in New York which impressed me most occurred while I was walking through Bowling Green at Castle Garden. I was caught up in the arms of one of the Wiscasset sailors, Robert Barryman, who was decked out in regular Jack-ashore fashion, with blue jacket and white trousers. I thought him the most beautiful man I had ever seen.

He took me to a refreshment stand and ordered a glass of sarsaparilla for me, which I drank with as much relish as if it were the nectar of the gods. To this day nothing that I have ever seen of the kind rivals the image which remains in my mind of the gorgeousness of the highly ornamented brass vessel out of which that nectar came foaming. Often as I have passed the identical spot I see standing there the old woman's sarsaparilla stand, and I marvel what became of the dear old sailor. I have tried to trace him, but in vain, hoping that if found he might be enjoying a ripe old age, and that it might be in my power to add to the pleasure of his declining years. He was my ideal Tom Bowling, and when that fine old song is sung I always see as the "form of manly beauty" my dear old friend Barryman. Alas! ere this he's gone aloft. Well; by his kindness on the voyage he made one boy his devoted friend and admirer.

We knew only Mr. and Mrs. Sloane in New York—parents of the well-known John, Willie, and Henry Sloane. Mrs. Sloane (Euphemia Douglas) was my mother's companion in childhood in Dunfermline. Mr. Sloane and my father had been fellow weavers. We called upon them and were warmly welcomed. It was a genuine pleasure when Willie, his son, bought ground from me in 1900 opposite our New York residence for his two married daughters so that our children of the third generation became playmates as our mothers were in Scotland.

My father was induced by emigration agents in New York to take the Erie Canal by way of Buffalo and Lake Erie to Cleveland, and thence down the canal to Beaver—a journey which then lasted three weeks, and is made to-day by rail in ten hours. There was no railway communication then with Pittsburgh, nor indeed with any western town. The Erie Railway was under construction and we saw gangs of men at work upon it as we traveled. Nothing comes amiss to youth, and I look back upon my three weeks as a passenger upon the canal-boat with unalloyed pleasure. All that was disagreeable in my experience has long since faded from recollection, excepting the night we were compelled to remain upon the wharf-boat at Beaver waiting for the steamboat to take us up the Ohio to Pittsburgh. This was our first introduction to the mosquito in all its ferocity. My mother suffered so severely that in the morning she could hardly see. We were all frightful sights, but I do not remember that even the stinging misery of that night kept me from sleeping soundly. I could always sleep, never knowing "horrid night, the child of hell."

Our friends in Pittsburgh had been anxiously waiting to hear from us, and in their warm and affectionate greeting all our troubles were forgotten. We took up our residence with them in Allegheny City. A brother of my Uncle Hogan had built a small weaver's shop at the back end of a lot in Rebecca Street. This had a second story in which there were two rooms, and it was in these (free of rent, for my Aunt Aitken owned them) that my parents began housekeeping. My uncle soon gave up weaving and my father took his place and began making tablecloths, which he had not only to weave, but afterwards, acting as his own merchant, to travel and sell, as no dealers could be found to take them in quantity. He was compelled to market them himself, selling from door to door. The returns were meager in the extreme.

As usual, my mother came to the rescue. There was no keeping her down. In her youth she had learned to bind shoes in her father's business for pin-money, and the skill then acquired was now turned to account for the benefit of the family. Mr. Phipps, father of my friend and partner Mr. Henry Phipps, was, like my grandfather, a master shoemaker. He was our neighbor in Allegheny City. Work was obtained from him, and in addition to attending to her household duties—for, of course, we had no servant—this wonderful woman, my mother, earned four dollars a week by binding shoes. Midnight would often find her at work. In the intervals during the day and evening, when household cares would permit, and my young brother sat at her knee threading needles and waxing the thread for her, she recited to him, as she had to me, the gems of Scottish minstrelsy which she seemed to have by heart, or told him tales which failed not to contain a moral.

This is where the children of honest poverty have the most precious of all advantages over those of wealth. The mother, nurse, cook, governess, teacher, saint, all in one; the father, exemplar, guide, counselor, and friend! Thus were my brother and I brought up. What has the child of millionaire or nobleman that counts compared to such a heritage?

My mother was a busy woman, but all her work did not prevent her neighbors from soon recognizing her as a wise and kindly woman whom they could call upon for counsel or help in times of trouble. Many have told me what my mother did for them. So it was in after years wherever we resided; rich and poor came to her with their trials and found good counsel. She towered among her neighbors wherever she went.

3
Letters to George "Dod" Lauder

No immigrant ever became more quickly Americanized than did the twelve-year-old Andrew Carnegie upon his arrival in Pennsylvania in 1848. In a series of letters written to his cousin George "Dod" Lauder back in Dunfermline, young Carnegie first sounded that note of flag-waving American boosterism which he would sustain throughout his life, earning for him the cognomen, "the Star-Spangled Scotchman."

Andrew, to be sure, could not brag about the luxurious life he had found in America. The back alley in Allegheny where the Carnegie family lived during their first years was certainly not paved with gold. Nor could he speak of attending school, for Carnegie went to work in a bobbin factory as soon as the family was settled. But he could boast of the American political system which contrasted with the rigid, class-oriented society of Britain from which the Carnegies had fled, and this he did with great enthusiasm.

These letters to Dod are remarkable both in style and content when one considers they were written by a teenager who had had only four years of formal education. They compare favorably with the best of the adult Carnegie's prose. Scotland may not have enjoyed the democracy that young Carnegie claimed he had found in America, but no one could fault the education it provided its youth.

In a letter dated 1 June 1853, Andrew encloses a copy of the United States Constitution and asks Dod to reciprocate:

Bye the bye, either send me your boasted British one or lets know what you understand by it. I have no doubt but what you will be surprised at its (i.e. the American constitution) simplicity and won't believe that such a Nation as this composed of 25,000,000 from all ends of the earth can be governed by such an insignificant looking document as that but thats because you have been brought up to think a Constitution should have something *mysterious* about it as it is the case with your own—a thing to be talked about but never seen. Our Con. was made by the People and can be altered amended or done away with by them whenever they see fit. (Letter in the possession of E. E. Moore, Pittsburgh)

Having given Dod the opportunity to read the American Constitution Andrew in a follow-up letter proceeded to enlighten his cousin as to the significance of the Ameri-

can political system in producing the good life for all its citizens. As usual, Carnegie's enthusiasm exceeded the bounds of reality. Pauperism was certainly known to many Americans, including the author of this letter.

In my last letter I promised to tell you how we were governed. Your Monarchial statesman if informed that we succeeded in *preserving order (that bugbear of the middle classes)* would at once conclude that the dominant race kept the others in absolute subjection denied them all civil rights. . . . But how erroneous his idea would be for our government is founded upon justice and our creed is that the will of the People is the *source* & their happiness the end of all legitimate "Government." Such a government needs none of the wretched props necessary to the existence of despotisms—Our army consists of a few thousand men employed in protecting our frontiers from Indian depredations. . . . We have perfect political Equality. . . . It is strange that with your immense Army and policy system you cannot keep the Peace. . . . Here they [newly arrived immigrants] find no Royal Family (increasing with fearful rapidity) to squander their hard made earnings—no aristocracy to support—No established Church with its enormous sinecures. . . . they find the various reforms which they struggled for at home in successful operation here. . . . We have all your good traits which are many with few or none of your bad ones which I must say are neither few nor far between. . . . We have the Charter which you have been fighting for for years as the Panacea for all Britian's [sic] woes, the bulwark of the people. . . . But we are not at a standstill we have only commenced the great work of reform.

. . . But the best proof of the superiority of our system is seen in the general prosperity & progress of its citizens. . . . We have now in the National Treasury nearly 22,000,000$ Our debt is being paid off as fast as it becomes due. . . . Our public Lands of almost unlimited extent are becoming settled with an enterprising people. . . . Pauperism is almost unknown. . . . Everything around us is motion—mind is freed from superstitious reverence for old customs, unawed by gorgeous and unmeaning shows & forms. . . . But you may reply, Government has little or nothing to do with this state of affairs—Why then I would ask the contrast between the U. States & the Canadas. They were settled by the same people, at the same time—under the same Government—& look at the difference—Where is her Rail Roads Telegraphs & Canals? . . . We have given to the world a Washington, a Franklin, a Fulton, a Morse—What has Canada ever produced—Ah Dod "There's something rotten in Denmark" How can you account for this—Is it not a fair sample of our respective systems. The one exhibits the vigor of manhood, the other the lassitude of old age. . . . the one is "old England" the other "young America"—that's where the secret lies. (18 August 1853, Carnegie Papers, Library of Congress; italics added)

When Dod, in defense of Britain, replied that at least there was no Negro slavery within the British Empire, he touched on a very sore point. Andrew did his best to meet this criticism:

Allow me to say that I am an enthusiastic & ultra abolitionist, admit and deplore the great evils that necessarily flow in the wake of slavery feel as keenly the great wrong perpetrated upon the African as you can do. It is the greatest evil in the world and I promise you that whatever influence I may acquire shall be used to overthrow it. In short I am a Republican and believe in our Noble declaration "That all men are born free and equal." You must not think then that I want to smooth it over & give you the bright side, for I hope I shall never be found upholding palliating oppression in any shape or form.

But, he continued, Britain was responsible for introducing slavery and the slave trade in the first place, and the Third Congress of the United States had abolished the slave trade. "Pennsylvania our own noble state abolished Slavery in 1798. N York did the same these two are the greatest states in the Union, containing more than a fifth of the total population." *He pointed out to his cousin that slavery was a state question and each state was properly jealous of its own rights.*

Indeed, I consider that doctrine one of the main pillars of our Republic. It would be impossible for a country as extensive as this is, to be properly governed by a Central Government. . . . And so if Mississippi holds slaves, what have we to do with it? What can we do to prevent it? . . . We are all abolitionists in the North, Uncle Tom's Cabin is lauded to the skies, read in every parlor, taught in some Sunday Schools & played in our theatres. . . . That a way will be opened by which they [the Southern states] can cast off this only blot on our glorious Republic is the earnest prayer of an overwhelming majority of the people. . . . Slavery is sectional, Liberty alone is National. (Andrew Carnegie to Dod Lauder, 12 November 1855, letter in the possession of E. E. Moore, Pittsburgh; Dod's letters to Carnegie unfortunately are not extant, and the contents must be inferred from Carnegie's replies)

If faults could be found in the consistency of Carnegie's arguments, none certainly could be found in his patriotism.

Part II

Carnegie at Work, Making Money

From the moment in 1856 that he received his first dividend check for five dollars on the ten shares he owned in Adams Express and cried exultantly, "Eureka, here's the goose that lays golden eggs," until that memorable day forty-five years later when J. P. Morgan, having purchased Carnegie Steel for $480 million, congratulated Carnegie on being "the richest man in the world," Carnegie was busy making money. It must at times have seemed to him that this was not so difficult a task. With Midas magic, everything he touched turned to gold, be it oil, sleeping cars, telegraph lines, railroads, bonds, bridges, iron, or steel. Money was never for Carnegie an end in itself. He was never a hoarder of wealth like those master Wall Street manipulators Daniel Drew and Hetty Green, never an avaricious collector of art like Henry Clay Frick. Carnegie, like J. P. Morgan and John D. Rockefeller, regarded money simply as an instrument of power, both in its accumulation and in its dispersal.

The selections in this section have been chosen to illustrate how Carnegie saw himself as a traveler on "The Road to Business Success."

4
How I Served My Apprenticeship

The following article was written in 1896 at the height of Carnegie's power as steel king of the world. Youth's Companion, *whose editors requested the essay, was in the late nineteenth and early twentieth centuries the most widely circulated periodical for boys in America. It was designed to instill in youth the same values of thrift, honesty, sobriety, industry, and the proper reverence for God and capitalism to which the churches, the schools, and such youth organizations as the YMCA and the Boy Scouts of America were also dedicated. The article was published in the issue of 25 April 1896.*

It is a great pleasure to tell how I served my apprenticeship as a businessman. But there seems to be a question preceding this: Why did I become a business man? I am sure that I should never have selected a business career if I had been permitted to choose.

The eldest son of parents who were themselves poor, I had, fortunately, to begin to perform some useful work in the world while still very young in order to earn an honest livelihood, and was thus shown even in early boyhood that my duty was to assist my parents and, like them, become, as soon as possible, a bread-winner in the family. What I could get to do, not what I desired, was the question.

When I was born my father was a well-to-do master weaver in Dunfermline, Scotland. He owned no less than four damask-looms and employed apprentices. This was before the days of steam-factories for the manufacture of linen. A few large merchants took orders, and employed master weavers, such as my father, to weave the cloth, the merchants supplying the materials.

As the factory system developed hand-loom weaving naturally declined, and my father was one of the sufferers by the change. The first serious lesson of my life came to me one day when he had taken in the last of his work to the merchant, and returned to our little home greatly distressed because there was no more work for him to do. I was then just about ten years of age, but the lesson burned into my heart, and I resolved then that the wolf of poverty should be driven from our door some day, if I could do it.

The question of selling the old looms and starting for the United States came up in the family council, and I heard it discussed from day to day. It was finally resolved to take the plunge and join relatives already in Pittsburg [sic]. I well remember that neither father nor mother thought the change would be otherwise than a great sacrifice for them, but that "it would be better for the two boys."

In after life, if you can look back as I do and wonder at the complete surrender of their own desires which parents make for the good of their children, you must reverence their memories with feelings akin to worship.

On arriving in Allegheny City (there were four of us: father, mother, my younger brother, and myself) my father entered a cotton factory. I soon followed, and served as a "bobbin-boy," and this is how I began my preparation for subsequent apprenticeship as a business man. I received one dollar and twenty cents a week, and was then just about twelve years old.

I cannot tell you how proud I was when I received my first week's own earnings. One dollar and twenty cents made by myself and given to me because I had been of some use in the world! No longer entirely dependent upon my parents, but at last admitted to the family partnership as a contributing member and able to help them! I think this makes a man out of a boy sooner than almost anything else, and a real man, too, if there be any germ of true manhood in him. It is everything to feel that you are useful.

I have had to deal with great sums. Many millions of dollars have since passed through my hands. But the genuine satisfaction I had from that one dollar and twenty cents outweighs any subsequent pleasure in money-getting. It was the direct reward of honest, manual labor; it represented a week of very hard work—so hard that, but for the aim and end which sanctified it, slavery might not be much too strong a term to describe it.

For a lad of twelve to rise and breakfast every morning, except for blessed Sunday morning, and go into the streets and find his way to the factory and begin to work while it was still dark outside, and not be released until after darkness came again in the evening, forty minutes' interval only being allowed at noon, was a terrible task.

But I was young and had my dreams, and something within always told me that this would not, could not, should not last—I should some day get into a better position. Besides this, I felt myself no longer a mere boy, but quite a little man, and this made me happy.

A change soon came, for a kind old Scotsman, who knew some of our relatives, made bobbins, and took me into his factory before I was thirteen. But here for a time it was even worse than in the cotton factory, because I was set to fire a boiler in the cellar, and actually to run the small steam-engine which drove the machinery. The firing of the boiler was all right, for fortunately we did not use coal, but the refuse wooden chips; and I always liked to work in wood. But the responsibility of keeping the water right and of running the engine, and the danger of my making a mistake and blowing the whole factory to pieces, caused too great a strain, and I often awoke and found myself sitting up in bed through the night, trying the steam-gages. But I never told them at home that I was having a hard tussle. No, no! everything must be bright to them.

This was a point of honor, for every member of the family was working hard, except, of course, my little brother, who was then a child, and we were telling each other only all the bright things. Besides this, no man would whine and give up—he would die first.

There was no servant in our family, and several dollars per week were earned by the mother by binding shoes after her daily work was done! Father was also hard at work in the factory. And could I complain?

My kind employer, John Hay—peace to his ashes!—soon relieved me of the undue strain, for he needed some one to make out bills and keep his accounts, and finding that I could write a plain school-boy hand and could "cipher," he made me his only clerk. But still I had to work hard upstairs in the factory, for the clerking took but little time.

You know how people moan about poverty as being a great evil, and it seems to be accepted that if people had only plenty of money and were rich, they would be happy and more useful, and get more out of life.

As a rule, there is more genuine satisfaction, a truer life, and more obtained from life in the humble cottages of the poor than in the palaces of the rich. I always pity the sons and daughters of rich men, who are attended by servants, and have governesses at a later age, but am glad to remember that they do not know what they have missed.

They have kind fathers and mothers, too, and think that they enjoy the sweetness of these blessings to the fullest: but this they cannot do; for the poor boy who has in his father his constant companion, tutor, and model, and in his mother—holy name!—his nurse, teacher, guardian angel, saint, all in one, has a richer, more precious fortune in life than any rich man's son who is not so favored can possibly know, and compared with which all other fortunes count for little.

It is because I know how sweet and happy and pure the home of honest poverty is, how free from perplexing care, from social envies and emulations, how loving and how united its members may be in the common interest of supporting the family, that I sympathize with the rich man's boy and congratulate the poor man's boy; and it is for these reasons that from the ranks of the poor so many strong, eminent, self-reliant men have always sprung and always must spring.

If you will read the list of the immortals who "were not born to die," you will find that most of them have been born to the precious heritage of poverty.

It seems, nowadays, a matter of universal desire that poverty should be abolished. We should be quite willing to abolish luxury, but to abolish honest, industrious, self-denying poverty would be to destroy the soil upon which mankind produces the virtues which enable our race to reach a still higher civilization than it now possesses.

I come now to the third step in my apprenticeship, for I had already taken two, as you see—the cotton factory and then the bobbin factory; and with the third—the third time is the chance, you know—deliverance came. I obtained a situation as messenger boy in the telegraph office at Pittsburg when I was fourteen. Here I entered a new world.

Amid books, newspapers, pencils, pens and ink and writing-pads, and a clean office, bright windows, and the literary atmosphere, I was the happiest boy alive.

My only dread was that I should some day be dismissed because I did not know the city; for it is necessary that a messenger boy should know all the firms and addresses of men who are in the habit of receiving telegrams. But I was a stranger in Pittsburg. However, I made up my mind that I would learn to repeat successively each business house in the principal streets, and was soon able to shut my eyes and begin at one side of Wood Street, and call every firm successively to the top, then pass to the other side and call every firm to the bottom. Before long I was able to do this with the business streets generally. My mind was then at rest upon that point.

Of course every ambitious messenger boy wants to become an operator, and before the operators arrive in the early mornings the boys slipped up to the instruments and practised. This I did, and was soon able to talk to the boys in the other offices along the line, who were also practising.

One morning I heard Philadelphia calling Pittsburg, and giving the signal, "Death message." Great attention was then paid to "death messages," and I thought I ought to try to take this one. I answered and did so, and went off and delivered it before the operator came. After that the operators sometimes used to ask me to work for them.

Having a sensitive ear for sound, I soon learned to take messages by the ear, which was then very uncommon—I think only two persons in the United States could then do it. Now every operator takes by ear, so easy is it to follow and do what any other boy can—if you only have to. This brought me into notice, and finally I became an operator, and received the, to me, enormous recompense of twenty-five dollars per month—three hundred dollars a year!

This was a fortune—the very sum that I had fixed when I was a factory-worker as the fortune I wished to possess, because the family could live on three hundred dollars a year and be almost or quite independent. Here it was at last! But I was soon to be in receipt of extra compensation for extra work.

The six newspapers of Pittsburg received telegraphic news in common. Six copies of each despatch were made by a gentleman who received six dollars per week for the work, and he offered me a gold dollar every week if I would do it, of which I was very glad indeed, because I always liked to work with news and scribble for newspapers.

The reporters came to a room every evening for the news which I had prepared, and this brought me into most pleasant intercourse with these clever fellows, and besides, I got a dollar a week as pocket-money, for this was not considered family revenue by me.

I think this last step of doing something beyond one's task is fully entitled to be considered "business." The other revenue, you see, was just salary obtained for regular work; but here was a little business operation upon my own account, and I was very proud indeed of my gold dollar every week.

The Pennsylvania Railroad shortly after this was completed to Pittsburg, and that genius, Thomas A. Scott, was its superintendent. He often came to the telegraph office to talk to his chief, the general superintendent, at Altoona, and I became known to him in this way.

When that great railway system put up a wire of its own, he asked me to be his clerk and operator; so I left the telegraph office—in which there is great danger that a young man may be permanently buried, as it were—and became connected with the railways.

The new appointment was accompanied by what was, to me, a tremendous increase of salary. It jumped from twenty-five to thirty-five dollars per month. Mr. Scott was then receiving one hundred and twenty-five dollars per month, and I used to wonder what on earth he could do with so much money.

I remained for thirteen years in the service of the Pennsylvania Railroad Company, and was at last superintendent of the Pittsburg division of the road, successor to Mr. Scott, who had in the meantime risen to the office of vice-president of the company.

One day Mr. Scott, who was the kindest of men, and had taken a great fancy to me, asked if I had or could find five hundred dollars to invest.

Here the business instinct came into play. I felt that as the door was opened for a business investment with my chief, it would be wilful flying in the face of providence if I did not jump at it; so I answered promptly:

"Yes, sir; I think I can."

"Very well," he said, "get it; a man has just died who owns ten shares in the Adams Express Company which I want you to buy. It will cost you fifty dollars per share, and I can help you with a little balance if you cannot raise it all."

Here was a queer position. The available assets of the whole family were not five hundred dollars. But there was one member of the family whose ability, pluck, and resource never failed us, and I felt sure the money could be raised somehow or other by my mother.

Indeed, had Mr. Scott known our position he would have advanced it himself; but the last thing in the world the proud Scot will do is to reveal his poverty and rely upon others. The family had managed by this time to purchase a small house and pay for it in order to save rent. My recollection is that it was worth eight hundred dollars.

The matter was laid before the council of three that night, and the oracle spoke: "Must be done. Mortgage our house. I will take the steamer in the morning for Ohio, and see uncle, and ask him to arrange it. I am sure he can." This was done. Of course her visit was successful—where did she ever fail?

The money was procured, paid over; ten shares of Adams Express Company stock was mine; but no one knew our little home had been mortgaged "to give our boy a start."

Adams Express stock then paid monthly dividends of one percent, and the first check for five dollars arrived. I can see it now, and I well remember the signature of "J. C. Babcock, Cashier," who wrote a big "John Hancock" hand.

The next day being Sunday, we boys—myself and my ever-constant companions—took our usual Sunday afternoon stroll in the country, and sitting down in the woods, I showed them this check, saying, "Eureka! We have found it."

Here was something new to all of us, for none of us had ever received anything but from toil. A return from capital was something strange and new.

How money could make money, how, without any attention from me, this mysterious golden visitor should come, led to much speculation upon the part of the young fellows, and I was for the first time hailed as a "capitalist."

You see, I was beginning to serve my apprenticeship as a business man in a satisfactory manner.

A very important incident in my life occurred when, one day in a train, a nice, farmer-looking gentleman approached me, saying that the conductor had told him I was connected with the Pennsylvania Railroad, and he would like to show me something. He pulled from a small green bag the model of the first sleeping-car. This was Mr. Woodruff, the inventor.

Its value struck me like a flash. I asked him to come to Altoona the following week, and he did so. Mr. Scott, with his usual quickness, grasped the idea. A contract was made with Mr. Woodruff to put two trial cars on the Pennsylvania Railroad. Before leaving Altoona Mr. Woodruff came and offered me an interest in the venture, which I promptly accepted. But how I was to make my payments rather troubled me, for the cars were to be paid for in monthly instalments after delivery, and my first monthly payment was to be two hundred and seventeen dollars and a half.

I had not the money, and I did not see any way of getting it. But I finally decided to visit the local banker and ask him for a loan, pledging myself to repay at the rate of fifteen dollars per month. He promptly granted it. Never shall I forget his putting his arm over my shoulder, saying, "Oh, yes, Andy; you are all right!"

I then and there signed my first note. Proud day this; and surely now no one will dispute that I was becoming a "businessman." I had signed my first note, and, most important of all—for any fellow can sign a note—I had found a banker willing to take it as "good."

My subsequent payments were made by the receipts from the sleeping-cars, and I really made my first considerable sum from this investment in the Woodruff Sleeping-car Company, which was afterwards absorbed by Mr. Pullman — a remarkable man whose name is now known over all the world.

Shortly after this I was appointed superintendent of the Pittsburg division, and returned to my dear old home, smoky Pittsburg. Wooden bridges were then used exclusively upon the railways, and the Pennsylvania Railroad was experimenting with a bridge built of cast-iron. I saw that wooden bridges would not do for the future, and organized a company in Pittsburg to build iron bridges.

Here again I had recourse to the bank, because my share of the capital was twelve hundred and fifty dollars, and I had not the money; but the bank lent it to me, and we began the Keystone Bridge Works, which proved a great success. This company built the first great bridge over the Ohio River, three hundred feet span, and has built many of the most important structures since.

This was my beginning in manufacturing; and from that start all our other works have grown, the profits of one building the other. My "apprenticeship" as a business man soon ended, for I resigned my position as an officer of the Pennsylvania Railroad Company to give exclusive attention to business.

I was no longer merely an official working for others upon a salary, but a full-fledged businessman working upon my own account.

I never was quite reconciled to working for other people. At the most, the railway officer has to look forward to the enjoyment of a stated salary, and he has a great many people to please; even if he gets to be president, he has sometimes a board of directors who cannot know what is best to be done; and even if this board be satisfied, he has a board of stockholders to criticize him, and as the property is not his own he cannot manage it as he pleases.

I always liked the idea of being my own master, of manufacturing something and giving employment to many men. There is only one thing to think of manufacturing if you are a Pittsburger, for Pittsburg even then had asserted her supremacy as the "Iron City," the leading iron- and steel-manufacturing city in America.

So my indispensable and clever partners, who had been my boy companions, I am delighted to say — some of the very boys who had met in the grove to wonder at the five-dollar check — began business, and still continue extending it to meet the ever-growing and ever-changing wants of our most progressive country, year after year.

Always we are hoping that we need expand no farther; yet ever we are finding that to stop expanding would be to fall behind; and even to-day the successive improvements and inventions follow each other so rapidly that we see just as much yet to be done as ever.

When the manufacturer of steel ceases to grow he begins to decay, so we must keep on extending. The result of all these developments is that three pounds of finished steel are now bought in Pittsburg for two cents, which is cheaper than anywhere else on the earth, and that our country has become the greatest producer of iron in the world.

And so ends the story of my apprenticeship and graduation as a businessman.

5
Memorandum of 1868

In late December 1868, Andrew Carnegie sat down at his desk in the St. Nicholas Hotel in New York where he and his mother the previous year had established their residency. He totaled up his diverse holdings in railroads, bridge and iron companies, and other miscellaneous investments and found that he now had assets of $400,000, which gave him an annual income of over $50,000.

The end of a year for a Scottish Calvinist is a time for reflecting upon man's sinful frailty and God's awesome majesty. Carnegie had never accepted the Calvinist view of either man or God, but the ethos of Scotland had been bred into him. That he had flourished in this new land there could be no doubt. In twenty years he had climbed from the poverty of a back alley in Allegheny, Pennsylvania, to the marble-fronted splendor of the St. Nicholas Hotel. In so doing, he had outstripped even the most ambitious dreams of his mother, but the nagging fear persisted that he had at the same time violated the noble ideals for social and economic justice that his father and grandfather had espoused in Dunfermline. With all the introspection of a Jonathan Edwards or a John Knox, he took a hard, unpitying look at himself. He then wrote down another kind of balance sheet to accompany the statement of his business holdings.

The following memorandum is a remarkable document of self-analysis and adjuration that is surely unique in American entrepreneurial history. One cannot imagine John D. Rockefeller, J. P. Morgan, or Donald Trump writing such a note. In the years that followed, Carnegie continued to "push inordinately," and his business contemporaries saw no evidence of his wanting to retire from "business cares." The self-addressed note lay undisturbed in his desk drawer, but it remained nevertheless disturbing to his self-evaluation. It would not find an answer satisfying to its author for another twenty years—not until Carnegie pontificated his Gospel of Wealth.

A photocopy of this memorandum can be found in the Andrew Carnegie Papers in the Manuscript Division of the New York Public Library. The original remained

Memorandum of 1868

in the possession of Louise Whitfield Carnegie and later in the possession of her daughter, Margaret Carnegie Miller.

Dec. '68
St. Nicholas Hotel
N York

Thirty three and an income of 50,000$ per annum. By this time two years I can so arrange all my business as to secure at least 50,000 per annum. Beyond this never earn — make no effort to increase fortune, but spend the surplus each year for benovelent [sic] purposes. Cast aside business forever except for others.

Settle in Oxford & get a thorough education making the acquaintance of literary men — this will take three years active work — pay especial attention to speaking in public.

Settle then in London & purchase a controlling interest in some newspaper or live review & give the general management of it attention, taking a part in public matters especially those connected with education & improvement of the poorer classes.

Man must have an idol — The amassing of wealth is one of the worst species of idolitary [sic]. No idol more debasing than the worship of money. Whatever I engage in I must push inordinately therefor should I be careful to choose that life which will be the most elevating in its character. To continue much longer overwhelmed by business cares and with most of my thoughts wholly upon the way to make more money in the shortest time, must degrade me beyond hope of permanent recovery.

I will resign business at Thirty five, but during the ensuing two years, I wish to spend the afternoons in securing instruction, and in reading systematically.

6
The Road to Business Success: A Talk to Young Men

In the late nineteenth century, business schools—or commercial colleges, as many institutions preferred to call themselves—were springing up in large cities and smaller towns throughout America. At these schools young men were trained in accounting, marketing, purchasing, and advertising, while young women were being taught to use the newly invented typewriter, to take shorthand, and to file. In this speech given to the male students at the Curry Commercial College in Pittsburgh, 23 June 1885, Carnegie offered his recipe for achieving business success. His address is a paean to that deeply embedded faith that Americans held in the self-made man who "begins by sweeping out the office," and ends up "on top." Carnegie, to be sure, had not himself in the beginning followed his own recipe for success. Early in his career, he had put "many eggs in many different baskets." It was not until 1872 that he found for his considerable clutch of eggs the single right depository in a basket made of steel.

It is well that young men should begin at the beginning and occupy the most subordinate positions. Many of the leading businessmen of Pittsburg had a serious responsibility thrust upon them at the very threshold of their career. They were introduced to the broom, and spent the first hours of their business lives sweeping out the office. I notice we have janitors and janitresses now in offices, and our young men unfortunately miss that salutary branch of a business education. But if by chance the professional sweeper is absent any morning the boy who has the genius of the future partner in him will not hesitate to try his hand at the broom. The other day a fond fashionable mother in Michigan asked a young man whether he had ever seen a young lady sweep in a room so grandly as her Priscilla. He said no, he never had, and the mother was gratified beyond measure, but then said he, after a pause, "What I should like to see her do is sweep out a room." It does not hurt the newest comer to sweep out the office if necessary. I was one of those sweepers myself, and who do you suppose were my fellow sweepers? David McCargo, now superintendent of the Alleghany Valley Railroad; Robert Pitcairn, Superintendent of the Pennsylvania Railroad, and Mr. Moreland, City Attorney. We all took turns, two each morning did the sweeping; and now I remember Davie was so proud of his clean white shirt bosom that he used to spread over it an old silk bandana handkerchief which he kept for the purpose, and we other boys thought he was putting on airs. So he was. None of us had a silk handkerchief.

Assuming that you have all obtained employment and are fairly started, my advice to you is "aim high." I would not give a fig for the young man who does not already see himself the partner or the head of an important firm. Do not rest content for a moment in your thoughts as head clerk, or foreman, or general manager in any concern, no matter how extensive. Say each to yourself, "My place is at the top." *Be king in your dreams.* Make your vow that you will reach that position, with untarnished reputation, and make no other vow to distract your attention, except the very commendable one that when you are a member of the firm or before that, if you have been promoted two or three times, you will form another partnership with the loveliest of her sex—a partnership to which our new partnership act has no application. The liability there is never limited.

Let me indicate two or three conditions essential to success. Do not be afraid that I am going to moralize, or inflict a homily upon you. I speak upon the subject only from the view of a man of the world, desirous of aiding you to become successful businessmen. You all know that there is no genuine, praiseworthy success in life if you are not honest, truthful, fair-dealing. I assume you are and will remain all these, and also that you are determined to live pure, respectable lives, free from pernicious or equivocal associations with one sex or the other. There is no creditable future for you else. Otherwise your learning and your advantages not only go for naught, but serve to accentuate your failure and your disgrace. I hope you will not take it amiss if I warn you against three of the gravest dangers which will beset you in your upward path.

The first and most seductive, and the destroyer of most young men, is the drinking of liquor. I am no temperance lecturer in disguise, but a man who knows and tells you what observation has proved to him; and I say to you that you are more likely to fail in your career from acquiring the habit of drinking liquor than from any, or all, the other temptations likely to assail you.

You may yield to almost any other temptation and reform—may brace up, and if not recover lost ground, at least remain in the race and secure and maintain a respectable position. But from the insane thirst for liquor escape is almost impossible. I have known but few exceptions to this rule. First, then, you must not drink liquor to excess. Better if you do not touch it at all—much better; but if this be too hard a rule for you then take your stand firmly here:— Resolve never to touch it except at meals. A glass at dinner will not hinder your advance in life or lower your tone; but I implore you hold it inconsistent with the dignity and self-respect of gentlemen, with what is due from yourselves to yourselves, being the men you are, and especially the men you are determined to become, to drink a glass of liquor at a bar. Be far too much of the gentleman ever to enter a barroom. You do not pursue your careers in safety unless you stand firmly upon this ground. Adhere to it and you have escaped danger from the deadliest of your foes.

The next greatest danger to a young business man in this community I believe to be that of speculation. When I was a telegraph operator here we had no Exchanges in the City, but the men or firms who speculated upon the Eastern Exchanges were necessarily known to the operators. They could be counted on the fingers of one hand. These men were not our citizens of first repute: they were regarded with suspicion. I have lived to see all of these speculators irreparably ruined men, bankrupt in money and bankrupt in character. There is scarcely an instance of a man who has made a fortune by speculation and kept it. Gamesters die poor, and there is certainly not an instance of a speculator who has lived a life creditable to himself, or advantageous to the community. The man who grasps the morning paper to see first how his speculative ventures upon the Exchanges are likely to result, unfits himself for the calm consideration and proper solution of business problems, with which he has to deal later in the day, and saps the sources of that persistent and concentrated energy upon which depend the permanent success, and often the very safety, of his main business.

The speculator and the businessman tread diverging lines. The former depends upon the sudden turn of fortune's wheel; he is a millionnaire today, a bankrupt tomorrow. But the man of business knows that only by years of patient, unremitting attention to affairs can he earn his reward, which is the result, not of chance, but of well-devised means for the attainment of ends. During all these years his is the cheering thought that by no possibility can he benefit himself without carrying prosperity to others. The speculator on the other hand had better never have lived so far as the good of others or the good of the community is concerned. Hundreds of young men were tempted in this city not long since to gamble in oil, and many were ruined; all were injured whether they lost or won. You may be, nay, you are certain to be similarly tempted; but when so tempted I hope you will remember this advice. Say to the tempter who asks you to risk your small savings, that if ever you decide to speculate you are determined to go to a regular and well-conducted house where they cheat fair. You can get fair play and about an equal chance upon the red and black in such a place; upon the Exchange you have neither. You might as well try your luck with the three-card-monte man. There is another point involved in speculation. Nothing is more essential to young businessmen than untarnished credit, credit begotten of confidence in their prudence, principles and stability of character. Well, believe me, nothing kills credit sooner in any Bank Board than the knowledge that either firms or men engage in speculation. It matters not a whit whether gains or losses be the temporary result of these operations. The moment a man is known to speculate, his credit is impaired, and soon thereafter it is gone. How can a man be credited whose resources may be swept away in one hour by a panic among gamesters? Who can tell how he stands among them? except that this is certain: he has given due notice that he may stand to lose all, so that those who credit him have themselves to blame. Resolve to be businessmen, but speculators never.

The third and last danger against which I shall warn you is one which has wrecked many a fair craft which started well and gave promise of a prosperous voyage. It is the perilous habit of indorsing—all the more dangerous, inasmuch as it assails one generally in the garb of friendship. It appeals to your generous instincts, and you say, "How can I refuse to lend my name only, to assist a friend?" It is because there is so much that is true and commendable in that view that the practice is so dangerous. Let me endeavour to put you upon safe honourable grounds in regard to it. I would say to you to make it a rule now, *never indorse:* but this is too much like never taste wine, or never smoke, or any other of the "nevers." They generally result in exceptions. You will as businessmen now and then probably become security for friends. Now, here is the line at which regard for the success of friends should cease and regard for your own honour begin.

If you owe anything, all your capital and all your effects are a solemn trust in your hands to be held inviolate for the security of those who have trusted you. Nothing can be done by you with honour which jeopardizes these first claims upon you. When a man in debt indorses for another, it is not his own credit or his own capital he risks, it is that of his own creditors. He violates a trust. Mark you then, never indorse until you have cash means not required for your own debts, and never indorse beyond those means.

Before you indorse at all, consider indorsements as gifts, and ask yourselves whether you wish to make the gift to your friend and whether the money is really yours to give and not a trust for your creditors.

You are not safe, gentlemen, unless you stand firmly upon this as the only ground which an honest businessman can occupy.

I beseech you avoid liquor, speculation and indorsement. Do not fail in either, for liquor and speculation are the Scylla and Charybdis of the young man's business sea, and indorsement his rock ahead.

Assuming you are safe in regard to these your gravest dangers, the question now is how to rise from the subordinate position we have imagined you in, through the successive grades to the position for which you are, in my opinion, and, I trust, in your own, evidently intended. I can give you the secret. It lies mainly in this. Instead of the question, "What must I do for my employer?" substitute "What can I do?" Faithful and conscientious discharge of the duties assigned you is all very well, but the verdict in such cases generally is that you perform your present duties so well that you had better continue performing them. Now, young gentlemen, this will not do. It will not do for the coming partners. There must be something beyond this. We make Clerks, Bookkeepers, Treasurers, Bank Tellers of this class, and there they remain to the end of the chapter. The rising man must do something exceptional, and beyond the range of his special department. HE MUST ATTRACT ATTENTION. A shipping clerk, he may do so by discovering in an invoice an error with which he has nothing to do, and which has escaped the attention of the proper party. If a weighing clerk, he may save for the firm by doubting the adjustment of the scales and having them corrected, even if this be the province of the master mechanic. If a messenger boy, even he can lay the seed of promotion by going beyond the letter of his instructions in order to secure the desired reply. There is no service so low and simple, neither any so high, in which the young man of ability and willing disposition cannot readily and almost daily prove himself capable of greater trust and usefulness, and, what is equally important, show his invincible determination to rise. Some day, in your own department, you will be directed to do or say something which you know will prove disadvantageous to the interest of the firm. Here is your chance. Stand up like a man and say so. Say it boldly, and give your reasons, and thus prove to your employer that, while his thoughts have been engaged upon other matters, you have been studying during hours when perhaps he thought you asleep, how to advance his interests. You may be right or you may be wrong, but in either case you have gained the first condition of success. You have attracted attention. Your employer has found that he has not a mere hireling in his service, but a man; not one who is content to give so many hours of work for so many dollars in return, but one who devotes his spare hours and constant thoughts to the business. Such an employe must perforce be thought of, and thought of kindly and well. It will not be long before his advice is asked in his special branch, and if the advice given be sound, it will soon be asked and taken upon questions of broader bearing. This means partnership; if not with present employers then with others. Your foot, in such a case, is upon the ladder; the amount of climbing done depends entirely upon yourself.

One false axiom you will often hear, which I wish to guard you against: "Obey orders if you break owners." Don't you do it. This is no rule for you to follow. Always break orders to save owners. There never was a great character who did not sometimes smash the routine regulations and make new ones for himself. The rule is only suitable for such as have no aspirations, and you have not forgotten that you are destined to be owners and to make orders and break orders. Do not hesitate to do it whenever you are sure the interests of your employer will be thereby promoted and when you are so sure of the result that you are willing to take the responsibility. You will never be a partner unless you know the business of your department far better than the owners possibly can. When called to account for your independent action, show him the result of your genius, and tell him that you knew that it would be so; show him how mistaken the orders were. Boss your boss just as soon as you can; try it on early. There is nothing he will like so well if he is the right kind of boss; if he is not, he is not the man for you to remain with—leave him whenever you can, even at a present sacrifice, and find one capable of discerning genius. Our young partners in the Carnegie firm have won their spurs by showing that we did not know half as well what was wanted as they did. Some of them have acted upon occasion with me as if they owned the firm and I was but some airy New Yorker presuming to advise upon what I knew very little about. Well, they are not interfered with much now. They were the true bosses—the very men we were looking for.

There is one sure mark of the coming partner, the future millionnaire; his revenues always exceed his expenditures. He begins to save early, almost as soon as he begins to earn. No matter how little it may be possible to save, save that little. Invest it securely, not necessarily in bonds, but in anything which you have good reason to believe will be profitable, but no gambling with it, remember. A rare chance will soon present itself for investment. The little you have saved will prove the basis for an amount of credit utterly surprising to you. Capitalists trust the saving young man. For every hundred dollars you can produce as the result of hard-won savings, Midas, in search of a partner, will lend or credit a thousand; for every thousand, fifty thousand. It is not capital that your seniors require, it is the man who has proved that he has the business habits which create capital, and to create it in the best of all possible ways, as far as self-discipline is concerned, is, by adjusting his habits to his means. Gentlemen, it is the first hundred dollars saved which tells. Begin at once to lay up something. The bee predominates in the future millionnaire.

Of course there are better, higher aims than saving. As an end, the acquisition of wealth is ignoble in the extreme; I assume that you save and long for wealth only as a means of enabling you the better to do some good in your day and generation. Make a note of this essential rule: Expenditure always within income.

You may grow important, or become discouraged when year by year you float on in subordinate positions. There is no doubt that it is becoming harder and harder as business gravitates more and more to immense concerns, for a young man without capital to get a start for himself, and in this city especially, where large capital is essential, it is unusually difficult. Still, let me tell you for your encouragement that there is no country in the world where able and energetic young men can so readily rise as this, nor any city where there is more room at the top. It has been impossible to meet the demand for capable, first-class bookkeepers (mark the adjectives), the supply has *never* been equal to the demand. Young men give all kinds of reasons why in their cases failure was clearly attributable to exceptional circumstances which render success impossible. Some never had a chance, according to their own story. This is simply nonsense. No young man ever lived who had not a chance, and a splendid chance, too, if he ever was employed at all. He is assayed in the mind of his immediate superior, from the day he begins work, and, after a time, if he has merit, he is assayed in the council chamber of the firm. His ability, honesty, habits, associations, temper, disposition, all these are weighed and analysed. The young man who never had a chance is the same young man who has been canvassed over and over again by his superiors, and found destitute of necessary qualifications, or is deemed unworthy of closer relations with the firm, owing to some objectionable act, habit, or association, of which he thought his employers ignorant.

Another class of young men attribute their failure to employers having relations or favourites whom they advanced unfairly. They also insist that their employers disliked brighter intelligences than their own, and were disposed to discourage aspiring genius, and delighted in keeping young men down. There is nothing in this. On the contrary, there is no one suffering so much for lack of the right man in the right place, nor so anxious to find him as the owner. There is not a firm in Pittsburg today which is not in the constant search for business ability, and every one of them will tell you that there is no article in the market at all times so scarce. There is always a boom in brains, cultivate that crop, for if you grow any amount of that commodity, here is your best market and you cannot overstock it, and the more brains you have to sell, the higher price you can exact. They are not quite so sure a crop as wild oats, which never fail to produce a bountiful harvest, but they have the advantage over these in always finding a market. Do not hesitate to engage in any legitimate business, for there is no business in America, I do not care what, which will not yield a fair profit if it receive the unremitting, exclusive attention, and all the capital of capable and industrious men. Every business will have its season of depression—years always come during which the manufacturers and merchants of the city are severely tried—years when mills must be run, not for profit, but at a loss, that the organization and men may be kept together and employed, and the concern may keep its products in the market. But on the other hand, every legitimate business producing or dealing in an article which man requires is bound in time to be fairly profitable, if properly conducted.

And here is the prime condition of success, the great secret: concentrate your energy, thought, and capital exclusively upon the business in which you are engaged. Having begun in one line, resolve to fight it out on that line, to lead in it; adopt every improvement, have the best machinery, and know the most about it.

The concerns which fail are those which have scattered their capital, which means that they have scattered their brains also. They have investments in this, or that, or the other, here, there and everywhere. "Don't put all your eggs in one basket" is all wrong. I tell you "put all your eggs in one basket, and then watch that basket." Look round you and take notice; men who do that do not often fail. It is easy to watch and carry the one basket. It is trying to carry too many baskets that breaks most eggs in this country. He who carries three baskets must put one on his head, which is apt to tumble and trip him up. One fault of the American businessman is lack of concentration.

To summarize what I have said: Aim for the highest; never enter a bar-room; do not touch liquor, or if at all only at meals; never speculate; never indorse beyond your surplus cash fund; make the firm's interest yours; break orders always to save owners; concentrate; put all your eggs in one basket, and watch that basket; expenditure always within revenue; lastly, be not impatient, for, as Emerson says, "no one can cheat you out of ultimate success but yourselves."

I congratulate poor young men upon being born to that ancient and honourable degree which renders it necessary that they should devote themselves to hard work. A basketful of bonds is the heaviest basket a young man ever had to carry. He generally gets to staggering under it. We have in this city creditable instances of such young men, who have pressed to the front rank of our best and most useful citizens. These deserve great credit. But the vast majority of the sons of rich men are unable to resist the temptations to which wealth subjects them, and sink to unworthy lives. I would almost as soon leave a young man a curse, as burden him with the almighty dollar. It is not from this class you have rivalry to fear. The partner's sons will not trouble you much, but look out that some boys poorer, much poorer than yourselves, whose parents cannot afford to give them the advantages of a course in this institute, advantages which should give you a decided lead in the race—look out that such boys do not challenge you at the post and pass you at the grand stand. Look out for the boy who has to plunge into work direct from the common school and who begins by sweeping out the office. He is the probable dark horse that you had better watch.

7
The Age of Steel

Living in Pittsburgh and busily engaged in running railroads and building bridges, Andrew Carnegie could hardly escape having a keen interest in the production of iron. It is not at all certain, however, that he would have eventually selected that particular industry in which to invest all his considerable entrepreneurial talent had he not in 1863 been quite reluctantly persuaded by his brother Tom and two of his closest boyhood friends, Henry Phipps and Tom Miller, to serve as arbiter in the managerial disputes that threatened the continued success of the Kloman iron company, a firm in which the three men had become partners. Carnegie was already well acquainted with this small company, for Andrew Kloman produced the best railroad axles on the market, and as superintendent of the Pittsburgh Division of the Pennsylvania Railroad, Carnegie had been one of his best customers.

Carnegie's entry into the troubled situation at the Kloman & Phipps Company resulted in the creation of the Union Iron Mills in 1865. The die had been cast. What had been for Carnegie at first simply a troublesome distraction that took him away from his major interests in bridge building and bond selling quickly became the one big basket he had been seeking in which he could invest all his remarkable skill for making money. As was often the case, serendipity played as large a part in Carnegie's life as did advance planning.

In the following selection, Carnegie gives us an insight into his methods for achieving business success: always emphasize the cost of production, not the profits of production; reinvest profits back into the company rather than pay them out as dividends; constantly rationalize the production process by making use of scientific research; find the best talent possible and reward that talent either with a partnership in the firm or, in the single case of Captain Bill Jones, America's greatest steel maker, with an extraordinarily high salary. It was a simple and obvious recipe for success, but few of his contemporaries had the wisdom or the freedom to adopt it. While other iron and steel companies became corporations that were obliged to disperse their profits in dividends to their stockholders, while they initially scorned "book larnin'" steel production by professional chemists, and while they continued to lose their most talented employees to other firms willing to pay higher salaries, Carnegie kept his company a simple partnership and tied his "young geniuses" to his company not by dividends or raising salaries, but by awarding them a small percentage of the ownership, thus promising them a fortune at some long future date if they stayed with him and continued to produce high grade steel at the lowest possible cost.

Included below are portions of chapters *10, 12, 13, 14, and 16 of* The Autobiography of Andrew Carnegie, *ed. John Van Dyke (Boston: Houghton Mifflin, 1920).*

The Keystone Works have always been my pet as being the parent of all the other works. But they had not been long in existence before the advantage of wrought- over cast-iron became manifest. Accordingly, to insure uniform quality, and also to make certain shapes which were not then to be obtained, we determined to embark in the manufacture of iron. My brother and I became interested with Thomas N. Miller, Henry Phipps, and Andrew Kloman in a small iron mill. Miller was the first to embark with Kloman and he brought Phipps in, lending him eight hundred dollars to buy a one-sixth interest, in November, 1861.

I must not fail to record that Mr. Miller was the pioneer of our iron manufacturing projects. We were all indebted to Tom, who still lives (July 20, 1911) and sheds upon us the sweetness and light of a most lovable nature, a friend who grows more precious as the years roll by. He has softened by age, and even his outbursts against theology as antagonistic to true religion are in his fine old age much less alarming. We are all prone to grow philosophic in age, and perhaps this is well. [In re-reading this—July 19, 1912—in our retreat upon the high moors at Aultnagar, I drop a tear for my bosom friend, dear Tom Miller, who died in Pittsburgh last winter. Mrs. Carnegie and I attended his funeral. Henceforth life lacks something, lacks much—my first partner in early years, my dearest friend in old age. May I go where he is, wherever that may be.]

Andrew Kloman had a small steel-hammer in Allegheny City. As a superintendent of the Pennsylvania Railroad I had found that he made the best axles. He was a great mechanic—one who had discovered, what was then unknown in Pittsburgh, that whatever was worth doing with machinery was worth doing well. His German mind made him thorough. What he constructed cost enormously, but when once started it did the work it was intended to do from year's end to year's end. In those early days it was a question with axles generally whether they would run any specified time or break. There was no analysis of material, no scientific treatment of it.

How much this German created! He was the first man to introduce the cold saw that cut cold iron the exact lengths. He invented upsetting machines to make bridge links, and also built the first "universal" mill in America. All these were erected at our works. When Captain Eads could not obtain the couplings for the St. Louis Bridge arches (the contractors failing to make them) and matters were at a standstill, Kloman told us that he could make them and why the others had failed. He succeeded in making them. Up to that date they were the largest semicircles that had ever been rolled. Our confidence in Mr. Kloman may be judged from the fact that when he said he could make them we unhesitatingly contracted to furnish them.

I have already spoken of the intimacy between our family and that of the Phippses. In the early days my chief companion was the elder brother, John. Henry was several years my junior, but had not failed to attract my attention as a bright, clever lad. One day he asked his brother John to lend him a quarter of a dollar. John saw that he had important use for it and handed him the shining quarter without inquiry. Next morning an advertisement appeared in the *Pittsburgh Dispatch:* "A willing boy wishes work."

This was the use the energetic and willing Harry had made of his quarter, probably the first quarter he had ever spent at one time in his life. A response came from the well-known firm of Dilworth and Bidwell. They asked the "willing boy" to call. Harry went and obtained a position as errand boy, and as was then the custom, his first duty every morning was to sweep the office. He went to his parents and obtained their consent, and in this way the young lad launched himself upon the sea of business. There was no holding back a boy like that. It was the old story. He soon became indispensable to his employers, obtained a small interest in a collateral branch of their business; and then, ever on the alert, it was not many years before he attracted the attention of Mr. Miller, who made a small investment for him with Andrew Kloman. That finally resulted in the building of the iron mill in Twenty-Ninth Street. He had been a schoolmate and great crony of my brother Tom. As children they had played together, and throughout life, until my brother's death in 1886, these two formed, as it were, a partnership within a partnership. They invariably held equal interests in the various firms with which they were connected. What one did the other did.

The errand boy is now one of the richest men in the United States and has begun to prove that he knows how to expend his surplus. Years ago he gave beautiful conservatories to the public parks of Allegheny and Pittsburgh. That he specified "that these should be open upon Sunday" shows that he is a man of his time. This clause in the gift created much excitement. Ministers denounced him from the pulpit and assemblies of the church passed resolutions declaring against the desecration of the Lord's Day. But the people rose, *en masse*, against this narrow-minded contention and the Council of the city accepted the gift with acclamation. The sound common sense of my partner was well expressed when he said in reply to a remonstrance by ministers: "It is all very well for you, gentlemen, who work one day in the week and are masters of your time the other six during which you can view the beauties of Nature—all very well for you—but I think it shameful that you should endeavor to shut out from the toiling masses all that is calculated to entertain and instruct them during the only day which you well know they have at their disposal."

These same ministers have recently been quarreling in their convention at Pittsburgh upon the subject of instrumental music in churches. But while they are debating whether it is right to have organs in churches, intelligent people are opening museums, conservatories, and libraries upon the Sabbath; and unless the pulpit soon learns how to meet the real wants of the people in this life (where alone men's duties lie) much better than it is doing at present, these rival claimants for popular favor may soon empty their churches.

Unfortunately Kloman and Phipps soon differed with Miller about the business and forced him out. Being convinced that Miller was unfairly treated, I united with him in building new works. These were the Cyclops Mills of 1864. After they were set running it became possible, and therefore advisable, to unite the old and the new works, and the Union Iron Mills were formed by their consolidation in 1867. I did not believe that Mr. Miller's reluctance to associate again with his former partners, Phipps and Kloman, could not be overcome, because they would not control the Union Works. Mr. Miller, my brother, and I would hold the controlling interest. But Mr. Miller proved obdurate and begged me to buy his interest, which I reluctantly did after all efforts had failed to induce him to let bygones be bygones. He was Irish, and the Irish blood when aroused is uncontrollable. Mr. Miller has since regretted (to me) his refusal of my earnest request, which would have enabled the pioneer of all of us to reap what was only his rightful reward—millionairedom for himself and his followers.

We were young in manufacturing then and obtained for the Cyclops Mills what was considered at the time an enormous extent of land—seven acres. For some years we offered to lease a portion of the ground to others. It soon became a question whether we could continue the manufacture of iron within so small an area. Mr. Kloman succeeded in making iron beams and for many years our mill was far in advance of any other in that respect. We began at the new mill by making all shapes which were required, and especially such as no other concern would undertake, depending upon an increasing demand in our growing country for things that were only rarely needed at first. What others could not or would not do we would attempt, and this was a rule of our business which was strictly adhered to. Also we would make nothing except of excellent quality. We always accommodated our customers, even although at some expense to ourselves, and in cases of dispute we gave the other party the benefit of the doubt and settled. These were our rules. We had no lawsuits.

As I became acquainted with the manufacture of iron I was greatly surprised to find that the cost of each of the various processes was unknown. Inquiries made of the leading manufacturers of Pittsburgh proved this. It was a lump business, and until stock was taken and the books balanced at the end of the year, the manufacturers were in total ignorance of results. I heard of men who thought their business at the end of the year would show a loss and had found a profit, and vice versa. I felt as if we were moles burrowing in the dark, and this to me was intolerable. I insisted upon such a system of weighing and accounting being introduced throughout our works as would enable us to know what our cost was for each process and especially what each man was doing, who saved material, who wasted it, and who produced the best results.

To arrive at this was a much more difficult task than one would imagine. Every manager in the mills was naturally against the new system. Years were required before an accurate system was obtained, but eventually, by the aid of many clerks and the introduction of weighing scales at various points in the mill, we began to know not only what every department was doing, but what each one of the many men working at the furnaces was doing, and thus to compare one with another. One of the chief sources of success in manufacturing is the introduction and strict maintenance of a perfect system of accounting so that responsibility for money or materials can be brought home to every man. Owners who, in the office, would not trust a clerk with five dollars without having a check upon him, were supplying tons of material daily to men in the mills without exacting an account of their stewardship by weighing what each returned in the finished form.

The Siemens Gas Furnace had been used to some extent in Great Britain for heating steel and iron, but it was supposed to be too expensive. I well remember the criticisms made by older heads among the Pittsburgh manufacturers about the extravagant expenditure we were making upon these newfangled furnaces. But in the heating of great masses of material, almost half the waste could sometimes be saved by using the new furnaces. The expenditure would have been justified, even if it had been doubled. Yet it was many years before we were followed in this new departure; and in some of those years the margin of profit was so small that the most of it was made up from the savings derived from the adoption of the improved furnaces.

Our strict system of accounting enabled us to detect the great waste possible in heating large masses of iron. This improvement revealed to us a valuable man in a clerk, William Borntraeger, a distant relative of Mr. Kloman, who came from Germany. He surprised us one day by presenting a detailed statement showing results for a period, which seemed incredible. All the needed labor in preparing this statement he had performed at night unasked and unknown to us. The form adapted was uniquely original. Needless to say, William soon became superintendent of the works and later a partner, and the poor German lad died a millionaire. He well deserved his fortune. . . .

The small shops put up originally for the Keystone Bridge Company had been leased for other purposes and ten acres of ground had been secured in Lawrenceville on which new and extensive shops were erected. Repeated additions to the Union Iron Mills had made them the leading mills in the United States for all sorts of structural shapes. Business was promising and all the surplus earnings I was making in other fields were required to expand the iron business. I had become interested, with my friends of the Pennsylvania Railroad Company, in building some railways in the Western States, but gradually withdrew from all such enterprises and made up my mind to go entirely contrary to the adage not to put all one's eggs in one basket. I determined that the proper policy was "to put all good eggs in one basket and then watch that basket."

I believe the true road to preeminent success in any line is to make yourself master in that line. I have no faith in the policy of scattering one's resources, and in my experience I have rarely if ever met a man who achieved preeminence in money-making—certainly never one in manufacturing—who was interested in many concerns. The men who have succeeded are men who have chosen one line and stuck to it. It is surprising how few men appreciate the enormous dividends derivable from investment in their own business. There is scarcely a manufacturer in the world who has not in his works some machinery that should be thrown out and replaced by improved appliances; or who does not for the want of additional machinery or new methods lose more than sufficient to pay the largest dividend obtainable by investment beyond his own domain. And yet most business men whom I have known invest in bank shares and in faraway enterprises, while the true gold mine lies right in their own factories.

I have tried always to hold fast to this important fact. It has been with me a cardinal doctrine that I could manage my own capital better than any other person, much better than any board of directors. The losses men encounter during a business life which seriously embarrass them are rarely in their own business, but in enterprises of which the investor is not master. My advice to young men would be not only to concentrate their whole time and attention on the one business in life in which they engage, but to put every dollar of their capital into it. If there be any business that will not bear extension, the true policy is to invest the surplus in first-class securities which will yield a moderate but certain revenue if some other growing business cannot be found. As for myself my decision was taken early. I would concentrate upon the manufacture of iron and steel and be master in that.

My visits to Britain gave me excellent opportunities to renew and make acquaintance with those prominent in the iron and steel business—Bessemer in the front, Sir Lothian Bell, Sir Bernard Samuelson. Sir Windsor Richards, Edward Martin, Bingley, Evans, and the whole host of captains in that industry. My election to the council, and finally to the presidency of the British Iron and Steel Institute soon followed, I being the first president who was not a British subject. That honor was highly appreciated, although at first declined, because I feared that I could not give sufficient time to its duties, owing to my residence in America.

As we had been compelled to engage in the manufacture of wrought-iron in order to make bridges and other structures, so now we thought it desirable to manufacture our own pig iron. And this led to the erection of the Lucy Furnace in the year 1870—a venture which would have been postponed had we fully appreciated its magnitude. We heard from time to time the ominous predictions made by our older brethren in the manufacturing business with regard to the rapid growth and extension of our young concern, but we were not deterred. We thought we had sufficient capital and credit to justify the building of one blast furnace.

The estimates made of its cost, however, did not cover more than half the expenditure. It was an experiment with us. Mr. Kloman knew nothing about blast-furnace operations. But even without exact knowledge no serious blunder was made. The yield of the Lucy Furnace (named after my bright sister-in-law) exceeded our most sanguine expectations and the then unprecedented output of a hundred tons per day was made from one blast furnace, for one week— an output that the world had never heard of before. We held the record and many visitors came to marvel at the marvel.

Looking back today it seems incredible that only forty years ago (1870) chemistry in the United States was an almost unknown agent in connection with the manufacture of pig iron. It was the agency, above all others, most needful in the manufacture of iron and steel. The blast-furnace manager of that day was usually a rude bully, generally a foreigner, who in addition to his other acquirements was able to knock down a man now and then as a lesson to the other unruly spirits under him. He was supposed to diagnose the condition of the furnace by instinct, to possess some almost supernatural power of divination, like his congener in the country districts who was reputed to be able to locate an oil well or water supply by means of a hazel rod. He was a veritable quack doctor who applied whatever remedies occurred to him for the troubles of his patient.

The Lucy Furnace was out of one trouble and into another, owing to the great variety of ores, limestone, and coke which were then supplied with little or no regard to their component parts. This state of affairs became intolerable to us. We finally decided to dispense with the rule-of-thumb-and-intuition manager, and to place a young man in charge of the furnace. We had a young shipping clerk, Henry M. Curry, who had distinguished himself, and it was resolved to make him manager.

Mr. Phipps had the Lucy Furnace under his special charge. His daily visits to it saved us from failure there. Not that the furnace was not doing as well as other furnaces in the West as to money-making, but being so much larger than other furnaces its variations entailed much more serious results. I am afraid my partner had something to answer for in his Sunday morning visits to the Lucy Furnace when his good father and sister left the house for more devotional duties. But even if he had gone with them his real earnest prayer could not but have had reference at times to the precarious condition of the Lucy Furnace then absorbing his thoughts.

The next step taken was to find a chemist as Mr. Curry's assistant and guide. We found the man in a learned German, Dr. Fricke, and great secrets did the doctor open up to us. Iron stone from mines that had a high reputation was now found to contain ten, fifteen, and even twenty percent less iron than it had been credited with. Mines that hitherto had a poor reputation we found to be now yielding superior ore. The good was bad and the bad was good, and everything was topsy-turvy. Nine-tenths of all the uncertainties of pig-iron making were dispelled under the burning sun of chemical knowledge.

At a most critical period when it was necessary for the credit of the firm that the blast furnace should make its best product, it had been stopped because an exceedingly rich and pure ore had been substituted for an inferior ore—an ore which did not yield more than two thirds of the quantity of iron of the other. The furnace had met with disaster because too much lime had been used to flux this exceptionally pure ironstone. The very superiority of the materials had involved us in serious losses.

What fools we had been! But then there was this consolation: we were not as great fools as our competitors. It was years after we had taken chemistry to guide us that it was said by the proprietors of some other furnaces that they could not afford to employ a chemist. Had they known the truth then, they would have known that they could not afford to be without one. Looking back it seems pardonable to record that we were the first to employ a chemist at blast furnaces—something our competitors pronounced extravagant.

The Lucy Furnace became the most profitable branch of our business, because we had almost the entire monopoly of scientific management. Having discovered the secret, it was not long (1872) before we decided to erect an additional furnace. This was done with great economy as compared with our first experiment. The mines which had no reputation and the products of which many firms would not permit to be used in their blast furnaces found a purchaser in us. Those mines which were able to obtain an enormous price for their products, owing to a reputation for quality, we quietly ignored. A curious illustration of this was the celebrated Pilot Knob mine in Missouri. Its product was, so to speak, under a cloud. A small portion of it only could be used, it was said, without obstructing the furnace. Chemistry told us that it was low in phosphorus, but very high in silicon. There was no better ore and scarcely any as rich, if it were properly fluxed. We therefore bought heavily of this and received the thanks of the proprietors for rendering their property valuable.

It is hardly believable that for several years we were able to dispose of the highly phosphoric cinder from the puddling furnaces at a higher price than we had to pay for the pure cinder from the heating furnaces of our competitors—a cinder which was richer in iron than the puddled cinder and much freer from phosphorus. Upon some occasion a blast furnace had attempted to smelt the flue cinder, and from its greater purity the furnace did not work well with a mixture intended for an impurer article; hence for years it was thrown over the banks of the river at Pittsburgh by our competitors as worthless. In some cases we were even able to exchange a poor article for a good one and obtain a bonus.

But it is still more unbelievable that a prejudice, equally unfounded, existed against putting into the blast furnaces the roll-scale from the mills which was pure oxide of iron. This reminds me of my dear friend and fellow-Dunfermline townsman, Mr. Chisholm, of Cleveland. We had many pranks together. One day, when I was visiting his works at Cleveland, I saw men wheeling this valuable roll-scale into the yard. I asked Mr. Chisholm where they were going with it, and he said:

"To throw it over the bank. Our managers have always complained that they had bad luck when they attempted to remelt it in the blast furnace."

I said nothing, but upon my return to Pittsburgh I set about having a joke at his expense. We had then a young man in our service named Du Puy, whose father was known as the inventor of a direct process in iron-making with which he was then experimenting in Pittsburgh. I recommended our people to send Du Puy to Cleveland to contract for all the roll-scale of my friend's establishment. He did so, buying it for fifty cents per ton and having it shipped to him direct. This continued for some time. I expected always to hear of the joke being discovered. The premature death of Mr. Chisholm occurred before I could apprise him of it. His successors soon, however, followed our example.

I had not failed to notice the growth of the Bessemer process. If this proved successful I knew that iron was destined to give place to steel; that the Iron Age would pass away and the Steel Age take its place. My friend, John A. Wright, president of the Freedom Iron Works at Lewiston, Pennsylvania, had visited England purposely to investigate the new process. He was one of our best and most experienced manufacturers, and his decision was so strongly in its favor that he induced his company to erect Bessemer works. He was quite right, but just a little in advance of his time. The capital required was greater than he estimated. More than this, it was not to be expected that a process which was even then in somewhat of an experimental stage in Britain could be transplanted to the new country and operated successfully from the start. The experiment was certain to be long and costly, and for this my friend had not made sufficient allowance.

At a later date, when the process had become established in England, capitalists began to erect the present Pennsylvania Steel Works at Harrisburg. These also had to pass through an experimental stage and at a critical moment would probably have been wrecked but for the timely assistance of the Pennsylvania Railroad Company. It required a broad and able man like President Thomson, of the Pennsylvania Railroad, to recommend to his board of directors that so large a sum as six hundred thousand dollars should be advanced to a manufacturing concern on his road, that steel rails might be secured for the line. The result fully justified his action.

The question of a substitute for iron rails upon the Pennsylvania Railroad and other leading lines had become a very serious one. Upon certain curves at Pittsburgh, on the road connecting the Pennsylvania with the Fort Wayne, I had seen new iron rails placed every six weeks or two months. Before the Bessemer process was known I had called President Thomson's attention to the efforts of Mr. Dodds in England, who had carbonized the heads of iron rails with good results. I went to England and obtained control of the Dodds patents and recommended President Thomson to appropriate twenty thousand dollars for experiments at Pittsburgh, which he did. We built a furnace on our grounds at the upper mill and treated several hundred tons of rails for the Pennsylvania Railroad Company and with remarkably good results as compared with iron rails. These were the first hard-headed rails used in America. We placed them on some of the sharpest curves and their superior service far more than compensated for the advance made by Mr. Thomson. Had the Bessemer process not been successfully developed, I verily believe that we should ultimately have been able to improve the Dodds process sufficiently to make its adoption general. But there was nothing to be compared with the solid steel article which the Bessemer process produced.

Our friends of the Cambria Iron Company at Johnstown, near Pittsburgh—the principal manufacturers of rails in America—decided to erect a Bessemer plant. In England I had seen it demonstrated, at least to my satisfaction, that the process could be made a grand success without undue expenditure of capital or great risk. Mr. William Coleman, who was ever alive to new methods, arrived at the same conclusion. It was agreed we should enter upon the manufacture of steel rails at Pittsburgh. He became a partner and also my dear friend Mr. David McCandless, who had so kindly offered aid to my mother at my father's death. The latter was not forgotten. Mr. John Scott and Mr. David A. Stewart, and others joined me; Mr. Edgar Thomson and Mr. Thomas Scott, president and vice-president of the Pennsylvania Railroad, also became stockholders, anxious to encourage the development of steel. The steel-rail company was organized January 1, 1873.

The question of location was the first to engage our serious attention. I could not reconcile myself to any location that was proposed, and finally went to Pittsburgh to consult with my partners about it. The subject was constantly in my mind and in bed Sunday morning the site suddenly appeared to me. I rose and called to my brother:

"Tom, you and Mr. Coleman are right about the location; right at Braddock's, between the Pennsylvania, the Baltimore and Ohio, and the river, is the best situation in America; and let's call the works after our dear friend Edgar Thomson. Let us go over to Mr. Coleman's and drive out to Braddock's."

We did so that day, and the next morning Mr. Coleman was at work trying to secure the property. Mr. McKinney, the owner, had a high idea of the value of his farm. What we had expected to purchase for five or six hundred dollars an acre cost us two thousand. But since then we have been compelled to add to our original purchase at a cost of five thousand dollars per acre.

There, on the very field of Braddock's defeat, we began the erection of our steel-rail mills. In excavating for the foundations many relics of the battle were found—bayonets, swords, and the like. It was there that the then provost of Dunfermline, Sir Arthur Halkett, and his son were slain. How did they come to be there will very naturally be asked. It must not be forgotten that, in those days, the provosts of the cities of Britain were members of the aristocracy—the great men of the district who condescended to enjoy the honor of the position without performing the duties. No one in trade was considered good enough for the provostship. We have remnants of this aristocratic notion throughout Britain today. There is scarcely any life assurance or railway company, or in some cases manufacturing company but must have at its head, to enjoy the honors of the presidency, some titled person totally ignorant of the duties of the position. So it was that Sir Arthur Halkett, as a gentleman, was Provost of Dunfermline, but by calling he followed the profession of arms and was killed on this spot. It was a coincidence that what had been the field of death to two native-born citizens of Dunfermline should be turned into an industrial hive by two others.

Another curious fact has recently been discovered. Mr. John Morley's address, in 1904 on Founder's Day at the Carnegie Institute, Pittsburgh, referred to the capture of Fort Duquesne by General Forbes and his writing Prime Minister Pitt that he had rechristened it "Pittsburgh" for him. This General Forbes was then Laird of Pittencrieff and was born in the Glen which I purchased in 1902 and presented to Dunfermline for a public park. So that two Dunfermline men have been Lairds of Pittencrieff whose chief work was in Pittsburgh. One named Pittsburgh and the other labored for its development.

In naming the steel mills as we did the desire was to honor my friend Edgar Thomson, but when I asked permission to use his name his reply was significant. He said that as far as American steel rails were concerned, he did not feel that he wished to connect his name with them, for they had proved to be far from creditable. Uncertainty was, of course, inseparable from the experimental stage; but, when I assured him that it was now possible to make steel rails in America as good in every particular as the foreign article, and that we intended to obtain for our rails the reputation enjoyed by the Keystone bridges and the Kloman axles, he consented.

He was very anxious to have us purchase land upon the Pennsylvania Railroad, as his first thought was always for that company. This would have given the Pennsylvania a monopoly of our traffic. When he visited Pittsburgh a few months later and Mr. Robert Pitcairn, my successor as superintendent of the Pittsburgh Division of the Pennsylvania, pointed out to him the situation of the new works at Braddock's Station, which gave us not only a connection with his own line, but also with the rival Baltimore and Ohio line, and with a rival in one respect greater than either—the Ohio River—he said, with a twinkle of his eye to Robert, as Robert told me:

"Andy should have located his works a few miles farther east." But Mr. Thomson knew the good and sufficient reasons which determined the selection of the unrivaled site.

The works were well advanced when the financial panic of September, 1873, came upon us. I then entered upon the most anxious period of my business life. All was going well when one morning in our summer cottage, in the Allegheny Mountains at Cresson, a telegram came announcing the failure of Jay

Cooke & Co. Almost every hour after brought news of some fresh disaster. House after house failed. The question every morning was which would go next. Every failure depleted the resources of other concerns. Loss after loss ensued, until a total paralysis of business set in. Every weak spot was discovered and houses that otherwise would have been strong were borne down largely because our country lacked a proper banking system.

We had not much reason to be anxious about our debts. Not what we had to pay of our own debts could give us much trouble, but rather what we might have to pay for our debtors. It was not our bills payable but our bills receivable which required attention, for we soon had to begin meeting both. Even our own banks had to beg us not to draw upon our balances. One incident will shed some light upon the currency situation. One of our paydays was approaching. One hundred thousand dollars in small notes were absolutely necessary, and to obtain these we paid a premium of twenty-four hundred dollars in New York and had them expressed to Pittsburgh. It was impossible to borrow money, even upon the best collaterals; but by selling securities, which I had in reserve, considerable sums were realized — the company undertaking to replace them later.

It happened that some of the railway companies whose lines centered in Pittsburgh owed us large sums for material furnished — the Fort Wayne road being the largest debtor. I remember calling upon Mr. Thaw, the vice-president of the Fort Wayne, and telling him we must have our money. He replied:

"You ought to have your money, but we are not paying anything these days that is not protestable."

"Very good," I said, "your freight bills are in that category and we shall follow your excellent example. Now I am going to order that we do not pay you one dollar for freight."

"Well, if you do that," he said, "we will stop your freight."

I said we would risk that. The railway company could not proceed to that extremity. And as a matter of fact we ran for some time without paying the freight bills. It was simply impossible for the manufacturers of Pittsburgh to pay their accruing liabilities when their customers stopped payment. The banks were forced to renew maturing paper. They behaved splendidly to us, as they always have done, and we steered safely through. But in a critical period like this there was one thought uppermost with me, to gather more capital and keep it in our business so that come what would we should never again be called upon to endure such nights and days of racking anxiety.

Speaking for myself in this great crisis, I was at first the most excited and anxious of the partners. I could scarcely control myself. But when I finally saw the strength of our financial position I became philosophically cool and found myself quite prepared, if necessary, to enter the directors' rooms of the various banks with which we dealt, and lay our entire position before their boards. I felt that this could result in nothing discreditable to us. No one interested in our business had lived extravagantly. Our manner of life had been the very reverse of this. No money had been withdrawn from the business to build costly homes, and, above all, not one of us had made speculative ventures upon the stock exchange, or invested in any other enterprises than those connected with the main business. Neither had we exchanged endorsements with others. Besides this we could show a prosperous business that was making money every year.

I was thus enabled to laugh away the fears of my partners, but none of them rejoiced more than I did that the necessity for opening our lips to anybody about our finances did not arise. Mr. Coleman, good friend and true, with plentiful means and splendid credit, did not fail to volunteer to give us his endorsements. In this we stood alone; William Coleman's name, a tower of strength, was for us only. How the grand old man comes before me as I write. His patriotism knew no bounds. Once when visiting his mills, stopped for the Fourth of July, as they always were, he found a corps of men at work repairing the boilers. He called the manager to him and asked what this meant. He ordered all work suspended.

"Work on the Fourth of July!" he exclaimed, "when there's plenty of Sundays for repairs!" He was furious.

When the cyclone of 1873 struck us we at once began to reef sail in every quarter. Very reluctantly did we decide that the construction of the new steel works must cease for a time. Several prominent persons, who had invested in them, became unable to meet their payments and I was compelled to take over their interests, repaying the full cost to all. In that way control of the company came into my hands.

The first outburst of the storm had affected the financial world connected with the Stock Exchange. It was some time before it reached the commercial and manufacturing world. But the situation grew worse and worse and finally led to the crash which involved my friends in the Texas Pacific enterprise, of which I have already spoken. This was to me the severest blow of all. People could, with difficulty, believe that occupying such intimate relations as I did with the Texas group, I could by any possibility have kept myself clear of their financial obligations.

Mr. Schoenberger, president of the Exchange Bank at Pittsburgh, with which we conducted a large business, was in New York when the news reached him of the embarrassment of Mr. Scott and Mr. Thomson. He hastened to Pittsburgh, and at a meeting of his board next morning said it was simply impossible that I was not involved with them. He suggested that the bank should refuse to discount more of our bills receivable. He was alarmed to find that the amount of these bearing our endorsement and under discount, was so large. Prompt action on my part was necessary to prevent serious trouble. I took the first train for Pittsburgh, and was able to announce there to all concerned that, although I was a shareholder in the Texas enterprise, my interest was paid for. My name was not upon one dollar of their paper or of any other outstanding paper. I stood clear and clean without a financial obligation or property which I did not own and which was not fully paid for. My only obligations were those connected with our business; and I was prepared to pledge for it every dollar I owned, and to endorse every obligation the firm had outstanding.

Up to this time I had the reputation in business of being a bold, fearless, and perhaps a somewhat reckless young man. Our operations had been extensive, our growth rapid and, although still young, I had been handling millions. My own career was thought by the elderly ones of Pittsburgh to have been rather more brilliant than substantial. I know of an experienced one who declared that if "Andrew Carnegie's brains did not carry him through his luck would." But I think nothing could be farther from the truth than the estimate thus suggested. I am sure that any competent judge would be surprised to find how little I ever risked for myself or my partners. When I did big things, some large corporation like the Pennsylvania Railroad Company was behind me and the responsible party. My supply of Scotch caution never has been small; but I was apparently something of a dare-devil now and then to the manufacturing fathers of Pittsburgh. They were old and I was young, which made all the difference.

The fright which Pittsburgh financial institutions had with regard to myself and our enterprises rapidly gave place to perhaps somewhat unreasoning confidence. Our credit became unassailable, and thereafter in times of financial pressure the offerings of money to us increased rather than diminished, just as the deposits of the old Bank of Pittsburgh were never so great as when the deposits in other banks ran low. It was the only bank in America which redeemed its circulation in gold, disdaining to take refuge under the law and pay its obligations in greenbacks. It had few notes, and I doubt not the decision paid as an advertisement.

In addition to the embarrassment of my friends Mr. Scott, Mr. Thomson, and others, there came upon us later an even severer trial in the discovery that our partner, Mr. Andrew Kloman, had been led by a party of speculative people into the Escanaba Iron Company. He was assured that the concern was to be made a stock company, but before this was done his colleagues had succeeded in creating an enormous amount of liabilities—about seven hundred thousand dollars. There was nothing but bankruptcy as a means of reinstating Mr. Kloman.

This gave us more of a shock than all that had preceded, because Mr. Kloman, being a partner, had no right to invest in another iron company, or in any other company involving personal debt, without informing his partners. There is one imperative rule for men in business—no secrets from partners. Disregard of this rule involved not only Mr. Kloman himself, but our company, in peril, coming, as it did, atop of the difficulties of my Texas Pacific friends with whom I had been intimately associated. The question for a time was whether there was anything really sound. Where could we find bedrock upon which we could stand?

Had Mr. Kloman been a businessman it would have been impossible ever to allow him to be a partner with us again after this discovery. He was not such, however, but the ablest of practical mechanics with some business ability. Mr. Kloman's ambition had been to be in the office, where he was worse than useless, rather than in the mill devising and running new machinery, where he was without a peer. We had some difficulty in placing him in his proper position and keeping him there, which may have led him to seek an outlet elsewhere. He was perhaps flattered by men who were well known in the community; and in this case he was led by persons who knew how to reach him by extolling his wonderful business abilities in addition to his mechanical genius—abilities which his own partners, as already suggested, but faintly recognized.

After Mr. Kloman had passed through the bankruptcy court and was again free, we offered him a ten percent interest in our business, charging for it only the actual capital invested, with nothing whatever for goodwill. This we were to carry for him until the profits paid for it. We were to charge interest only on the cost, and he was to assume no responsibility. The offer was accompanied by the condition that he should not enter into any other business or endorse for others, but give his whole time and attention to the mechanical and not the business management of the mills. Could he have been persuaded to accept this, he would have been a multimillionaire; but his pride, and more particularly that of his family, perhaps, would not permit this. He would go into business on his own account, and, notwithstanding the most urgent appeals on my part, and that of my colleagues, he persisted in the determination to start a new rival concern with his sons as business managers. The result was failure and premature death.

How foolish we are not to recognize what we are best fitted for and can perform, not only with ease but with pleasure, as masters of the craft. More than one able man I have known has persisted in blundering in an office when he had great talent for the mill, and has worn himself out, oppressed with cares and anxieties, his life a continual round of misery, and the result at last failure. I never regretted parting with any man so much as Mr. Kloman. His was a good heart, a great mechanical brain, and had he been left to himself I believe he would have been glad to remain with us. Offers of capital from others—offers which failed when needed—turned his head, and the great mechanic soon proved the poor man of affairs.[1]

When Mr. Kloman had severed his connection with us there was no hesitation in placing William Borntraeger in charge of the mills. It has always been with especial pleasure that I have pointed to the career of William.

---

1. Long after the circumstances here recited, Mr. Isidor Straus called upon Mr. Henry Phipps and asked him if two statements which had been publicly made about Mr. Carnegie and his partners in the steel company were true. Mr. Phipps replied they were not. Then said Mr. Straus: "Mr. Phipps, you owe it to yourself and also to Mr. Carnegie to say so publicly." This Mr. Phipps did in the *New York Herald*, January 30, 1904, in the following handsome manner and without Mr. Carnegie's knowledge:

Question: "In a recent publication mention was made of Mr. Carnegie's not having treated Mr. Miller, Mr. Kloman, and yourself properly during your early partnership, and at its termination. Can you tell me anything about this?"

Answer: "Mr. Miller has already spoken for himself in this matter, and I can say that the treatment received from Mr. Carnegie during our partnership, so far as I was concerned, was always fair and liberal.

"My association with Mr. Kloman in business goes back forty-three years. Everything in connection with Mr. Carnegie's partnership with Mr. Kloman was of a pleasant nature.

"At a much more recent date, when the firm of Carnegie, Kloman and Company was formed, the partners were Andrew Carnegie, Thomas M. Carnegie, Andrew Kloman, and myself. The Carnegies held the controlling interest.

"After the partnership agreement was signed, Mr. Kloman said to me that the Carnegies, owning the larger interest, might be too enterprising in making improvements, which might lead us into serious

He came direct from Germany—a young man who could not speak English, but being distantly connected with Mr. Kloman was employed in the mills, at first in a minor capacity. He promptly learned English and became a shipping clerk at six dollars per week. He had not a particle of mechanical knowledge, and yet such was his unflagging zeal and industry for the interests of his employer that he soon became marked for being everywhere about the mill, knowing everything, and attending to everything.

William was a character. He never got over his German idioms and his inverted English made his remarks very effective. Under his superintendence the Union Iron Mills became a most profitable branch of our business. He had overworked himself after a few years' application and we decided to give him a trip to Europe. He came to New York by way of Washington. When he called upon me in New York he expressed himself as more anxious to return to Pittsburgh than to revisit Germany. In ascending the Washington Monument he had seen the Carnegie beams in the stairway and also at other points in public buildings, and as he expressed it:

"It yust make me so broud dat I want to go right back and see dat everyting is going right at de mill."

Early hours in the morning and late in the dark hours at night William was in the mills. His life was there. He was among the first of the young men we admitted to partnership, and the poor German lad at his death was in receipt of an income, as I remember, of about $50,000 a year, every cent of which was deserved. Stories about him are many. At a dinner of our partners to cele-

---

trouble; and he thought that they should consent to an article in the partnership agreement requiring the consent of three partners to make effective any vote for improvements. I told him that we could not exact what he asked, as their larger interest assured them control, but I would speak to them. When the subject was broached, Mr. Carnegie promptly said that if he could not carry Mr. Kloman or myself with his brother in any improvements he would not wish them made. Other matters were arranged by courtesy during our partnership in the same manner."

Question: "What you have told me suggests the question, why did Mr. Kloman leave the firm?"

Answer: "During the great depression which followed the panic of 1873, Mr. Kloman, through an unfortunate partnership in the Escanaba Furnace Company, lost his means, and his interest in our firm had to be disposed of. We bought it at book value at a time when manufacturing properties were selling at ruinous prices, often as low as one-third or one-half their cost.

"After the settlement had been made with the creditors of the Escanaba Company, Mr. Kloman was offered an interest by Mr. Carnegie of $100,000 in our firm, to be paid only from future profits. This Mr. Kloman declined, as he did not feel like taking an interest which formerly had been much larger. Mr. Carnegie gave him $40,000 from the firm to make a new start. This amount was invested in a rival concern, which soon closed.

"I knew of no disagreement during this early period with Mr. Carnegie, and their relations continued pleasant as long as Mr. Kloman lived. Harmony always marked their intercourse, and they had the kindliest feeling one for the other."

brate the year's business, short speeches were in order from every one. William summed up his speech thus: "What we haf to do, shentlemens, is to get brices up and costs down and efery man *stand on his own bottom.*" There was loud, prolonged, and repeated laughter.

Captain Evans ("Fighting Bob") was at one time government inspector at our mills. He was a severe one. William was sorely troubled at times and finally offended the Captain, who complained of his behavior. We tried to get William to realize the importance of pleasing a government official. William's reply was: "But he gomes in and smokes my cigars" (bold Captain! William reveled in one-cent Wheeling tobies) "and then he goes and contems my iron. What does you tinks of a man like dat? But I apologize and dreat him right to-morrow."

The Captain was assured William had agreed to make due amends, but he laughingly told us afterward that William's apology was: "Vell, Captain, I hope you vas all right dis morning. I haf noting against you, Captain," holding out his hand, which the Captain finally took and all was well.

William once sold to our neighbor, the pioneer steelmaker of Pittsburgh, James Park, a large lot of old rails which we could not use. Mr. Park found them of a very bad quality. He made claims for damages and William was told that he must go with Mr. Phipps to meet Mr. Park and settle. Mr. Phipps went into Mr. Park's office, while William took a look around the works in search of the condemned material, which was nowhere to be seen. Well did William know where to look. He finally entered the office, and before Mr. Park had time to say a word William began: "Mr. Park, I vas glad to hear dat de old rails what I sell you don't suit for steel. I will buy dem all from you back, five dollars ton profit for you." Well did William know that they had all been used. Mr. Park was nonplussed, and the affair ended. William had triumphed.

Upon one of my visits to Pittsburgh William told me he had something "particular" he wished to tell me—something he couldn't tell any one else. This was upon his return from the trip to Germany. There he had been asked to visit for a few days a former schoolfellow, who had risen to be a professor:

"Well, Mr. Carnegie, his sister who kept his house was very kind to me, and ven I got to Hamburg I tought I sent her yust a little present. She write me a letter, then I write her a letter. She write me and I write her, and den I ask her would she marry me. She was very educated, but she write yes. Den I ask her to come to New York, and I meet her dere, but, Mr. Carnegie, dem people don't know noting about business and de mills. Her bruder write me dey want me to go dere again and marry her in Chairmany, and I can go away not again from de mills. I tought I yust ask you aboud it."

"Of course you can go again. Quite right, William, you should go. I think the better of her people for feeling so. You go over at once and bring her home. I'll arrange it." Then, when parting, I said: "William, I suppose your sweetheart is a beautiful, tall, 'peaches-and-cream' kind of German young lady."

"Vell, Mr. Carnegie, she is a leetle stout. If *I had the rolling of her I give her yust one more pass.*" All William's illustrations were founded on mill practice. [I find myself bursting into fits of laughter this morning (June, 1912) as I re-read this story. But I did this also when reading that "Every man must stand on his own bottom."]

Mr. Phipps had been head of the commercial department of the mills, but when our business was enlarged, he was required for the steel business. Another young man, William L. Abbott, took his place. Mr. Abbott's history is somewhat akin to Borntraeger's. He came to us as a clerk upon a small salary and was soon assigned to the front in charge of the business of the iron mills. He was no less successful than was William. He became a partner with an interest equal to William's, and finally was promoted to the presidency of the company.

Mr. Curry had distinguished himself by this time in his management of the Lucy Furnaces, and he took his place among the partners, sharing equally with the others. There is no way of making a business successful that can vie with the policy of promoting those who render exceptional service. We finally converted the firm of Carnegie, McCandless & Co. into the Edgar Thomson Steel Company, and included my brother and Mr. Phipps, both of whom had declined at first to go into the steel business with their too enterprising senior. But when I showed them the earnings for the first year and told them if they did not get into steel they would find themselves in the wrong boat, they both reconsidered and came with us. It was fortunate for them as for us.

My experience has been that no partnership of new men gathered promiscuously from various fields can prove a good working organization as at first constituted. Changes are required. Our Edgar Thomson Steel Company was no exception to this rule. Even before we began to make rails, Mr. Coleman became dissatisfied with the management of a railway official who had come to us with a great and deserved reputation for method and ability. I had, therefore, to take over Mr. Coleman's interest. It was not long, however, before we found that his judgment was correct. The new man had been a railway auditor, and was excellent in accounts, but it was unjust to expect him, or any other office man, to be able to step into manufacturing and be successful from the start. He had neither the knowledge nor the training for this new work. This does not mean that he was not a splendid auditor. It was our own blunder in expecting the impossible.

The mills were at last about ready to begin[2] and an organization the auditor proposed was laid before me for approval. I found he had divided the works into two departments and had given control of one to Mr. Stevenson, a Scotsman who afterwards made a fine record as a manufacturer, and control of the other to a Mr. Jones. Nothing, I am certain, ever affected the success of the steel company more than the decision which I gave upon that proposal. Upon no account could two men be in the same works with equal authority. An army with two commanders-in-chief, a ship with two captains, could not fare more disastrously than a manufacturing concern with two men in command upon the same ground, even though in two different departments. I said: "This will not do. I do not know Mr. Stevenson, nor do I know Mr. Jones, but one or the other must be made captain and he alone must report to you."

The decision fell upon Mr. Jones and in this way we obtained "The Captain," who afterward made his name famous wherever the manufacture of Bessemer steel is known.

The Captain was then quite young, spare and active, bearing traces of his Welsh descent even in his stature, for he was quite short. He came to us as a two-dollar-a-day mechanic from the neighboring works at Johnstown. We soon saw that he was a character. Every movement told it. He had volunteered as a private during the Civil War and carried himself so finely that he became captain of a company which was never known to flinch. Much of the success of the Edgar Thomson Works belongs to this man.

In later years he declined an interest in the firm which would have made him a millionaire. I told him one day that some of the young men who had been given an interest were now making much more than he was and we had voted to make him a partner. This entailed no financial responsibility, as we always provided that the cost of the interest given was payable only out of profits.

"No," he said, "I don't want to have my thoughts running on business. I

---

2. The steel-rail mills were ready and rails were rolled in 1874.

The Age of Steel

have enough trouble looking after these works. Just gived me a h—l of a salary if you think I'm worth it."

"All right, Captain, the salary of the President of the United States is yours."

"That's the talk," said the little Welshman.[3]

Our competitors in steel were at first disposed to ignore us. Knowing the difficulties they had in starting their own steel works, they could not believe we would be ready to deliver rails for another year and declined to recognize us as competitors. The price of steel rails when we began was about seventy dollars per ton. We sent our agent through the country with instructions to take orders at the best prices he could obtain; and before our competitors knew it, we had obtained a large number—quite sufficient to justify us in making a start.

So perfect was the machinery, so admirable the plans, so skillful were the men selected by Captain Jones, and so great a manager was he himself, that our success was phenomenal. I think I place a unique statement on record when I say that the result of the first month's operations left a margin of profit of $11,000. It is also remarkable that so perfect was our system of accounts that we knew the exact amount of the profit. We had learned from experience in our iron works what exact accounting meant. There is nothing more profitable than clerks to check up each transfer of material from one department to another in process of manufacture.

The one vital lesson in iron and steel that I learned in Britain was the necessity for owning raw materials and finishing the completed article ready for its purpose. Having solved the steel-rail problem at the Edgar Thomson Works, we soon proceeded to the next step. The difficulties and uncertainties of obtaining regular supplies of pig iron compelled us to begin the erection of blast furnaces. Three of these were built, one, however, being a reconstructed blast furnace purchased from the Escanaba Iron Company, with which Mr. Kloman had been connected. As is usual in such cases, the furnace cost us as much as a new one, and it never was as good. There is nothing so unsatisfactory as purchases of inferior plants.

---

3. The story is told that when Mr. Carnegie was selecting his younger partners he one day sent for a young Scotsman, Alexander R. Peacock, and asked him rather abruptly:

"Peacock, what would you give to be made a millionaire?"

"A liberal discount for cash, sir," was the answer.

He was a partner owning a two percent interest when the Carnegie Steel Company was merged into the United States Steel Corporation.

But although this purchase was a mistake, directly considered, it proved, at a subsequent date, a source of great profit because it gave us a furnace small enough for the manufacture of spiegel and, at a later date, of ferro-manganese. We were the second firm in the United States to manufacture our own spiegel, and the first, and for years the only, firm in America that made ferro-manganese. We had been dependent upon foreigners for a supply of this indispensable article, paying as high as eighty dollars a ton for it. The manager of our blast furnaces, Mr. Julian Kennedy, is entitled to the credit of suggesting that with the ores within reach we could make ferro-manganese in our small furnace. The experiment was worth trying and the result was a great success. We were able to supply the entire American demand and prices fell from eighty to fifty dollars per ton as a consequence.

While testing the ores of Virginia we found that these were being quietly purchased by Europeans for ferro-manganese, the owners of the mine being led to believe that they were used for other purposes. Our Mr. Phipps at once set about purchasing that mine. He obtained an option from the owners, who had neither capital nor skill to work it efficiently. A high price was paid to them for their interests, and (with one of them, Mr. Davis, a very able young man) we became the owners, but not until a thorough investigation of the mine had proved that there was enough of manganese ore in sight to repay us. All this was done with speed; not a day was lost when the discovery was made. And here lies the great advantage of a partnership over a corporation. The president of the latter would have had to consult a board of directors and wait several weeks and perhaps months for their decision. By that time the mine would probably have become the property of others.

We continued to develop our blast-furnace plant, every new one being a great improvement upon the preceding, until at last we thought we had arrived at a standard furnace. Minor improvements would no doubt be made, but so far as we could see we had a perfect plant and our capacity was then fifty thousand tons per month of pig iron.

The blast-furnace department was no sooner added than another step was seen to be essential to our independence and success. The supply of superior coke was a fixed quantity—the Connellsville field being defined. We found that we could not get on without a supply of the fuel essential to the smelting of pig iron; and a very thorough investigation of the question led us to the conclusion that the Frick Coke Company had not only the best coal and coke property, but that it had in Mr. Frick himself a man with a positive genius for its management. He had proved his ability by starting as a poor railway clerk and succeeding. In 1882 we purchased one-half of the stock of this company, and by subsequent purchases from other holders we became owners of the great bulk of the shares.

There now remained to be acquired only the supply of iron stone. If we could obtain this we should be in the position occupied by only two or three of the European concerns. We thought at one time we had succeeded in discovering in Pennsylvania this last remaining link in the chain. We were misled, however, in our investment in the Tyrone region, and lost considerable sums as the result of our attempts to mine and use the ores of that section. They promised well at the edges of the mines, where the action of the weather for ages had washed away impurities and enriched the ore, but when we penetrated a small distance they proved too "lean" to work.

Our chemist, Mr. Prousser, was then sent to a Pennsylvania furnace among the hills which we had leased, with instructions to analyze all the materials brought to him from the district, and to encourage people to bring him specimens of minerals. A striking example of the awe inspired by the chemist in those days was that only with great difficulty could he obtain a man or a boy to assist him in the laboratory. He was suspected of illicit intercourse with the Powers of Evil when he undertook to tell by his suspicious-looking apparatus what a stone contained. I believe that at last we had to send him a man from our office at Pittsburgh.

One day he sent us a report of analyses of ore remarkable for the absence of phosphorus. It was really an ore suitable for making Bessemer steel. Such a discovery attracted our attention at once. The owner of the property was Moses Thompson, a rich farmer, proprietor of seven thousand acres of the most beautiful agricultural land in Center County, Pennsylvania. An appointment was made to meet him upon the ground from which the ore had been obtained. We found the mine had been worked for a charcoal blast furnace fifty or sixty years before, but it had not borne a good reputation then, the reason no doubt being that its product was so much purer than other ores that the same amount of flux used caused trouble in smelting. It was so good it was good for nothing in those days of old.

We finally obtained the right to take the mine over at any time within six months, and we therefore began the work of examination, which every purchaser of mineral property should make most carefully. We ran lines across the hillside fifty feet apart, with cross-lines at distances of a hundred feet apart, and at each point of intersection we put a shaft down through the ore. I believe there were eighty such shafts in all and the ore was analyzed at every few feet of depth, so that before we paid over the hundred thousand dollars asked we knew exactly what there was of ore. The result hoped for was more than realized. Through the ability of my cousin and partner, Mr. Lauder, the cost of mining and washing was reduced to a low figure, and the Scotia ore made good all the losses we had incurred in the other mines, paid for itself, and left a profit besides. In this case, at least, we snatched victory from the jaws of defeat. We trod upon sure ground with the chemist as our guide. It will be seen that we were determined to get raw materials and were active in the pursuit.

We had lost and won, but the escapes in business affairs are sometimes very narrow. Driving with Mr. Phipps from the mills one day we passed the National Trust Company office on Penn Street, Pittsburgh. I noticed the large gilt letters across the window, "Stockholders individually liable." That very morning in looking over a statement of our affairs I had noticed twenty shares "National Trust Company" on the list of assets. I said to Harry: "If this is the concern we own shares in, won't you please sell them before you return to the office this afternoon?"

He saw no need for haste. It would be done in good time.

"No, Harry, oblige me by doing it instantly."

He did so and had it transferred. Fortunate, indeed, was this, for in a short time the bank failed with an enormous deficit. My cousin, Mr. Morris, was among the ruined shareholders. Many others met the same fate. Times were panicky, and had we been individually liable for all the debts of the National Trust Company our credit would inevitably have been seriously imperiled. It was a narrow escape. And with only twenty shares (two thousand dollars' worth of stock), taken to oblige friends who wished our name on their list of shareholders! The lesson was not lost. The sound rule in business is that you may give money freely when you have a surplus, but your name never—neither as endorser nor as member of a corporation with individual liability. A trifling investment of a few thousand dollars, a mere trifle—yes, but a trifle possessed of deadly explosive power.

The rapid substitution of steel for iron in the immediate future had become obvious to us. Even in our Keystone Bridge Works, steel was being used more and more in place of iron. King Iron was about to be deposed by the new King Steel, and we were becoming more and more dependent upon it. We had about concluded in 1886 to build alongside of the Edgar Thomson Mills new works for the manufacture of miscellaneous shapes of steel when it was suggested to us that the five or six leading manufacturers of Pittsburgh, who had combined to build steel mills at Homestead, were willing to sell their mills to us.

These works had been built originally by a syndicate of manufacturers, with the view of obtaining the necessary supplies of steel which they required in their various concerns, but the steel-rail business, being then in one of its booms, they had been tempted to change plans and construct a steel-rail mill. They had been able to make rails as long as prices remained high, but, as the mills had not been specially designed for this purpose, they were without the indispensable blast furnaces for the supply of pig iron, and had no coke lands for the supply of fuel. They were in no condition to compete with us.

It was advantageous for us to purchase these works. I felt there was only one way we could deal with their owners, and that was to propose a consolidation with Carnegie Brothers & Co. We offered to do so on equal terms, every dollar they had invested to rank against our dollars. Upon this basis the negotiation was promptly concluded. We, however, gave to all parties the option to take cash, and most fortunately for us, all elected to do so except Mr. George Singer, who continued with us to his and our entire satisfaction. Mr. Singer told us afterwards that his associates had been greatly exercised as to how they could meet the proposition I was to lay before them. They were much afraid of being overreached but when I proposed equality all around, dollar for dollar, they were speechless.

This purchase led to the reconstruction of all our firms. The new firm of Carnegie, Phipps & Co. was organized in 1886 to run the Homestead Mills. The firm of Wilson, Walker & Co. was embraced in the firm of Carnegie, Phipps & Co., Mr. Walker being elected chairman. My brother was chairman of Carnegie Brothers & Co. and at the head of all. A further extension of our business was the establishing of the Hartman Steel Works at Beaver Falls, designed to work into a hundred various forms the product of the Homestead Mills. So now we made almost everything in steel from a wire nail up to a twenty-inch steel girder, and it was then not thought probable that we should enter into any new field.

It may be interesting here to note the progress of our works during the decade 1888 to 1897. In 1888 we had twenty millions of dollars invested; in 1897 more than double or over forty-five millions. The 600,000 tons of pig iron we made per annum in 1888 was trebled; we made nearly 2,000,000. Our product of iron and steel was in 1888, say, 2000 tons per day; it grew to exceed 6000 tons. Our coke works then embraced about 5000 ovens; they were trebled in number, and our capacity, then 6000 tons, became 18,000 tons per day. Our Frick Coke Company in 1897 had 42,000 acres of coal land, more than two-thirds of the true Connellsville vein. Ten years hence increased production may be found to have been equally rapid. It may be accepted as an axiom that a manufacturing concern in a growing country like ours begins to decay when it stops extending.

To make a ton of steel one and a half tons of iron stone has to be mined, transported by rail a hundred miles to the Lakes, carried by boat hundreds of miles, transferred to cars, transported by rail one hundred and fifty miles to Pittsburgh; one and a half tons of coal must be mined and manufactured into coke and carried fifty-odd miles by rail; and one ton of limestone mined and carried one hundred and fifty miles to Pittsburgh. How then could steel be manufactured and sold without loss at three pounds for two cents? This, I confess, seemed to me incredible, and little less than miraculous, but it was so.

America is soon to change from being the dearest steel manufacturing country to the cheapest. Already the shipyards of Belfast are our customers. This is but the beginning. Under present conditions America can produce steel as cheaply as any other land, notwithstanding its higher-priced labor. There is no labor so cheap as the dearest in the mechanical field, provided it is free, contented, zealous, and reaping reward as it renders service. And here America leads.

One great advantage which America will have in competing in the markets of the world is that her manufacturers will have the best home market. Upon this they can depend for a return upon capital, and the surplus product can be exported with advantage, even when the prices received for it do not more than cover actual cost, provided the exports be charged with their proportion of all expenses. The nation that has the best home market, especially if products are standardized, as ours are, can soon outsell the foreign producer. The phrase I used in Britain in this connection was: "The Law of the Surplus." It afterward came into general use in commercial discussions.

8
My Experience with Railway Rates and Rebates

In 1887, Andrew Carnegie brought into Carnegie Brothers as a major partner Henry Clay Frick, the Coke King of America. In so doing, he obtained not only control of a raw material essential to the making of steel, but also the most able lieutenant he would ever employ during his long career of empire building.

The two men, so very different in personality and temperament, were nevertheless in complete accord as to the most basic principle of business policy that led to success. Cost of production should always be the company's greatest concern. The cutting of costs was of far greater importance to achieving success than were either the raising of prices or the distribution of profits.

Each man, however, had his own particular area of concern for cutting the cost of production. For Frick, it was the cost of the labor that was the most troublesome, but for Carnegie it was the cost of transportation. The railroad, more specifically the Pennsylvania Railroad, was Carnegie's bête noire. As a former employee, Carnegie knew all about secret rebates and the great discrepancy between published rates and the actual rates paid by certain customers who were favored because they had access to a competing line. He greatly resented the monopolistic position that the Pennsylvania Railroad held in Pittsburgh, and a consuming ambition which constantly tormented and goaded him was to break that monopoly by a competitive road, preferably one that he himself controlled. He had chosen the site of the Edgar Thomson plant at Braddock because of its proximity to the Baltimore and Ohio line, but unfortunately the B&O did not have facilities adequate to make it a true competitor of the Pennsylvania in handling the freight demands of the plant.

Carnegie assiduously sought and learned, by one means or another—usually illegally, the rates that his competitors were being charged. His general freight manager, George E. McCague, was especially efficient in obtaining these data, probably through bribery. The information was usually sufficient for Carnegie to receive the rates or the rebates that he wanted.

80   *Carnegie at Work, Making Money*

> *In the following article, first published in* Century Magazine *in March 1908, Carnegie gives a highly sanitized version of "My Experience with Railway Rates and Rebates." Here the reader is given the impression that Carnegie was the noble hero battling only for equality of treatment for all manufacturers and for the end of secret rebates. His former freight agent employee, M. M. Bosworth, in an angry letter to Carnegie written in 1907, gives a much more candid account of Carnegie's experiences:*

> Why don't you tell the public that through the great volume of your business you were able to take railroads by the throat and to compel them to secretly violate state and Federal laws . . . ? Why are you apparently afraid to acknowledge that you were the "chiefest rebater" of the Pennsylvania R R Co. . . . It takes Carnegie-Frick millionaire hogs to receive vast financial benefits through secret violations . . . and leave old pals in the lurch. (4 May 1907, Carnegie Papers, Library of Congress, vol. 142)

> *It would seem that Carnegie's experiences with rebates were more varied and rewarding than this highly acclaimed article indicated.*

This subject carries one back to his early days. It was in 1856 that my chief Thomas A. Scott, superintendent of the Pittsburg division of the Pennsylvania Railroad, was made general superintendent, with headquarters at Altoona. I was his secretary and telegraph-operator in Pittsburg, and he took me with him.

The duties of the superintendent of the line, then in its infancy, included the making of local freight rates. These I entered in the rate-book, and naturally grew to take a share in their making. Our great aim in these days was to develop local traffic. Of through traffic little was expected, although President Thomson, the great railroad man of his day, had ventured to predict that a hundred carloads of through freight would in time pass Pittsburg daily. This prophecy was often quoted to show the length to which that sanguine, but far-sighted, official could go. Now every day thousands pass through the city in each direction.

Local traffic—that is, traffic originating and ending upon the line—was then depended upon to yield revenue. One enterprising man would write or call to say that he was thinking of opening a stone quarry on the line and shipping dressed stone to the towns and cities, if he could get rates enabling him to do so. Because traffic paying much less than we might think fair was better than no traffic at all, we would hold out every inducement to pioneers, with the result that the quarry was opened.

Another was willing to make the experiment of cutting bark and shipping it to tanneries, intending later, however, to erect a tannery in the forest. Here was a tempting new enterprise, and rates were readily agreed upon. Another thought a peculiar quality of sand was suitable for glassmaking, and was willing to open the deposit and test it. He was promptly accorded a siding, which was usually necessary, and rates low enough to permit him to begin.

The plot began to thicken when a second man came with a proposition to open another similar factory or quarry, which he could not do unless he received rates equal to those given to his predecessor, although his railway haul might be longer. If two factories were to be only a few miles apart, it was obvious that they had to receive the same rates, and so the question of "special rates," starting very simply, soon became a complicated one. Areas had to be established in which the rates were uniform, although this involved the seeming injustice of charging more per ton per mile upon the traffic of one than of the other. This could not be avoided.

At a later date, corporations were found desirous of establishing ironworks and of opening coal mines, etc.

From such small beginnings was built up the enormous local traffic of the Pennsylvania Railroad, unequalled, it is believed, by any other line in the world. All these rates, it will be understood, referred to traffic within the State of Pennsylvania, Pittsburg and Philadelphia being the terminals of the line. Beyond Philadelphia was the Camden & Amboy Railway; beyond Pittsburg, the Fort Wayne & Chicago, separate organisations with which we had nothing to do.

During this period, through traffic occupied an entirely subordinate position. Rates for it were made in Philadelphia by a "freight agent," who then was an official of little importance compared with what he soon became.

Upon the completion of the Erie, New York Central, Baltimore & Ohio, and the Pennsylvania systems between the Atlantic seaboard and the great West, a strong competition for through traffic at once began. At first it was a scramble, and each road got what it could, at the best rate it could, regardless of everything. The position was peculiar, and is so still, and must long remain so. Eastbound tonnage from Chicago, St. Louis, and other points in the West to the Atlantic seaboard is far greater than that from the East to the West;

hence long trains of empty freight-cars have to be hauled westward empty.

It is evident why westward-bound freight was eagerly sought by all lines. Each had its freight agents, all scrambling to secure the prize. What rates might be obtained for westbound freight was a secondary consideration, for any rate was clear gain, since cars must go west in any case, and might as well go loaded as empty.

Hence bitter wars broke out between the roads at intervals, and the four presidents would meet and make what was called a "gentlemen's agreement." These worthy presidents would give their word of honor that certain rates would be strictly adhered to, and gave orders to that effect, we may be sure, in good faith to their subordinates. But it is a remarkable fact, notwithstanding, that these "gentlemen's agreements" did not last long, but required renewal at short intervals. The rates agreed upon were too easily evaded. The assistant freight agent or one of his staff could promise certain favors to shippers upon other traffic, while adhering strictly to the agreed-upon charge for that he was securing, or could remit charges upon other freight not involved in the agreement.

So gentlemen's agreements were made and remade, but meanwhile freight from Pittsburg was often sent by way of the Ohio River, some five hundred miles, to Cincinnati, transferred from boat to railroad car there, and transported back to Pittsburg by rail, passing through its streets to the seaboard, for less than the fixed rate upon the same articles from Pittsburg direct to the seaboard. It was the same with freight from the East to the West. Many a trainload of iron from the East has passed through the streets of Pittsburg, paying less freight than was charged upon the same articles from Pittsburg to the same points west. The Pennsylvania Railroad had a monopoly of the traffic, and much grievous wrong had we manufacturers in that state to suffer in consequence.

We must not be understood as blaming the Pennsylvania officials severely. They did not raise our Pittsburg rates, and these in themselves might be considered fair; but they lowered the rates to our competitors in their warfare with the trunk-lines. This bore hard upon the manufacturers of Pennsylvania, and especially of Pittsburg. It would have been a wiser and broader policy if the Pennsylvania Railroad had been bold enough to say: "Come what may, we will protect manufacturers upon our own lines"; but it required more than the ordinary railroad official of that day to reach this height. A perfect system of rates over the various routes could not be reached without first passing for a season through great irregularities and making many mistakes. Order had to be hammered out of chaos.

These were the days when the much-talked-of "rebates" had their origin. "Gentlemen's agreement" rates were charged, and the bills of lading were fair and square on the surface, but the understanding with the shipper was that rebates would be allowed and settled for at some future time. The keener members soon discovered that evidence might be called for by competing lines, and the question asked, "Have any rebates been paid on this shipment?" The party concerned might be able to say that he had paid none, but had he been questioned a month or two afterward, perhaps, or asked if advantages in other directions had not been granted to the shipper, he could not have so stated truthfully. In short, every conceivable way of keeping the word of promise to the ear and breaking it to the hope was indulged in. At least we shippers over the Pennsylvania road heard from its officials from time to time that the other lines were most unscrupulous competitors and solely blamable for the reigning disorder.

The sentiment aroused in Pittsburg because of these unequal rates became dangerous. The Pennsylvania Railroad was regarded as a monopoly strangling to local interests, and so it was. The manufacturers of Pittsburg, never in a position to get rebates, were in fact being driven to the wall by the competition of manufacturers upon other lines whose products passed their doors and were carried a thousand miles over the Pennsylvania system for less than they were compelled to pay for half the distance. Remonstrances were constantly made, but without avail, until the time came when the railway company had a dispute with its men, which gave occasion for an outburst of the smoldering bitterness Pittsburg felt. Grave riots took place, and the spirit of hostility shown by all classes to the great monopoly brought from Philadelphia my former chief, then vice-president, to Pittsburg. At a conference with the manufacturers it was agreed by him that no matter what the through rates fell to, the local traffic on their lines from Pittsburg would be carried to Chicago or Philadelphia and New York at a small difference less than the through rate between the seaboard and Chicago and other points. That is to say, Pittsburg traffic would be charged only a shade less for half the distance than Philadelphia and Chicago through traffic paid for double the distance. Rates according to distance were denied. With this the Pittsburg manufacturers had to be content. Matters went along tolerably well until railway rates were again thoroughly demoralised by war between the trunk-lines. Our Carnegie Steel Company upon this occasion had had what it thought the certainty of a contract of great value for material with the Newport News Shipbuilding Company, freight from

Pittsburg to Newport News being much less than from Chicago. The contract, however, went to Chicago, and upon investigation we found that the rate given to our Chicago competitor to Newport News was less than the Pennsylvania Railroad rate from Pittsburg, the distance not one-half so great. President Ingalls of the Chesapeake & Ohio, then beginning his brilliant career, had made the lower rate for his new line, not yet embraced in the "gentlemen's agreement." We investigated, and found several rates of a similar nature prevailing to other points, and having a list of these made, the writer carried it to President Roberts of the Pennsylvania Railroad, with a request that he place us upon his own line on an equality with manufacturers on other lines. When the paper was presented to him, showing the overcharges we labored under, he pushed it aside, saying: "I have enough business of my own to attend to; don't wish to have anything to do with yours, Andy."

I said: "All right, Mr. Roberts; when you wish to see me again, you will ask an interview. Good morning."

The situation had become intolerable, and we looked about for the best means of protecting ourselves. A railroad line of our own from Pittsburg to the Lakes would be an invaluable acquisition, rendering us independent of any monopoly and enabling us to transport all our ironstone traffic from the lakes to Pittsburg, and our coal and coke from Pittsburg to the lakes, also giving us connection with the other through lines. I purchased the harbor at Conneaut and a few miles of railroad connected with it, and began extending the line to Pittsburg.

My partners had good reason to dread the consequences of the reckless challenge to the monster monopoly, and I could not blame them; for it undoubtedly had the power to cripple our operations. An intimation to the superintendent that the car-supply for our works or the movement of our traffic, need not receive undue attention would be serious, indeed. As a precaution, I took good care that the authorities in Philadelphia were advised of the policy I had determined to pursue if there was the slightest interruption to our business: all our works would be stopped, I would visit each in succession, and inform the workmen why they were idle; publish the monopoly rates; explain why Pittsburg needed our new railroad; and ask them, and all the workmen from other mills, to stand with folded arms upon the streets over which the Pennsylvania trains passed for miles, in peaceful protest and as an intimation that justice had better be done to Pittsburg. No interference with our operations came.

Railway Rates and Rebates

It was not long before I received a note from Vice-President Thomson, saying that President Roberts and himself would like an interview. I agreed to call as I passed through Philadelphia, and did so. I write this in the first person because my partners did not see their way to fight the great Pennsylvania Railroad; but my Scotch blood was up, and I was in to fight to the death, determined no longer to stand what we had been groaning under. It was indeed a fearful thing to fall into the hands of a railroad monopoly in those early days, and yet this is to be said for the railroad: while its rates for competitive traffic were being reduced beyond reason by competition, the company needed all the more the high rates upon local traffic if these could be enforced. This was no doubt taking a very narrow view, but railroading was then in its infancy, and public sentiment was not the force it has since become.

What I needed for the interview with my former railway associates were the secret rebate rates prevailing elsewhere. Our freight agent Mr. McCague, then a clever young man, obtained these and placed them in my hands in a few days. He had left me with the word of Richelieu ringing in his ears.

> From the hour I grasp that packet,
> Think your guardian stars rains fortune on you!

Some time after that he was of course admitted to partnership; that was the turning point in his career.

Entering President Roberts's room, I found him and my dear friend, Frank Thomson, vice-president, sitting together. My reception was cordial.

"How are you, Andy?"

"How are you, Mr. Roberts? How are you, Frank? Gentlemen, you asked me for an interview, and here is the culprit before you. Put me in the dock and question me as you wish."

Frank said: "This is just what we want to do. May I be examiner?"

"Yes," I said, "you are just the man."

"What are you fighting the Pennsylvania Railroad for?" he asked. "You were brought up in its service. We were boys together."

"Well, Frank, I knew you would ask me that question, and here is the answer."

I handed him the packet of secret rates, and, begging to be excused for a few minutes, left the room, desirous of giving them an opportunity of looking it over together. Upon my return they were still sitting with the packet lying before them.

Frank raised his head and exclaimed: "Andy, I feel like Rip Van Winkle."

"Frank, the Pennsylvania Railroad officials have slept just about as long."

"Well, tell us what you want."

"I don't want anything. I did not ask to see you. You asked to see me."

"Don't talk that way. What do you want? We wish to make an arrangement satisfactory to you. We did not know these things were going on. We can hardly believe it; but we shall now find out. Tell us what you think we ought to do."

I said: "Gentlemen, all we have ever asked was that the rates charged us shall be at all times as low as those which competitors on other lines are paying on the same articles for similar distances. We ask for nothing else. Other lines are carrying freight for our competitors cheaper than you are carrying it for us, and you take part of this freight at the cut rates. We cannot stand that. We have never asked for lower rates than our competitors, but we shall never rest satisfied with less."

"If you will stop building that line from the lakes to your works, we will do what you ask," was his response.

"Gentlemen, that cannot be. I have agreed to build that line, and certain parties have taken action in consequence of my promise. It has to be built."

Repeated efforts were made to induce me to forego building, until finally I said to President Roberts: "You have just given a rival concern about to build works on your line in Pittsburg an agreement to give them everything you give us. We make no complaint; but if I had come to you and asked you, Mr. Roberts, to withdraw that agreement, and you had told me you were pledged to give it, I should say no more; I should expect you to keep your word. If abandoning the new line is a condition of anything you will do for us, we must part." No more was said upon that subject.

Then came the extension of the lake line we had decided to build from Pittsburg to our coke ovens. They wished that stopped, and as I was not yet pledged to build it, I said that was a matter for negotiation. If they wished to carry our coke over their line from the ovens to our works at Pittsburg at the same rate agreed upon with the new proposed line for that service, they could have the contract. This they gladly accepted. The result of the meeting was that I got all I asked for, and greatly obliged the Pennsylvania Railroad by allowing them to retain transportation of our own coke traffic from the coke fields to Pittsburg. Everything was satisfactorily arranged, and we were all "boys together" again. I was the ally of the P. R. R., much to my delight.

It was estimated that the agreement saved us about one and a half millions of dollars per year, a large sum upon our business then. Railway officials, free from restrictions, could make or unmake mining and manufacturing concerns in those days, and could do so still, had we not at last a court of appeal and laws against obvious discriminations.

The Interstate Commerce Commission is to become one of our greatest safeguards.

I must not forget to mention that one part of the understanding was that so long as the Pennsylvania Railroad gave us the same rates our competitors paid for similar distances anywhere in the United States, we would not be parties to building any additional lines in the Pittsburg district in competition with the Pennsylvania Railroad, and this agreement lasted until Mr. Cassatt returned to power.

I was in Europe when he changed the coke and other rates, not knowing their origin or the details of our agreement with his predecessors. All that we asked and obtained, as I have explained, was the same rates given by other lines to our competitors, and nothing lower than these. It was impossible, I am told, for the railroad company to do anything however, but charge the regular rates on some of our shipments as made, and at the end of each month to compare these rates with any they had given to others, or which we could show their competitors had given to others, for similar traffic. Therefore, the necessary deductions, if any, that had to be made to us, might be considered in one sense technically "rebates" upon the higher rates charged although not such in any true sense; for the net result to us was that, according to the agreement, we got just the rates that the Pennsylvania Railroad officials were satisfied our competitors were paying in other districts over other lines. Thus we were given, as it were, the "most favored nation" clause, nothing more. The new rate on coke was in a different category. Here the Pennsylvania Railroad Company elected to take the place of a threatened rival railroad and had to meet its terms. The Carnegie Steel Company only got what the new line was to give it.

The efforts of Pittsburg manufacturers to escape the thrall of the great monopoly were, first, the making of an independent line to the lakes, and connecting with the New York & Erie, New York Central, etc., which was done, but subsequently sold to the Vanderbilt interests, who offered three dollars for one invested. It proved to be a great mistake to sell, because it permitted the two railroad systems to confer and come to terms upon fixed rates and probably division of traffic. Thus ended effort number one.

Some time after, when war again broke out between the rival systems, the late William H. Vanderbilt asked me what I thought of the project of his able and enterprising son-in-law, Mr. Twombly, to extend the Reading system to Pittsburg through Pennsylvania. I thought so well of it that I said: "If you will undertake it, I and my friends will go with you to the extent of $5,000,000," a prodigious sum then—at least to us.

"If you will, then I will put in $5,000,000 also," he replied. Thus the South Pennsylvania was organised, and its construction begun. Here was a chance for the New York Central to grip and hold its antagonist by the throat; but the Pennsylvania interests, seeing what the movement involved, approached Mr. Vanderbilt while I was absent in Europe and induced him to surrender. Exactly what advantage the New York Central system received, I do not know, but it should have been great indeed, for this was probably the greatest mistake in its history. Mr. Twombly had found the key to masterdom for the Vanderbilt interests, but it was foolishly thrown away. The work on the South Pennsylvania was stopped, and our investment returned. Thus ended effort number two.

My personal effort to build the Bessemer Railroad to the Lakes came after these vain efforts of united Pittsburg to emancipate herself.

When Mr. Cassatt ended the agreement entered into between his predecessor and myself, I was quite prepared to take up the challenge. We were once more free. An idea struck me one morning. I called upon Mr. George Gould and said to him: "Years ago, soon after I had taken up residence in New York, your father approached me in the Windsor Hotel and said he would buy the control of the Pennsylvania Railroad, and divide profits equally with me, if I would promise to devote myself to its management. It was a great compliment to be paid to one so young; but my heart was already in steel development, and I declined. This morning I come to you and offer an opportunity to create and control a through line from the Atlantic to the Pacific. Extend your line to Pittsburg, and we will give you a contract for one-third of all our business, provided you agree to give us the rates prevailing elsewhere and enjoyed by our competitors." I offered to build west to meet him, and also to join him in building east. Fortunately he agreed, and the result is that the Gould system to-day is in Pittsburg, enjoying that contract. We were just upon the eve of arranging to extend the line eastward, taking in our coke works en route, which would have been a hard blow to the Pennsylvania Railroad, since we controlled our own coke traffic, when Mr. Morgan asked Mr. Schwab, if I wished to retire from business; if so, he thought he could let me out. I replied in the affirmative, having resolved early in life not to spend my old age struggling for more dollars. I had seen so many pitiable cases of men with fortunes to retire upon but nothing to retire to, condemned to continue like flies held fast by the revolving wheel, to whom change means misery. Of course we stopped all negotiations looking to Eastern extension after this, and the result was my retirement from business.

With Mr. Cassatt's return to power as president of the Pennsylvania system, came needed reform, and it gives me pleasure to record the great service that companion of my youth did to the railroad interests of the country. In doing so, he broke the constitution of Pennsylvania, which prohibits any of its railroads from controlling competing lines by purchase or otherwise. He bought large interests in the Baltimore & Ohio and other competing lines; but when he did this, I do not believe he knew he was breaking the constitution, for in those days railway officials thought little about the law, because it rarely touched transportation operations. These investments have since been sold by the Pennsylvania company.

His influence upon competing lines became decisive. He enforced uniform rates honestly on the Pennsylvania system, and he gradually induced the other lines to adhere to them. Then was established what is called the "community of interest" idea.

In the interval, the Government had taken up the subject of interstate commerce, which the states were and are clearly unable to control. Wise laws were passed, and a national commission appointed, and the evils of rebates are today already unknown. Under present laws no corporation can afford to offer, neither can any person or company afford to receive rebates, the risk of exposure and punishment being now fortunately far too great.

Thus the conditions described as prevailing in the past in railway transportation, then still in the formative stage, are rapidly being succeeded by a system finally to become as perfect as is possible for man to create and maintain.

The President has performed a great service, focusing the attention of the country upon certain crying evils, and the present position of the Government is all that could be desired. The dead past is to bury its past. It is rapidly doing so. It was the custom for different rates to prevail in the beginning of railroad development, when all was chaos, but our conditions are soon to be those which the old lands have been led by experience to establish. We are only following their example in supervising railway and other corporations strictly, as we do national banks. Leases, mergers, purchases of shares, control of other lines or corporations, the issue of bonds and stocks, and the rates of freight, must all be reported, examined, and approved by the tribunal which is to become our Industrial Supreme Court.

We may rest assured that the Interstate Commission, progressing from year to year as it gains experience, will sustain fair rates for the railroad companies and establish what is indispensable—equality of rates throughout the whole country. The equality of the shipper will soon become an axiom ranking with the equality of the citizen—one shipper's privilege over any railroad every shipper's right. Different rates per ton or per mile may prevail in different sections or under different conditions but these will be open to all.

This will give to shareholders in corporations a degree of security hitherto unknown, enhance the value of their investments, and prove as beneficial for the corporations as for the shareholders and the country. Capital, both domestic and foreign, will be attracted more than ever to this field.

The creation of the commission is the most important addition that has been made in our day to the machinery of government. It should be proclaimed by the Administration and leading statesmen of both parties, and kept clearly before the people that no radical action has either been taken or is contemplated. On the contrary, all that is desired is only what other nations already possess, and is in the truest sense conservative and preservative in the highest degree.

The ease and rapidity with which the commission was established, which has already abolished demoralising rebates and is rapidly giving to corporate investments the security they possess in other lands by bringing them under supervision, is a great triumph for our governmental system in all departments, legislative, executive, and judicial, and gives to all the assurance that no emergency can arise in our country which will not be promptly and successfully met—an intelligent, just, and fairminded people at the base cordially approving the salutary measures of their representatives with the President, a great reforming force, at the head, leading the way.

9
An Employer's View of the Labor Question

Of all of the many articles, books, pamphlets, and letters-to-the-editor that Andrew Carnegie wrote during his long career as a writer, none created as much discussion and controversy as did the two articles that appeared in Forum *magazine in 1886.*

In the first essay, published in April 1886, Carnegie paints a picture of sweetness and light in American labor relations. It can be seen as a companion piece to his magnum opus, Triumphant Democracy, *which was published in the same year. It trumpets the same exultant theme of progress, ever onward and upward, as it sketches the remarkable advances the worker had made in the past three centuries from serfdom to a position of being, as Carnegie saw it, on "equal terms with the purchaser of his labor." Carnegie looks forward to the time in the near future when "collisions" between labor and capital will be as rare as international war, and he discusses various proposals to eliminate such strife, including cooperatives, compulsory arbitration, profit-sharing through wages on a sliding scale, and trade unions. He gives special emphasis to the "right of men to form themselves into these unions. . . . The right of the working men to combine . . . is no less sacred than the right of the manufacturer to enter into associations. . . . My experience has been that trades-unions upon the whole are beneficial both to labor and capital."*

Small wonder that organized labor everywhere hailed Carnegie's Forum *article as its Magna Carta, given willingly by a new, far more benevolent King John. As might be expected, the managerial class and the conservative press reacted quite differently. His own partners in both the steel and coke companies were highly embarrassed by Carnegie's pronouncements. Frick, in particular, must have read this essay in grim, tight-lipped anger. He later blamed this article in part for his difficulties with labor in the coal fields the following spring.*

The question naturally arises as to why Carnegie felt compelled to write these two Forum *articles. (The second, "Results of the Labor Struggle," appears as selection #10 below). No one expected the late-nineteenth-century industrialist to provide labor with* a Bill of Rights. Why had Carnegie gone out of his way to enunciate a policy which he was not prepared to implement and which could not fail to embarrass him and make him vulnerable to the charge of hypocrisy?

The only satisfactory answer, it would seem, is to be found in Carnegie's lifelong quest to reconcile the radical egalitarianism of his Dunfermline childhood with the capitalistic success he had gained in manhood. For his own peace of mind he had to believe that he had not betrayed the faith of his father and grandfather when he became the employer of tens of thousands of men. He once wrote that of all the lines in Robert Burns's poems, the one that meant the most to him was, "Thine own reproach alone do fear." Somehow he had to justify his own life to himself. He wanted to believe that his enlightened views on labor were really possible to implement and that he would make them a reality.

The struggle in which labor has been engaged during the past three hundred years, first against authority and then against capital, has been a triumphal march. Victory after victory has been achieved. Even so late as in Shakespere's time, remains of villeinage or serfdom still existed in England. Before that, not only the labor but the person of the laborer belonged to the chief. The workers were either slaves or serfs; men and women were sold with the estate upon which they worked, and became the property of the new lord, just as did the timber which grew on the land. In those days we hear nothing of strikes or of trades-unions, or differences of opinion between employer and employed. The fact is, labor had then no right which the chief, or employer, was bound to respect. Even as late as the beginning of this century, the position of the laborer in some departments was such as can scarcely be credited. What do our laboring friends think of this, that down to 1779 the miners of Britain were in a state of serfdom. They "were compelled by law to remain in the pits as long as the owner chose to keep them at work there, and were actually sold as part of the capital invested in the works. If they accepted an engagement elsewhere, their master could always have them fetched back and flogged as thieves for having attempted to rob him of their labor. This law was modified in 1779, but was not repealed till after the acts passed in 1797 and 1799" ("The Trades-Unions of England," p. 119). This was only ninety-seven years ago. Men are still living who were living then. Again, in France, as late as 1806, every workman had to procure a license; and in Russia, down to our own days, agricultural laborers were sold with the soil they tilled.

Consider the change, nay, the revolution! Now the poorest laborer in America or in England, or indeed throughout the civilized world, who can handle a pick or a shovel, stands upon equal terms with the purchaser of his labor. He sells or withholds it as may seem best to him. He negotiates, and thus rises to the dignity of an independent contractor. When he has performed the work he bargained to do, he owes his employer nothing, and is under no obligation to him. Not only has the laborer conquered his political and personal freedom: he has achieved industrial freedom as well, as far as the law can give it, and he now fronts his master, proclaiming himself his equal under the law.

But, notwithstanding this complete revolution, it is evident that the permanent relations to each other of labor and capital have not yet evolved. The present adjustment does not work without friction, and changes must be made before we can have industrial peace. Today we find collisions between these forces, capital and labor, when there should be combination. The mill hands of an industrial village in France have just risen against their employers, attacked the manager's home and killed him. The streets of another French village are barricaded against the expected forces of order. The shipbuilders of Sunderland, in England, are at the verge of starvation, owing to a quarrel with their employers; and Leicester has just been the scene of industrial riots. In our country, labor disputes and strikes were never so numerous as now. East and West, North and South, everywhere, there is unrest, showing that an equilibrium has not yet been reached between employers and employed.

A strike or lockout is, in itself, a ridiculous affair. Whether a failure or a success, it gives no direct proof of its justice or injustice. In this it resembles war between two nations. It is simply a question of strength and endurance between the contestants. The gage of battle, or the duel, is not more senseless, as a means of establishing what is just and fair, than an industrial strike or lockout. It would be folly to conclude that we have reached any permanent adjustment between capital and labor until strikes and lockouts are as much things of the past as the gage of battle or the duel have become in the most advanced communities.

Taking for granted, then, that some further modifications must be made between capital and labor, I propose to consider the various plans that have been suggested by which labor can advance another stage in its development in relation to capital. And, as a preliminary, let it be noted that it is only labor and capital in their greatest masses which it is necessary to consider. It is only in large establishments that the industrial unrest of which I have spoken ominously manifests itself. The farmer who hires a man to assist him, or the gentleman who engages a groom or a butler, is not affected by strikes. The innumerable cases in which a few men only are directly concerned, which comprise in the aggregate the most of labor, present upon the whole a tolerably satisfactory condition of affairs. This clears the ground of much, and leaves us to deal only with the immense mining and manufacturing concerns of recent growth, in which capital and labor often array themselves in alarming antagonism.

Among the expedients suggested for their better reconciliation, the first place must be assigned to the idea of cooperation, or the plan by which the workers are to become part owners in enterprises, and share their fortunes. There is no doubt that if this could be effected it would have the same beneficial effect upon the workman which the ownership of land has upon the man who has hitherto tilled the land for another. The sense of ownership would make of him more of a man as regards himself, and hence more of a citizen as regards the commonwealth. But we are here met by a difficulty which I confess I have not yet been able to overcome, and which renders me less sanguine than I should like to be in regard to cooperation. The difficulty is this, and it seems to me to be inherent in all gigantic manufacturing, mining, and commercial operations. Two men or two combinations of men will erect blast furnaces, iron mills, cotton mills, or piano manufactories adjoining each other, or engage in shipping or commercial business. They will start with equal capital and credit; and to those only superficially acquainted with the personnel of these concerns, success will seem as likely to attend the one as the other. Nevertheless, one will fail after dragging along a lifeless existence, and pass into the hands of its creditors; while the neighboring mill or business will make a fortune for its owners. Now, the successful manufacturer, dividing every month or every year a proportion of his profits among his workmen, either as a bonus or as dividends upon shares owned by them, will not only have a happy and contented body of operatives, but he will inevitably attract from his rival the very best workmen in every department. His rival, having no profits to divide among his workmen, and paying them only a small assured minimum to enable them to live, finds himself despoiled of foremen and of workmen necessary to carry on his business successfully. His workmen are discontented and, in their own opinion, defrauded of the proper fruits of their skill, through incapacity or inattention of their employers. Thus, unequal business capacity in the management produces unequal results.

It will be precisely the same if one of these manufactories belongs to the workmen themselves; but in this case, in the present stage of development of the workmen, the chances of failure will be enormously increased. It is, indeed, greatly to be doubted whether any body of workingmen in the world could today organize and successfully carry on a mining or manufacturing or commercial business in competition with concerns owned by men trained to affairs. If any such cooperative organization succeeds, it may be taken for granted that it is principally owing to the exceptional business ability of one of the managers, and only in a very small degree to the efforts of the mass of workmen-owners. This business ability is excessively rare, as is proved by the incredibly large proportion of those who enter upon the stormy sea of business only to fail. I should say that twenty cooperative concerns would fail to every one that would succeed. There are, of course, a few successful establishments, notably two in France and one in England, which are organized upon the cooperative plan, in which the workmen participate directly in the profits. But these were all created by the present owners, who now generously share the profits with their workmen, and are making the success of their manufactories upon the cooperative plan the proud work of their lives. What these concerns will become when the genius for affairs is no longer with them to guide, is a matter of grave doubt and, to me, of foreboding. I can, of course, picture in my mind a state of civilization in which the most talented businessmen shall find their most cherished work in carrying on immense concerns, not primarily for their own personal aggrandizement, but for the good of the masses of workers engaged therein, and their families; but this is only a foreshadowing of a dim and distant future. When a class of such men has evolved, the problem of capital and labor will be permanently solved to the entire satisfaction of both. But as this manifestly belongs to a future generation, I cannot consider cooperation, or common ownership, as the next immediate step in advance which it is possible for labor to make in its upward path.

The next suggestion is that peaceful settlement of differences should be reached through arbitration. Here we are upon firmer ground. I would lay it down as a maxim that there is no excuse for a strike or a lockout until arbitration of differences has been offered by one party and refused by the other. No doubt serious trouble attends even arbitration at present, from the difficulty of procuring suitable men to judge intelligently between the disputants. There is a natural disinclination among businessmen to expose their business to men in whom they have not entire confidence. We lack, so far, in America a retired class of men of affairs. Our vile practice is to keep on accumulating more dollars until we die. If it were the custom here, as it is in England, for men to withdraw from active business after acquiring a fortune, this class would furnish the proper arbitrators. On the other hand, the ex-presidents of trades-unions, such as Mr. Jarrett or Mr. Wihle, after they have retired from active control, would commend themselves to the manufacturers and to the men as possessed of the necessary technical knowledge, and educated to a point where commercial reasons would not be without their proper weight upon them. I consider that of all the agencies immediately available to prevent wasteful and embittering contests between capital and labor, arbitration is the most powerful and most beneficial.

The influence of trades-unions upon the relations between the employer and employed has been much discussed. Some establishments in America have refused to recognize the right of the men to form themselves into these unions, although I am not aware that any concern in England would dare to take this position. This policy, however, may be regarded as only a temporary phase of the situation. The right of the workingmen to combine and to form trades-unions is no less sacred than the right of the manufacturer to enter into associations and conferences with his fellows, and it must sooner or later be conceded. Indeed, it gives one but a poor opinion of the American workman if he permits himself to be deprived of a right which his fellow in England long since conquered for himself. My experience has been that trades-unions, upon the whole, are beneficial both to labor and to capital. They certainly educate the workingmen, and give them a truer conception of the relations of capital and labor than they could otherwise form. The ablest and best workmen eventually come to the front in these organizations; and it may be laid down as a rule that the more intelligent the workman the fewer the contests with employers. It is not the intelligent workman, who knows that labor without his brother capital is helpless, but the blatant ignorant man, who regards capital as the natural enemy of labor, who does so much to embitter the relations between employer and employed; and the power of this ignorant demagogue arises chiefly from the lack of proper organization among the men through which their real voice can be expressed. This voice will always be found in favor of the judicious and intelligent representative. Of course, as men become intelligent more deference must be paid to them personally and to their rights, and even to their opinions and prejudices; and, upon the whole, a greater share of profits must be paid in the day of prosperity to the intelligent than to the ignorant workman. He cannot be imposed upon so readily. On the other hand, he will be found much readier to accept reduced compensation when business is depressed; and it is better in the long run for capital to be served by the highest intelligence, and to be made well aware of the fact that it is dealing with men who know what is due to them, both as to treatment and compensation.

One great source of the trouble between employers and employed arises from the fact that the immense establishments of today, in which alone we find serious conflicts between capital and labor, are not managed by their owners, but by salaried officers, who cannot possibly have any permanent interest in the welfare of the workingmen. These officials are chiefly anxious to present a satisfactory balance sheet at the end of the year, that their hundreds of shareholders may receive the usual dividends, and that they may therefore be secure in their positions, and be allowed to manage the business without unpleasant interference either by directors or shareholders. It is notable that bitter strikes seldom occur in small establishments where the owner comes into direct contact with his men, and knows their qualities, their struggles, and their aspirations. It is the chairman, situated hundreds of miles away from his men, who only pays a flying visit to the works and perhaps finds time to walk through the mill or mine once or twice a year, that is chiefly responsible for the disputes which break out at intervals. I have noticed that the manager who confers oftenest with a committee of his leading men has the least trouble with his workmen. Although it may be impracticable for the presidents of these large corporations to know the workingmen personally, the manager at the mills, having a committee of his best men to present their suggestions and wishes from time to time, can do much to maintain and strengthen amicable relations, if not interfered with from headquarters. I, therefore, recognize in trades-unions, or, better still, in organizations of the men of each establishment, who select representatives to speak for them, a means, not of further embittering the relations between employer and employed, but of improving them.

It is astonishing how small a sacrifice upon the part of the employer will sometimes greatly benefit the men. I remember that at one of our meetings with a committee, it was incidentally remarked by one speaker that the necessity for obtaining credit at the stores in the neighborhood was a grave tax upon the men. An ordinary workman, he said, could not afford to maintain himself and family for a month, and as he only received his pay monthly, he was compelled to obtain credit and to pay exorbitantly for everything, whereas, if he had the cash, he could buy at twenty-five percent less. "Well," I said, "why cannot we overcome that by paying every two weeks?" The reply was: "We did not like to ask it, because we have always understood that it would cause much trouble; but if you do that it will be worth an advance of five percent in our wages." We have paid semi-monthly since. Another speaker happened to say that although they were in the midst of coal, the price charged for small lots delivered at their houses was a certain sum per bushel. The price named was double what our best coal was costing us. How easy for us to deliver to our men such coal as they required, and charge them cost! This was done without a cent's loss to us, but with much gain to the men. Several other points similar to these have arisen by which their labors might be lightened or products increased, and others suggesting changes in machinery or facilities which, but for the conferences referred to, would have been unthought of by the employer and probably never asked for by the men. For these and other reasons I attribute the greatest importance to an organization of the men, through whose duly elected representatives the managers may be kept informed from time to time of their grievances and suggestions. No matter how able the manager, the clever workman can often show him how beneficial changes can be made in the special branch in which that workman labors. Unless the relations between manager and workmen are not only amicable but friendly, the owners miss much; nor is any man a first-class manager who has not the confidence and respect, and even the admiration, of his workmen. No man is a true gentleman who does not inspire the affection and devotion of his servants. The danger is that such committees may ask conferences too often; three or four meetings per year should be regarded as sufficient.

I come now to the greatest cause of the friction which prevails between capital and labor in the largest establishments, the real essence of the trouble, and the remedy I have to propose.

The trouble is that the men are not paid at any time the compensation proper to that time. All large concerns necessarily keep filled with orders, say for six months in advance, and these orders are taken, of course, at prices prevailing when they are booked. This year's operations furnish perhaps the best illustration of the difficulty. Steel rails at the end of last year for delivery this year were $29 per ton at the works. Of course the mills entered orders freely at this price, and kept on entering them until the demand growing unexpectedly great carried prices up to $35 per ton. Now, the various mills in America are compelled for the next six months or more to run upon orders which do not average $31 per ton at the seaboard and Pittsburg, and say $34 at Chicago.

Transportation, ironstone, and prices of all kinds have advanced upon them in the meantime, and they must therefore run for the bulk of the year upon very small margins of profit. But the men, noticing in the papers the "great boom in steel rails," very naturally demand their share of the advance, and, under our existing faulty arrangements between capital and labor, they have secured it. The employers, therefore, have grudgingly given what they know under proper arrangements they should not have been required to give, and there has been friction, and still is dissatisfaction upon the part of the employers. Reverse this picture. The steel-rail market falls again. The mills have still six months' work at prices above the prevailing market, and can afford to pay men higher wages than the then existing state of the market would apparently justify. But having just been amerced in extra payments for labor which they should not have paid, they naturally attempt to reduce wages as the market price of rails goes down, and there arises discontent among the men, and we have a repetition of the negotiations and strikes which have characterized the beginning of this year. In other words, when the employer is going down the employee insists on going up, and vice versa. What we must seek is a plan by which the men will receive high wages when their employers are receiving high prices for the product, and hence are making large profits; and, *per contra*, when the employers are receiving low prices for product, and therefore small if any profits, the men will receive low wages. If this plan can be found, employers and employed will be "in the same boat," rejoicing together in their prosperity, and calling into play their fortitude together in adversity. There will be no room for quarrels, and instead of a feeling of antagonism there will be a feeling of partnership between employers and employed.

There is a simple means of producing this result, and to its general introduction both employers and employed should steadily bend their energies. Wages should be based upon a sliding scale, in proportion to the net prices received for product month by month. And I here gladly pay Mr. Potter, president of the North Chicago Rolling Mill Company, the great compliment to say that he has already taken a step in this direction, for today he is working his principal mill upon this plan. The result is that he has had no stoppage whatever this year, nor any dissatisfaction. All has gone smoothly along, and this in itself is worth at least as much to the manufacturer and to the men as the difference in wages one way or another which can arise from the new system.

The celebrated Crescent Steel Works of Pittsburg, manufacturers of the highest grades of tool steel, pay their skilled workmen by a sliding scale, based upon prices received for product—an important factor in the eminent success of that firm. The scale adopted by the iron manufacturers and workmen is only an approach to the true sliding scale; nevertheless it is a decided gain both to capital and labor, as it is adopted from year to year, and hence eliminates strikes on account of wages during the year, and limits these interruptions from that cause to the yearly negotiation as to the justice or injustice of the scale. As this scale, however, is not based upon the prices actually received for product, but upon the published list of prices, which should be received in theory, there is not complete mutuality between the parties. In depressed times, such as the iron industry has been passing through in recent years, enormous concessions upon the published card prices have been necessary to effect sales, and in these the workmen have not shared with their employers. If, however, there was added to the scale, even in its present form, a stipulation that all causes of difference which could not be postponed till the end of the year, and then considered with the scale, should be referred to arbitration, and that, in case of failure of the owners and workmen to agree at the yearly conference, arbitration should also be resorted to, strikes and lockouts would be entirely eliminated from the iron business; and if the award of the arbitrators took effect from the date of reference the works could run without a day's interruption.

Dismissing, therefore, for the present all consideration of cooperation as not being within measurable distance, I believe that the next steps in the advance toward permanent, peaceful relations between capital and labor are:

First. That compensation be paid the men based upon a sliding scale in proportion to the prices received for product.

Second. A proper organization of the men of every works to be made, by which the natural leaders, the best men, will eventually come to the front and confer freely with the employers.

Third. Peaceful arbitration to be in all cases resorted to for the settlement of differences which the owners and the mill committee cannot themselves adjust in friendly conference.

Fourth. No interruption ever to occur to the operations of the establishment, since the decision of the arbitrators shall be made to take effect from the date of reference.

If these measures were adopted by an establishment, several important advantages would be gained:

First. The employer and employed would simultaneously share their prosperity or adversity with each other. The scale once settled, the feeling of antagonism would be gone, and a feeling of mutuality would ensue. Capital and labor would be shoulder to shoulder, supporting each other.

Second. There could be neither strike nor lockout, since both parties had agreed to abide by a forthcoming decision of disputed points. Knowing that in the last resort strangers were to be called in to decide what should be a family affair, the cases would, indeed, be few which would not be amicably adjusted by the original parties without calling in others to judge between them.

Whatever the future may have in store for labor, the evolutionist, who sees nothing but certain and steady progress for the race, will never attempt to set bounds to its triumphs, even to its final form of complete and universal industrial cooperation, which I hope is some day to be reached. But I am persuaded that the next step forward is to be in the direction I have here ventured to point out; and as one who is now most anxious to contribute his part toward helping forward the day of amicable relations between the two forces of capital and labor, which are not enemies, but are really auxiliaries who stand or fall together, I ask at the hands of both capital and labor a careful consideration of these views.

10
Results of the Labor Struggle

Carnegie had had bad fortune in the timing of his first Forum *article. This Pollyanna-like version of "the labor question" had appeared at the very moment when all hell seemed to be breaking loose on the American labor front, culminating in the Chicago Haymarket Square explosion and the national hysteria that ensued. Carnegie rushed back into print in August (1886) with this second* Forum *article in which he attempted to minimize the significance of the labor disorders of that year. He points out that there had been only 250,000 men involved in the strikes out of a total labor force of 20 million workers. He blames the press for magnifying the crisis and creating a national panic. Most significantly, he places the major responsibility for the strikes not upon labor but upon management.*

Carried away with his zeal for occupying Solomon's throne in industrial America, Carnegie then writes the fateful paragraph decrying management's use of scab labor to break a strike and ends with the memorable sentence, "There is an unwritten law among the best workers: 'Thou shalt not take thy neighbor's job.'" Labor would never forget that Eleventh Commandment which Carnegie, with this article, had carved in stone. Nor would labor ever let Carnegie forget it either.

When "An Employer's View of the Labor Question" was written, labor and capital were at peace, each performing its proper function; capital providing for the wants of labor, and labor regularly discharging its daily task. But before that paper reached the public the most serious labor revolt that ever occurred in this country was upon us. Capital, frightened almost into panic, began to draw back into its strongholds, and many leaders of public opinion seemed to lose self-command. Among the number were not a few of our foremost political economists. These writers of the closet, a small but important class in this country, removed from personal contact with everyday affairs, and uninformed of the solid basis of virtue in the wage-receiving class upon which American society rests, necessarily regarded such phenomena from a purely speculative standpoint. Some of them apparently thought that the fundamental institutions upon which peaceful development depends had been, if not completely overthrown, at least gravely endangered, and that civilization itself had received a rude shock from the disturbance. More than one did not hesitate to intimate that the weakness of democratic institutions lay at the foundation of the revolt. Suggestions were made that the suffrage should be confined to the educated; that the masses might be held in stricter bonds. When we hear the cry of these alarmists we are tempted to reverse the rebuke of the sacred Teacher: they are always troubled more by the mote in their own country's eye than by the beam in the eye of other lands. They forget that not sixty days before monarchical Belgium was convulsed with labor revolts, compared with which ours were insignificant and practically harmless. That country, with its five and a half millions of inhabitants, had more rioters than the United States, with its fifty-six millions; and instead of restoring peace, as this country did, by means of the established forces of order, the Belgian government had to abandon, for a time, all law, and publicly authorize every citizen to wage private war against the insurgents.

Our magazines, reviews, and newspapers have been filled with plans involving radical changes considered necessary by these sciolists for the restoration and maintenance of proper relations between capital and labor. The pulpit has been equally prolific. Thirty days have not elapsed since the excitement was at its height, and yet today capital and labor are again cooperating everywhere, as at the date of my first paper, and we are now in position to judge of the extent of the disturbance and to reduce the specter to its real dimensions. It will soon be seen that what occurred was a very inadequate cause for the alarm created. The eruption was not, in itself, a very serious matter, either in its extent or in its consequences. Its lesson lay in the indications it gave of the forces underlying it. There are in the United States today a total of more than twenty millions of workers who earn their bread by the sweat of their brow; in trade and transportation alone there are more than seven millions. At the very height of the revolt, not more than 250,000 of these had temporarily ceased to labor. This was the estimate given by "Bradstreet's" on the 14th of May. Three days later it was 80,000, and four days after that only 47,000. The remaining millions continued to pursue their usual vocations in peace. It is fair to assume that the number reported on the 14th of May included all those who were dissatisfied and had requested advance of wages or redress of grievances, but were not really strikers at all. A demonstration that shrinks to one-fourth its size from the 14th to the 17th of May, and then again to one-half its remaining proportions in the next three days, can scarcely be called a contest. The number of those involved in a serious struggle with capital did not, therefore, at any one time exceed 50,000 — not one percent of the total wage-receiving class, in the branches where alone labor troubles occurred. How then, one is tempted to ask, did so small an interruption seem so great? Why was it taken for granted that a general revolt of labor had taken place, when not one worker in a hundred had really entered upon a contest? The reason for the delusion is obvious. The omnipresent press, with the electric telegraph at its command, spreads the report of a local disturbance in East St. Louis over the entire three million square miles of the land. It is felt almost as distinctly in New Orleans, Boston, and San Francisco as in the city of St. Louis itself, upon the opposite side of the river. The thoughts of men throughout the country concentrate upon this one point of outbreak. Excitable natures fancy the trouble to be general, and even imagine that the very ground trembles under their own feet. In this way the petty, local difficulty upon the Wabash system of railways, which involved only 3,700 Knights of Labor, and a strike of a few hundred men on the Third Avenue Railway, New York, together with a few trifling and temporary disputes at other points, were magnified into a general warfare between capital and labor. There were but a few local skirmishes; peace already reigns; and our professors and political economists and the whole school of pessimists who tremble for the safety of human society in general, and of the Republic in particular, and the ministers that have bodily essayed to revolutionize existing conditions, are free to find another subject for their anxious fears and forebodings. The relations between capital and labor which have slowly evolved themselves in the gradual development of the race will not be readily changed. The solid walls with which humanity fortifies itself in each advanced position gained in its toilsome march forward will not fall to the ground at the blast of trumpets. Present conditions have grown up slowly, and can be changed for the better only slowly and by small, successive steps. A short history of the disturbances will, however, furnish many useful and needed lessons.

The trouble grew, as many serious troubles do grow, from a trifle. A leader of the Knights of Labor was dismissed. Whether the fact that he was a labor leader influenced his superior to dismiss him will probably never be known; but this much is to be said, that it was very likely to do so. Salaried officials in the service of large corporations are naturally disposed to keep under them only such men as give them no trouble.

On the other hand, the safety of its leaders is the key of labor's position. To surrender that is to surrender everything. Even if the leader in question had not been as regularly at work as other men, even if he had to take days now and then to attend to official duties for his brethren, the superior of that man should have dealt very leniently with him. The men cannot know whether their leader is stricken down for proper cause or not; but, at the same time, they cannot help suspecting. And here I call the attention of impartial minds to the elements of manhood and the high sense of honor and loyalty displayed upon the part of workingmen who sacrifice so much and throw themselves in the front of the conflict to secure the safety of their standard-bearers. Everything reasonable can be done with men of this spirit. The loyalty which they show to their leaders can be transferred to their employers by treating them as such men deserve. Society has nothing to fear from men so stanch and loyal to one another. Nor is the loyalty shown in this instance exceptional; it distinguishes workingmen as a class. Mr. Irons has said that "one hour's gentlemanly courtesy on the part of the manager would have averted all this disaster." Whether this be true or not, the statement should not be overlooked, for it is true that one hour of courtesy on the part of employers would prevent many strikes. Whether the men ask in proper manner for interviews, or observe all the rules of etiquette, is immaterial. We expect from the presumably better-informed party representing capital much more in this respect than from labor; and it is not asking too much of men intrusted with the management of great properties that they should devote some part of their attention to searching out the causes of disaffection among their employees, and, where any exist, that they should meet the men more than halfway in the endeavor to allay them. There is nothing but good for both parties to be derived from labor teaching the representative of capital the dignity of man, as man. The workingman, becoming more and more intelligent, will hereafter demand the treatment due to an equal.

The strikers at first were excusable, even if mistaken, in imagining that their leader had been stricken down; but, under the excitement of conflict, violence was resorted to; and further, an attempt was made to drag into the quarrel railway lines that had nothing to do with it. The men took up these wrong positions and were deservedly driven from them. And labor here received a salutary lesson — namely, that nothing is to be gained by violence and lawlessness, nor by endeavoring to unjustly punish the innocent for the sins of the guilty. Public sentiment, always disposed to side with labor, was with the men at first, but soon finding itself unable to sanction their doings, it veered to the other side. When the strikers lost that indispensable ally they lost all.

The other branch of the revolt of labor occurred in New York City, where the employees of the Third Avenue Railway struck for fewer hours and better pay. If ever a strike was justifiable this one was. It is simply disgraceful for a corporation to compel its men to work fifteen or sixteen hours a day. Such was the verdict of the public, and the men won a deserved victory. Here again, as at St. Louis, for lack of proper leadership, they went too far; and in their demand for the employment of certain men and the dismissal of others they lost their only sure support—public sentiment. This was compelled to decide against their final demands, and consequently they failed, and deservedly failed. How completely public sentiment, when aroused, compels obedience, as we have seen it did both at St. Louis and in New York City, is further shown by the result of the order, issued June 6, requiring the men of all the city railroads in Brooklyn and New York to stop work until the striking employees of the Third Avenue line were reinstated. The edict was disregarded by the men themselves, who found that compliance would not be approved by the community, and that, therefore, the attempt would fail. It was an attempt that the worst foe of labor might have instigated.

These were the two chief strikes from which came the epidemic of demands and strikes throughout the country.

None of these ebullitions proved of much moment. A rash had broken out upon the body politic, but it was only skin-deep, and disappeared as rapidly as it had come. At a somewhat later date the disturbance took a different form. A demand was made that the hours of labor should be reduced from ten to eight hours a day. To state this demand is to pronounce its fate. Existing conditions are not changed by twenty percent leaps and bounds, and especially in times like these, when business is not even moderately profitable. Such a request simply meant that many employers of labor would not be able to keep their men at work at all. History proves, nevertheless, that the hours of labor are being gradually reduced. The percentage of men working from ten to eleven hours in this country in 1830 was 29.7. These ten-hour workers increased in 1880 to 59.6 percent of the whole; while the classes who in 1830 worked excessively hours—from twelve to thirteen—constituted 32.5 percent. In 1880 they were only 14.6 percent; while the number of men compelled to work between thirteen and fourteen hours, which was in 1830 13.5 percent, had fallen in 1880 to 2.3 percent. Those working twelve hours are generally employed in double shifts, night and day. I do not believe that we have reached the limit of this reduction, but I do believe that any permanent reduction will be secured only by the half-hour at a time. If labor be guided by wise counsel, it will ask for reductions of half-hours, and then wait until a reduction to this extent is firmly established, and surrounding circumstances have adjusted themselves to that.

In considering the reasonableness of the demand for fewer hours of labor, we must not lose sight of the fact that the American works more hours, on an average, than his fellow in Great Britain. Twenty-three trades in Massachusetts are reported as working sixty hours and seventeen minutes a week, on an average, while the same crafts in Great Britain work only fifty-three hours and fifty minutes, showing that the American works an hour a day longer than his English brother. In British textile factories, the number of working hours in a week ranges from fifty-four to fifty-six. In mines, foundries, and machine shops, fifty-four hours make a week's work, which is equivalent to nine hours a day, six days a week; but the men, in all cases, work enough overtime each day to insure them a half-holiday on Saturday. In some districts, notably in Glasgow, the men prefer to work two weeks, and make every other Saturday a whole holiday. This gives them an opportunity to leave on early morning trains, on excursions, and to spend Saturday and Sunday with friends. The Allegheny Valley Railroad Company, under the management of my friend Mr. McCargo, introduced the half-Saturday holiday in the shops some time ago, with the happiest results. Mr. McCargo found, by years of experience, that workingmen lose about half a day a week. Since the half-holiday was established no more time has been lost than before. The men work five and one-half days a week regularly. While they are not paid, of course, for the half-holiday, they could not be induced to give it up. This example should be followed, not only by all the railroads of the country, but by every employer of labor, and should be supported by every man who seeks to improve the condition of the wage-receiving classes.

I venture to suggest to the representatives of labor, however, that before they demand any reduction upon ten hours per day, they should concentrate their efforts upon making ten hours the universal practice, and secure this. At present, every ton of pig iron made in the world, except at two establishments, is made by men working in double shifts of twelve hours each, having neither Sunday or holiday the year round. Every two weeks the day men change to the night shift by working twenty-four hours consecutively. Gas works, paper mills, flour mills, and many other industries, are run by twelve-hour shifts, and breweries exact fifteen hours a day, on an average, from their men. I hold that it is not possible for men working ten hours a day to enlist public sentiment on their side in a demand for the shortening of their task, as long as many of their fellows are compelled to work twelve or more hours a day.

The eight-hour movement is not, however, without substantial foundation. Works that run day and night should be operated with three sets of men, each working eight hours. The steel-rail mills in this country are generally so run. The additional cost of the three sets of men has been divided between the workmen and the employers, the latter apparently having to meet an advance of wages to the extent of 16⅔ percent, but against this is to be placed the increased product which can be obtained. This is not inconsiderable, especially during the hot months, for it has been found that men working twelve hours a day continuously cannot produce as much per hour as men working eight hours a day; so that, if there be any profit at all in the business, the employer derives some advantage from the greater productive capacity of his works and capital, while the general expenses of the establishment remain practically as they were before. Since electric lighting has been perfected, many establishments which previously could not be run at night can be run with success. I therefore look for a large increase in the number of establishments working men only eight hours, but employing the machinery that now runs only ten hours the entire twenty-four. Each shift, of course, takes turn of each of the three parts into which the twenty-four hours are divided, and thus the lives of the men are rendered less monotonous and many hours for recreation and self-improvement are obtained.

The literature called forth by the recent excitement is preponderatingly favorable to cooperation, or profit-sharing, as the only true remedy for all disputes between labor and capital. My April article has been criticized because it relegated that to the future. But the advocates of this plan should weigh well the fact that the majority of enterprises are not profitable; that most men who embark in business fail—indeed, it is stated that only five in every hundred succeed, and that, with the exception of a few wealthy and partially retired manufacturers, and a very few wealthy corporations, men engaged in business affairs are in the midst of an anxious and unceasing struggle to keep their heads above water. How to pay maturing obligations, how to obtain cash for the payment of their men, how to procure orders or how to sell product, and, in not a few instances, how to induce their creditors to be forbearing, are the problems which tax the minds of businessmen during the dark hours of night, when their employees are asleep. I attach less and less value to the teaching of those doctrinaires who sit in their cozy studies and spin theories concerning the relations between capital and labor, and set before us divers high ideals. The banquet to which they invite the workingman when they propose industrial cooperation is not yet quite prepared, and would prove to most of those who accepted the invitation a Barmecide feast. Taken as a whole, the condition of labor today would not be benefited, but positively injured, by cooperation.

Let me point out, however, to the advocates of profit-sharing that ample opportunity already exists for workingmen to become part-owners in almost any department of industrialism, without changing present relations. The great railway corporations, in all cases, as well as the great manufacturing companies generally, are stock concerns, with shares of fifty or a hundred dollars each, which are bought and sold daily in the market. Not an employee of any of these but can buy any number of shares, and thus participate in the dividends and in the management. That capital is a unit is a popular error. On the contrary, it is made up of hundreds and thousands of small component parts, owned, for the most part, by people of limited means. The Pennsylvania Railway proper, for instance, which embraces only the 350 miles of line between Pittsburg and Philadelphia, is today owned by 19,340 shareholders, in lots of from one fifty-dollar share upward. The New York Central Railway, of 450 miles, between New York and Buffalo, belongs not to one, or two, or several capitalists, but to 10,418 shareholders, of whom about one-third are women and executors of estates. The entire railway system of America will show a similar wide distribution of ownership among the people. There are but three railway corporations in which the great capitalists hold a considerable interest; and the interest in two of these is held by various members of a family, and in no case does it amount to the control of the whole. In one of these very cases, the New York Central, as we have seen, there are more than ten thousand owners.

Steel-rail mills, with only one exception, show a like state of affairs. One of them belongs to 215 shareholders; of whom 7 are employees, 32 are estates, and 57 are women. Another of these concerns is owned by 302 stockholders; of whom 101 are women, 29 are estates, representing an unknown number of individuals, and 20 are employees of the company. A large proportion of the remaining owners and small holders of comparatively limited means, who have, from time to time, invested their savings where they had confidence both as to certainty of income and safety of principal. The Merrimac Manufacturing Company (cotton), of Lowell, is owned by 2,500 shareholders, of whom forty-two percent are holders of one share, twenty-one percent of two, and ten percent of three shares. Twenty-seven percent are holders of over three shares; and not less than thirty-eight percent of the whole stock is held by trustees, guardians, and executors of charitable, religious, educational, and financial institutions.

I have obtained from other concerns similar statements, which need not be published. They prove without exception that from one-fourth to one-third of the number of shareholders in corporations are women and executors of estates. The number of shareholders I have given are those of record, each holding a separate certificate. But it is obvious, in the case of executors, that this one certificate may represent a dozen owners. Many certificates issued in the name of a firm represent several persons, while shares held by a corporation may represent hundreds; but if we assume that every certificate of stock issued by the Pennsylvania Railroad Company represents only two owners, which is absurdly under the truth, it follows that, should every employee of that great company quarrel with it, the contest would be not against a few, but against a much larger body than they themselves constitute. It is within the mark to say that every striking employee would oppose his personal interest against that of three or four other members of the community. The total number of men employed by the Pennsylvania Railroad Company is 18,911 — not as many as there are shareholders of record. And what is true of the Pennsylvania Railway Company is true of the railway system as a whole, and, in a greater or less degree, of mining and manufacturing corporations generally. When one, therefore, denounces great corporations for unfair treatment of their men, he is not denouncing the act of some monster capitalist, but that of hundreds and thousands of small holders, scarcely one of whom would be a party to unfair or illiberal treatment of the workingman; the majority of them, indeed, would be found on his side; and, as we have seen, many of the owners themselves would be workingmen. Labor has only to bring its just grievances to the attention of owners to secure fair and liberal treatment. The "great capitalist" is almost a myth, and exists, in any considerable number or degree, only in the heated imagination of the uninformed. Aggregate capital in railway corporations consists of many more individuals than it employs.

Following the labor disturbances, there came the mad work of a handful of foreign anarchists in Chicago and Milwaukee, who thought they saw in the excitement a fitting opportunity to execute their revolutionary plans. Although labor is not justly chargeable with their doings, nevertheless the cause of labor was temporarily discredited in public opinion by these outbreaks. The promptitude with which one labor organization after another not only disclaimed all sympathy with riot and disorder, but volunteered to enroll itself into armed force for the maintenance of order, should not be overlooked by the student of labor problems desirous of looking justly at the question from the laborer's point of view. It is another convincing proof, if further proof were necessary, that whenever the peace of this country is seriously threatened, the masses of men, not only in the professions and in the educated classes, but down to and through the very lowest ranks of industrious workers, are determined to maintain it. A survey of the field, now that peace is restored, gives the results as follows:

First. The "dead line" has been definitely fixed between the forces of disorder and anarchy and those of order. Bomb-throwing means swift death to the thrower. Rioters assembling in numbers and marching to pillage will be remorselessly shot down; not by the order of a government above the people, not by overwhelming standing armies, not by troops brought from a distance, but by the masses of peaceable and orderly citizens of all classes in their own community, from the capitalist down to and including the steady workingman, whose combined influence constitutes that irresistible force, under democratic institutions, known as public sentiment. That sentiment has not only supported the officials who shot down disturbers of the peace, but has extolled them in proportion to the promptitude of their action.

Second. Another proof of the indestructibility of human society, and of its determination and power to protect itself from every danger as it arises and to keep marching forward to higher states of development, has been given in Judge Mallory's words: "Every person who counsels, hires, procures, or incites others to the commission of any unlawful or criminal act, is equally guilty with those who actually perpetrate the act, though such person may not have been present at the time of the commission of the offense." The difference between liberty and license of speech is now clearly defined—a great gain.

Third. It has likewise been clearly shown that public sentiment sympathizes with the efforts of labor to obtain from capital a fuller recognition of its position and claims than has hitherto been accorded. And in this expression, "a fuller recognition," I include not only pecuniary compensation, but what I conceive to be even more important today—a greater consideration of the workingman as a man and a brother. I trust the time has gone by when corporations can hope to work men fifteen or sixteen hours a day. And the time approaches, I hope, when it will be impossible, in this country, to work men twelve hours a day continuously.

Fourth. While public sentiment has rightly and unmistakably condemned violence, even in the form for which there is the most excuse, I would have the public give due consideration to the terrible temptation to which the workingman on a strike is sometimes subjected. To expect that one dependent upon his daily wage for the necessaries of life will stand by peaceably and see a new man employed in his stead, is to expect much. This poor man may have a wife and children dependent upon his labor. Whether medicine for a sick child, or even nourishing food for a delicate wife, is procurable, depends upon his steady employment. In all but a very few departments of labor it is unnecessary, and, I think, improper, to subject men to such an ordeal. In the case of railways and a few other employments it is, of course, essential for the public wants that no interruption occur, and in such case substitutes must be employed; but the employer of labor will find it much more to his interest, wherever possible, to allow his works to remain idle and await the result of a dispute, than to employ the class of men that can be induced to take the place of other men who have stopped work. Neither the best men as men, nor the best men as workers, are thus to be obtained. There is an unwritten law among the best workmen: "Thou shalt not take thy neighbor's job." No wise employer will lightly lose his old employees. Length of service counts for much in many ways. Calling upon strange men should be the last resort.

Fifth. The results of the recent disturbances have given indubitable proof that trades-unions must, in their very nature, become more conservative than the mass of the men they represent. If they fail to be conservative, they go to pieces through their own extravagance. I know of three instances in which threatened strikes were recently averted by the decision of the Master Workman of the Knights of Labor, supported by the best workmen, against the wishes of the less intelligent members of that organization. Representative institutions eventually bring to the front the ablest and most prudent men, and will be found as beneficial in the industrial as they have proved themselves to be in the political world. Leaders of the stamp of Mr. Powderly, Mr. Arthur, of the Brotherhood of Locomotive Engineers, and Messrs. Wihle and Martin, of the Amalgamated Iron and Steel Association, will gain and retain power;

while such as the radical and impulsive Mr. Irons, if at first clothed with power, will soon lose it.

Thus, as the result of the recent revolt, we see advantages gained by both capital and labor. Capital is more secure because of what has been demonstrated, and labor will hereafter be more respectfully treated and its claims more carefully considered, in deference to an awakened public opinion in favor of the laborer. Labor won while it was reasonable in its demands and kept the peace; it lost when it asked what public sentiment pronounced unreasonable, and especially when it broke the peace.

The disturbance is over and peace again reigns; but let no one be unduly alarmed at frequent disputes between capital and labor. Kept within legal limits, they are encouraging symptoms, for they betoken the desire of the workingman to better his condition; and upon this desire hang all hopes of advancement of the masses. It is the stagnant pool of Contentment, not the running stream of Ambition, that breeds disease in the body social and political. The workingmen of this country can no more be induced to sanction riot and disorder than can any other class of the community. Isolated cases of violence under strong provocation may break out upon the surface, but the body underneath is sound to the core, and resolute for the maintenance of order.

For the first time within my knowledge, the leading organs of public opinion in England have shown a more correct appreciation of the forces at work in the Republic than some of our own despondent writers. The London *Daily News* said truly that "the territorial democracy of America can be trusted to deal with such outbreaks"; and the *Daily Telegraph* spoke as follows:

There is no need for any fear to be entertained lest the lawbreakers of Chicago should get the better of the police, and, if it be necessary to invoke their aid, of the citizens of that astonishing young city. Frankly speaking, such rioters would have a better chance of intimidating Birmingham than of overawing Chicago, St. Louis, or New York. In dealing with the insurgents of this class the record of the great Republic is singularly clear.

Not only the democracy, but the industrious workingmen of which the democracy is so largely composed, have amply fulfilled the flattering predictions of our English friends, and may safely be trusted in the future to stand firmly for the maintenance of peace.

II
The Homestead Strike

With the purchase of the Homestead steel plant in October 1883, Carnegie Brothers & Company not only acquired the most modern rail mill and the best Bessemer plant in the country, but it also, unhappily for Carnegie, obtained six highly organized and well-disciplined labor lodges of the powerful Amalgamated Association of Iron and Steel Workers. Indeed, it had been a succession of labor disputes with this union that finally resulted in the original owners' willingness to accept Carnegie's offer to buy the plant at little more than its original cost.

The aggressive and highly successful tactics of the union at Homestead would soon put to a test the noble pro-labor sentiments Andrew Carnegie had extravagantly expressed in his Forum *articles. Would the Steel King actually abide by his Magna Carta or would he renege in favor of profits? In the first critical test put to Carnegie by labor in 1889, the union was recognized as the sole bargaining agent for Homestead, and a three-year contract was signed. Carnegie had passed the test with flying colors, but at a considerable discomfiture to his partners and at a considerable cost to his own pocketbook.*

By the spring of 1892, as the time for new contract negotiations approached, cost began to weigh more heavily than principle in Carnegie's scale of values. He became convinced that his company could no longer continue part union, part non-union, and that as "the vast majority of our employees are non-union, the minority must give place to the majority." The "sacred right of workers to combine" must be violated after all. In the name of company unity, unionism must be sacrificed.

As he did every summer, Carnegie left for Scotland in April 1892. Upon his arrival in Britain, Carnegie sent Frick a note: "We will approve of anything you do, not stopping short of approval of a contest. We are with you to the end" (Carnegie to Frick, 4 May 1892, quoted in George Harvey, Henry Clay Frick, The Man *[New York: Privately printed, 1936], pp. 165–66). Having given Frick carte blanche, Carnegie had made the tragedy at Homestead inevitable.*

The following selection from Andrew Carnegie's Autobiography, *ed. John Van*

Dyke (Boston: Houghton Mifflin, 1920), chapters 17 and 18, must have been the most difficult single piece that he ever had to write. Undoubtedly, he would have found it much more pleasant to omit this account entirely, just as he had failed to mention in his autobiography many other unpleasant episodes in his life, including his irreconcilable break with Frick in 1900. But the most traumatic and most highly publicized episode in his business career could hardly be ignored. Carnegie, moreover, seized this opportunity to absolve himself before the public of all responsibility for what had happened at Homestead. In this short chapter, the reader has a classic example of "mea non culpa." Carnegie had surely convinced himself that if only he had been on the scene, there would have been no bloodshed at Homestead. It is doubtful, however, that he convinced the general public.

Carnegie's account bears little resemblance to what actually happened at Homestead. It is in error both by omission and commission on many points, including Carnegie's assertion that the company had offered what amounted to a 30 percent increase in the wage-scale, or that only the 218 skilled union men wanted a strike. The entire labor force, skilled and unskilled, union and non-union, was united in its opposition to Frick's offer, and labor had the backing of the entire Homestead community.

For a far more accurate account of what occurred at Homestead in July 1892, the following are recommended: the contemporary works by Margaret Byington, Homestead: The Households of a Mill Town *(1910; rpt. Pittsburgh: University of Pittsburgh Press, 1974), and Arthur G. Burgoyne,* The Homestead Strike of 1892 *(1893; rpt. Pittsburgh: University of Pittsburgh Press, 1979); and three more recent studies, Leon Wolff's* Lockout: The Story of the Homestead Strike of 1892 *(New York: Harper & Row, 1965), Joseph F. Wall's* Andrew Carnegie *(1970; rpt. Pittsburgh: University of Pittsburgh Press, 1989), and Paul Krause,* The Battle for Homestead, 1880–1892: Culture, Politics, and Steel *(Pittsburgh: University of Pittsburgh Press, 1992).*

While upon the subject of our manufacturing interests, I may record that on July 1, 1892, during my absence in the Highlands of Scotland, there occurred the one really serious quarrel with our workmen in our whole history. For twenty-six years I had been actively in charge of the relations between ourselves and our men, and it was the pride of my life to think how delightfully satisfactory these had been and were. I hope I fully deserved what my chief partner, Mr. Phipps, said in his letter to the *New York Herald,* January 30, 1904, in reply to one who had declared I had remained abroad during the Homestead strike, instead of flying back to support my partners. It was to the effect that "I was always disposed to yield to the demands of the men, however unreasonable"; hence one or two of my partners did not wish me to return.[1] Taking no account of the reward that comes from feeling that you and your employees are friends and judging only from economical results, I believe that higher wages to men who respect their employers and are happy and contented are a good investment, yielding, indeed, big dividends.

The manufacture of steel was revolutionized by the Bessemer open-hearth and basic inventions. The machinery hitherto employed had become obsolete, and our firm, recognizing this, spent several millions at Homestead reconstructing and enlarging the works. The new machinery made about sixty percent more steel than the old. Two hundred and eighteen tonnage men (that is, men who were paid by the ton of steel produced) were working under a three years' contract, part of the last year being with the new machinery. Thus their earnings had increased almost sixty percent before the end of the contract.

The firm offered to divide this sixty percent with them in the new scale to be made thereafter. That is to say, the earnings of the men would have been thirty percent greater than under the old scale and the other thirty percent would have gone to the firm to recompense it for its outlay. The work of the men would not have been much harder than it had been hitherto, as the improved machinery did the work. This was not only fair and liberal, it was generous, and under ordinary circumstances would have been accepted by the men with thanks. But the firm was then engaged in making armor for the United States Government, which we had declined twice to manufacture and which was urgently needed. It had also the contract to furnish material for the Chicago Exhibition. Some of the leaders of the men, knowing these conditions, insisted upon demanding the whole sixty percent, thinking the firm would be compelled to give it. The firm could not agree, nor should it have

---

1. The full statement of Mr. Phipps is as follows:

Question: "It was stated that Mr. Carnegie acted in a cowardly manner in not returning to America from Scotland and being present when the strike was in progress at Homestead."

Answer: "When Mr. Carnegie heard of the trouble at Homestead he immediately wired that he would take the first ship for America, but his partners begged him not to appear, as they were of the opinion that the welfare of the Company required that he should not be in this country at the time. They knew of his extreme disposition to always grant the demands of labor, however unreasonable.

"I have never known of any one interested in the business to make any complaint about Mr. Carnegie's absence at that time, but all the partners rejoiced that they were permitted to manage the affair in their own way." (Henry Phipps in the *New York Herald*, January 30, 1904.)

agreed to such an attempt as this to take it by the throat and say, "Stand and deliver." It very rightly declined. Had I been at home nothing would have induced me to yield to this unfair attempt to extort.

Up to this point all had been right enough. The policy I had pursued in cases of difference with our men was that of patiently waiting, reasoning with them, and showing them that their demands were unfair; but never attempting to employ new men in their places—never. The superintendent of Homestead, however, was assured by the three thousand men who were not concerned in the dispute that they could run the works, and were anxious to rid themselves of the two hundred and eighteen men who had banded themselves into a union and into which they had hitherto refused to admit those in other departments—only the "heaters" and "rollers" of steel being eligible.

My partners were misled by this superintendent, who was himself misled. He had not had great experience in such affairs, having recently been promoted from a subordinate position. The unjust demands of the few union men, and the opinion of the three thousand non-union men that they were unjust, very naturally led him into thinking there would be no trouble and that the workmen would do as they had promised. There were many men among the three thousand who could take, and wished to take, the places of the two hundred and eighteen—at least so it was reported to me.

It is easy to look back and say that the vital step of opening the works should never have been taken. All the firm had to do was to say to the men: "There is a labor dispute here and you must settle it between yourselves. The firm has made you a most liberal offer. The works will run when the dispute is adjusted, and not till then. Meanwhile your places remain open to you." Or, it might have been well if the superintendent had said to the three thousand men, "All right, if you will come and run the works without protection," thus throwing upon them the responsibility of protecting themselves—three thousand men as against two hundred and eighteen. Instead of this it was thought advisable (as an additional precaution by the state officials, I understand) to have the sheriff with guards to protect the thousands against the hundreds. The leaders of the latter were violent and aggressive men; they had guns and pistols, and, as was soon proved, were able to intimidate the thousands.

I quote what I once laid down in writing as our rule: "My idea is that the Company should be known as determined to let the men at any works stop work; that it will confer freely with them and wait patiently until they decide to return to work, never thinking of trying new men—never." The best men as men, and the best workmen, are not walking the streets looking for work. Only the inferior class as a rule is idle. The kind of men we desired are rarely allowed to lose their jobs, even in dull times. It is impossible to get new men to run successfully the complicated machinery of a modern steel plant. The attempt to put in new men converted the thousands of old men who desired to work, into lukewarm supporters of our policy, for workmen can always be relied upon to resent the employment of new men. Who can blame them?

If I had been at home, however, I might have been persuaded to open the works, as the superintendent desired, to test whether our old men would go to work as they had promised. But it should be noted that the works were not opened at first by my partners for new men. On the contrary, it was, as I was informed upon my return, at the wish of the thousands of our old men that they were opened. This is a vital point. My partners were in no way blamable for making the trial so recommended by the superintendent. Our rule never to employ new men, but to wait for the old to return, had not been violated so far. In regard to the second opening of the works, after the strikers had shot the sheriff's officers, it is also easy to look back and say, "How much better had the works been closed until the old men voted to return"; but the Governor of Pennsylvania, with eight thousand troops, had meanwhile taken charge of the situation.

I was traveling in the Highlands of Scotland when the trouble arose, and did not hear of it until two days after. Nothing I have ever had to meet in all my life, before or since, wounded me so deeply. No pangs remain of any wound received in my business career save that of Homestead. It was so unnecessary. The men were outrageously wrong. The strikers, with the new machinery, would have made from four to nine dollars a day under the new scale—thirty percent more than they were making with the old machinery. While in Scotland I received the following cable from the officers of the union of our workmen:

"Kind master, tell us what you wish us to do and we shall do it for you."

This was most touching, but, alas, too late. The mischief was done, the works were in the hands of the Governor; it was too late.

I received, while abroad, numerous kind messages from friends conversant with the circumstances, who imagined my unhappiness. The following from Mr. Gladstone was greatly appreciated:

My Dear Mr. Carnegie,

My wife has long ago offered her thanks, with my own, for your most kind congratulations. But I do not forget that you have been suffering yourself from anxieties, and have been exposed to imputations in connection with your gallant efforts to direct rich men into a course of action more enlightened than that which they usually follow. I wish I could relieve you from these imputations of journalists, too often rash, conceited or censorious, rancorous, ill-natured. I wish to do the little, the very little, that is in my power, which is simply to say how sure I am that no one who knows you will be prompted by the unfortunate occurrences across the water (of which manifestly we cannot know the exact merits) to qualify in the slightest degree either his confidence in your generous views or his admiration of the good and great work you have already done.

Wealth is at present like a monster threatening to swallow up the moral life of man; you by precept and by example have been teaching him to disgorge. I for one thank you.

Believe me

Very faithfully yours
(Signed) W. E. Gladstone

I insert this as giving proof, if proof were needed, of Mr. Gladstone's large, sympathetic nature, alive and sensitive to everything transpiring of a nature to arouse sympathy—Neapolitans, Greeks, and Bulgarians one day, or a stricken friend the next.

The general public, of course, did not know that I was in Scotland and knew nothing of the initial trouble at Homestead. Workmen had been killed at the Carnegie Works, of which I was the controlling owner. That was sufficient to make my name a by-word for years. But at last some satisfaction came. Senator Hanna was president of the National Civic Federation, a body composed of capitalists and workmen which exerted a benign influence over both employers and employed, and the Honorable Oscar Straus, who was then vice-president, invited me to dine at his house and meet the officials of the Federation. Before the date appointed Mark Hanna, its president, my lifelong friend and former agent at Cleveland, had suddenly passed away. I attended the dinner. At its close Mr. Straus arose and said that the question of a successor to Mr. Hanna had been considered, and he had to report that every labor organization heard from had favored me for the position. There were present several of the labor leaders who, one after another, arose and corroborated Mr. Straus.

I do not remember so complete a surprise and, I shall confess, one so grateful to me. That I deserved well from labor I felt. I knew myself to be warmly sympathetic with the workingman, and also that I had the regard of our own workmen; but throughout the country it was naturally the reverse, owing to the Homestead riot. The Carnegie Works meant to the public Mr. Carnegie's war upon labor's just earnings.

I arose to explain to the officials at the Straus dinner that I could not possibly accept the great honor, because I had to escape the heat of the summer and the head of the Federation must be on hand at all seasons ready to grapple with an outbreak, should one occur. My embarrassment was great, but I managed to let all understand that this was felt to be the most welcome tribute I could have received—a balm to the hurt mind. I closed by saying that if elected to my lamented friend's place upon the Executive Committee I should esteem it an honor to serve. To this position I was elected by unanimous vote. I was thus relieved from the feeling that I was considered responsible by labor generally, for the Homestead riot and the killing of workmen.

I owe this vindication to Mr. Oscar Straus, who had read my articles and speeches of early days upon labor questions, and who had quoted these frequently to workmen. The two labor leaders of the Amalgamated Union, White and Schaeffer from Pittsburgh, who were at this dinner, were also able and anxious to enlighten their fellow-workmen members of the Board as to my record with labor, and did not fail to do so.

A mass meeting of the workmen and their wives was afterwards held in the Library Hall at Pittsburgh to greet me, and I addressed them from both my head and my heart. The one sentence I remember, and always shall, was to the effect that capital, labor, and employer were a three-legged stool, none before or after the others, all equally indispensable. Then came the cordial handshaking and all was well. Having thus rejoined hands and hearts with our employees and their wives, I felt that a great weight had been effectually lifted, but I had had a terrible experience although thousands of miles from the scene.

An incident flowing from the Homestead trouble is told by my friend, Professor John C. Van Dyke, of Rutgers College.

"In the spring of 1900, I went up from Guaymas, on the Gulf of California, to the ranch of a friend at La Noria Verde, thinking to have a week's shooting in the mountains of Sonora. The ranch was far enough removed from civilization, and I had expected meeting there only a few Mexicans and many Yaqui Indians, but much to my surprise I found an English-speaking man, who proved to be an American. I did not have long to wait in order to find out what brought him there, for he was very lonesome and disposed to talk. His name was Mc-

Luckie, and up to 1892 he had been a skilled mechanic in the employ of the Carnegie Steel Works at Homestead. He was what was called a 'top hand,' received large wages, was married, and at that time had a home and considerable property. In addition, he had been honored by his fellow-townsmen and had been made burgomaster of Homestead.

"When the strike of 1892 came McLuckie naturally sided with the strikers, and in his capacity as burgomaster gave the order to arrest the Pinkerton detectives who had come to Homestead by steamer to protect the works and preserve order. He believed he was fully justified in doing this. As he explained it to me, the detectives were an armed force invading his bailiwick, and he had a right to arrest and disarm them. The order led to bloodshed, and the conflict was begun in real earnest.

"The story of the strike is, of course, well known to all. The strikers were finally defeated. As for McLuckie, he was indicted for murder, riot, treason, and I know not what other offenses. He was compelled to flee from the State, was wounded, starved, pursued by the officers of the law, and obliged to go into hiding until the storm blew over. Then he found that he was blacklisted by all the steel men in the United States and could not get employment anywhere. His money was gone, and, as a final blow, his wife died and his home was broken up. After many vicissitudes he resolved to go to Mexico, and at the time I met him he was trying to get employment in the mines about fifteen miles from La Noria Verde. But he was too good a mechanic for the Mexicans, who required in mining the cheapest kind of unskilled peon labor. He could get nothing to do and had no money. He was literally down to his last copper. Naturally, as he told the story of his misfortunes, I felt very sorry for him, especially as he was a most intelligent person and did no unnecessary whining about his troubles.

"I do not think I told him at the time I knew Mr. Carnegie and had been with him at Cluny in Scotland shortly after the Homestead strike, nor that I knew from Mr. Carnegie the other side of the story. But McLuckie was rather careful not to blame Mr. Carnegie, saying to me several times that if 'Andy' had been there the trouble would never have arisen. He seemed to think 'the boys' could get on very well with 'Andy' but not so well with some of his partners.

"I was at the ranch for a week and saw a good deal of McLuckie in the evenings. When I left there, I went directly to Tucson, Arizona, and from there I had occasion to write to Mr. Carnegie, and in the letter I told him about meeting with McLuckie. I added that I felt very sorry for the man and thought he had been treated rather badly. Mr. Carnegie answered at once, and on the margin of the letter wrote in lead pencil: 'Give McLuckie all the money he wants, but don't mention my name.' I wrote to McLuckie immediately, offering him what money he needed, mentioning no sum, but giving him to understand that it would be sufficient to put him on his feet again. He declined it. He said he would fight it out and make his own way, which was the right-enough American spirit. I could not help but admire it in him.

"As I remember now, I spoke about him later to a friend, Mr. J. A. Naugle, the general manager of the Sonora Railway. At any rate, McLuckie got a job with the railway at driving wells, and made a great success of it. A year later, or perhaps it was in the autumn of the same year, I again met him at Guaymas, where he was superintending some repairs on his machinery at the railway shops. He was much changed for the better, seemed happy, and to add to his contentment, had taken unto himself a Mexican wife. And now that his sky was cleared, I was anxious to tell him the truth about my offer that he might not think unjustly of those who had been compelled to fight him. So before I left him, I said,

"'McLuckie, I want you to know now that the money I offered you was not mine. That was Andrew Carnegie's money. It was his offer, made through me.'

"McLuckie was fairly stunned, and all he could say was:

"'Well, that was damned white of Andy, wasn't it?'"

I would rather risk that verdict of McLuckie's as a passport to Paradise than all the theological dogmas invented by man. I knew McLuckie well as a good fellow. It was said his property in Homestead was worth thirty thousand dollars. He was under arrest for the shooting of the police officers because he was the burgomaster, and also the chairman of the Men's Committee of Homestead. He had to fly, leaving all behind him. . . .

Upon my return to Pittsburgh in 1892, after the Homestead trouble, I went to the works and met many of the old men who had not been concerned in the riot. They expressed the opinion that if I had been at home the strike would never have happened. I told them that the company had offered generous terms and beyond its offer I should not have gone; that before their cable reached me in Scotland, the Governor of the State had appeared on the scene with troops and wished the law vindicated; that the question had then passed out of my partners' hands. I added:

"You were badly advised. My partners' offer should have been accepted. It was very generous. I don't know that I would have offered so much."

To this one of the rollers said to me:

"Oh, Mr. Carnegie, it wasn't a question of dollars. The boys would have let you kick 'em, but they wouldn't let that other man stroke their hair."

So much does sentiment count for in the practical affairs of life, even with the laboring classes. This is not generally believed by those who do not know them, but I am certain that disputes about wages do not account for one half the disagreements between capital and labor. There is lack of due appreciation and of kind treatment of employees upon the part of the employers.

Suits had been entered against many of the strikers, but upon my return these were promptly dismissed. All the old men who remained, and had not been guilty of violence, were taken back. I had cabled from Scotland urging that Mr. Schwab be sent back to Homestead. He had been only recently promoted to the Edgar Thomson Works. He went back, and "Charlie," as he was affectionately called, soon restored order, peace, and harmony. Had he remained at the Homestead Works, in all probability no serious trouble would have arisen. "Charlie" liked his workmen and they liked him; but there still remained at Homestead an unsatisfactory element in the men who had previously been discarded from our various works for good reasons and had found employment at the new works before we purchased them.

Part III

Carnegie at Work, Giving Away Money

After having written himself a note of instructions in 1868 as to what he should do upon reaching the age of thirty-five, Carnegie conveniently ignored his own warning and advice. He continued to "push inordinately" and to make ever more money. Within twenty years his 1868 wealth which produced an annual income of $50,000 had expanded to a fortune of $30 million. The self-addressed memorandum had been ignored, but it could not be dismissed from his thoughts.

By 1888, Carnegie had, to be sure, dispersed a small part of his largesse in good works. He had given a swimming bath and a library to his native town of Dunfermline; a library to the town of Braddock, Pennsylvania; an organ to the small Swedenborgian church in Allegheny, which his father had attended; and a gift of $6,000 to the Western University of Pennsylvania (now the University of Pittsburgh). This was hardly an impressive list of benefactions and certainly offered "little hope of permanent recovery" from what he believed to be the degrading pursuit of wealth. Carnegie had yet to find a satisfactory release from the stern admonition, "Thine own reproach alone do fear."

Carnegie was to find absolution in an article entitled "Wealth" which he submitted to the North American Review *the following year. The editor of this publication, Allen Thorndike Rice, called it "the finest article I have ever published in the Review." "Wealth" appeared in two installments, subtitled "The Problem of the Administration of Wealth," in the June 1889 issue, and "The Best Fields for Phi-*

lanthropy," in December 1889. "Wealth" was later reprinted in the British journal Pall Mall Gazette, whose editor, W. T. Stead, retitled the two-part article "The Gospel of Wealth," by which it has been known ever since.

Carnegie had made his response to his own conscience, but his wealth continued to accumulate at an alarming rate. It was not until he finally retired from business and sold his steel plants to the J. P. Morgan syndicate in 1901 that he was ready to start practicing the gospel he had been preaching for the past twelve years. He was determined that his benevolent giving would not be simply charitable handouts to the needy but would demonstrate what he was pleased to call "scientific philanthropy." His giving would be, he was convinced, the capitalists's answer to Karl Marx's "scientific socialism."

As he did with any venture into which he entered, Carnegie again "pushed inordinately." In the next few years, he provided hundreds of communities throughout the United States, Canada, and Great Britain with libraries; gave thousands of organs to churches; established the Carnegie Institute of Pittsburgh; the Carnegie Institution of Washington, D.C.; the Carnegie Foundation for the Advancement of Teaching to provide pensions for college professors; and the Carnegie Dunfermline Trust to bring "sweetness and light" to his native town. In the city of New York, he built a great music hall and an imposing headquarters for the National Engineering Societies of America.

Just as he had done in business, Carnegie eventually put all his philanthropic energy and resources into one basket labeled Peace. To promote the establishment of world peace and international order he created four foundations: the Carnegie Hero Fund with branches in several countries to reward heroes of peace who saved lives; the Simplified Spelling Board to make English a feasible world language; the Carnegie Endowment for International Peace; and the Church Peace Union. He built three "temples of peace": the Pan American Union building in Washington, D.C.; the Central American Court of Justice in Cartago, Costa Rica; and most imposing of all, the Palace of Peace at The Hague, Netherlands, to house the World Court.

Carnegie's dazzling gifts attracted much public attention. Box scores began to appear in the press comparing Carnegie's gifts with those of his most important convert to the Gospel of Wealth, John D. Rockefeller. In 1904, the London Times reported Carnegie's gifts to have totaled $21 million, Rockefeller's $10 million. By 1910, the score stood: Carnegie, $179,300,000; Rockefeller, $134,271,000.

To Carnegie's surprise, however, the Gospel of Wealth had brought him not only the expected public acclaim but also the unexpected public criticism. He must have known that he could not please everyone with his gifts, but he had not anticipated that he would be pilloried from both the right and the left in his efforts to "benefit all mankind." Yet with the possible exception of Homestead, nothing he had done in his business career was subjected to such scorching criticism as was his philanthropy. Conservatives regarded him a socialist, and liberals accused him of trying to prostitute the colleges, science, and the general public with his millions. How Carnegie had made his millions was his own business, how he gave it away was apparently everyone's business.

Most discouraging of all was the fact that no matter how fast he had run during these ten years of giving, he had not run fast enough. Like Alice, Carnegie in the strange wonderland of philanthropy discovered that he had to run as fast as he could simply to stay in the same place. The interest on all those 5 percent United States Steel bonds he had acquired kept gaining on his dispersal of those bonds. By 1911 he had given away $180 million, but he still had almost the same amount left. "The final dispensation of one's wealth preparing for the final exit is I found a heavy task — all sad.... You have no idea the strain I have been under," he wrote his Scottish solicitor, John Ross (11 February 1913, Carnegie Papers, Library of Congress, vol. 213).

Finally in desperation, Carnegie followed the suggestion of his good friend Elihu Root. He created two more foundations, quite open-ended as to their program for benefiting the general welfare of Americans and British: the Carnegie Corporation of New York, to which he transferred the bulk of his remaining fortune, $125 million; and the United Kingdom Trust two years later, with a much smaller endowment of $10 million. In that year, the New York Herald ran the final score on the contest between Carnegie and Rockefeller: "Carnegie, $332 million; Rockefeller, $175 million." Rockefeller still had many more millions to go in his pursuit of the Gospel of Wealth, but for Carnegie the race was thankfully over.

12
The Gospel of Wealth According to Saint Andrew

Mark Twain was a frequent supplicant for a handout from Andrew Carnegie. He addressed his begging letters to "Saint Andrew," and Carnegie in turn would address his response to "Saint Mark." Close friend and great admirer of Twain though he was, Carnegie never enclosed the requested funds. Except for a few select persons, mostly relatives and old Dunfermline friends whom he placed on his private pension list, Carnegie rarely responded favorably to individual requests for financial aid. He regarded such giving as mere charity, which was a violation of the tenets he had set forth in his article "Wealth." (It was published under this title in the North American Review, *June and December 1889; a British editor later gave it the title "The Gospel of Wealth.")*

In this two-part article, Carnegie first justifies the accumulation of great wealth as inevitable within the capitalist system, but also beneficial, provided that the amasser of wealth realizes that he or she is but a steward responsible for returning that fortune to the society out of which it has come. The stewardship concept of wealth was, of course, not original with Carnegie. None of his predecessors in philanthropy, however, had ever analyzed or tried to make the art of giving into a science as he does in the first section of his article dealing with "The Problem of the Administration of Wealth."

In the second part of his article, Carnegie becomes more specific in listing "The Best Fields of Philanthropy." In descending order of importance, Carnegie states the seven areas in which "the wise trustee of surplus wealth should invest" to benefit and advance the general welfare. Carnegie's specificity aroused great criticism. As might be expected, many of these critics were American and British clergymen who were outraged to find that Carnegie had placed churches last on his list, just after swimming baths.

The most penetrating criticism from the clerics came from the liberal professor of religion at Andover Seminary, William Jewett Tucker. He did not plead the claims of sectarian religion to the capitalist's surplus wealth as did his fellow clergymen, how-

ever. He instead struck at the heart of Carnegie's thesis. The basic assumption of Carnegie as to the inevitability of great wealth, Tucker found especially reprehensible. Carnegie was indeed giving a new gospel statement, not Saint Matthew's, "For ye have the poor always with you," but "Saint Andrew's," "For ye have the rich always with you." This Tucker found to be in a true democratic society not inevitable but inconsistent with democracy and unjust. Nor would Tucker accept Carnegie's premise that the successful amasser of wealth is the best administrator of its redistribution. This doctrine smacked of noblesse oblige, *more appropriate to feudalism than to democracy, "and in the long run, [a democratic] society cannot afford to be patronized,"* Tucker wrote. *"For I can conceive of no greater mistake . . . than that of trying to make charity do the work of justice. . . . The ethical question of today centres, I am sure, in the* distribution *rather than in the* redistribution *of wealth" (William Jewett Tucker, "The Gospel of Wealth,"* Andover Review, *June 1891).*

Here was criticism that Carnegie must have found truly disturbing. Professed believer as he was in the democratic process and in progress, Carnegie, for his own peace of mind, had to ignore the Reverend Dr. Tucker's trenchant criticism. Certain that his way was the right way, he wrote to his good friend John Morley, *"Tenacity and steady sailing to the haven we clear for — supreme confidence in one's own ideas, or conclusion rather, after thought — and above all, placing* use *above popularity" (9 April 1901, Carnegie Papers, Library of Congress, vol. 82).* This was his answer to those of little faith who dared doubt the truth of his Gospel of Wealth.

The Problem of the Administration of Wealth

The problem of our age is the proper administration of wealth, that the ties of brotherhood may still bind together the rich and poor in harmonious relationship. The conditions of human life have not only been changed, but revolutionized, within the past few hundred years. In former days there was little difference between the dwelling, dress, food, and environment of the chief and those of his retainers. The Indians are today where civilized man then was. When visiting the Sioux, I was led to the wigwam of the chief. It was like the others in external appearance, and even within the difference was trifling between it and those of the poorest of his braves. The contrast between the palace of the millionaire and the cottage of the laborer with us today measures the change which has come with civilization. This change, however, is not to be deplored, but welcomed as highly beneficial. It is well, nay, essential, for the progress of the race that the houses of some should be homes for all that is highest and best in literature and the arts, and for all the refinements of civilization, rather than that none should be so. Much better this great irregularity than universal squalor. Without wealth there can be no Mæcenas. The "good old times" were not good old times. Neither master nor servant was as well situated then as today. A relapse to old conditions would be disastrous to both—not the least so to him who serves—and would sweep away civilization with it. But whether the change be for good or ill, it is upon us, beyond our power to alter, and, therefore, to be accepted and made the best of. It is a waste of time to criticize the inevitable.

It is easy to see how the change has come. One illustration will serve for almost every phase of the cause. In the manufacture of products we have the whole story. It applies to all combinations of human industry, as stimulated and enlarged by the inventions of this scientific age. Formerly, articles were manufactured at the domestic hearth, or in small shops which formed part of the household. The master and his apprentices worked side by side, the latter living with the master, and therefore subject to the same conditions. When these apprentices rose to be masters, there was little or no change in their mode of life, and they, in turn, educated succeeding apprentices in the same routine. There was, substantially, social equality, and even political equality, for those engaged in industrial pursuits had then little or no voice in the State.

The inevitable result of such a mode of manufacture was crude articles at high prices. Today the world obtains commodities of excellent quality at prices which even the preceding generation would have deemed incredible. In the commercial world similar causes have produced similar results, and the race is benefited thereby. The poor enjoy what the rich could not before afford. What were the luxuries have become the necessaries of life. The laborer has now more comforts than the farmer had a few generations ago. The farmer has more luxuries than the landlord had, and is more richly clad and better housed. The landlord has books and pictures rarer and appointments more artistic than the king could then obtain.

The price we pay for this salutary change is, no doubt, great. We assemble thousands of operatives in the factory, and in the mine, of whom the employer can know little or nothing, and to whom he is little better than a myth. All intercourse between them is at an end. Rigid castes are formed, and, as usual, mutual ignorance breeds mutual distrust. Each caste is without sympathy with the other, and ready to credit anything disparaging in regard to it. Under the law of competition, the employer of thousands is forced into the strictest economies, among which the rates paid to labor figure prominently, and often there is friction between the employer and the employed, between capital and labor, between rich and poor. Human society loses homogeneity.

The price which society pays for the law of competition, like the price it pays for cheap comforts and luxuries, is also great; but the advantages of this law are also greater still than its cost—for it is to this law that we owe our wonderful material development, which brings improved conditions in its train. But, whether the law be benign or not, we must say of it, as we say of the change in the conditions of men to which we have referred: It is here; we cannot evade it; no substitutes for it have been found; and while the law may be sometimes hard for the individual, it is best for the race, because it insures the survival of the fittest in every department. We accept and welcome, therefore, as conditions to which we must accommodate ourselves, great inequality of environment; the concentration of business, industrial and commercial, in the hands of a few; and the law of competition between these, as being not only beneficial, but essential to the future progress of the race. Having accepted these, it follows that there must be great scope for the exercise of special ability in the merchant and in the manufacturer who has to conduct affairs upon a great scale. That this talent for organization and management is rare among men is proved by the fact that it invariably secures enormous rewards for its possessor, no matter where or under what laws or conditions. The experienced in affairs always rate the MAN whose services can be obtained as a partner as not only the first consideration, but such as render the question of his capital scarcely worth considering: for able men soon create capital; in the hands of those without the special talent required, capital soon takes wings. Such men become interested in firms or corporations using millions; and, estimating only simple interest to be made upon the capital invested, it is inevitable that their income must exceed their expenditure and that they must, therefore, accumulate wealth. Nor is there any middle ground which such men can occupy, because the great manufacturing or commercial concern which does not earn at least interest upon its capital soon becomes bankrupt. It must either go forward or fall behind; to stand still is impossible. It is a condition essential to its successful operation that it should be thus far profitable, and even that, in addition to interest on capital, it should make profit. It is a law, as certain as any of the others named, that men possessed of this peculiar talent for affairs, under

The Gospel of Wealth

the free play of economic forces must, of necessity, soon be in receipt of more revenue than can be judiciously expended upon themselves; and this law is as beneficial for the race as the others.

Objections to the foundations upon which society is based are not in order, because the condition of the race is better with these than it has been with any other which has been tried. Of the effect of any new substitutes proposed we cannot be sure. The Socialist or Anarchist who seeks to overturn present conditions is to be regarded as attacking the foundation upon which civilization itself rests, for civilization took its start from the day when the capable, industrious workman said to his incompetent and lazy fellow, "If thou dost not sow, thou shalt not reap," and thus ended primitive Communism by separating the drones from the bees. One who studies this subject will soon be brought face to face with the conclusion that upon the sacredness of property civilization itself depends—the right of the laborer to his hundred dollars in the savings-bank, and equally the legal right of the millionaire to his millions. Every man must be allowed "to sit under his own vine and fig-tree, with none to make afraid," if human society is to advance, or even to remain so far advanced as it is. To those who propose to substitute Communism for this intense Individualism, the answer therefore is: The race has tried that. All progress from that barbarous day to the present time has resulted from its displacement. Not evil, but good, has come to the race from the accumulation of wealth by those who have had the ability and energy to produce it. But even if we admit for a moment that it might be better for the race to discard its present foundation, Individualism—that it is a nobler ideal that man should labor, not for himself alone, but in and for a brotherhood of his fellows, and share with them all in common, realizing Swedenborg's idea of heaven, where, as he says, the angels derive their happiness, not from laboring for self, but for each other—even admit all this, and a sufficient answer is, This is not evolution, but revolution. It necessitates the changing of human nature itself—a work of eons, even if it were good to change it, which we cannot know.

It is not practicable in our day or in our age. Even if desirable theoretically, it belongs to another and long-succeeding sociological stratum. Our duty is with what is practicable now—with the next step possible in our day and generation. It is criminal to waste our energies in endeavoring to uproot, when all we can profitably accomplish is to bend the universal tree of humanity a little in the direction most favorable to the production of good fruit under existing circumstances. We might as well urge the destruction of the highest existing type of man because he failed to reach our ideal as to favor the destruction of Individualism, Private Property, the Law of Accumulation of Wealth, and the Law of Competition; for these are the highest result of human experience, the soil in which society, so far, has produced the best fruit. Unequally or unjustly, perhaps, as these laws sometimes operate, and imperfect as they appear to the Idealist, they are, nevertheless, like the highest type of man, the best and most valuable of all that humanity has yet accomplished.

We start, then, with a condition of affairs under which the best interests of the race are promoted, but which inevitably gives wealth to the few. Thus far, accepting conditions as they exist, the situation can be surveyed and pronounced good. The question then arises—and if the foregoing be correct, it is the only question with which we have to deal—What is the proper mode of administering wealth after the laws upon which civilization is founded have thrown it into the hands of the few? And it is of this great question that I believe I offer the true solution. It will be understood that fortunes are here spoken of, not moderate sums saved by many years of effort, the returns from which are required for the comfortable maintenance and education of families. This is not wealth, but only competence, which it should be the aim of all to acquire, and which it is for the best interests of society should be acquired.

There are but three modes in which surplus wealth can be disposed of. It can be left to the families of the decedents; or it can be bequeathed for public purposes; or, finally, it can be administered by its possessors during their lives. Under the first and second modes most of the wealth of the world that has reached the few has hitherto been applied. Let us in turn consider each of these modes. The first is the most injudicious. In monarchical countries, the estates and the greatest portion of the wealth are left to the first son, that the vanity of the parent may be gratified by the thought that his name and title are to descend unimpaired to succeeding generations. The condition of this class in Europe today teaches the failure of such hopes or ambitions. The successors have become impoverished through their follies, or from the fall in the value of land. Even in Great Britain the strict law of entail has been found inadequate to maintain an hereditary class. Its soil is rapidly passing into the hands of the stranger. Under republican institutions the division of property among the children is much fairer; but the question which forces itself upon thoughtful men in all lands is, Why should men leave great fortunes to their children? If this is done from affection, is it not misguided affection? Observation teaches that, generally speaking, it is not well for the children that they should be so burdened. Neither is it well for the State. Beyond providing for the wife and daughters moderate sources of income, and very moderate allowances indeed, if any, for the sons, men may well hesitate; for it is no longer questionable that great sums bequeathed often work more for the injury than for the good of the recipients. Wise men will soon conclude that, for the best interests of the members of their families, and of the State, such bequests are an improper use of their means.

It is not suggested that men who have failed to educate their sons to earn a livelihood shall cast them adrift in poverty. If any man has seen fit to rear his sons with a view to their living idle lives, or, what is highly commendable, has instilled in them the sentiment that they are in a position to labor for public ends without reference to pecuniary considerations, then, of course, the duty of the parent is to see that such are provided for in moderation. There are instances of millionaires' sons unspoiled by wealth, who, being rich, still perform great services to the community. Such are the very salt of the earth, as valuable as, unfortunately, they are rare. It is not the exception, however, but the rule, that men must regard; and, looking at the usual result of enormous sums conferred upon legatees, the thoughtful man must shortly say, "I would as soon leave to my son a curse as the almighty dollar," and admit to himself that it is not the welfare of the children, but family pride, which inspires these legacies.

As to the second mode, that of leaving wealth at death for public uses, it may be said that this is only a means for the disposal of wealth, provided a man is content to wait until he is dead before he becomes of much good in the world. Knowledge of the results of legacies bequeathed is not calculated to inspire the brightest hopes of much posthumous good being accomplished by them. The cases are not few in which the real object sought by the testator is not attained, nor are they few in which his real wishes are thwarted. In many cases the bequests are so used as to become only monuments of his folly. It is well to remember that it requires the exercise of not less ability than that which acquired it, to use wealth so as to be really beneficial to the community. Besides this, it may fairly be said that no man is to be extolled for doing what he cannot help doing, nor is he to be thanked by the community to which he only leaves wealth at death. Men who leave vast sums in this way may fairly be thought men who would not have left it at all had they been able to take it with them. The memories of such cannot be held in grateful remembrance, for there is no grace in their gifts. It is not to be wondered at that such bequests seem so generally to lack the blessing.

The growing disposition to tax more and more heavily large estates left at death is a cheering indication of the growth of a salutary change in public opinion. The State of Pennsylvania now takes—subject to some exceptions—one tenth of the property left by its citizens. The budget presented in the British Parliament the other day proposes to increase the death duties; and, most significant of all, the new tax is to be a graduated one. Of all forms of taxation this seems the wisest. Men who continue hoarding great sums all their lives, the proper use of which for public ends would work good to the community from which it chiefly came, should be made to feel that the community, in the form of the State, cannot thus be deprived of its proper share. By taxing estates heavily at death the State marks its condemnation of the selfish millionaire's unworthy life.

It is desirable that nations should go much further in this direction. Indeed, it is difficult to set bounds to the share of a rich man's estate which should go at his death to the public through the agency of the State, and by all means such taxes should be graduated, beginning at nothing upon moderate sums to dependants, and increasing rapidly as the amounts swell, until of the millionaire's hoard, as of Shylock's, at least

> The other half
> Comes to the privy coffer of the State.

This policy would work powerfully to induce the rich man to attend to the administration of wealth during his life, which is the end that society should always have in view, as being by far the most fruitful for the people. Nor need it be feared that this policy would sap the root of enterprise and render men less anxious to accumulate, for, to the class whose ambition it is to leave great fortunes and be talked about after their death, it will attract even more attention, and, indeed, be a somewhat nobler ambition, to have enormous sums paid over to the State from their fortunes.

There remains, then, only one mode of using great fortunes; but in this we have the true antidote for the temporary unequal distribution of wealth, the reconciliation of the rich and the poor—a reign of harmony, another ideal, differing, indeed, from that of the Communist in requiring only the further evolution of existing conditions, not the total overthrow of our civilization. It is founded upon the present most intense Individualism, and the race is prepared to put it in practice by degrees whenever it pleases. Under its sway we shall have an ideal State, in which the surplus wealth of the few will become, in the best sense, the property of the many, because administered for the common good; and this wealth, passing through the hands of the few, can be made a much more potent force for the elevation of our race than if distributed in small sums to the people themselves. Even the poorest can be made to see this, and to agree that great sums gathered by some of their fellow-citizens and spent for public purposes, from which the masses reap the principal benefit, are more valuable to them than if scattered among themselves in trifling amounts through the course of many years.

If we consider the results which flow from the Cooper Institute, for instance, to the best portion of the race in New York not possessed of means, and compare these with those which would have ensued for the good of the masses from an equal sum distributed by Mr. Cooper in his lifetime in the form of wages, which is the highest form of distribution, being for work done and not for charity, we can form some estimate of the possibilities for the improvement of the race which lie embedded in the present law of the accumulation of wealth. Much of this sum, if distributed in small quantities among the people, would have been wasted in the indulgence of appetite, some of it in excess, and it may be doubted whether even the part put to the best use, that of adding to the comforts of the home, would have yielded results for the race, as a race, at all comparable to those which are flowing and are to flow from the Cooper Institute from generation to generation. Let the advocate of violent or radical change ponder well this thought.

We might even go so far as to take another instance—that of Mr. Tilden's bequest of five millions of dollars for a free library in the city of New York; but in referring to this one cannot help saying involuntarily: How much better if Mr. Tilden had devoted the last years of his own life to the proper administration of this immense sum; in which case neither legal contest nor any other cause of delay could have interfered with his aims. But let us assume that Mr. Tilden's millions finally become the means of giving to this city a noble public library, where the treasures of the world contained in books will be open to all forever, without money and without price. Considering the good of that part of the race which congregates in and around Manhattan Island, would its permanent benefit have been better promoted had these millions been allowed to circulate in small sums through the hands of the masses? Even the most strenuous advocate of Communism must entertain a doubt upon this subject. Most of those who think will probably entertain no doubt whatever.

Poor and restricted are our opportunities in this life, narrow our horizon, our best work most imperfect; but rich men should be thankful for one inestimable boon. They have it in their power during their lives to busy themselves in organizing benefactions from which the masses of their fellows will derive lasting advantage, and thus dignify their own lives. The highest life is probably to be reached, not by such imitation of the life of Christ as Count Tolstoi gives us, but, while animated by Christ's spirit, by recognizing the changed conditions of this age, and adopting modes of expressing this spirit suitable to the changed conditions under which we live, still laboring for the good of our fellows, which was the essence of his life and teaching, but laboring in a different manner.

This, then, is held to be the duty of the man of wealth: To set an example of modest, unostentatious living, shunning display or extravagance; to provide moderately for the legitimate wants of those dependent upon him; and, after doing so, to consider all surplus revenues which come to him simply as trust funds, which he is called upon to administer, and strictly bound as a matter of duty to administer in the manner which, in his judgment, is best calculated to produce the most beneficial results for the community—the man of wealth thus becoming the mere trustee and agent for his poorer brethren, bringing to their service his superior wisdom, experience, and ability to administer, doing for them better than they would or could do for themselves.

We are met here with the difficulty of determining what are moderate sums to leave to members of the family; what is modest, unostentatious living; what is the test of extravagance. There must be different standards for different conditions. The answer is that it is as impossible to name exact amounts or actions as it is to define good manners, good taste, or the rules of propriety; but, nevertheless, these are verities, well known, although indefinable. Public sentiment is quick to know and to feel what offends these. So in the case of wealth. The rule in regard to good taste in the dress of men or women applies here. Whatever makes one conspicuous offends the canon. If any family be chiefly known for display, for extravagance in home, table, or equipage, for enormous sums ostentatiously spent in any form upon itself—if these be its chief distinctions, we have no difficulty in estimating its nature or culture. So likewise in regard to the use or abuse of its surplus wealth, or to generous, free-handed cooperation in good public uses, or to unabated efforts to accumulate and hoard to the last, or whether they administer or bequeath. The verdict rests with the best and most enlightened public sentiment. The community will surely judge, and its judgments will not often be wrong.

The best uses to which surplus wealth can be put have already been indicated. Those who would administer wisely must, indeed, be wise; for one of the serious obstacles to the improvement of our race is indiscriminate charity. It were better for mankind that the millions of the rich were thrown into the sea than so spent as to encourage the slothful, the drunken, the unworthy. Of every thousand dollars spent in so-called charity today, it is probable that nine hundred and fifty dollars is unwisely spent—so spent, indeed, as to produce the very evils which it hopes to mitigate or cure. A well-known writer of philosophic books admitted the other day that he had given a quarter of a dollar to a man who approached him as he was coming to visit the house of his friend. He knew nothing of the habits of this beggar, knew not the use that would be made of this money, although he had every reason to suspect that it would be spent improperly. This man professed to be a disciple of Herbert Spencer; yet the quarter-dollar given that night will probably work more injury than all the money will do good which its thoughtless donor will ever be able to give in true charity. He only gratified his own feelings, saved himself from annoyance—and this was probably one of the most selfish and very worst actions of his life, for in all respects he is most worthy.

In bestowing charity, the main consideration should be to help those who will help themselves; to provide part of the means by which those who desire to improve may do so; to give those who desire to rise the aids by which they may rise; to assist, but rarely or never to do all. Neither the individual nor the race is improved by almsgiving. Those worthy of assistance, except in rare cases, seldom require assistance. The really valuable men of the race never do, except in case of accident or sudden change. Every one has, of course, cases of individuals brought to his own knowledge where temporary assistance can do genuine good, and these he will not overlook. But the amount which can be wisely given by the individual for individuals is necessarily limited by his lack of knowledge of the circumstances connected with each. He is the only true reformer who is as careful and as anxious not to aid the unworthy as he is to aid the worthy, and, perhaps, even more so, for in almsgiving more injury is probably done by rewarding vice than by relieving virtue.

The rich man is thus almost restricted to following the examples of Peter Cooper, Enoch Pratt of Baltimore, Mr. Pratt of Brooklyn, Senator Stanford, and others, who know that the best means of benefiting the community is to place within its reach the ladders upon which the aspiring can rise—free libraries, parks, and means of recreation, by which men are helped in body and mind; works of art, certain to give pleasure and improve the public taste; and public institutions of various kinds, which will improve the general condition of the people; in this manner returning their surplus wealth to the mass of their fellows in the forms best calculated to do them lasting good.

Thus is the problem of rich and poor to be solved. The laws of accumulation will be left free, the laws of distribution free. Individualism will continue, but the millionaire will be but a trustee for the poor, intrusted for a season with a great part of the increased wealth of the community, for administering it for the community far better than it could or would have done for itself. The best minds will thus have reached a stage in the development of the race in which it is clearly seen that there is no mode of disposing of surplus wealth creditable to thoughtful and earnest men into whose hands it flows, save by using it year by year for the general good. This day already dawns. Men may die without incurring the pity of their fellows, still sharers in great business enterprises from which their capital cannot be or has not been withdrawn, and which is left chiefly at death for public uses; yet the day is not far distant when the man who dies leaving behind him millions of available wealth, which was free for him to administer during life, will pass away "unwept, unhonored, and unsung," no matter to what uses he leaves the dross which he cannot take with him. Of such as these the public verdict will then be: "The man who dies thus rich dies disgraced."

Such, in my opinion, is the true gospel concerning wealth, obedience to which is destined some day to solve the problem of the rich and the poor, and to bring "Peace on earth, among men good will."

The Best Fields for Philanthropy

While "The Gospel of Wealth" has met a cordial reception upon this side of the Atlantic, it is natural that in the motherland it should have attracted more attention, because the older civilization is at present brought more clearly face to face with socialistic questions. The contrast between the classes and the masses, between rich and poor, is not yet quite so sharp in this vast, fertile, and developing continent, with less than twenty persons per square mile, as in crowded little Britain, with fifteen times that number and no territory unoccupied. Perhaps the *Pall Mall Gazette* in its issue of September 5 puts most pithily the objections that have been raised to what the English have been pleased to call "The Gospel of Wealth." I quote: "Great fortunes, says Mr. Carnegie, are great blessings to a community, because such and such things may be done with them. Well, but they are also a great curse, for such and such things are done with them. Mr. Carnegie's preaching, in other words, is altogether vitiated by Mr. Benzon's practice. The gospel of wealth is killed by the acts."

To this the reply seems obvious: the gospel of Christianity is also killed by the acts. The same objection that is urged against the gospel of wealth lies against the commandment, "Thou shalt not steal." It is no argument against a gospel that it is not lived up to; indeed, it is an argument in its favor, for a gospel must be higher than the prevailing standard. It is no argument against a law that it is broken: in that disobedience lies the reason for making and maintaining the law; the law which is never to be broken is never required.

Undoubtedly the most notable incident in regard to "The Gospel of Wealth" is that it was fortunate enough to attract the attention of Mr. Gladstone, and bring forth the following note from him: "I have asked Mr. Lloyd Bryce [*North American Review*] kindly to allow the republication in this country of the extremely interesting article on 'Wealth,' by Mr. Andrew Carnegie, which has just appeared in America." This resulted in the publication of the article in several newspapers and periodicals, and an enterprising publisher issued it in pamphlet form, dedicated by permission to Mr. Gladstone.

All this is most encouraging, proving as it does that society is alive to the great issue involved, and is in a receptive mood. Your request, Mr. Editor, that I should continue the subject and point out the best fields for the use of surplus wealth, may be taken as further proof that whether the ideas promulgated are to be received or rejected, they are at least certain to obtain a hearing.

The first article held that there is but one right mode of using enormous fortunes—namely, that the possessors from time to time during their own lives should so administer these as to promote the permanent good to the communities from which they were gathered. It was held that public sentiment would soon say of one who died possessed of available wealth which he was free to administer: "The man who dies thus rich dies disgraced."

The purpose of this paper is to present some of the best methods of performing this duty of administering surplus wealth for the good of the people. The first requisite for a really good use of wealth by the millionaire who has accepted the gospel which proclaims him only a trustee of the surplus that comes to him, is to take care that the purposes for which he spends it shall not have a degrading, pauperizing tendency upon its recipients, but that his trust shall be so administered as to stimulate the best and most aspiring poor of the community to further efforts for their own improvement. It is not the irreclaimably destitute, shiftless, and worthless which it is truly beneficial or truly benevolent for the individual to attempt to reach and improve. For these there exists the refuge provided by the city or the State, where they can be sheltered, fed, clothed, and kept in comfortable existence, and—most important of all—where they can be isolated from the well-doing and industrious poor, who are liable to be demoralized by contact with these unfortunates. One man or woman who succeeds in living comfortably by begging is more dangerous to society, and a greater obstacle to the progress of humanity, than a score of wordy Socialists. The individual administrator of surplus wealth has as his charge the industrious and ambitious; not those who need everything done for them, but those who, being most anxious and able to help themselves, deserve and will be benefited by help from others and by the extension of their opportunities by the aid of the philanthropic rich.

It is ever to be remembered that one of the chief obstacles which the philanthropist meets in his efforts to do real and permanent good in this world, is the practice of indiscriminate giving; and the duty of the millionaire is to resolve to cease giving to objects that are not clearly proved to his satisfaction to be deserving. He must remember Mr. Rice's belief, that nine hundred and fifty out of every thousand dollars bestowed today upon so-called charity had better be thrown into the sea. As far as my experience of the wealthy extends, it is unnecessary to urge them to give of their superabundance in charity so called. Greater good for the race is to be achieved by inducing them to cease impulsive and injurious giving. As a rule, the sins of millionaires in this respect are not those of omission, but of commission, because they do not take time to think, and chiefly because it is much easier to give than to refuse. Those who have surplus wealth give millions every year which produce more evil than good, and really retard the progress of the people, because most of the forms in vogue today for benefiting mankind only tend to spread among the poor a spirit of dependence upon alms, when what is essential for progress is that they should be inspired to depend upon their own exertions. The miser millionaire who hoards his wealth does less injury to society than the careless millionaire who squanders his unwisely, even if he does so under cover of the mantle of sacred charity. The man who gives to the individual beggar commits a grave offense, but there are many societies and institutions soliciting alms, to aid which is none the less injurious to the community. These are as corrupting as individual beggars. Plutarch's "Morals" contains this lesson: "A beggar asking an alms of a Lacedæmonian, he said: 'Well, should I give thee anything, thou wilt be the greater beggar, for he that first gave thee money made thee idle, and is the cause of this base and dishonorable way of living.'" As I know them, there are few millionaires, very few indeed, who are clear of the sin of having made beggars.

Bearing in mind these considerations, let us endeavor to present some of the best uses to which a millionaire can devote the surplus of which he should regard himself as only the trustee.

First. Standing apart by itself there is the founding of a university by men enormously rich, such men as must necessarily be few in any country. Perhaps the greatest sum ever given by an individual for any purpose is the gift of Senator Stanford, who undertakes to establish a complete university upon the Pacific coast, where he amassed his enormous fortune, which is said to involve the expenditure of ten millions of dollars, and upon which he may be expected to bestow twenty millions of his surplus. He is to be envied. A thousand years hence some orator, speaking his praise upon the then crowded shores of the Pacific, may thus adapt Griffith's eulogy of Wolsey:

> In bestowing, madam,
> He was most princely. Ever witness for him
> This seat of learning, . . .
>   though unfinished, yet so famous,
> So excellent in art, and still so rising,
> That Christendom shall ever speak his virtue.

Here is a noble use of wealth. We have many such institutions—Johns Hopkins, Cornell, Packer, and others—but most of these have only been bequeathed, and it is impossible to extol any man greatly for simply leaving what he cannot take with him. Cooper and Pratt and Stanford, and others of this class, deserve credit and admiration as much for the time and attention given during their lives as for their expenditure upon their respective monuments.

We cannot think of the Pacific coast without recalling another important work of a different character which has recently been established there—the Lick Observatory. If any millionaire be interested in the ennobling study of astronomy—and there should be and would be such if they but gave the subject the slightest attention—here is an example which could well be followed, for the progress made in astronomical instruments and appliances is so great and continuous that every few years a new telescope might be judiciously given to one of the observatories upon this continent, the last being always the largest and the best, and certain to carry further and further the knowledge of the universe and of our relation to it here upon the earth. As one among many of the good deeds of the late Mr. Thaw of Pittsburg, his constant support of the observatory there may be mentioned. This observatory enabled Professor Langley to make his wonderful discoveries. He is now at the head of the Smithsonian Institution, a worthy successor to Professor Henry. Connected with him was Mr. Braeshier [sic] of Pittsburg, whose instruments are in most of the principal observatories of the world. He was a common millwright, but Mr. Thaw recognized his genius and was his main support through trying days. This common workman has been made a professor by one of the foremost scientific bodies of the world. In applying part of his surplus in aiding these two now famous men, the millionaire Thaw did a noble work. Their joint labors have brought great credit, and are destined to bring still greater credit, upon their country in every scientific center throughout the world.

It is reserved for very few to found universities, and, indeed, the use for many, or perhaps any, new universities does not exist. More good is henceforth to be accomplished by adding to and extending those in existence. But in this department a wide field remains for the millionaire as distinguished from the Crœsus among millionaires. The gifts to Yale University have been many, but there is plenty of room for others. The School of Fine Arts, founded by Mr. Street, the Sheffield Scientific School, endowed by Mr. Sheffield, and Professor Loomis's fund for the observatory, are fine examples. Mrs. C. J. Osborne's building for reading and recitation is to be regarded with especial pleasure as being the wise gift of a woman. Harvard University has not been forgotten; the Peabody Museum and the halls of Wells, Matthews, and Thayer may be cited. Sever Hall is worthy of special mention, as showing what a genius like Richardson could do with the small sum of a hundred thousand dollars. The Vanderbilt University, at Nashville, Tennessee, may be mentioned as a true product of the gospel of wealth. It was established by the members of the Vanderbilt family during their lives—mark this vital feature, during their lives; for nothing counts for much that is left by a man at his death. Such funds are torn from him, not given by him. If any millionaire be at a loss to know how to accomplish great and indisputable good with his surplus, here is a field which can never be fully occupied, for the wants of our universities increase with the development of the country.

Second. The result of my own study of the question, What is the best gift which can be given to a community? is that a free library occupies the first place, provided the community will accept and maintain it as a public institution, as much a part of the city property as its public schools, and, indeed, an adjunct to these. It is, no doubt, possible that my own personal experience may have led me to value a free library beyond all other forms of beneficence. When I was a working-boy in Pittsburg, Colonel Anderson of Allegheny—a name I can never speak without feelings of devotional gratitude—opened his little library of four hundred books to boys. Every Saturday afternoon he was in attendance at his house to exchange books. No one but he who has felt it can ever know the intense longing with which the arrival of Saturday was awaited, that a new book might be had. My brother and Mr. Phipps, who have been my principal business partners through life, shared with me Colonel Anderson's precious generosity, and it was when reveling in the treasures which he opened to us that I resolved, if ever wealth came to me, that it should be used to establish free libraries, that other poor boys might receive opportunities similar to those for which we were indebted to that noble man.

Great Britain has been foremost in appreciating the value of free libraries for its people. Parliament passed an act permitting towns and cities to establish and maintain these as municipal institutions; whenever the people of any town or city voted to accept the provisions of the act, the authorities were authorized to tax the community to the extent of one penny in the pound valuation. Most of the towns already have free libraries under this act. Many of these are the gifts of rich men, whose funds have been used for the building, and in some cases for the books also, the communities being required to maintain and to develop the libraries. And to this feature I attribute most of their usefulness. An endowed institution is liable to become the prey of a clique. The public ceases to take interest in it, or, rather, never acquires interest in it. The rule has been violated which requires the recipients to help themselves. Everything has been done for the community instead of its being only helped to help itself, and good results rarely ensue.

Many free libraries have been established in our country, but none that I know of with such wisdom as the Pratt Library in Baltimore. Mr. Pratt built and presented the library to the city of Baltimore, with the balance of cash handed over; the total cost was one million dollars, upon which he required the city to pay five percent per annum, fifty thousand dollars per year, to trustees for the maintenance and development of the library and its branches. During

1888, 430,217 books were distributed; 37,196 people of Baltimore are registered upon the books as readers. And it is safe to say that 37,000 frequenters of the Pratt Library are of more value to Baltimore, to the State, and to the country, than all the inert, lazy, and hopelessly poor in the whole nation. And it may further be safely said that, by placing books within the reach of 37,000 aspiring people which they were anxious to obtain, Mr. Pratt has done more for the genuine progress of the people than has been done by all the contributions of all the millionaires and rich people to help those who cannot or will not help themselves. The one wise administrator of his surplus has poured a fertilizing stream upon soil that was ready to receive it and return a hundredfold. The many squanderers have not only poured their streams into sieves which can never be filled—they have done worse: they have poured them into stagnant sewers that breed the diseases which most afflict the body politic. And this is not all. The million dollars of which Mr. Pratt has made so grand a use are something, but there is something greater still. When the fifth branch library was opened in Baltimore, the speaker said:

Whatever may have been done in these four years, it is my pleasure to acknowledge that much, very much, is due to the earnest interest, the wise counsels, and the practical suggestions of Mr. Pratt. He never seemed to feel that the mere donation of great wealth for the benefit of his fellow-citizens was all that would be asked of him, but he wisely labored to make its application as comprehensive and effective as possible. Thus he constantly lightened burdens that were, at times, very heavy, brought good cheer and bright sunshine when clouds flitted across the sky, and made every officer and employee feel that good work was appreciated, and loyal devotion to duty would receive hearty commendation.

This is the finest picture I have ever seen of any of the millionaire class. As here depicted, Mr. Pratt is the ideal disciple of the gospel of wealth. We need have no fear that the mass of toilers will fail to recognize in such as he their best leaders and their most invaluable allies; for the problem of poverty and wealth, of employer and employed, will be practically solved whenever the time of the few is given, and their wealth is administered during their lives, for the best good of that portion of the community which has not been burdened with the responsibilities which attend the possession of wealth. We shall have no antagonism between classes when that day comes, for the high and the low, the rich and the poor, shall then indeed be brothers.

No millionaire will go far wrong in his search for one of the best forms for the use of his surplus who chooses to establish a free library in any community that is willing to maintain and develop it. John Bright's words should ring in his ear: "It is impossible for any man to bestow a greater benefit upon a young man than to give him access to books in a free library." Closely allied to the library, and, where possible, attached to it, there should be rooms for an art gallery and museum, and a hall for such lectures and instruction as are provided in the Cooper Union. The traveler upon the Continent is surprised to find that every town of importance has its art gallery and museum; these may be large or small, but each has a receptacle for the treasures of the locality, in which are constantly being placed valuable gifts and bequests. The Free Library and Art Gallery of Birmingham are remarkable among such institutions, and every now and then a rich man adds to their value by presenting books, fine pictures, or other works of art. All that our cities require, to begin with, is a proper fire-proof building. Their citizens who travel will send to it rare and costly things from every quarter of the globe they visit, while those who remain at home will give or bequeath to it of their treasures. In this way collections will grow until our cities will ultimately be able to boast of permanent exhibitions from which their own citizens will derive incalculable benefit, and which they will be proud to show to visitors. In the Metropolitan Museum of Art in New York we have made an excellent beginning. Here is another avenue for the proper use of surplus wealth.

Third. We have another most important department in which great sums can be worthily used—the founding or extension of hospitals, medical colleges, laboratories, and other institutions connected with the alleviation of human suffering, and especially with the prevention rather than with the cure of human ills. There is no danger in pauperizing a community in giving for such purposes, because such institutions relieve temporary ailments or shelter only those who are hopeless invalids. What better gift than a hospital can be given to a community that is without one?—the gift being conditioned upon its proper maintenance by the community in its corporate capacity. If hospital accommodation already exists, no better method for using surplus wealth can be found than in making additions to it. The late Mr. Vanderbilt's gift of half a million dollars to the Medical Department of Columbia College for a chemical laboratory was one of the wisest possible uses of wealth. It strikes at the prevention of disease by penetrating into its causes. Several others have established such laboratories, but the need for them is still great.

If there be a millionaire in the land who is at a loss what to do with the surplus that has been committed to him as trustee, let him investigate the good that is flowing from these chemical laboratories. No medical college is complete without its laboratory. As with universities, so with medical colleges: it is not new institutions that are required, but additional means for the more thorough equipment of those that exist. The forms that benefactions to these may wisely take are numerous, but probably none is more useful than that adopted by Mr. Osborne when he built a school for training female nurses at Bellevue College. If from all gifts there flows one-half of the good that comes from this wise use of a millionaire's surplus, the most exacting may well be satisfied. Only those who have passed through a lingering and dangerous illness can rate at their true value the care, skill, and attendance of trained female nurses. Their employment as nurses has enlarged the sphere and influence of woman. It is not to be wondered at that a senator of the United States, and a physician distinguished in this country for having received the highest distinctions abroad, should recently have found their wives in this class.

Fourth. In the very front rank of benefactions public parks should be placed, always provided that the community undertakes to maintain, beautify, and preserve them inviolate. No more useful or more beautiful monument can be left by any man than a park for the city in which he was born or in which he has long lived, nor can the community pay a more graceful tribute to the citizen who presents it than to give his name to the gift. Mrs. Schenley's gift last month of a large park to the city of Pittsburg deserves to be noted. This lady, although born in Pittsburg, married an English gentleman while yet in her teens. It is forty years and more since she took up her residence in London among the titled and the wealthy of the world's metropolis, but still she turns to the home of her childhood and by means of Schenley Park links her name with it forever. A noble use this of great wealth by one who thus becomes her own administrator. If a park be already provided, there is still room for many judicious gifts in connection with it. Mr. Phipps of Allegheny has given conservatories to the park there, which are visited by many every day of the week, and crowded by thousands of working people every Sunday; for, with rare wisdom, he has stipulated as a condition of the gift that the conservatories shall be open on Sundays. The result of his experiment has been so gratifying that he finds himself justified in adding to them from his surplus, as he is doing largely this year. To lovers of flowers among the wealthy I commend a study of what is possible for them to do in the line of Mr. Phipps's example; and may they please note that Mr. Phipps is a wise as well as a liberal giver, for he requires the city to maintain these conservatories, and thus secures for them forever the public ownership, the public interest, and the public criticism of their management. Had he undertaken to manage and maintain them, it is probable that popular interest in the gift would never have been awakened.

The parks and pleasure-grounds of small towns throughout Europe are not less surprising than their libraries, museums, and art galleries. I saw nothing more pleasing during my recent travels than the hill at Bergen, in Norway. It has been converted into one of the most picturesque of pleasure-grounds; fountains, cascades, waterfalls, delightful arbors, fine terraces, and statues adorn what was before a barren mountainside. Here is a field worthy of study by the millionaire who would confer a lasting benefit upon his fellows. Another beautiful instance of the right use of wealth in the direction of making cities more and more attractive is to be found in Dresden. The owner of the leading paper there bequeathed its revenues forever to the city, to be used in beautifying it. An art committee decides, from time to time, what new artistic feature is to be introduced, or what hideous feature is to be changed, and as the revenues accrue, they are expended in this direction. Thus, through the gift of this patriotic newspaper proprietor his native city of Dresden is fast becoming one of the most artistic places of residence in the whole world. A work having been completed, it devolves upon the city to maintain it forever. May I be excused if I commend to our millionaire newspaper proprietors the example of their colleague in the capital of Saxony?

Scarcely a city of any magnitude in the older countries is without many structures and features of great beauty. Much has been spent upon ornament, decoration, and architectural effect. We are still far behind in these things upon this side of the Atlantic. Our Republic is great in some things — in material development unrivaled; but let us always remember that in art and in the finer touches we have scarcely yet taken a place. Had the exquisite Memorial Arch recently erected temporarily in New York been shown in Dresden, the art committee there would probably have been enabled, from the revenue of the newspaper given by its owner for just such purposes, to order its permanent erection to adorn the city forever.

While the bestowal of a park upon a community will be universally approved as one of the best uses of surplus wealth, in embracing such additions to it as conservatories, or in advocating the building of memorial arches and works of adornment, it is probable that many will think I go too far, and consider these somewhat fanciful. The material good to flow from them may not be so directly visible; but let not any practical mind, intent only upon material good, depreciate the value of wealth given for these or for kindred esthetic purposes as being useless as far as the mass of the people and their needs are concerned. As with libraries and museums, so with these more distinctively artistic works: they perform their great use when they reach the best of the masses of the people. It is better to reach and touch the sentiment for beauty in the naturally bright minds of this class than to pander to those incapable of being so touched. For what the improver of the race must endeavor is to reach those who have the divine spark ever so feebly developed, that it may be strengthened and grow. For my part, I think Mr. Phipps put his money to better use in giving the workingmen of Allegheny conservatories filled with beautiful flowers, orchids, and aquatic plants, which they, with their wives and children, can enjoy in their spare hours, and upon which they can feed their love for the beautiful, than if he had given his surplus money to furnish them with bread; for those in health who cannot earn their bread are scarcely worth considering by the individual giver, the care of such being the duty of the State. The man who erects in a city a conservatory or a truly artistic arch, statue, or fountain, makes a wise use of his surplus. "Man does not live by bread alone."

Fifth. We have another good use for surplus wealth in providing our cities with halls suitable for meetings of all kinds, and for concerts of elevating music. Our cities are rarely possessed of halls for these purposes, being in this respect also very far behind European cities. Springer Hall, in Cincinnati, a valuable addition to the city, was largely the gift of Mr. Springer, who was not content to bequeath funds from his estate at death, but gave during his life, and in addition, gave—what was equally important—his time and business ability to insure the successful results which have been achieved. The gift of a hall to any city lacking one is an excellent use for surplus wealth for the good of a community. The reason why the people have only one instructive and elevating, or even amusing, entertainment when a dozen would be highly beneficial, is that the rent of a hall, even when a suitable hall exists, which is rare, is so great as to prevent managers from running the risk of financial failure. If every city in our land owned a hall which could be given or rented for a small sum for such gatherings as a committee or the mayor of the city judged advantageous, the people could be furnished with proper lectures, amusements, and concerts at an exceedingly small cost. The town halls of European cities, many of which have organs, are of inestimable value to the people, utilized as they are in the manner suggested. Let no one underrate the influence of entertainments of an elevating or even of an amusing character, for these do much to make the lives of the people happier and their natures better. If any millionaire born in a small village which has now become a great city is prompted in the day of his success to do something for his brithplace with part of his surplus, his grateful remembrance cannot take a form more useful than that of a public hall with an organ, provided the city agrees to maintain and use it.

Sixth. In another respect we are still much behind Europe. A form of beneficence which is not uncommon there is providing swimming-baths for the people. The donors of these have been wise enough to require the city benefited to maintain them at its own expense, and as proof of the contention that everything should never be done for any one or for any community, but that the recipients should invariably be called upon to do a part, it is significant that it is found essential for the popular success of these healthful establishments to exact a nominal charge for their use. In many cities, however, the schoolchildren are admitted free at fixed hours upon certain days; different hours being fixed for the boys and the girls to use the great swimming-baths, hours or days being also fixed for the use of these baths by women. In addition to the highly beneficial effect of these institutions upon the public health in inland cities, the young of both sexes are thus taught to swim. Swimming clubs are organized, and matches are frequent, at which medals and prizes are given. The reports published by the various swimming-bath establishments throughout Great Britain are filled with instances of lives saved because those who fortunately escaped shipwreck had been taught to swim in the baths; and not a few instances are given in which the pupils of certain bathing establishments have saved the lives of others. If any disciple of the gospel of wealth gives his favorite city large swimming and private baths, provided the municipality undertakes their management as a city affair, he will never be called to account for an improper use of the funds intrusted to him.

Seventh. Churches as fields for the use of surplus wealth have purposely been reserved until the last, because, these being sectarian, every man will be governed in his action in regard to them by his own attachments; therefore gifts to churches, it may be said, are not, in one sense, gifts to the community at large, but to special classes. Nevertheless, every millionaire may know of a district where the little cheap, uncomfortable, and altogether unworthy wooden structure stands at the crossroads, in which the whole neighborhood gathers on Sunday, and which, independently of the form of the doctrines taught, is the center of social life and source of neighborly feeling. The administrator of wealth makes a good use of a part of his surplus if he replaces that building with a permanent structure of brick, stone, or granite, up whose sides the honeysuckle and columbine may climb, and from whose tower the sweet-tolling bell may sound. The millionaire should not figure how cheaply this structure can be built, but how perfect it can be made. If he has the money, it should be made a gem, for the educating influence of a pure and noble specimen of architecture, built, as the pyramids were built, to stand for ages, is not to be measured by dollars. Every farmer's home, heart, and mind in the district will be influenced by the beauty and grandeur of the church; and many a bright boy, gazing enraptured upon its richly colored windows and entranced by the celestial voice of the organ, will there receive his first message from and in spirit be carried away to the beautiful and enchanting realm which lies far from the material and prosaic conditions which surround him in this workaday world—a real world, this new realm, vague and undefined though its boundaries be. Once within its magic circle, its denizens live there an inner life more precious than the external, and all their days and all their ways, their triumphs and their trials, and all they see, and all they hear, and all they think, and all they do, are hallowed by the radiance which shines from afar upon this inner life, glorifying everything, and keeping all right within. But having given the building, the donor should stop there; the support of the church should be upon its own people. There is not much genuine religion in the congregation or much good to come from the church which is not supported at home.

Many other avenues for the wise expenditure of surplus wealth might be indicated. I enumerate but a few—a very few—of the many fields which are open, and only those in which great or considerable sums can be judiciously used. It is not the privilege, however, of millionaires alone to work for or aid measures which are certain to benefit the community. Every one who has but a small surplus above his moderate wants may share this privilege with his richer brothers, and those without surplus can give at least a part of their time, which is usually as important as funds, and often more so.

It is not expected, neither is it desirable, that there should be general concurrence as to the best possible use of surplus wealth. For different men and different localities there are different uses. What commends itself most highly to the judgment of the administrator is the best use for him, for his heart should be in the work. It is as important in administering wealth as it is in any other branch of a man's work that he should be enthusiastically devoted to it and feel that in the field selected his work lies.

Besides this, there is room and need for all kinds of wise benefactions for the common weal. The man who builds a university, library, or laboratory performs no more useful work than he who elects to devote himself and his surplus means to the adornment of a park, the gathering together of a collection of pictures for the public, or the building of a memorial arch. These are all true laborers in the vineyard. The only point required by the gospel of wealth is that the surplus which accrues from time to time in the hands of a man should be administered by him in his own lifetime for that purpose which is seen by him, as trustee, to be best for the good of the people. To leave at death what he cannot take away, and place upon others the burden of the work which it was his own duty to perform, is to do nothing worthy. This requires no sacrifice, nor any sense of duty to his fellows.

Time was when the words concerning the rich man entering the kingdom of heaven were regarded as a hard saying. Today, when all questions are probed to the bottom and the standards of faith receive the most liberal interpretations, the startling verse has been relegated to the rear, to await the next kindly revision as one of those things which cannot be quite understood, but which, meanwhile, it is carefully to be noted, are not to be understood literally. But is it so very improbable that the next stage of thought is to restore the doctrine in all its pristine purity and force, as being in perfect harmony with sound ideas upon the subject of wealth and poverty, the rich and the poor, and the contrasts everywhere seen and deplored? In Christ's day, it is evident, reformers were against the wealthy. It is none the less evident that we are fast recurring to that position today; and there will be nothing to surprise the student of sociological development if society should soon approve the text which has caused so much anxiety: "It is easier for a camel to enter the eye of a needle than for a rich man to enter the kingdom of heaven." Even if the needle were the small casement at the gates, the words betoken serious difficulty for the rich. It will be but a step for the theologian from the doctrine that he who dies rich dies disgraced, to that which brings upon the man punishment or deprivation hereafter.

The gospel of wealth but echoes Christ's words. It calls upon the millionaire to sell all that he hath and give it in the highest and best form to the poor by administering his estate himself for the good of his fellows, before he is called upon to lie down and rest upon the bosom of Mother Earth. So doing, he will approach his end no longer the ignoble hoarder of useless millions; poor, very poor indeed, in money, but rich, very rich, twenty times a millionaire still, in the affection, gratitude, and admiration of his fellow-men, and—sweeter far—soothed and sustained by the still, small voice within, which, whispering, tells him that, because he has lived, perhaps one small part of the great world has been bettered just a little. This much is sure: against such riches as these no bar will be found at the gates of Paradise.

13
Carnegie's Report on Spreading the Gospel

In his Autobiography *(ed. John Van Dyke [Boston: Houghton Mifflin, 1920]), Andrew Carnegie devotes surprisingly little space to that activity which occupied much of his attention and energy after his retirement from business in 1901. In the chapter given below, entitled "The 'Gospel of Wealth'," he touches but lightly and smilingly upon the implementation of the program of philanthropy which he had first enunciated two decades earlier. Except for one brief allusion to "the task of distribution before me [which] would tax me in my old age to the utmost," there is no suggestion of just how difficult and frequently painful that task had proved to be. Like the sundial in his garden, Carnegie in his autobiography was determined to record only the sunny hours.*

In this chapter, he singles out for emphasis only four of his many philanthropies: the library gifts, the best known and most widely acclaimed of all his benefactions; the Andrew Carnegie Relief Fund, established in 1901 to provide financial assistance for his former employees in need, which in this account gives him a splendid opportunity to tell his readers that he loved his workers and they loved him in spite of Homestead; the Carnegie Institution of Washington, which provides the funds "to encourage investigations, research and discovery" and whose early accomplishments in surveying the oceans and discovering new worlds in the skies thrilled its founder; and the Carnegie Hero Fund, which Carnegie would always insist was his favorite philanthropy because it was "my ain bairn . . . no one suggested it to me."

There was much else that Carnegie could have given as evidence of the effectiveness of his Gospel of Wealth. He could have bragged of being the innovator of the modern philanthropic foundation, at a time when there was no personal income or inheritance tax to provide motivation. Above all, he might have pointed out the wisdom he had demonstrated in setting up most of his major foundations by providing an escape clause that allowed the trustees to use the funds as needed for purposes different from those originally specified. For example, in his Letter of Gift to the Carnegie Corporation of New York, he wrote: "Conditions upon erth [sic—Carnegie's simplified spelling to encourage the use of English] inevitably change; hence no wise men will bind Trustees forever to certain paths, causes or institutions.... I giv [sic] my Trustees full authority to change policy or causes hitherto aided... when this, in their opinion, has become necessary or desirable. They shall best conform to my wishes by using their own judgment." And again, in establishing the Carnegie Endowment for International Peace, Carnegie stipulated that "when the establishment of universal peace is attained, the donor provides that the revenue shall be devoted to the banishment of the next most degrading evil or evils, the suppression of which would most advance the progress, elevation and happiness of man." Always with Carnegie there was change and progress "onward and upward to perfection." The officers of many closely bound foundations must surely envy the flexibility which Carnegie wisely provided to his trustees.

Carnegie apparently felt no need in his autobiography to publicize his good works. Nor did he need to chew over past quarrels and criticisms concerning the distribution of his wealth. He liked what he had done, and his gifts spoke for themselves. He had, moreover, found release from his own self-reproach. In defending his Gospel of Wealth, Carnegie had once written that persons of great wealth, by following his tenets, "can, perhaps, also find refuge from self-questioning." Here almost as an incidental aside, Carnegie revealed an underlying motivation for his gospel. He had at last fulfilled the demands he had placed upon himself in the 1868 memorandum. He had once written, "The man who dies thus rich, dies disgraced." Carnegie could now die in a state of grace.

After my book, "The Gospel of Wealth," was published, it was inevitable that I should live up to its teachings by ceasing to struggle for more wealth. I resolved to stop accumulating and begin the infinitely more serious and difficult task of wise distribution. Our profits had reached forty millions of dollars per year and the prospect of increased earnings before us was amazing. Our successors, the United States Steel Corporation, soon after the purchase, netted sixty millions in one year. Had our company continued in business and adhered to our plans of extension, we figured that seventy millions in that year might have been earned.

Steel had ascended the throne and was driving away all inferior material. It was clearly seen that there was a great future ahead; but so far as I was concerned I knew the task of distribution before me would tax me in my old age to the utmost. As usual, Shakespeare had placed his talismanic touch upon the thought and framed the sentence—

> So distribution should undo excess,
> And each man have enough.

At this juncture—that is March, 1901—Mr. Schwab told me Mr. Morgan had said to him he should really like to know if I wished to retire from business; if so he thought he could arrange it. He also said he had consulted our partners and that they were disposed to sell, being attracted by the terms Mr. Morgan had offered. I told Mr. Schwab that if my partners were desirous to sell I would concur, and we finally sold.

There had been so much deception by speculators buying old iron and steel mills and foisting them upon innocent purchasers at inflated values—hundred-dollar shares in some cases selling for a trifle—that I declined to take anything for the common stock. Had I done so, it would have given me just about one hundred millions more of five percent bonds, which Mr. Morgan said afterwards I could have obtained. Such was the prosperity and such the money value of our steel business. Events proved I should have been quite justified in asking the additional sum named, for the common stock has paid five percent continuously since.[1] But I had enough, as has been proved, to keep me busier than ever before, trying to distribute it.

My first distribution was to the men in the mills. The following letters and papers will explain the gift:

New York, N.Y., March 12, 1901

I make this first use of surplus wealth, four millions of first mortgage 5% Bonds, upon retiring from business, as an acknowledgment of the deep debt which I owe to the workmen who have contributed so greatly to my success. It is designed to relieve those who may suffer from accidents, and provide small pensions for those needing help in old age.

---

1. The Carnegie Steel Company was bought by Mr. Morgan at Mr. Carnegie's own price. There was some talk at the time of his holding out for a higher price than he received, but testifying before a committee of the House of Representatives in January, 1912, Mr. Carnegie said: "I considered what was fair: and that is the option Morgan got. Schwab went down and arranged it. I never saw Morgan on the subject or any man connected with him. Never a word passed between him and me. I gave my memorandum and Morgan saw it was eminently fair. I have been told many times since by insiders that I should have asked $100,000,000 more and could have got it easily. Once for all, I want to put a stop to all this talk about Mr. Carnegie 'forcing high prices for anything.'"

In addition I give one million dollars of such bonds, the proceeds thereof to be used to maintain the libraries and halls I have built for our workmen.

In return, the Homestead workmen presented the following address:

Munhall, Pa., Feb'y 23, 1903

Mr. Andrew Carnegie
New York, N.Y.

Dear Sir:

We, the employees of the Homestead Steel Works, desire by this means to express to you through our Committee our great appreciation of your benevolence in establishing the "Andrew Carnegie Relief Fund," the first annual report of its operation having been placed before us during the past month.

The interest which you have always shown in your workmen has won for you an appreciation which cannot be expressed by mere words. Of the many channels through which you have sought to do good, we believe that the "Andrew Carnegie Relief Fund" stands first. We have personal knowledge of cares lightened and of hope and strength renewed in homes where human prospects seemed dark and discouraging.

Respectfully yours

Committee
- Harry F. Rose, Roller
- John Bell, Jr., Blacksmith
- J. A. Horton, Timekeeper
- Walter A. Greig, Electric Foreman
- Harry Cusack, Yardmaster

The Lucy Furnace men presented me with a beautiful silver plate and inscribed upon it the following address:

Andrew Carnegie Relief Fund
Lucy Furnaces

Whereas, Mr. Andrew Carnegie, in his munificent philanthropy, has endowed the "Andrew Carnegie Relief Fund" for the benefit of employees of the Carnegie Company, Therefore be it

Resolved, that the employees of the Lucy Furnaces, in special meeting assembled, do convey to Mr. Andrew Carnegie their sincere thanks for and appreciation of his unexcelled and bounteous endowment, and furthermore be it

Spreading the Gospel

Resolved, that it is their earnest wish and prayer that his life may be long spared to enjoy the fruits of his works.

Committee
- James Scott, Chairman
- Louis A. Hutchison, Secretary
- James Daly
- R. C. Taylor
- John V. Ward
- Frederick Voelker
- John M. Veigh

I sailed soon for Europe, and as usual some of my partners did not fail to accompany me to the steamer and bade me good-bye. But, oh! the difference to me! Say what we would, do what we would, the solemn change had come. This I could not fail to realize. The wrench was indeed severe and there was pain in the good-bye which was also a farewell.

Upon my return to New York some months later, I felt myself entirely out of place, but was much cheered by seeing several of "the boys" on the pier to welcome me—the same dear friends, but so different. I had lost my partners, but not my friends. This was something; it was much. Still a vacancy was left. I had now to take up my self-appointed task of wisely disposing of surplus wealth. That would keep me deeply interested.

One day my eyes happened to see a line in that most valuable paper, the *Scottish American*, in which I had found many gems. This was the line: "The gods send thread for a web begun."

It seemed almost as if it had been sent directly to me. This sank into my heart, and I resolved to begin at once my first web. True enough, the gods sent thread in the proper form. Dr. J. S. Billings, of the New York Public Libraries, came as their agent, and of dollars, five and a quarter millions went at one stroke for sixty-eight branch libraries, promised for New York City. Twenty more libraries for Brooklyn followed.

My father, as I have stated, had been one of the five pioneers in Dunfermline who combined and gave access to their few books to their less fortunate neighbors. I had followed in his footsteps by giving my native town a library—its foundation stone laid by my mother—so that this public library was really my first gift. It was followed by giving a public library and hall to Allegheny City—our first home in America. President Harrison kindly accompanied me from Washington and opened these buildings. Soon after this, Pittsburgh asked for a library, which was given. This developed, in due course, into a group of buildings embracing a museum, a picture gallery, technical schools, and the Margaret Morrison School for Young Women. This group of buildings I opened to the public November 5, 1895. In Pittsburgh I had made my fortune and in the twenty-four millions already spent on this group,[2] she gets back only a small part of what she gave, and to which she is richly entitled.

The second large gift was to found the Carnegie Institution of Washington. The 28th of January, 1902, I gave ten million dollars in five percent bonds, to which there has been added sufficient to make the total cash value twenty-five millions of dollars, the additions being made upon record of results obtained. I naturally wished to consult President Roosevelt upon the matter, and if possible to induce the Secretary of State, Mr. John Hay, to serve as chairman, which he readily agreed to do. With him were associated as directors my old friend Abram S. Hewitt, Dr. Billings, William E. Dodge, Elihu Root, Colonel Higginson, D. O. Mills, Dr. S. Weir Mitchell, and others.

When I showed President Roosèvelt the list of the distinguished men who had agreed to serve, he remarked: "You could not duplicate it." He strongly favored the foundation, which was incorporated by an act of Congress April 28, 1904, as follows: "To encourage in the broadest and most liberal manner investigations, research and discovery, and the application of knowledge to the improvement of mankind; and, in particular, to conduct, endow and assist investigation in any department of science, literature and art, and to this end to cooperate with governments, universities, colleges, technical schools, learned societies, and individuals."

I was indebted to Dr. Billings as my guide, in selecting Dr. Daniel C. Gilman as the first President. He passed away some years later. Dr. Billings then recommended the present highly successful president, Dr. Robert S. Woodward. Long may he continue to guide the affairs of the Institution! The history of its achievements is so well known through its publications that details here are unnecessary. I may, however, refer to two of its undertakings that are somewhat unique. It is doing a worldwide service with the wood-and-bronze yacht, *Carnegie*, which is voyaging around the world correcting the errors of the earlier surveys. Many of these ocean surveys have been found misleading,

---

2. The total gifts to the Carnegie Institute at Pittsburgh amounted to about twenty-eight million dollars.

owing to variations of the compass. Bronze being nonmagnetic, while iron and steel are highly so, previous observations have proved liable to error. A notable instance is that of the stranding of a Cunard steamship near the Azores. Captain Peters, of the *Carnegie*, thought it advisable to test this case and found that the captain of the ill-fated steamer was sailing on the course laid down upon the admiralty map, and was not to blame. The original observation was wrong. The error caused by variation was promptly corrected.

This is only one of numerous corrections reported to the nations who go down to the sea in ships. Their thanks are our ample reward. In the deed of gift I expressed the hope that our young Republic might some day be able to repay, at least in some degree, the great debt it owes to the older lands. Nothing gives me deeper satisfaction than the knowledge that it has to some extent already begun to do so.

With the unique service rendered by the wandering *Carnegie*, we may rank that of the fixed observatory upon Mount Wilson, California, at an altitude of 5886 feet. Professor Hale is in charge of it. He attended the gathering of leading astronomers in Rome one year, and such were his revelations there that these savants resolved their next meeting should be on top of Mount Wilson. And so it was.

There is but one Mount Wilson. From a depth seventy-two feet down in the earth photographs have been taken of new stars. On the first of these plates many new worlds — I believe sixteen — were discovered. On the second I think it was sixty new worlds which had come into our ken, and on the third plate there were estimated to be more than a hundred — several of them said to be twenty times the size of our sun. Some of them were so distant as to require eight years for their light to reach us, which inclines us to bow our heads whispering to ourselves, "All we know is as nothing to the unknown." When the monster new glass, three times larger than any existing, is in operation, what revelations are to come! I am assured if a race inhabits the moon they will be clearly seen.

The third delightful task was founding the Hero Fund, in which my whole heart was concerned. I had heard of a serious accident in a coal pit near Pittsburgh, and how the former superintendent, Mr. Taylor, although then engaged in other pursuits, had instantly driven to the scene, hoping to be of use in the crisis. Rallying volunteers, who responded eagerly, he led them down the pit to rescue those below. Alas, alas, he the heroic leader lost his own life.

I could not get the thought of this out of my mind. My dear, dear friend, Mr. Richard Watson Gilder, had sent me the following true and beautiful poem, and I re-read it the morning after the accident, and resolved then to establish the Hero Fund.

> In the Time of Peace
> 'T was said: "When roll of drum and battle's roar
> Shall cease upon the earth, O, then no more
>
> The deed—the race—of heroes in the land."
> But scarce that word was breathed when one small hand
>
> Lifted victorious o'er a giant wrong
> That had its victims crushed through ages long;
>
> Some woman set her pale and quivering face
> Firm as a rock against a man's disgrace;
>
> A little child suffered in silence lest
> His savage pain should wound a mother's breast;
>
> Some quiet scholar flung his gauntlet down
> And risked, in Truth's great name, the synod's frown;
>
> A civic hero, in the calm realm of laws,
> Did that which suddenly drew a world's applause;
>
> And one to the pest his lithe young body gave
> That he a thousand thousand lives might save.

Hence arose the five-million-dollar fund to reward heroes, or to support the families of heroes, who perish in the effort to serve or save their fellows, and to supplement what employers or others do in contributing to the support of the families of those left destitute through accidents. This fund, established April 15, 1904, has proved from every point of view a decided success. I cherish a fatherly regard for it since no one suggested it to me. As far as I know, it never had been thought of; hence it is emphatically "my ain bairn." Later I extended it to my native land, Great Britain, with headquarters at Dunfermline—the Trustees of the Carnegie Dunfermline Trust undertaking its administration, and splendidly have they succeeded. In due time it was extended to France, Germany, Italy, Belgium, Holland, Norway, Sweden, Switzerland, and Denmark.

Regarding its workings in Germany, I received a letter from David Jayne Hill, our American Ambassador at Berlin, from which I quote:

My main object in writing now is to tell you how pleased His Majesty is with the working of the German Hero Fund. He is enthusiastic about it and spoke in most complimentary terms of your discernment, as well as your generosity in founding it. He did not believe it would fill so important a place as it is doing. He told me of several cases that are really touching, and which would otherwise have been wholly unprovided for. One was that of a young man who saved a boy from drowning and just as they were about to lift him out of the water, after passing up the child into a boat, his heart failed, and he sank. He left a lovely young wife and a little boy. She has already been helped by the Hero Fund to establish a little business from which she can make a living, and the education of the boy, who is very bright, will be looked after. This is but one example.

Valentini (Chief of the Civil Cabinet), who was somewhat skeptical at first regarding the need of such a fund, is now glowing with enthusiasm about it, and he tells me the whole Commission, which is composed of carefully chosen men, is earnestly devoted to the work of making the very best and wisest use of their means and has devoted much time to their decisions.

They have corresponded with the English and French Commission, arranged to exchange reports, and made plans to keep in touch with one another in their work. They were deeply interested in the American report and have learned much from it.

King Edward of Britain was deeply impressed by the provisions of the fund, and wrote me an autograph letter of appreciation of this and other gifts to my native land, which I deeply value, and hence insert.

Windsor Castle, November 21, 1908

Dear Mr. Carnegie:

I have for some time past been anxious to express to you my sense of your generosity for the great public objects which you have presented to this country, the land of your birth.

Scarcely less admirable than the gifts themselves is the great care and thought you have taken in guarding against their misuse.

I am anxious to tell you how warmly I recognize your most generous benefactions and the great services they are likely to confer upon the country.

As a mark of recognition, I hope you will accept the portrait of myself which I am sending to you.

Believe me, dear Mr. Carnegie,

Sincerely yours
Edward R. & I.

Some of the newspapers in America were doubtful of the merits of the Hero Fund and the first annual report was criticized, but all this has passed away and the action of the fund is now warmly extolled. It has conquered, and long will it be before the trust is allowed to perish! The heroes of the barbarian past wounded or killed their fellows; the heroes of our civilized day serve or save theirs. Such the difference between physical and moral courage, between barbarism and civilization. Those who belong to the first class are soon to pass away, for we are finally to regard men who slay each other as we now do cannibals who eat each other; but those in the latter class will not die as long as man exists upon the earth, for such heroism as they display is god-like.

The Hero Fund will prove chiefly a pension fund. Already it has many pensioners, heroes or the widows or children of heroes. A strange misconception arose at first about it. Many thought that its purpose was to stimulate heroic action, that heroes were to be induced to play their parts for the sake of reward. This never entered my mind. It is absurd. True heroes think not of reward. They are inspired and think only of their fellows endangered; never of themselves. The fund is intended to pension or provide in the most suitable manner for the hero should he be disabled, or for those dependent upon him should he perish in his attempt to save others. It has made a fine start and will grow in popularity year after year as its aims and services are better understood. Today we have in America 1430 hero pensioners or their families on our list.

I found the president for the Hero Fund in a Carnegie veteran, one of the original boys, Charlie Taylor. No salary for Charlie—not a cent would he ever take. He loves the work so much that I believe he would pay highly for permission to live with it. He is the right man in the right place. He has charge also, with Mr. Wilmot's able assistance, of the pensions for Carnegie workmen (Carnegie Relief Fund); also the pensions for railway employees of my old division. Three relief funds and all of them benefiting others.

I got my revenge one day upon Charlie, who was always urging me to do for others. He is a graduate of Lehigh University and one of her most loyal sons. Lehigh wished a building and Charlie was her chief advocate. I said nothing, but wrote President Drinker offering the funds for the building conditioned upon my naming it. He agreed, and I called it "Taylor Hall." When Charlie discovered this, he came and protested that it would make him ridiculous, that he had only been a modest graduate, and was not entitled to have his name publicly honored, and so on. I enjoyed his plight immensely, waiting until he had finished, and then said that it would probably make him somewhat ridiculous if I insisted upon "Taylor Hall," but he ought to be willing to sacrifice himself somewhat for Lehigh. If he wasn't consumed with vanity he would not care much how his name was used if it helped his Alma Mater. Taylor was not much of a name anyhow. It was his insufferable vanity that made such a fuss. He should conquer it. He could make his decision. He could sacrifice the name of Taylor or sacrifice Lehigh, just as he liked, but: "No Taylor, no Hall." I had him! Visitors who may look upon that structure in after days and wonder who Taylor was may rest assured that he was a loyal son of Lehigh, a working, not merely a preaching, apostle of the gospel of service to his fellow-men, and one of the best men that ever lived. Such is our Lord High Commissioner of Pensions.

Part IV
Carnegie at Work, Playing

John Morley, the British statesman and Carnegie's closest friend, frequently complained of his weariness and exhaustion from carrying out the duties of state. In one such letter to Carnegie, he observed, "Of one thing be sure — that your poor friend with this load on his back craves Rest. That's a feeling unknown, I do believe, to Mr. A. Carnegie?" (15 January 1909, Carnegie Papers, Library of Congress, vol. 161).

Carnegie's restless energy had always been a source of amazement to his associates in both business and social activities. One reason for Carnegie's exceptional vitality was that he had early learned the importance of play. Even as a teen-age boy, working fifteen to eighteen hours a day, Carnegie, as he relates in his autobiography, managed to find time to read a book, to sneak into the upper gallery to watch a production at the old Pittsburgh Theatre, or to get up early on Sunday mornings to ice-skate on the river.

Once he had become an independent entrepreneur, Carnegie resolutely refused throughout his business career to become tied to an office. In 1867, he established his residence in New York, far removed from the smoke and provincialism of Pittsburgh. He had only disdain for his associates who dedicated their lives solely to business. He claimed that he had met just one successful businessman, the president of the Baltimore & Ohio, John Garrett, who could quote from memory a single line of Burns or Shakespeare. The vast majority of entrepreneurs were as limited in their interests as they were in knowledge.

Carnegie preferred to have in his parlor the company of Andrew White, Mark Twain, Rudyard Kipling, Herbert Spencer, John Morley, Matthew Arnold, and Walter Damrosch rather than Pullman, Gould, or Rockefeller. The diamond-encrusted Four Hundred—the elite of New York society—had no appeal for Carnegie. He wanted to socialize with those who could display their minds, not their pocketbooks, and stimulate his own thoughts, not his cupidity.

Having suffered a mild sunstroke in the summer of 1861 while supervising the repair of a railroad bridge, Carnegie for the rest of his life used his unusual sensitivity to heat as a convenient excuse to go into pleasant retreat each summer—at first with his mother to their cottage in the little mountain village of Cresson near Pittsburgh, and later, after his marriage to Louise Whitfield, to a castle in Scotland.

Carnegie loved travel by any form of conveyance—canal boat, train, ship, and especially a four-in-hand coach, where, seated on top with a bevy of friends, he could survey the countryside with an imperial gaze. No matter how critically pressing his business affairs might be, he was always ready to take time out, be it for a coaching trip from Brighton to Inverness, or a ship cruise "Round the World."

For Carnegie, relaxation never meant rest. He always played as hard as he worked, perhaps even harder. At the advanced age of sixty-two, he for the first time took up golf and quickly became addicted to that ancient Scottish game. Duffer though he remained, he was frequently and pleasantly surprised to discover that he could best those who were much better golfers than he, never suspecting that there might be any ulterior motive underlying his opponents' defeat.

No businessman ever took more seriously the old adage that "all work and no play makes Jack a dull boy." And no one would ever accuse Andy of being a dull boy in either work or play.

14
On Books, Theater, Music, and Keeping the Sabbath

Chapter 4 of the Autobiography of Andrew Carnegie, *ed. John Van Dyke (Boston: Houghton Mifflin, 1920).*

With all their pleasures the messenger boys were hard worked. Every other evening they were required to be on duty until the office closed, and on these nights it was seldom that I reached home before eleven o'clock. On the alternating nights we were relieved at six. This did not leave much time for self-improvement, nor did the wants of the family leave any money to spend on books. There came, however, like a blessing from above, a means by which the treasures of literature were unfolded to me.

Colonel James Anderson—I bless his name as I write—announced that he would open his library of four hundred volumes to boys, so that any young man could take out, each Saturday afternoon, a book which could be exchanged for another on the succeeding Saturday. My friend, Mr. Thomas N. Miller, reminded me recently that Colonel Anderson's books were first opened to "working boys," and the question arose whether messenger boys, clerks, and others, who did not work with their hands, were entitled to books. My first communication to the press was a note, written to the *Pittsburgh Dispatch*, urging that we should not be excluded; that although we did not now work with our hands, some of us had done so, and that we were really working boys.[1] Dear Colonel Anderson promptly enlarged the classification. So my first appearance as a public writer was a success.

---

1. The note was signed "Working Boy." The librarian responded in the columns of the *Dispatch* defending the rules, which he claimed meant that "a Working Boy should have a trade." Carnegie's rejoinder was signed "A Working Boy, though without a Trade," and a day or two thereafter the *Dispatch* had an item on its editorial page which read: "Will 'a Working Boy without a Trade' please call at this office." (David Homer Bates in *Century Magazine*, July, 1908.)

My dear friend, Tom Miller, one of the inner circle, lived near Colonel Anderson and introduced me to him, and in this way the windows were opened in the walls of my dungeon through which the light of knowledge streamed in. Every day's toil and even the long hours of night service were lightened by the book which I carried about with me and read in the intervals that could be snatched from duty. And the future was made bright by the thought that when Saturday came a new volume could be obtained. In this way I became familiar with Macaulay's essays and his history, and with Bancroft's "History of the United States," which I studied with more care than any other book I had then read. Lamb's essays were my special delight, but I had at this time no knowledge of the great master of all, Shakespeare, beyond the selected pieces in the school books. My taste for him I acquired a little later at the old Pittsburgh Theater.

John Phipps, James R. Wilson, Thomas N. Miller, William Cowley — members of our circle — shared with me the invaluable privilege of the use of Colonel Anderson's library. Books which it would have been impossible for me to obtain elsewhere were, by his wise generosity, placed within my reach; and to him I owe a taste for literature which I would not exchange for all the millions that were ever amassed by man. Life would be quite intolerable without it. Nothing contributed so much to keep my companions and myself clear of low fellowship and bad habits as the beneficence of the good Colonel. Later, when fortune smiled upon me, one of my first duties was the erection of a monument to my benefactor. It stands in front of the Hall and Library in Diamond Square, which I presented to Allegheny, and bears this inscription:

To Colonel James Anderson, Founder of Free Libraries in Western Pennsylvania. He opened his Library to working boys and upon Saturday afternoons acted as librarian, thus dedicating not only his books but himself to the noble work. This monument is erected in grateful remembrance by Andrew Carnegie, one of the "working boys" to whom were thus opened the precious treasures of knowledge and imagination through which youth may ascend.

This is but a slight tribute and gives only a faint idea of the depth of gratitude which I feel for what he did for me and my companions. It was from my own early experience that I decided there was no use to which money could be applied so productive of good to boys and girls who have good within them and ability and ambition to develop it, as the founding of a public library in a community which is willing to support it as a municipal institution. I am sure that the future of those libraries I have been privileged to found will prove the correctness of this opinion. For if one boy in each library district, by having access to one of these libraries, is half as much benefited as I was by having access to Colonel Anderson's four hundred well-worn volumes, I shall consider they have not been established in vain.

"As the twig is bent the tree's inclined." The treasures of the world which books contain were opened to me at the right moment. The fundamental advantage of a library is that it gives nothing for nothing. Youths must acquire knowledge themselves. There is no escape from this. It gave me great satisfaction to discover, many years later, that my father was one of the five weavers in Dunfermline who gathered together the few books they had and formed the first circulating library in that town.

The history of that library is interesting. It grew, and was removed no less than seven times from place to place, the first move being made by the founders, who carried the books in their aprons and two coal scuttles from the hand-loom shop to the second resting place. That my father was one of the founders of the first library in his native town, and that I have been fortunate enough to be the founder of the last one, is certainly to me one of the most interesting incidents of my life. I have said often, in public speeches, that I had never heard of a lineage for which I would exchange that of a library-founding weaver.[2] I followed my father in library founding unknowingly—I am tempted almost to say providentially—and it has been a source of intense satisfaction to me. Such a father as mine was a guide to be followed—one of the sweetest, purest, and kindest natures I have ever known.

I have stated that it was the theater which first stimulated my love for Shakespeare. In my messenger days the old Pittsburgh Theater was in its glory under the charge of Mr. Foster. His telegraphic business was done free, and the telegraph operators were given free admission to the theater in return. This privilege extended in some degree also to the messengers, who, I fear, sometimes withheld telegrams that arrived for him in the late afternoon until they could be presented at the door of the theater in the evening, with the timid request that the messenger might be allowed to slip upstairs to the second tier—a request which was always granted. The boys exchanged duties to give each the coveted entrance in turn.

In this way I became acquainted with the world that lay behind the green

---

2. "It's a God's mercy we are all from honest weavers; let us pity those who haven't ancestors of whom they can be proud, dukes or duchesses though they be." (*Our Coaching Trip*, by Andred Carnegie, New York, 1882.)

curtain. The plays, generally, were of the spectacular order; without much literary merit, but well calculated to dazzle the eye of a youth of fifteen. Not only had I never seen anything so grand, but I had never seen anything of the kind. I had never been in a theater, or even a concert room, or seen any form of public amusement. It was much the same with "Davy" McCargo, "Harry" Oliver, and "Bob" Pitcairn. We all fell under the fascination of the footlights, and every opportunity to attend the theater was eagerly embraced.

A change in my tastes came when "Gust" Adams,[3] one of the most celebrated tragedians of the day, began to play in Pittsburgh a round of Shakespearean characters. Thenceforth there was nothing for me but Shakespeare. I seemed to be able to memorize him almost without effort. Never before had I realized what magic lay in words. The rhythm and the melody all seemed to find a resting place in me, to melt into a solid mass which lay ready to come at call. It was a new language and its appreciation I certainly owe to dramatic representation, for, until I saw *Macbeth* played, my interest in Shakespeare was not aroused. I had not read the plays.

At a much later date, Wagner was revealed to me in *Lohengrin*. I had heard at the Academy of Music in New York, little or nothing by him when the overture to *Lohengrin* thrilled me as a new revelation. Here was a genius, indeed, differing from all before, a new ladder upon which to climb upward—like Shakespeare, a new friend.

I may speak here of another matter which belongs to this same period. A few persons in Allegheny—probably not above a hundred in all—had formed themselves into a Swedenborgian Society, in which our American relatives were prominent. My father attended that church after leaving the Presbyterian, and, of course, I was taken there. My mother, however, took no interest in Swedenborg. Although always inculcating respect for all forms of religion, and discouraging theological disputes, she maintained for herself a marked reserve. Her position might best be defined by the celebrated maxim of Confucius: "To perform the duties of this life well, troubling not about another, is the prime wisdom."

She encouraged her boys to attend church and Sunday school; but there was no difficulty in seeing that the writings of Swedenborg, and much of the Old and New Testaments had been discredited by her as unworthy of divine authorship or of acceptance as authoritative guides for the conduct of life. I

---

3. Edwin Adams.

became deeply interested in the mysterious doctrines of Swedenborg, and received the congratulations of my devout Aunt Aitken upon my ability to expound "spiritual sense." That dear old woman fondly looked forward to a time when I should become a shining light in the New Jerusalem, and I know it was sometimes not beyond the bounds of her imagination that I might blossom into what she called a "preacher of the Word."

As I more and more wandered from man-made theology these fond hopes weakened, but my aunt's interest in and affection for her first nephew, whom she had dandled on her knee in Scotland, never waned. My cousin, Leander Morris, whom she had some hopes of saving through the Swedenborgian revelation, grievously disappointed her by actually becoming a Baptist and being dipped. This was too much for the evangelist, although she should have remembered her father passed through that same experience and often preached for the Baptists in Edinburgh.

Leander's reception upon his first call after his fall was far from cordial. He was made aware that the family record had suffered by his backsliding when at the very portals of the New Jerusalem revealed by Swedenborg and presented to him by one of the foremost disciples—his aunt. He began deprecatingly:

"Why are you so hard on me, aunt? Look at Andy, he is not a member of any church and you don't scold him. Surely the Baptist Church is better than none."

The quick reply came:

"Andy! Oh! Andy, he's naked, but you are clothed in rags."

He never quite regained his standing with dear Aunt Aitken. I might yet be reformed, being unattached; but Leander had chosen a sect and that sect not of the New Jerusalem.

It was in connection with the Swedenborgian Society that a taste for music was first aroused in me. As an appendix to the hymnbook of the society there were short selections from the oratorios. I fastened instinctively upon these, and although denied much of a voice, yet credited with "expression," I was a constant attendant upon choir practice. The leader, Mr. Koethen, I have reason to believe, often pardoned the discords I produced in the choir because of my enthusiasm in the cause. When, at a later date, I became acquainted with the oratorios in full, it was a pleasure to find that several of those considered in musical circles as the gems of Handel's musical compositions were the ones that I as an ignorant boy had chosen as favorites. So the beginning of my musical education dates from the small choir of the Swedenborgian Society of Pittsburgh.

I must not, however, forget that a very good foundation was laid for my love of sweet sounds in the unsurpassed minstrelsy of my native land as sung by my father. There was scarcely an old Scottish song with which I was not made familiar, both words and tune. Folksongs are the best possible foundation for sure progress to the heights of Beethoven and Wagner. My father being one of the sweetest and most pathetic singers I ever heard, I probably inherited his love of music and of song, though not given his voice. Confucius' exclamation often sounds in my ears: "Music, sacred tongue of God! I hear thee calling and I come."

An incident of this same period exhibits the liberality of my parents in another matter. As a messenger boy I had no holidays, with the exception of two weeks given me in the summertime, which I spent boating on the river with cousins at my uncle's at East Liverpool, Ohio. I was very fond of skating, and in the winter about which I am speaking, the slack water of the river opposite our house was beautifully frozen over. The ice was in splendid condition, and reaching home late Saturday night the question arose whether I might be permitted to rise early in the morning and go skating before church hours. No question of a more serious character could have been submitted to ordinary Scottish parents. My mother was clear on the subject, that in the circumstances I should be allowed to skate as long as I liked. My father said he believed it was right I should go down and skate, but he hoped I would be back in time to go with him to church.

I suppose this decision would be arrived at today by nine hundred and ninety-nine out of every thousand homes in America, and probably also in the majority of homes in England, though not in Scotland. But those who hold today that the Sabbath in its fullest sense was made for man, and who would open picture galleries and museums to the public, and make the day somewhat of a day of enjoyment for the masses instead of pressing upon them the duty of mourning over sins largely imaginary, are not more advanced than were my parents forty years ago. They were beyond the orthodox of the period when it was scarcely permissible, at least among the Scotch, to take a walk for pleasure or read any but religious books on the Sabbath.

15
Round the World

In May 1865, Andrew Carnegie set off for that Grand Tour of the European continent expected of all young men of means, accompanied by two of his boyhood friends, Henry Phipps and John Vandevort. It had been only a month since Carnegie had resigned his position as superintendent of the Pittsburgh Division of the Pennsylvania Railroad to strike out on his own as a freelance capitalist, and he was eager to celebrate both his own independence and the glorious reunion of his nation after four long years of bloody civil conflict. So grand did this tour prove to be that while standing in the crater of Mount Vesuvius, the three young men vowed that someday, "instead of turning back as we had then to do, we would make a tour round the Ball."

Thirteen years later that time had arrived for two of the three. In October 1878, Andy and Vandy departed from San Francisco aboard the SS Belgic for a five-month journey that took them to Japan, China, Malaya, India, Egypt, and through the Mediterranean to the bay of Naples where their globe-circling tour had first been mutually pledged.

Carnegie kept a journal of the trip which he later revised and expanded for publication as Round the World *(New York: Charles Scribner's Sons, 1883). This was not the tourist's ordinary recording of marvelous sights seen, of exotic foods tasted, and of the usual mishaps of lost luggage, dysentery attacks, or pickpocket raids. In this journal there are, to be sure, the expected oohs and ahs over Japanese gardens, Chinese temples, and especially India's Taj Mahal, a structure that Carnegie reluctantly had to admit was even more magnificent than Edinburgh's monument to Sir Walter Scott, which hitherto he had always regarded as the acme of architectural achievement. But as with much of his writing, Carnegie was here using the travel book not just to amuse his audience with anecdotes or to provide a vicarious pleasure in viewing foreign lands through another's eyes. It was primarily a didactic exercise to instruct the reading public on a theme that Carnegie had enthusiastically adopted as a universal truth—the inevitable evolutionary progress of man toward perfection, a progress that has been delayed by superstitious religion but could never be deflected from reaching the ultimate goal.*

In the short selections given below, Carnegie reveals an attitude of cultural relevancy toward alien peoples that is remarkably advanced and much at variance with most British and American tourists of his day—or of this day. He has as much contempt and pity for the Protestant missionaries on board the Belgic *headed for China to "convert the heathen to the true faith" as he does for the Japanese woman he saw kneeling before the statue of a fat goddess to pray for a man-child. Gross generalizations of entire ethnic groups abound in these pages, but they are softened by the saving graces of tolerance, understanding, and above all, the assurance that all peoples—even the most backward peoples of India—are moving toward the light, no matter how difficult the superstition-strewn road they are traveling may be.*

New York, Saturday, October 12, 1878.

Bang! click! the desk closes, the key turns and good-bye for a year to my my wards—that goodly cluster over which I have watched with parental solicitude for many a day; their several cribs full of records and labelled Union Iron Mills, Lucy Furnaces, Keystone Bridge Works, Union Forge, Cokevale Works, and last, but not least, that infant Hercules the Edgar Thomson Steel Rail Works—good lusty bairns all, and well calculated to survive in the struggle for existence—great things are expected of them in the future, but for the present I bid them farewell; I'm off for a holiday, and the rise and fall of iron and steel "affecteth me not."

Years ago, Vandy, Harry, and I, standing in the very bottom of the crater of Mount Vesuvius, where we had roasted eggs and drank to the success of our next trip, resolved that some day, instead of turning back as we had then to do, we would make a tour round the Ball. My first return to Scotland and journey through Europe was an epoch in my life, I had so early in my days determined to do it; today another epoch comes—our tour fulfils another youthful aspiration. There is a sense of supreme satisfaction in carrying out these early dreams which I think nothing else can give, it is such a triumph to realize one's castles in the air. Other dreams remain, which in good time also *must* come to pass; for nothing can defeat these early inborn hopes, if one lives, and if death comes there is, until the latest day, the exaltation which comes from victory if one but continues true to his guiding star and manfully struggles on.

Harbor of San Francisco, Thursday, October 24.

At last! noon, 24th, and there she lies—the *Belgic* at her dock! What a crowd! but not of us; eight hundred Chinamen are to return to the Flowery Land. One looks like another; but how quiet they are! Are they happy? overjoyed at being homeward bound? We cannot judge. Those sphinx-like, copper-colored faces tell us no tales. We had asked a question last night by telegraph, and here is the reply brought to us on the deck. It ends with a tender good-bye. How near and yet how far! but even if the message had sought us out at the Antipodes, its power to warm the heart with the sense of the near presence and companionship of those we love would only have been enhanced. In this we seem almost to have reached the dream of the Swedish seer, who tells us that thought brings presence, annihilating space in heaven.

We start promptly at noon. Our ship is deeply laden with flour, which China needs in consequence of the famine prevailing in its northern provinces, not owing to a failure of the rice, as I had understood, but of the millet, which is used by the poor instead of rice. Some writers estimate that five millions of people must die from starvation before the next crop can be gathered; but this seems incredible. And now America comes to the rescue, so that at this moment, while from its Eastern shores it pours forth its inexhaustible stores to feed Europe, it sends from the West of its surplus to the older races of the far East. Thus from all sides, fabled Ceres as she is, she scatters to all peoples from the horn of plenty. Favored land, may you prove worthy of all your blessings and show to the world that after ages of wars and conquests there comes at last to the troubled earth the glorious reign of peace. But no new steel cruisers, no standing army. These are the devil's tools in monarchies; the Republic's weapons are the ploughshare and the pruning hook.

At sea, Thursday, October 31
Sunday, November 3

We have a reverend missionary and wife, with two young lady missionaries in embryo, who are on their way to begin their labors among the Chinese. They are busily engaged learning the language. Poor girls! what a life they have before them! But apart from all question of its true usefulness, they have the grand thought to sustain them, and ennoble their lives, that they go at the call of what seems to them their duty.

Our second Sunday at sea. As I write, the bell tolls for church. Our missionary will have a small congregation, for there are only twenty-two passengers. I trust he will be moved to speak to us, away in mid-ocean, of the great works of the Unknown, the mighty deep, the universe, the stars, at which we nightly wonder, and not drag us down to the level of dogmas we can know nothing of, and about which we care less. The sermon is over. Pshaw! He spent the morning attempting to prove to us that the wine Christ made at the marriage feast was not fermented, as if it mattered, or as if this could ever be known! and I was in the mood to preach such a magnificent sermon myself, too, if I had had his place. No; I shall never forgive him—never!

It is an even chance that this missionary will one day inflict such frivolous stuff upon the heathen as part of the divine message; for of the majesty, the sweetness, and the reforming power of Christ's teaching and character, he seems to have not the faintest conception. To the enquiry one constantly hears in the East—why churches send forth as missionaries such inferior men as they generally do, whose task is to eradicate error and plant truth—there is this to be said: churches must take the best material at their disposal, and men who have the ability to influence their fellows through the pulpit find their best and highest work at home. This leaves the incapables for foreign service. The other class from which missionaries must be drawn are the over-zealous, who have plenty of enthusiastic emotional fervor, but combined in most cases with narrow, dogmatic views—

Monday, November 4.

Our course is the southerly one, 5,120 miles to Yokohama, some five hundred miles farther than that of the great circle; but for the increased distance we have full compensation in the delightful weather and calm seas we experience. The water is about 72°, the air 73°, so that it is genial on deck. We are really in summer weather—something so different from Atlantic sailing that I get accustomed to it with difficulty. Last night at ten o'clock was passed the halfway point ten days and eight hours out. The captain showed us his chart today, and it was reassuring to see that tomorrow we shall pass within 120 miles of land—the Midway Islands. Upon one of this coral group the Pacific Mail Company has deposited 3,000 tons of coal and a large amount of mess pork as a reserve supply in case any steamer should be disabled. We passed the Sandwich Islands, not more than 450 miles to the southward, when one-quarter of the way over, and the Bonin Islands occupy about the same relative position in our course to the eastward, so that the immense distance between San Francisco and Yokohama is finely provided for in case of accident. You have but to sail southward and find a port of refuge. Indeed, there is along this entire parallel of latitude a new strip of land under process of manufacture. A good chart shows islands dotting the South Pacific Ocean, all of coral formation; these millions of toilers are hard at work, and it is only a question of time when our posterity will run by rail from the Sandwich to the Philippine Islands, always provided that the work of these little builders is not interfered with by forces which destroy. Thus the grand, never-ending work of creation goes on, cycle upon cycle, revealing new wonders at every turn and knowing no rest or pause.

Tokio, November 20

The most wonderful sights of Tokio are the temples and the famous tombs of the Tycoons. There is much similarity in the latter, but that of the sixth Tycoon, at Shibba, is by far the most magnificent. It is gorgeous in color, and the extreme delicacy of the gold is surprising; upon it, too, are found the finest known specimens of the old lacquer. But these tombs totally failed to impress me with any feeling akin to reverence; indeed, nothing in Japan seems calculated to do so—the odor of the toyshop pervades everything, even their temples. As for their religious belief, it is hard to tell what it is, or whether they have any. One thing is sure, the educated classes have discarded the faith of the multitude, if they ever really entertained it, and no longer worship the gods of old. The ignorant classes, however, are seen pouring into the temples with their modest offerings, and asking for prayers in their behalf. It is in Japan as it was in Greece—one religion for the masses, and another, or rather none in the ordinary sense, for the educated few.

As in Catholic countries, some shrines are esteemed more than others. The Temple of the Foxes is the most popular in the Empire. It is adorned with statues of Master Reynard in various postures. His votaries are numerous, for the sagacity of the fox has passed into a proverb, and these people hope by prayers and gifts to move the fox-god to bestow upon them the shrewdness of the symbol. The fox may be justly rated as the most successful preacher in Japan: he draws better than any other, and his congregation is the largest; but he has a rival not without pretensions in the favorite goddess "Emma." We found her to be a large, very fat woman, sitting in Japanese style, and surrounded by images of children. Babies cluster like cherubs around the principal figure, while an attendant sells for a cent apiece ugly painted ones made out of clay, many of which have been placed by worshippers before the goddess. As we approached, a young woman—married, for her teeth were black, and respectably but not richly dressed—was on her knees before the goddess so earnestly engaged in prayer that she appeared wholly unconscious of our presence. There was no mistaking that this was sincere devotion—a lifting up of the soul to some power considered higher than itself. I became most anxious to know what sorrow could so move her, and our interpreter afterward told us that she asked but one gift from the goddess. It was the prayer of old that a man-child should be born to her; and, poor woman! when one knows what her life must be in this country should this prayer remain unanswered, it saddens one to think of it. A living death; another installed in her place; all that woman holds dear trembling in the balance. How I pitied her! I also saw men praying before other idols and working themselves into a state of frenzy. Indeed I saw so much in the temples to make me unhappy that I wished I had never visited any of them. It gives one such desponding hopes of our race, of its present and of its future, when so many are so bound down to the lowest form of superstition.

Canton, China, December 21

Amid much which causes one to mourn for the backwardness of this country, here is the bright jewel in her crown. China is, as far as I know, the only nation which has advanced beyond the so-called heroic age when the soldier claims precedence. England and America must be content to claim that

> Peace hath her victories
> No less renowned than war,

while here the triumphs of peace are held in chief esteem. No general, no conqueror, be his victories what they may, can ever in China attain the highest rank. That is held only by successful scholars who have shown the possession of literary talent. When the news reaches a town or village that a townsman has been victorious at Peking, a general rejoicing takes place, and triumphal arches are built in his honor to witness for centuries how deeply they appreciate the honor conferred upon the town by their illustrious fellow-citizen. Upon his return the whole population turns out to meet and welcome him, and his career inspires other young men to emulate his virtues. Henceforth his life is one of honor, for from this class the rulers of China are taken. These are the Mandarins, and there is no other aristocracy in China. Nor are his honors hereditary. His sons, if they would be ennobled, must outstrip their fellows in knowledge, as their father did before them. An aristocracy founded upon learning, and composed of those who know the most, is an institution with which we have no serious quarrel. It is claims from birth which make my blood boil. These are an insult to every commoner, and we must not rest until every trace of hereditary privilege is swept from the earth. Neither king, queen, prince, nor lord should live in our native isle to insult us if I had my way—and my way may come ere I depart if I get the three score and ten allotted to mortals by the psalmist.

Calcutta, Wednesday, January 29

Today our Sunday-school recollections were again aroused by a sight of the terrible car of Juggernaut. It is really an immense affair, elaborately carved in bold relief, and on the top is a platform for the priests. I should say the car is twenty-five feet high and about eight by twelve at the base; it has six wheels, four outside and two in the centre, the former nine feet in diameter and the latter six, all of solid wood clamped together with iron bands, and all at least two feet in width of tread. Such a mass, drawn through the streets by elephants and accompanied by excited devotees, its hundred bells jangling as it rolled along where there was not another vehicle of any kind with which to compare it, or a house more than one small story high, must have appeared to the ignorant natives something akin to the supernatural; and I can now well understand how wretches, working themselves into a state of frenzy, should have felt impelled to dash under its wheels. It is still paraded upon certain festival days, invariably surrounded, however, by policemen, who keep the natives clear of the wheels, for even today, if they were not prevented, its victims would be as numerous as ever. Imagine, if you can, with what feelings we stood and gazed upon this car, which has crushed under its ponderous wheels religious enthusiasts by the thousand, and which still retains its fascination over men anxious to be allowed the glory of such self-immolation, at the supposed call of God, who would be a fiend if he desired such sacrifice.

It is not rare for fakirs to stand in postures that cripple them for life. One elects to stand on one foot until it becomes impossible for him ever to put the other to the ground. Another determines to raise his arms to heaven, never taking them down. In a short time, after excruciating pain, the joints stiffen so as to render any change impossible, and the arms shrivel until little but bone is left. Some let their nails grow into their flesh and through their hands. The forms of these penances are innumerable, and those who undergo them are regarded as holy men and are worshipped and supported by their less religious fellows. Kali must still have her blood, and hundreds of kids, goats, buffaloes, and other animals are sacrificed daily at her shrine. We saw the bloody work going forward. Crowds of pilgrims, numbering at least three hundred during our short stay, came in bands from the country to propitiate the goddess. Each one presents an offering as the idol is shown. It is the most disgusting object I have ever seen, and a sight of it would, I am sure, frighten children into crying. The business is skilfully managed. A small dark hall, capable of holding about twenty-five worshippers, occupies the space before the idol. This is filled with people and the doors closed; then, amid the murmurs of priests and beating of gongs, two sliding-doors are drawn aside, and the horrible she-demon, with swollen blood-red tongue, comes into view for a moment only, and the gifts are thrown at her. The crowd is excited by fear and awe, but ere the figure can be closely scrutinized the doors close, and the poor ignorant wretches seem stupefied with what has been revealed. They pass slowly out, looking as if they had been almost blinded with a glimpse of the forbidden mysteries, and another batch crowds in to be similarly worked upon. We saw other forms and figures of worship too gross to speak of. Nothing yet seen can be called idolatry when compared with this, and I felt like giving up all hope of improvement in these people; but then when one sees the extent and character of the superstitions of the East he cannot help having doubts of the advancement or elevation of the species. There is, however, this consoling knowledge, that the worshippers, such young girls and boys as we saw today excepted, know that Kali is but the symbol of power, not the power itself. Around this fact the forces able to overthrow superstition may be evolved hereafter. The germ is there.

The hundreds of young, pretty, innocent children whom we saw brought today to witness such rites by kind, dutiful, religious parents—the most conscientious and most respectable of the native race—were dressed with as much care and pride as a corresponding number of young Christians would be when taken to the rite of confirmation. How could I be otherwise than sad and murmur, "Forgive them, for they know not what they do." Thus far is plain sailing, for every one will agree with me; but when I denounced to the priests the pools of clotted blood as offensive, even to coarse men, and wholly unfit as a satisfactory offering to any power to whom we can ascribe the name of God, they retorted by saying this is also part of the Christian system: the God of Abraham demands his sacrifice of blood also. It is in vain to intimate that this day is past and that our Father in heaven no longer takes delight in the blood of rams or of bullocks. I shall never forget the malicious inquiry: "Does your God *change*, then?" "No, certainly not; but our conceptions of him change year by year as we gain knowledge." They smile, and I am troubled. Let us pause and reflect before we rashly assail any form of religion until we know that what we have to offer in its place is really free from the errors we mourn over in others. In the progress of the race such dreadful conceptions of God must apparently exist for a time. Has not Herbert Spencer himself assured us that, "Speaking generally, the religion current in each age and among each people has been as near an approximation to the truth as it was then and there possible for men to receive."

I needed all this from the philosopher to restrain my indignation at first and afterward to mitigate my sorrow. Even this was not quite sufficient, but how much an anecdote will sometimes do, and this one the philosopher above quoted told me himself. At times, when disposed to take gloomy views of man's advance, and sickened by certain of his still barbarous beliefs and acts, he had found relief in the story Emerson tells of himself when in similar moods. After attending a meeting—perhaps the one where he was hissed from the platform for denouncing human slavery—he walked home burning with indignation; but entering his grounds, and wandering among the green grass and the flowers, silently growing in the cool moonlight, he looked up at the big trees and the big trees looking down upon him seemed to say: "What! *so hot, my little sir!*" Yes, we must upon our "distemper sprinkle cool patience." If all is not well, yet all is coming well. In this faith we find peace. The endless progress of the race is assured now that evolution has come with its message and shed light where before there was darkness, reassuring those who thought and who therefore doubted most.

Bay of Naples, Thursday, March 20.

Early morning! Yes, my dear friends, *is is round*. Here stands Mount Vesuvius in full view this morning, making for itself pure white clouds of steam, which float in the otherwise clear, cloudless sky of Italy. No entering the crater now as we did before, for the volcano is no longer at rest. Vandy and I shake hands and recall our pledge made in the crater years ago, and say, "Well, that is now fulfilled, and may life only have for us in its unknown future another such five months of unalloyed happiness (save where the dark shades of death among friends at home have saddened the hours) as those we have been so privileged to enjoy."

London, undated

Go, therefore, my friends—all you who are so situated as to be able to avail yourselves of this privilege—go and see for yourselves how greatly we are bound by prejudices, how checkered and uncertain are many of our own advances, how very nearly all is balanced. No nation has all that is best, neither is any bereft of some advantages, and no nation, or tribe, or people is so unhappy that it would be willing to exchange its condition for that of any other. See, also, that in every society there are many individuals distinguished for traits of character which place them upon a par with the best and highest we know at home, and that such are everywhere regarded with esteem, and held up as models for lower and baser natures to emulate.

The traveller will not see in all his wanderings so much abject, repulsive misery among human beings in the most heathen lands, as that which startles him in his civilized Christian home, for nowhere are the extremes of wealth and poverty so painfully presented. He will learn, too, if he be observant, that very little is required after all to make mankind happy, and that the prizes of life worth contending for are, generally speaking, within the reach of the great mass.

Did you ever sum up these prizes and think how very little the millionaire has beyond the peasant, and how very often his additions tend not to happiness but to misery? What constitutes the choice food of the world? Plain beef, common vegetables and bread, and the best of all fruits—the apple; the only nectar bubbles from the brook without money and without price. All that our race eats or drinks beyond this range must be inferior, if not positively injurious. Dress—what man, or rather what woman wears—is less and less comfortable in proportion to its frills and its cost, and no jewel is so refined as the simple flower in the hair, which the village maid has for the plucking. All that women overload themselves with beyond this range is a source of unhappiness. To be the most simply attired is to be the most elegantly dressed. So much for true health and happiness in all that we eat, and drink, and wear.

If we extend the inquiry to the luxuries and adornments of life, is there any music—which of course comes first—comparable in grandeur to that of the wave, stirring the soul with its mighty organ tones as it breaks upon the beach, or any so exquisitely fine as that of the murmuring brook which sings its song forever to every listener upon its banks, while above birds warble and the zephyr plays its divine accompaniment among the trees! We spend fortunes for picture galleries, but what are the tiny painted copies compared to the great originals, the mountains, the glens, the streams and waterfalls, the fertile fields, the breezy downs, the silver sea! These are the gems of the universal gallery, the common heritage of man, the property of the humblest who has eyes to see, and as free as the air we breathe. We have our conservatories and spend our thousands upon orchids, but which of nature's smiles ranks with the rose and the mignonette, the daisy and the bluebell, and the sweet forget-me-not blooming for all earth's children, and which grow upon the window-sill of the artisan and which the laborer blesses at his cottage door!

If we go higher still in the scale, we find that the companionship of the gods is not denied to the steady wage receiving man, for Shakespeare and our Burns and our Scott can be had for sixpence per volume. In this blessed age in which we are privileged to live even the immortals are cheap and visit the toiler. We see the rich rolling over the land in their carriages, but blessed beyond these is the man who strolls along the hedgerows. The connoisseur in his gallery misses the health-giving breeze which brings happiness to the devotee who seeks the original afield. The lady in her overheated conservatory knows nothing of the joyous rapture of her more fortunate sister who gathers the spoils of the glen. Ah, my friends, ponder well over this truth: the more one dwells with her, the more one draws from her, the closer one creeps to her bosom, the sweeter is nature's kiss. From man's neglect of her for meaner substitutes come most of the disappointment and unhappiness of life. The masses of mankind are happy all round the world because their pleasures are drawn so largely from sources which lie open to all. The rich are not to be envied, for truly "there is no purchase in money" of any real happiness. When used for our own gratification, it injures us; when used ostentatiously, it brings care; when hoarded, it narrows the soul. Nature has not provided a means by which any man can use riches for selfish purposes without suffering therefrom. There is only one source of true blessedness in wealth, and that comes from giving it away for ends that tend to elevate our brothers and enable them to share it with us. Nature is gloriously communistic after all, God bless her! and sees that a pretty fair division is made, let man hoard as he may. The secret of happiness is renunciation.

Another advantage to be derived from a journey round the world is, I think, that the sense of the brotherhood of man, the unity of the race, is very greatly strengthened thereby, for one sees that the virtues are the same in all lands, and produce their good fruits, and render their possessors blessed in Benares and Kioto as in London or New York; that the vices, too, are akin, and also that the motives which govern men and their actions and aims are very much the same the world over. In their trials and sufferings, as in their triumphs and rejoicings, men do not differ, and so the heart swells and the sympathies extend, and we embrace all men in our thoughts, leaving not one outside the range of our solicitude and wishing every one well. The Japanese, Chinese, Cingalese, Indians, Egyptians, all have been made our friends through individuals of each race of whom we have heard much that was good and noble, pure lives, high aims, good deeds, and how can we, therefore, any longer dwell apart, believing our own land or our own people in any respect the chosen of God! No, no; we know now in a sense much more vivid than before that all the children of the earth dwell under the reign of the same divine law, and that for each and every one that law evolves through all the ages, the higher from the lower, the good from evil, slowly but surely separating the dross from the pure gold, disintegrating what is pernicious, consolidating what is beneficial to the race, so that the feeling that formerly told us that we alone had special care bestowed upon us gives place to the knowledge that every one in his day and generation, wherever found, receives the truth best fitted for his elevation from that state to the next higher, and so "Ilka blade of grass keps its ain drap o' dew," and grows its own fruit after its kind. For those and many other reasons, let all thoughtful souls follow my example and visit their brethren from one land to another till the circle is complete.

The unprecedented advance made by western nations in the past and present generations, upon which we continually plume ourselves, is shared by the world in general. Wherever we have been, one story met us. Everywhere there is progress, not only material but intellectual as well, and rapid progress too. The oldest inhabitant has always his comparison to offer between the days of his youth and the advantages possessed by the youth of today. Matters are not as they were. We saw no race which had retrograded, if we except Egypt, which is now in a transitional state, and will ultimately prove no exception to the rule. The whole world moves, and moves in the right direction—upward and onward—the things that are better than those that have been and those to come to be better than those of today. The law of evolution—the higher from the lower—is not discredited by a voyage round the world and the knowledge of what is transpiring from New York round to New York again gives us joy this morning as we sum it all up.

The trip has been without a single unpleasant incident. We have not missed one connection, nor ever been beyond the reach of all the comforts of life, nor have we had one unhappy or even lonely hour. Every day has brought something new or interesting. And sitting here in our quiet mountain home this morning, I feel that there is scarcely a prize that could be offered for which I would exchange the knowledge obtained and the memories of things seen during my trip. One of the great pleasures of travel in the East is the unbounded hospitality—excessive kindness—everywhere met with. With the numerous kind friends to whom we are so deeply indebted—a host far too great to name—please accept this general acknowledgment as at least a slight evidence that their goodness to us is not unappreciated? At every stage of our travels I have been struck with the cheering thought, that notwithstanding the indisputable fact that a vast amount of misery seems inseparable from human life, still the general condition of mankind is a happy one. Even the Hindoo in India, or the Malay in the Archipelago—and these seem to exist under the worst conditions—each of these constantly sees cause to bless his good fortune and render thanks—sincere, heartfelt thanks—to a kind Providence for casting his life in pleasant places, and not in damp, foggy England, or amid American frosts and snows. We have their sincere sympathy, I assure you. Nor is patriotism a peculiarly western virtue. No matter who or what he is, the man of the East in his heart exalts his own country and his own race, and esteems them specially favored of the gods. And indeed it is with nations as with individuals: as none are entirely good, so none are entirely bad. The unseen power is at work in all lands, evolving the higher from the lower and steadily improving all, so the traveller finds much to commend in every country, and seeing this he grows tolerant and liberal, and able more heartily to sing with Burns—

> Then let us pray that come it may—
>   As come it will, for a' that—
> That sense and worth, o'er a' the earth,
>   May bear the gree, for a' that;
>
> For a' that, and a' that,
>   It's coming yet, for a' that,
> That man to man, the warld o'er
>   Shall brothers be, for a' that.

In which hope, nay, in the confident and inspiring belief in the sure coming of the day of the Brotherhood of Man, I lay down my pen and bring to a close this record of my tour round the world.

16
Our Coaching Trip

On the first of June 1881, Carnegie set off on another pleasure trip to fulfill a promise made at a much earlier date than his pledge with John Vandevort to circle the globe. As a young boy living in the slums of "Slabtown" Allegheny, Carnegie had been surprised one evening to find his mother sitting before her cobbler bench and weeping. He had never before seen his stout, resolute little mother break down. From the moment in 1848 that she had made the decision for the family to emigrate to America, she had been the strength and the de facto head of the family. It was she who kept the family alive by repairing shoes for the neighborhood, and it was she who kept insisting that the decision to leave Scotland had been correct. Now for the first time she doubted her judgment and wondered if perhaps her scoffing neighbors in Dunfermline had been right after all. And so she wept in a quite unaccustomed moment of despair.

In an effort to console her, Andrew grasped her hand and promised, "Someday, I'll be rich, and we'll ride in a fine coach drawn by four horses." At which Margaret snorted, "That will do no good over here, if no one in Dunfermline can see us."

Thirty years later, her son was rich. He now could take his mother and a select group of friends on a trip in a resplendent four-in-hand coach from the southern coastal town of Brighton through England to Inverness, in Scotland. They would sweep into Dunfermline in so grand a style that the whole town would marvel over the family's success in the new world.

As with his earlier trip Round the World, Carnegie kept a travel diary of the coaching trip with an eye for future publication. He wrote later, comparing the published journals of his two trips: "I think them different. While coaching I was more joyously happy; during the journey round the World I was gaining more knowledge." The coaching trip journal, first published in 1882 for private circulation, and later by Charles Scribner's Sons in 1883 under the title An American Four-in-Hand in Britain, is indeed a rollicking account of a joyous trip. It is not the polemic against organized religion and for Herbert Spencer's social philosophy of evolutionary progress that Round the World is. Nevertheless, Carnegie finds opportunity throughout this *triumphant tour of his native land to attack the British monarchy, the established church, and the social inequality against which his Chartist forebears had railed. There are also some rather surprising asides scattered throughout the selections given below: he condemns the textile mills for polluting the environment of the English Midlands almost as much as (he admits) his own steel mills were polluting the air of Pittsburgh; he pleads for sane temperance in the use of alcoholic beverages and opposes the absolute prohibition which many were advocating; and he wishes that all American workers might have more time for rest and recreation. These are hardly the sentiments to be expected from a hard-driving, successful industrialist, but the lines were written while their author was on a happy holiday, keeping his promise to his proud mother and enjoying to the fullest the playtime that few of his contemporaries would ever experience except through these pages—providing, of course, they could find time to read them.*

Harbor of New York, June 1, 1881.
On board Steamer *Bothnia*.

Call the roll.

Lady Dowager Mother, Head of the Clan (no Salic Law in our family); Miss Jeannie Johns (Prima Donna); Miss Alice French (Stewardess); Mr. and Mrs. McCargo (Dainty Davie); Mr. and Mrs. King (Paisley Troubadours, Aleck good for fun and Aggie good for everything); Benjamin F. Vandevort (Benjie); Henry Phipps, Jr. (H. P., Our Pard) G. F. McCandless (General Manager); ten in all, making together with the scribe the All-coaching Eleven.

Ting-a-ling-a-ling! The tears are shed, the kisses ta'en. The helpless hulk breathes the breath of life. The pulsations of its mighty heart are felt; the last rope that binds us to land cast off, and now see the hundreds of handkerchiefs waving from the pier fading and fading away....

The *Bothnia* turned her face to the east, and out upon old ocean's gray and melancholy waste sailed the Gay Charioteers. As we steamed down the bay three steamers crowded with the most enterprising of Europe's people passed us, emigrants coming to find in the bounteous bosom of the Great Republic the blessings of equality, the just reward of honest labor. Ah, favored land! the best of the Old World seek your shores to swell to still grander proportions your assured greatness. That all come only for the material benefits you confer, I do not believe. Crowning these material considerations, I insist that the more intelligent of these people feel the spirit of true manhood stirring within them, and glory in the thought that they are to become part of a powerful people, of a government founded upon the born equality of man, free from military despotism and class distinctions. There is a trace of the serf in the man who lives contentedly in a land with ranks above him. One hundred and seventeen thousand came last month, and the cry is still they come! O ye self-constituted rulers of men in Europe, know you not that the knell of dynasties and of rank is sounding? Are you so deaf that you do not hear the thunders, so blind that you do not see the lightnings which now and then give warning of the storm that is to precede the reign of the people?

There is everything in the way one takes things. "Whatever is, is right," is a good maxim for travellers to adopt, but the Charioteers improved on that. The first resolution they passed was, "Whatever is, is lovely; all that does happen and all that doesn't shall be altogether lovely." We shall quarrel with nothing, admire everything and everybody. A surly beggar shall afford us sport, if any one can be surly under our smiles; and stale bread and poor fare shall only serve to remind us that we have banqueted at the Windsor. Even no dinner at all shall pass for a good joke. Rain shall be hailed as good for the growing corn; a cold day pass as invigorating, a warm one welcomed as suggestive of summer at home, and even a Scotch mist serve to remind us of the mysterious ways of Providence. In this mood the start was made. Could any one suggest a better for our purpose?

Now comes a splendid place to skip—the ocean voyage. Everybody writes that up upon the first trip, and every family knows all about it from the long descriptive letters of the absent one doing Europe.

When one has crossed the Atlantic twenty odd times there seems just about as much sense in boring one's readers with an account of the trip as if the journey were by rail from New York to Chicago. We had a fine, smooth run, and though some of us were a trifle distrait, most of us were supremely happy. A sea voyage compared with land travel is a good deal like matrimony compared with single blessedness, I take it: either decidedly better or decidedly worse. To him who finds himself comfortable at sea, the ocean is the grandest of treats. He never fails to feel himself a boy again while on the waves. There is an exaltation about it. "He walks the monarch of the peopled deck," glories in the storm, rises with and revels in it. Heroic song comes to him. The ship becomes a live thing, and if the monster rears and plunges it is akin to bounding on his thoroughbred who knows its rider. Many men feel thus, and I am happily of them, but the ladies who are at their best at sea are few.

The travellers, however, bore the journey well, though one or two proved indifferent sailors. One morning I had to make several calls upon members below and administer my favorite remedy; but pale and dejected as the patients were, not one failed to smile a ghastly smile, and repeat after a fashion the cabalistic words—"Altogether lovely."

London, Friday, June 10, 1881

The House of Commons claimed the first place with our party, all being anxious to see the Mother of Parliaments. It is not so easy a matter to do this as to see our Congress in session; but thanks to our friend Mr. Robert Clark and to others, we were fortunate in being able to do so frequently. . . .

We really heard John Bright speak—the one of all men living whom our party wished most to see and to hear. . . .

A grand character, that of the sturdy Quaker; once the best hated man in Britain, but one to whom both continents are now glad to confess their gratitude. He has been wiser than his generation, but has lived to see it grow up to him. Certainly no American can look down from the gallery upon that white head without beseeching heaven to shower its choicest blessings upon it. He spoke calmly upon the Permissive Liquor Bill, and gave the ministerial statement in regard to it. All he said was good common sense; we could do something by regulating the traffic and confining it to reasonable hours, but after all the great cure must come from the better education of the masses, who must be brought to feel that it is unworthy of their manhood to brutalize themselves with liquor. England has set herself at last to the most important of all work—the thorough education of her people; and we may confidently expect to see a great improvement in their habits in the next generation. My plan for mastering the monster evil of intemperance is that our temperance societies, instead of pledging men never to taste alcoholic beverages, should be really temperance agencies and require their members to use them only at meals—never to drink wines or spirits without eating. The man who takes a glass of wine, or beer, or spirits at dinner is clearly none the worse for it. I judge that if the medical fraternity were polled, a large majority would say he was the better for it. Why can't we recognize the fact that all races indulge in stimulants and will continue to do so? It is the regulation, not the eradication, of this appetite that is practical. The coming man is to consider it low to walk up to a bar and gulp down liquor. The race will come to this platform generations before they will accept that of Sir Wilfred Lawson and his total abstinence ideas.

Brighton, Friday Morning, June 17.

Let us call the roll once more at the door of the Grand Hotel, Brighton, that our history may be complete: Mr. and Miss Beck, London; Mr. and Mrs. Thomas Graham, Wolverhampton; Cousin Maggie Lauder, Dunfermline; dear Emma Franks, Liverpool; Mr. and Mrs. McCargo, Miss Jeannie Johns, Miss Alice French, Benjamin F. Vandevort, Henry Phipps, Jr., G. F. McCandless, Mother and the Scribe. These be the names of the new and delectable order of the Gay Charioteers, who mounted their coach at Brighton and began the long journey to the North Countrie on the day and date aforesaid. And here, O my good friends, let me say that until a man has stood at the door and unexpectedly seen his own four-in-hand drive up before him, the horses—four noble bays—champing the bits, their harness buckles glistening in the sun; the coach spick and span new and as glossy as a mirror, with the coachman on the box and the footman behind; and then, enchanted, has called to his friends, "Come, look, there it is, just as I had pictured it!" and has then seen them mount to their places with beaming faces—until, I say, he has had that experience, don't tell me that he has known the most exquisite sensation in life, for I know he hasn't. It was Izaak Walton, I believe, who when asked what he considered the most thrilling sensation in life, answered that he supposed it was the tug of a thirty-pound salmon. Well, that was not a bad guess. I have taken the largest trout of the season on bonnie Loch Leven, have been drawn over Spirit Lake in Iowa in my skiff for half an hour by a monster pickerel, and have played with the speckled beauties in Dead River. It is glorious; making a hundred thousand is nothing to it; but there's a thrill beyond that, my dear old quaint Izaak. I remember in one of my sweet strolls "ayont the wood mill braes" with a great man, my Uncle Bailie Morrison—and I treasure the memory of these strolls as among the chief of my inheritance—this very question came up. I asked him what he thought the most thrilling thing in life. He mused awhile, as was the Bailie's wont, and I said, "I think I can tell you, Uncle." "What is it then, Andrea?" (Not Andrew for the world, mother and the Bailie have the other.) "Well, Uncle, I think that when, in making a speech, one feels himself lifted, as it were, by some divine power into regions beyond himself, in which he seems to soar without effort, and swept by enthusiasm into the expression of some burning truth, which has laid brooding in his soul, throwing policy and prudence to the winds, he feels words whose eloquence surprises himself, burning hot, hissing through him like molten lava coursing the veins, he throws it forth, and panting for breath hears the quick, sharp, explosive roar of his fellow-men in thunder of assent, the precious moment which tells him that the audience is his own, but one soul in it and that his; I think this the supreme moment of life." "Go! Andrea, ye've hit it!" cried the Bailie, and didn't the dark eye sparkle! He had felt this often, had the Bailie; his nephew had only now and then been near enough to imagine the rest.

Mr. Adam Johnston once told me that, though he had heard the most noted orators of Britain, he never yet heard any one whose mastery of a popular audience was as complete as uncle's. Great praise this from such a source; but the head of our family, Uncle Tom, was even more than a natural orator; with all his glowing fire he was characterized by rare sagacity and sound common sense. And how sterling his honesty! All men knew where Tammy Morrison was to be found. A grand Radical, like his father before him, and this nephew after him, who will try, politically speaking at least, never to disgrace the family.

The happiness of giving happiness is far sweeter than the pleasure direct, and I recall no moments of my life in which the rarer pleasure seemed to suffuse my whole heart as when I stood at Brighton and saw my friends take their places that memorable morning. In this variable, fantastic climate of Britain the weather is ever a source of solicitude. What must it have been to me, when a good start was all important! I remember I awoke early that day and wondered whether it was sunny or rainy. If a clear day could have been purchased, it would have been obtained at almost any outlay. I could easily tell our fate by raising the window-blind, but I philosophically decided that it was best to lie still and take what heaven might choose to send us. I should know soon enough. If rain it was, I could not help it; if fair, it was all right. But let me give one suggestion to those who in England are impious enough to ask heaven to change its plans: don't ask for dry weather; always resort to that last extremity when it is "a drizzle-drozzle" you wish. Your supplications are so much more likely to be answered, you know.

There never was a lovelier morning in England than that which greeted me when I pulled up the heavy Venetian blind and gazed on the rippling sea before me, with its hundreds of pretty little sails. I repeated to myself these favorite lines as I stood entranced:

> The Bridegroom Sea is toying with the shore,
> His wedded bride; and in the fulness of his marriage joy
> He decorates her tawny brow with shells,
> Retires a space to see how fair she looks,
> Then proud runs up to kiss her.

That is what old ocean was doing that happy morning. I saw him at it, and I felt that if all created beings had one mouth I should like to kiss them too.

All seated! Mother next the coachman, and I at her side. The horn sounds, the crowd cheers, and we are off. A mile or two are traversed and there is a unanimous verdict upon one point—this suits us! Finer than we had dreamt! As we pass the pretty villas embossed in flowers and vines and all that makes England the home of happy homes, there comes the sound of increasing exclamations. How pretty! Oh, how beautiful! See, see, the roses! oh the roses! Look at that lawn! How lovely! Enchanting! entrancing! superb! exquisite! Oh, I never saw anything like this in all my life! And then the hum of song—La-*la*-LA-LA, Ra-da-*da*-DUM! Yes, it is all true, all we dreamt or imagined and beyond it. And so on we go through Brighton and up the hills to the famous Weald of Sussex.

While we make our first stop to water the horses at the wayside inn, and some of the men as well, for a glass of beer asserts its attractions, let me introduce you to two worthies whose names will occupy important places in our narrative, and dwell in our memories forever; men to whom we are indebted in a large measure for the success of the coaching experiment.

Ladies and gentlemen, this is Perry, Perry our coachman; and what he doesn't know about horses and how to handle them you needn't overtask yourselves trying to learn. And this is Joe—Joey, my lad—footman and coach manager. A good head and an eloquent tongue has Joe. Yes, and a kind heart. There is nothing he can do or think of doing for any of us—and he can do much—that he is not off and doing ere we ask him. "Skid, Joe!" "Right, Perry!" these talismanic words of our order we heard to-day for the first time. It will be many a long day before they cease to recall to the Charioteers some of the happiest recollections of life. Even as I write I am in English meadows far away and hear them tingling in my ears.

It was soon discovered that no mode of travel could be compared with coaching. By all other modes the views are obstructed by the hedges and walls; upon the top of the coach the eye wanders far and wide,

Our Coaching Trip

> O'er deep waving fields and pastures green,
> With gentle slopes and groves between.

Everything of rural England is seen, and how exquisitely beautiful it all is, this quiet, peaceful, orderly land!

> The ground's most gentle dimplement
> (As if God's finger touched, but did not press,
> In making England) — such an up and down
> Of verdure; nothing too much up and down,
> A ripple of land, such little hills the sky
> Can stoop to tenderly and the wheat-fields climb;
> Such nooks of valleys lined with orchises,
> Fed full of noises by invisible streams,
> I thought my father's land was worthy too of being Shakespeare's.

. . . Having got the party fairly started, let me tell you something of our general arrangements for the campaign. The coach, horses, and servants are engaged at a stipulated sum per week, which includes their travelling expenses. We have nothing to do with their bills or arrangements, neither are we in any wise responsible for accidents to the property. Every one is allowed a small handbag and a strap package; the former contains necessary articles for daily use, the latter waterproofs, shawls, shoes, etc. The Gay Charioteers march with supplies for one week. The trunks are forwarded every week to the point where we are to spend the succeeding Sunday, so that every Saturday evening we replenish our wardrobe, and at the Sunday evening dinner our ladies appear in grand toilette. In no case did any failure of this plan occur, nor were we ever put to the slightest inconvenience about clothing. Our hotel accommodations were secured by telegraph. Mr. Graham, previous to our start, had engaged these for our first week's stage.

The questions of luncheon soon came to the front, for should we be favored with fine weather, much of the poetry and romance of the journey was sure to cluster round the midday halt. It was by a process of natural selection that she who had proved her genius for making salads on many occasions during the voyage should be unanimously appointed to fill the important position of stewardess, and given full and unlimited control of the hampers. Miss French lived up to a well-deserved reputation by surprising us day after day with luncheons far excelling any dinner. Two coaching hampers, very complete affairs, were obtained in London. These the stewardess saw filled at the inn every morning with the best the country could afford, giving this her personal supervision, a labor of love. Harry's sweet tooth led him to many early excursions before breakfast in quest of sweets and flowers for us. Aleck was butler, and upon him we placed implicit reliance, and with excellent reason too, for the essential corkscrew and the use thereof—which may be rated as of prime necessity upon such a tour—and Aleck never failed us as superintendent of the bottles.

It was in obedience to the strictest tenets of our civil service reform association that the most important appointment of all was made with a unanimity which must ever be flattering to the distinguished gentleman who received the highly responsible appointment of general manager. Gardiner had evidently been born for the position. A man does not generally learn until he is forty what he can do to perfection; but there are thirty-two ready to certify that our general manager has not needed to wait so long. If he ever requires backers as the best manager—the very ideal manager of a coaching party—apply within. He had ten days' instruction from a master hand, friend Graham, who resigned office and retired to the shades of private life at Wolverhampton. It was Mr. Graham who arranged all the preliminaries, so that none of us had a thing to do at Brighton but to mount into our seats. He and Gardiner are twins in greatness, and, as far as our party is concerned, neither could be equalled except by the other. Just here let me note, for the peace of mind of any gentleman who may be tempted to try the coaching experiment: *Don't,* unless you have a dear friend with a clear head, an angelic disposition, a great big heart, and the tact essential for governing, who for your sake is willing to relieve you from the cares incident to such a tour—that is, if you expect to enjoy it as a recreation, and have something that forever after will linger in the memory as an adventure in wonderland.

There must always be a tendency toward grouping in a large party: groups of four or five, and in extreme cases a group of two; and especially is this so when married people, cousins, or dear friends are of the company. To prevent anything like this, and insure our being one united party, I asked the gentlemen not to occupy the same seat twice in succession—a rule which gave the ladies a different companion at each meal. This was understood to apply in a general way to our strolls, although in this case the general manager, with rare discretion, winked at many infringements, which insured him grateful constituents of both sexes. Young people should never be held too strictly to such rules, and a chaperon's duties, as we all know, are often most successfully performed by a wise and salutary neglect. Our general manager and even the Lady Dowager were considerate.

We generally started about half-past nine in the morning, half an hour earlier or later as the day's journey was to be long or short; and here let me record, to the credit of all, that not in any instance had we ever to wait for any of the party beyond the five minutes allowed upon all well-managed lines for "variation of watches." The horn sounded, and we were off through the crowds which were usually around the hotel door awaiting the start. Nor even at meals were we less punctual or less mindful of the comfort of others. I had indeed a model party in every way, and in none more praiseworthy than in this, that the Charioteers were always "on time." Jeannie's explanation may have reason in it: "Who wouldn't be ready and waiting to mount the coach! I'd as soon be late, and a good deal sooner, maybe, for my wedding as for meals; there was even a better reason why we were always ready then: we could hardly wait." We did indeed eat like hawks, especially at luncheon — a real boy's hunger — the ravenous gnawing after a day at the sea gathering whilks. I thought this had left me, but that with many another characteristic of glorious youth came once more to make daft callants of us. O those days! those happy, happy days! Can they be brought back once more? Will a second coaching trip do it? I would be off next summer. But one hesitates to put his luck to the test a second time, lest the perfect image of the first be marred. We shall see.

During the evening we had learned the next day's stage — where we were to stay over night, and, what is almost as important, in what pretty nook we were to rest at midday; on the banks of what classic stream or wimpling burn, or in what shady, moss-covered dell. Several people of note in the neighborhood dropped into the inn, as a rule, to see the American coaching party, whose arrival in the village had made as great a stir as if it were the advance show wagon of Barnum's menagerie. From these the best route and objects of interest to be seen could readily be obtained. The ordnance maps which we carried kept us from trouble about the right roads; not only this, they gave us the name of every estate we passed, and of its owner.

The horses have to be considered in selecting a luncheon place, which should be near an inn, where they can be baited. This was rarely inconvenient; but upon a few occasions, when the choice spot was in some glen or secluded place, we took oats along, and our horses were none the worse off for nibbling the roadside grass and drinking from the brook. Nor did the party look less like the aristocratic gypsies they felt themselves to be from having their coach standing on the moor or in the glen, and the horses picketed near by, as if we were just the true-born gypsies. And was there ever a band of gypsies happier than we, or freer from care? Didn't we often dash off in a roar:

> See! the smoking bowl before us,
>   Mark our jovial ragged ring!
> Round and round take up the chorus,
>   And in raptures let us sing.
> A fig for those by law protected!
>   Liberty's a glorious feast!
> Courts for cowards were erected,
>   Churches built to please the priest. . . .

Although we were coaching, it must not be thought that we neglected the pleasures of walking. No, indeed, we had our daily strolls. Sometimes the pedestrians started in advance of the coach from the inn or the luncheon ground, and walked until overtaken, and at other times we would dismount some miles before we reached the end of the day's journey, and walk into the village. This was a favorite plan, as we found by arriving later than the main body our rooms were ready and all the friends in our general sitting-room standing to welcome us.

Hills upon the route were always hailed as giving us an opportunity for a walk or a stroll, and all the sport derivable from a happy party in country lanes. It was early June, quite near enough to

> The flowery May who from her green lap throws
> The yellow cowslip and the pale primrose,

and the hundreds of England's wild beauties with

>   quaint enamell'd eyes,
> That on the green turf suck the honeyed showers,
> And purple all the ground with vernal flowers.

We carried perpetual flowering summer with us as we travelled from south to north, plucking the wild roses and the honeysuckles from the hedges near Brighton, never missing their sweet influences, and finding them ready to welcome us at Inverness, as if they had waited till our approach to burst forth in their beauty in kindly greeting of their kinsmen from over the sea. A dancing, laughing, welcome did the wild flowers of my native land give to us, God bless them!

Coventry, June 24

The rain ceased, as usual, before we had gone far, and we had a clear dry run until luncheon. We see the Black Country now, rows of little dingy houses beyond, with tall smoky chimneys vomiting smoke, mills and factories at every turn, coal pits and rolling mills and blast furnaces, the very bottomless pit itself; and such dirty, careworn children, hard-driven men, and squalid women. To think of the green lanes, the larks, the Arcadia we have just left. How can people be got to live such terrible lives as they seem condemned to here? Why do they not all run away to the green fields just beyond? Pretty rural Coventry suburbs in the morning and Birmingham at noon; the lights and shadows of human existence can rarely be brought into sharper contrast. If "Better fifty years of Europe than a cycle of Cathay," surely better a month in Leamington than life's span in the Black Country! But do not let us forget that it is just Pittsburgh over again; nay, not even quite so bad, for that city bears the palm for dirt against the world. The fact is, however, that life in such places seems attractive to those born to rural life, and large smoky cities drain the country; but surely this may be safely attributed to necessity. With freedom to choose, one would think the rush would be the other way. The working classes in England do not work so hard or so unceasingly as do their fellows in America. They have ten holidays to the American's one. Neither does their climate entail such a strain upon men as ours does.

I remember after Vandy and I had gone round the world and were walking Pittsburgh streets, we decided that the Americans were the saddest looking race we had seen. Life is so terribly earnest here. Ambition spurs us all on, from him who handles the spade to him who employs thousands. We know no rest. It is different in the older lands—men rest oftener and enjoy more of what life has to give. The young Republic has some things to teach the parent land, but the elder has an important lesson to teach the younger in this respect. In this world we must learn not to lay up our treasures, but to enjoy them day by day as we travel the path we never return to. If we fail in this we shall find when we do come to the days of leisure that we have lost the taste for and the capacity to enjoy them. There are so many unfortunates cursed with plenty to retire upon, but with nothing to retire to! Sound wisdom that schoolboy displayed who did not "believe in putting away for tomorrow the cake he could eat today." It might not be fresh on the morrow, or the cat might steal it. The cat steals many a choice bit from Americans intended for the morrow. Among the saddest of all spectacles to me is that of an elderly man occupying his last years grasping for more dollars. "The richest man in America sailing suddenly for Europe to escape business cares," said a wise Scotch gentleman to me, one morning, as he glanced over the *Times* at breakfast. Make a note of that, my enterprising friends.

It was on Saturday, July 16th, that we went over the border, Mr. Wilson, the coach-owner, going with us, on his way to his native town.

The bridge across the boundary line was soon reached. When midway over a halt was called, and vent given to our enthusiasm. With three cheers for the land of the heather, shouts of "Scotland forever," and the waving of hats and handkerchiefs, we dashed across the border. And, oh Scotland, my own, my native land, your exiled son returns with love for you as ardent as ever warmed the heart of man for his country. It's a God's mercy I was born a Scotchman, for I do not see how I could ever have been contented to be anything else. The little plucky dour deevil, set in her own ways and getting them too, level-headed and shrewd, with an eye to the main chance always and yet so lovingly weak, so fond, so led away by song or story, so easily touched to fine issues, so leal, so true! Ah! you suit me, Scotia, and proud am I that I am your son. . . .

Dunfermline, July 27–28

A man stopped us at the junction of the roads to inform us that we were expected to pass through the ancient borough of Innerkeithing, but I forgot myself there. It seemed a fair chance to escape part of the excitement (we had not yet begun the campaign as it were); at all events I dodged, to escape the first fire, as raw troops are always said to do, and so we took the direct road. When the top of the Ferry Hills was reached we saw the town, all as dead as if the holy Sabbath lay upon it, without one evidence of life. How beautiful is Dunfermline seen from the Ferry Hills, its grand old abbey towering over all, seeming to hallow the city and to lend a charm and dignity to the lowliest tenement. Nor is there in all broad Scotland, nor in many places elsewhere that I know of, a more varied and delightful view than that obtained from the park upon a fine day. What Benares is to the Hindoo, Mecca to the Mohammedan, Jerusalem to the Christian, all that Dunfermline is to me. . . .

[There follow lengthy quotations from the Dunfermline *Press* and the Dunfermline *Journal* of July 30, 1881, describing the celebrations in Dunfermline, including the laying of the cornerstone of the Free Public Library, which Carnegie had given to his native town. This building was Carnegie's first library gift. JFW]

It was all up after this. Perry and Joe, the coach and the horses were speeding away by rail to their homes; we were no longer *the* coaching party, but only ordinary tourists buying our tickets like other people instead of travelling as it were in style upon annual passes. . . .

We returned from Inverness by the usual tourist route: canal and boat to Oban, where we rested over night, thence next day to Glasgow. . . .

We landed at the Broomielaw, whither father and mother and Tom and I sailed thirty odd years ago, on the 800-ton ship *Wiscasset*, and began our seven weeks' voyage to the land of promise, poor emigrants in quest of fortune; but, mark you, not without thoughts in the radical breasts of our parents that it was advisable to leave a land which tolerated class distinctions for the *one* government of the people, by the people, and for the people, which welcomed them to its fold and insured for their sons as far as laws can give it equality with the highest and a fair and free field for the exercise of their powers.

My father saw through not only the sham but the injustice of rank, from king to knight, and loved America because she knows no difference in her sons. He was a Republican, aye, every inch, and his sons glory in that and follow where he led. . . .

Forever and ever may the parent land and the child land grow fonder and fonder of each other, and their people mingle more and more till they become as one and the same. All good educated Americans love England, for they know that she alone among the nations has

> On with toil of heart and knees and hand
> Through the long gorge to the far light hath won
> Her path upward and prevailed.

She it was who pointed out to America what to plant, and how, and where. The people of England should love America, for she has taught them in return that all the equal rights of man they are laboring for at home are bearing goodly fruit in the freer atmosphere of the West. May the two peoples therefore grow in love for each other, and with this fond wish, and many a sad farewell, the Gay Charioteers disband forever afterward in life to rally round each other in case of need at the mystic call of "Skid, Joe," "Right, Perry"; and certain of this, that whatever else fades from the memory, the recollection of our coaching trip from Brighton to Inverness remains a sacred possession forever.

17
Letters from Skibo

At the somewhat advanced age of fifty-one, Andrew Carnegie in April 1887 married Louise Whitfield, who was twenty-two years his junior. He took his bride on an extended wedding trip to Scotland. Louise quickly became as enamoured of her husband's native land as he himself was, and thus began their annual six-month residency in Scotland which would continue until the outbreak of World War I. In 1888, the Carnegies leased Cluny Castle in the central Highlands from its laird, Ewen Macpherson. Louise dearly loved Cluny, and with the birth of their only child, Margaret, in 1897 she asked her husband to purchase Cluny, but Macpherson refused to sell his ancestral home. Carnegie was obliged to find another "hieland hame" for his family. In June 1897, while on a coaching trip with some Scottish friends, he found the place he was looking for, the estate of Skibo on Dornoch Firth in the county of Sutherland. The original Skibo castle, built in the late twelfth century, had served as the residency of the bishops of Caithness until the Protestant Reformation in the sixteenth century. The then ruling bishop was forced to cede the 22,000-acre estate to the John Gray family.

By the time of Carnegie's purchase of Skibo from the current owner, Evan Sutherland-Walker, the ancient castle had been replaced by a nineteenth-century Victorian stone mansion. Over the next three years, Carnegie trebled the size of the manor house and added an additional 18,000 acres to his estate. By 1902, the imposing Skibo Castle was finally completed to Andrew's and Louise's satisfaction. To Skibo came a steady stream of political leaders, British royalty, poets, novelists, journalists, and educators. Here the visitors could swim in the huge, glass-enclosed pool filled with salt water piped from the Firth, play golf on Carnegie's private course, fish for salmon in the River Shin, stalk red deer and shoot grouse on the upper moors, or take short coastal cruises aboard Carnegie's yacht, Seabreeze.

Given below are a few brief excerpts of letters from both Louise and Andrew extolling the glories of Skibo and urging (especially by Andrew) ever more visitors to experience what he was pleased to call "our heaven on earth."

Louise Carnegie wrote to her New York pastor, Dr. Charles H. Eaton, sometime in the summer of 1898, shortly after taking over Skibo.

We are all very pleased with our new home. The surroundings are more of the English type than Scotch. The sweet pastoral scenery is perfect of its kind. A beautiful undulating park with cattle grazing, a stately avenue of fine old beeches, glimpses of the Dornoch Firth, about a mile away, all seen through the picturesque cluster of lime and beech trees. All make such a peaceful picture that already a restful home feeling has come. The Highland features to which our hearts turn longingly are not wanting, but are more distant.

To show you the unique range of attractions, yesterday Mr. Carnegie was trout fishing on a wild moorland loch surrounded by heather while I took Margaret to the *sea* and she had her first experience of rolling upon the soft white sand and digging her little hands in it to her heart's content, while the blue waters of the ocean came rolling in at her feet and the salt sea breeze brought the roses to her cheeks. She is strong and hearty and so full of mischief—a perfect little sunbeam. With all our fullness of life before we have never really lived till now. (Burton J. Hendrick and Daniel Henderson, *Louise Whitfield Carnegie* [New York: Hastings House, 1950], p. 152)

And Andrew wrote his favorite cousin, George "Dod" Lauder: "I am so busy working at fun! Fishing, yachting, golfing. Skibo never so delightful; all so quiet! A home at last" *(undated, quoted in Burton J. Hendrick,* The Life of Andrew Carnegie *[New York: Doubleday, Doran, 1932] vol. 2, p. 154).*

Skibo had been purchased largely at the insistence of Louise to provide a real home for their daughter Margaret, whom they affectionately called Baba. On one of Louise's rare visits away from the castle by herself, Andrew wrote her a short note:

Good morning, dear one. Entrancing is the only word for it up here. Such days! Cool, bright—so bright! Yesterday I thought the links never were so fine. How grateful for being here at home! Baba has just had her bite with me at breakfast and jelly on it! When you are away I find myself going to her as the connecting link, as indeed she is, part of both which makes us more truly one! (Quoted in Hendrick and Henderson, *LWC*, p. 155)

Although Louise often wearied of the steady stream of visitors who made their way to Skibo, Andrew was never as happy as when the castle was filled to capacity with admiring guests. There were the regular formal visits each year by the heads of the four Scottish universities and by the trustees of the Carnegie-Dunfermline and United Kingdom trusts which Carnegie had established, but the most welcome guests were those whom Carnegie called the "Old Shoes"—dear friends and relatives like the Lauder family, the Yates Thompsons, Herbert Gladstone, Lord Bryce, Nicholas Murray But-

ler, Mark Twain, Walter Damrosch, and Rudyard Kipling who needed no special occasion to visit. The "Oldest Shoe" of all was Carnegie's closest friend, John Morley. Every summer, Carnegie's letters were as frequent as they were urgent in requesting Lord Morley to come to Skibo as the following illustrates:

Don't fail to come as soon as you can next week. You may have trouble getting a Berth—better engage it. Sunday, August 9th would suit. We shall be ready for you the tenth & perhaps this would save you from the rush. Monday eve the tenth might be crowded—so why not Saturday eve & arrive Sunday noon. We can send for you even that day without shocking the people too much when we can urge a Cabinet official's needs. For any ordinary man this appliation would be insufficient. I hope you are to be greatly benefited by your stay with us which must not be short—stretch it as much as possible. Bryce's may be here ere you go. Montrose Room will be ready for its rightful occupant & I'll be happy. (5 August 1908, Carnegie Papers, Library of Congress, vol. 155)

In the great baronial front hall of Skibo Castle, its former owner had installed a pipe organ. Both Andrew and Louise were particularly fond of organ music, and along with the Scottish bagpipes, the organ became a central feature in the daily life of the castle, as Louise Carnegie describes in an early letter from Skibo to an American friend.

This year, when I heard we had an organ in the hall, I arranged, as a surprise to Mr. Carnegie, to have an organist here, who greeted us as we stepped on the threshold of our new home with Beethoven's *Fifth Symphony*. The organist has now become a permanent institution. Every morning we come down to breakfast greeted by swelling tones, beginning with a hymn or chorale, and swelling into selections from the oratorios, etc. In the evening our musician plays for us on our fine Bechstein piano, which we now are really enjoying for the first time. We are all delighted with our musical atmosphere. (Undated, quoted in Hendrick and Henderson, *LWC*, pp. 152-53)

Andrew Carnegie was scrupulously attentive to every small detail that would contribute to the perfection of life at Skibo. In the following letter to his solicitor, John Ross, he evinces as keen an interest in the selection of a new organist for Skibo as he previously had showed in the cost of production for a ton of steel:

We are particular about the music. . . . No fancy pieces—these prostitute the organ. the fine old hymns—Wagner's finest *religious* pieces Loghengrin [sic]—Siegfried March &. Played slowly, feelingly—no *bounce*—no flare. . . . You ask what terms? We can't tell—we wish him to feel he is liberally dealt with—pay the best price for the best is the rule. Your musical director ought to know a real musician from a claptrap splurger. Want him Skibo early July. (18 May 1906, Carnegie Papers, Library of Congress, vol. 29)

Part v

Carnegie, the Pundit

The press loved Andrew Carnegie, for unlike most of his fellow industrialists, who usually responded to questioning with a tight-lipped "no comment," Carnegie was willing to talk openly and volubly on any subject broached to him, and he was always good copy. Upon arrival or departure in his annual migrations to Scotland, he would welcome to his stateroom a bevy of reporters eager to query him on the state of the economy, the current political scene in Britain or the United States, and the latest radical threat to the established order.

If the press did not come often enough as a pilgrim to satisfy this mountain of pontifical judgment, then most assuredly the mountain would go to the press. In books, magazine articles, pamphlets, and in public addresses delivered on formal occasions, Carnegie scattered the sunshine light of his wisdom throughout the United Kingdom and the United States. And if the issue at hand was urgent enough to brook no delay, Carnegie was never too proud to use the letters-to-the-editor pages of the New York Herald or the London Times as an immediate outlet for his views.

Carnegie, in short, was the self-appointed pundit for the Anglo-American world long before there were the syndicated columnists like Walter Lippmann, James Reston, or William Safire to instruct the public on what to think about current events. In this section, samples are given of Carnegie's punditry on the important issues of his day: democracy, capitalism, Populism, Progressivism, Socialism, race relations in America, imperialism, pacifism, and the quest for interna-

tional order and collective security. These published pronouncements were received with the same seriousness by their readers as they were delivered by their author. A few, such as "The A B C of Money" and "The Parting of the Ways" had a direct political impact that present-day pundits might well envy.

18
Democracy: "The Republic"

In 1886, Charles Scribner's Sons published Andrew Carnegie's Triumphant Democracy, *which the author would always consider his magnum opus. Carnegie had reason to be proud of this effort, for the book created a sensation on both sides of the Atlantic. In the United States, it went through four printings and then a fifth, completely revised and updated edition. The British, for whom the book was particularly targeted, bought in even greater numbers. There were several printings, including a cheap, paperback edition which alone sold 40,000 copies. It was translated into French and German and had a sizable sale on the Continent. From the outside cover, designed by Carnegie himself (showing two golden pyramids, one standing firmly on its base and labeled "Republic," and the other teetering precariously on its apex and labeled "Monarchy"), to the final sentence some 509 pages later, the book is an exultant paean to Carnegie's adopted land.*

With statistical data taken from the 1880 census and from Scribner's Statistical Atlas, *Carnegie sought to prove his basic thesis that the United States was rich, progressive, and capitalistic because of the political order that had been established in 1787. The resulting book is a Fourth of July oration with numerical tables, expressing the American belief in the supreme importance of the political forms of democracy, in the signal value of material progress, in individualism, and in sheer numbers. The implicit faith in democracy so fervently expressed throughout the book does much to explain why the European doctrinaire found few rewards in the United States. The Spencerian evolutionist and the Marxist socialist both failed to understand America because they tended to see political bourgeois democracy as a product rather than the producer. Herbert Spencer believed that American political democracy was the result of the free enterprise system. Marx saw all forms of government as but manifestations of the prevailing economic order. In turning both Spencer and Marx upside down, Carnegie spoke for his Chartist forebears as well as for most of his contemporary Americans in emphasizing form over function.*

Carnegie also spoke for himself. As the historian Robert G. McClosky so aptly stated, Carnegie *"wrote* Triumphant Democracy *because he had an imperious need to explain and justify himself and his environment, because he had to convince both the world and himself that what he was doing was good and that the context within which he operated was just. The book appears to be a defense of democracy; actually, it is a defense of nineteenth-century capitalism—and Carnegie"* (American Conservatism in the Age of Enterprise *[Cambridge, Mass.: Harvard University Press, 1951], p. 136).*

This book was part of Carnegie's continuing search for a reconciliation between his radical Dunfermline past and his plutocratic present. That quest would not be entirely satisfied with this book, however. Carnegie's "imperious need" for self-justification would finally be met only with his Gospel of Wealth.

The selection given below is the first chapter of the book. It sets the thesis and tone for all that follows. One American critic, George William Curtis, complained that the book reminded him of the Californian's boasting over the weather in his state. "It's all sunshine, sunshine, sunshine. Where are the shadows?" To this charge, Carnegie had a ready reply. "The book was written at high noon when the sun casts no shadows." And when a skeptical Scottish reporter in an interview in Aberdeen sought to pursue the matter further by asking, "But you mean to say in America you have no long standing abuses to correct as we in Britain have?" Carnegie with quiet assurance replied, "No, that is true, and it is a blessing. The system is perfect.... We have only the proper administration of perfect institutions to look after." Against such a faith in form, the shafts of criticism were useless.

The Republic

Methinks I see in my mind a noble and puissant nation rousing herself like a strong man after sleep, and shaking her invincible locks; methinks I see her as an eagle mewing her mighty youth, and kindling her undazzled eyes at the full mid-day beam; purging and unscaling her long abused sight at the fountain itself of heavenly radiance; while the whole noise of timorous and flocking birds, with those also that love the twilight, flutter about, amazed at what she means.—Milton

The old nations of the earth creep on at a snail's pace; the Republic thunders past with the rush of the express. The United States, the growth of a single century, has already reached the foremost rank among nations, and is destined soon to out-distance all others in the race. In population, in wealth, in annual savings, and in public credit; in freedom from debt, in agriculture, and in manufactures, America already leads the civilized world.

France, with her fertile plains and sunny skies, requires a hundred and sixty years to grow two Frenchmen where one grew before. Great Britain, whose rate of increase is greater than that of any other European nation, takes seventy years to double her population. The Republic has repeatedly doubled hers in twenty-five years.

In 1831, Great Britain and Ireland contained twenty-four millions of people, and fifty years later (1881) thirty-four millions. France increased, during the same period, from thirty-two and a half to thirty-seven and a half millions. The Republic bounded from thirteen to fifty millions. England gained ten, France five, the United States thirty-seven millions! Thus the Republic, in one half-century, added to her numbers as many as the present total population of France, and more than the present population of the United Kingdom. Think of it! A Great Britain and Ireland called forth from the wilderness, as if by magic, in less than the span of a man's few days upon earth, almost

> As if the yawning earth to heaven,
> A subterranean host had given.

Truly the Republic is the Minerva of nations; full armed has she sprung from the brow of Jupiter Britain. The thirteen millions of Americans of 1830 have now increased to fifty-six millions—more English-speaking people than exist in all the world besides; more than in the United Kingdom and all her colonies, even were the latter doubled in population!

Startling as is this statement, it is tame in comparison with that which is to follow. In 1850 the total wealth of the United States was but $8,430,000,000 (£1,686,000,000), while that of the United Kingdom exceeded $22,500,000,000 (£4,500,000,000), or nearly three times that sum. Thirty short years sufficed to reverse the positions of the respective countries. In 1882 the Monarchy was possessed of a golden load of no less than eight thousand, seven hundred and twenty million sterling. Just pause a moment to see how this looks when strung out in cold figures; but do not try to realize what it means, for mortal man cannot conceive it. Herbert Spencer need not travel so far afield to reach the "unknowable!" He has it right here under his very eyes. Let him try to "know" the import of this—$43,600,000,000 (£8,720,000,000)! It is impossible. But stupendous as this seems, it is exceeded by the wealth of the Republic, which in 1880, two years before, amounted to $48,950,000,000 (£9,790,000,000). What a mercy we write for 1880; for had we to give the wealth of one year later another figure would have to be found, and added to the interminable row. America's wealth today greatly exceeds ten thousand millions sterling. Nor is this altogether due to her enormous agricultural resources, as may at first glance be thought; for all the world knows she is first among nations in agriculture. It is largely attributable to her manufacturing industries, for, as all the world does not know, she, and not Great Britain, is also the greatest manufacturing country. In 1880, British manufactures amounted in value to eight hundred and eighteen millions sterling; those of America to eleven hundred and twelve millions[1] — nearly half as much as those of the whole of Europe, which amounted to twenty-six hundred millions. Thus, although Great Britain manufactures for the whole world, and the Republic is only gaining, year after year, greater control of her own markets, Britain's manufactures in 1880 were not two-thirds the value of those of the one-century-old Republic, which is not generally considered a manufacturing country at all.

In the savings of nations America also comes first, her annual savings of two hundred and ten millions sterling exceeding those of the United Kingdom by fifty-six millions, and those of France by seventy millions sterling. The fifty million Americans of 1880 could have bought up the one hundred and forty millions of Russians, Austrians, and Spaniards; or, after purchasing wealthy France, would have had enough pocket money to acquire Denmark, Norway, Switzerland, and Greece. The Yankee Republican could even buy the home of his ancestors — the dear old home with all its exquisite beauty, historical associations, and glorious traditions, which challenge our love — and hold it captive,

> The cloud-capp'd towers, the gorgeous palaces,
> The solemn temples,

aye, every acre of Great Britain and Ireland could he buy, and hold it as a pretty little Isle of Wight to his great continent; and after doing this he could turn round and pay off the entire national debt of that deeply indebted land, and yet not exhaust his fortune, the product of a single century! What will he not be able to do ere his second century closes! Already the nations which have played great parts in the world's history grow small in comparison. In a hundred years they will be as dwarfs, in two hundred mere pigmies to this giant; he the Gulliver of nations, they but Liliputians who may try to bind him with their spider threads in vain.

The shipping of the Republic ranks next to that of the world's carrier, Brit-

---

1. British returns do not include flour mills and sawmills, but sixty millions sterling, a sum far beyond their possible value, have been allowed for these in the above estimate.

ain. No other nation approaches her in the race for place. In 1880, the carrying power of Great Britain was eighteen millions of tons; that of the Republic nine millions, being about one-half the motherland's commercial fleet, but more than that of France, Germany, Norway, Italy, and Spain combined, these being the five largest carrying powers of Europe after Britain. The Western Republic has more than four times the carrying capacity of its European sister France, and quite four times as much as Germany. Her ships earned nearly twenty percent of the total shipping earnings of the world in 1880. France and Germany each earned but a shade over five percent. The exports and imports of America are already equal to those of either of those countries—about £300,000,000 sterling. Notwithstanding those facts, which are corroborated by Mulhall, and are known to be correct, the general impression is that the Republic, gigantic as she is on land, has very little footing upon the water. This is one of many popular delusions about the "kin beyond sea." But while she is next to Britain herself as a maritime power, it is when we turn to her internal commerce—her carrying power on land—that she reverses positions with her great mother. The internal commerce of the United States exceeds the entire foreign commerce of Great Britain and Ireland, France, Germany, Russia, Holland, Austria-Hungary, and Belgium combined. For railway freight over a hundred and ten millions sterling are annually paid, a greater sum than the railway freightage of Great Britain, France, and Italy collectively, and more than is earned by all the ships in the world, exclusive of America's own earnings from ships. The Pennsylvania Railroad system alone transports more tonnage than all Britain's merchant ships.

In military and naval power the Republic is at once the weakest and the strongest of nations. Her regular army consists of but twenty-five thousand men scattered all over the continent in companies of fifty or a hundred. Her navy, thank God! is as nothing. But twenty years ago, as at the blast of a trumpet, she called into action two millions of armed men, and floated six hundred and twenty-six warships. Even the vaunted legions of Xerxes, and the hordes of Attila and Timour were exceeded in numbers by the citizen soldiers who took up arms in 1861 to defend the unity of the nation, and who, when the task was done, laid them quietly down, and returned to the avocations of peace. As Macaulay says of the soldiers of the Commonwealth: "In a few months there remained not a trace indicating that the most formidable army in the world had just been absorbed into the mass of the community." And the character of the Republic's soldiers, too, recalls his account of this republican army of Cromwell's. "The Royalists themselves confessed that, in every department of honest industry, the discarded warriors prospered beyond other men, that none was charged with any theft or robbery, that none was heard to ask for alms, and that if a baker, a mason, or a waggoner attracted notice by his diligence and sobriety, he was in all probability one of Oliver's old soldiers." This was when the parent land was free from hereditary rulers and under the invigorating influence of republican institutions. Thus do citizens fight on one side of the Atlantic as on the other, and, grander far, thus return to the pursuits of peace. Not for throne, for king, or for privileged class, but for *Country*, for a country which gives to the humblest every privilege accorded to the greatest. One says instinctively,

> Where's the coward that would not dare
> To fight for such a land!

Britons as republicans were of course invincible. What chance in the struggle has a royalist who cries, "My king!" against the citizen whose patriotic ardor glows as he whispers, "My country!" The "God save the King" of the monarchist grows faint before the nobler strain of the republican,

> God bless our native land!

Our king, poor trifler, may be beneath consideration. Our country is ever sure of our love. There be words to conjure and work miracles with, and "our country" is of these. Others, having ceased to be divine, have become ridiculous, and "king" and "throne" are of these.

The twenty thousand Englishmen who met in Bingley Hall, Birmingham, to honor the sturdiest Englishman of all, John Bright, dispersed not with the paltry and puerile "God save the Queen," but with these glorious words sung to the same tune:

> God bless our native land,
> May heaven's protecting hand
>   Still guard her shore;
> May peace her fame extend,
> Foe be transformed to friend,
> And Britain's power depend
>   On war no more.

Worthy this of England, blessed mother of nations which now are, and of others yet to be. To hear it was worth the voyage across the Atlantic. Never crept the thrill of triumph more wildly through my frame than when I lifted up my voice and sang with the exulting mass the coming national hymn which is to live and vibrate round the world when Royal families are as extinct as dodos. God speed the day! A royal family is an insult to every other family in the land. I found no trace of them at Birmingham.

The Republic wants neither standing army nor navy. In this lies her chief glory and her strength. Resting securely upon the love and devotion of all her sons, she can, Cadmus-like, raise from the soil vast armed hosts who fight only in her defence, and who, unlike the seed of the dragon, return to the avocations of peace when danger to the Republic is past. The American citizen who will not fight for his country if attacked is unworthy the name, and the American citizen who could be induced to engage in aggressive warfare is equally so. Happily "there is no such man."

Of more importance even than commercial or military strength is the Republic's commanding position among nations in intellectual activity; for she excels in the number of schools and colleges, in the number and extent of her libraries, and in the number of newspapers and other periodicals published.

In the application of science to social and industrial uses, she is far in advance of other nations. Many of the most important practical inventions which have contributed to the progress of the world during the past century originated with Americans. No other people have devised so many labor-saving machines and appliances. The first commercially successful steamboat navigated the Hudson, and the first steamship to cross the Atlantic sailed under the American flag from an American port. America gave to the world the cotton gin, and the first practical mowing, reaping, and sewing machines. In the most spiritual, most ethereal of all departments in which man has produced great triumphs, viz., electricity, the position of the American is specially noteworthy. He may be said almost to have made this province his own, for, beginning with Franklin's discovery of the identity of lightning and electricity, it was an American who devised the best and most widely used system of telegraphy, and an American who boldly undertook to bind together the old and the new land with electric chains. In the use of electricity for illuminating purposes America maintains her position as first wherever this subtle agent is invoked. The recent addition to the world's means of communication, the telephone, is also to be credited to the new land.

Into the distant future of this giant nation we need not seek to peer; but if we cast a glance forward, as we have done backward, for only fifty years, and assume that in that short interval no serious change will occur, the astounding fact startles us that in 1935, fifty years from now, when many in manhood will still be living, one hundred and eighty millions of English-speaking republicans will exist under one flag and possess more than two hundred and fifty thousand millions of dollars, or fifty thousand millions sterling of national wealth. Eighty years ago the whole of America and Europe did not contain so many people; and, if Europe and America continue their normal growth, it will be little more than another eighty years from now ere the Republic may boast as many loyal citizens as all the rulers of Europe combined, for before the year 1980 Europe and America will each have a population of about six hundred millions.

The causes which have led to the rapid growth and aggrandizement of this latest addition to the family of nations constitute one of the most interesting problems in the social history of mankind. What has brought about such stupendous results—so unparalleled a development of a nation within so brief a period! The most important factors in this problem are three: the ethnic character of the people, the topographical and climatic conditions under which they developed, and the influence of political institutions founded upon the equality of the citizen.

Certain writers in the past have maintained that the ethnic type of a people has less influence upon its growth as a nation than the conditions of life under which it is developing. The modern ethnologist knows better. We have only to imagine what America would be today if she had fallen, in the beginning, into the hands of any other people than the colonizing British, to see how vitally important is this question of race. America was indeed fortunate in the seed planted upon her soil. With the exception of a few Dutch and French it was wholly British; and, as will be shown in the next chapter, the American of today remains true to this noble strain and is four-fifths British. The special aptitude of this race for colonization, its vigor and enterprise, and its capacity for governing, although brilliantly manifested in all parts of the world, have never been shown to such advantage as in America. Freed here from the pressure of feudal institutions no longer fitted to their present development, and freed also from the dominion of the upper classes, which have kept the people at home from effective management of affairs and sacrificed the nation's interest for their own, as is the nature of classes, these masses of the lower ranks of Britons, called upon to found a new state, have proved themselves possessors of a positive genius for political administration.

The second, and perhaps equally important factor in the problem of the rapid advancement of this branch of the British race, is the superiority of the conditions under which it has developed. The home which has fallen to its lot, a domain more magnificent than has cradled any other race in the history of the world, presents no obstructions to unity—to the thorough amalgamation of its dwellers, North, South, East, and West, into one homogeneous mass—for the conformation of the American continent differs in important respects from that of every other great division of the globe. In Europe the Alps occupy a central position, forming on each side watersheds of rivers which flow into opposite seas. In Asia the Himalaya, the Hindu Kush, and the Altai Mountains divide the continent, rolling from their sides many great rivers which pour their floods into widely separated oceans. But in North America the mountains rise up on each coast, and from them the land slopes gradually into great central plains, forming an immense basin where the rivers flow together in one valley, offering to commerce many thousand miles of navigable streams. The map thus proclaims the unity of North America, for in this great central basin, three million square miles in extent, free from impassable rivers or mountain barriers great enough to hinder free intercourse, political integration is a necessity and consolidation a certainty.

Herbert Spencer has illustrated by numerous examples the principle that "mountain-haunting peoples and peoples living in deserts and marshes are difficult to consolidate, while peoples penned in by barriers are consolidated with facility." Nations so separated, moreover, regard those beyond the barrier as natural enemies; and in Europe the ambition and selfishness of ruling dynasties have helped to make this belief the political creed of the people. Cowper has seized upon this idea in the well-known lines:

> Mountains interposed
> Make enemies of nations, who had else
> Like kindred drops been mingled into one.

Europe has thus been kept in a state of perpetual war or of preparation for war among some of its several divisions, entailing much misery and loss of life as well as of material wealth, and retarding civilization.

Besides the rivers, the great lakes of America, estimated to contain one-third of all the fresh water in the world, are another important element in aid of consolidation. A ship sailing from any part of the world may discharge its cargo at Chicago in the northwest, a thousand miles inland. The Mississippi and its tributaries traverse the great western basin, a million and a quarter square miles in extent, and furnish an internal navigable system of twenty thousand miles. A steamer starting from Pittsburgh in Pennsylvania, four hundred and fifty miles inland from New York, and two thousand from the mouth of the Mississippi, passing through these water highways, and returning to its starting place at that smoky metropolis of iron and steel, will sail a distance much greater than round the world. Nor will it in all its course be stopped by any government official, or be taxed by any tariff. The flag it carries will ensure free passage for ship and cargo, unimpeded by any fiscal charge whatever, for the whole continent enjoys the blessings of absolute freedom of intercourse among its citizens. In estimating the influences which promote the consolidation of the people much weight must be given to this cause. Fifty-six millions of people, occupying an area which includes climatic differences so great that everything necessary for the wants of man can be readily produced, exchange their products without inspection or charge. Truly here is the most magnificent exhibition of free trade which the world has ever seen. It would be difficult to set bounds to the beneficial effects of the wise provision of the national Constitution which guarantees to every member of the vast confederacy the blessings of unrestricted commercial intercourse.

Not only from an economical point of view, but from the higher standpoint of its bearing upon the unity and brotherhood of the people, this unrestricted freedom of trade must rank as one of the most potent agencies for the preservation of the Union. Were each of the thirty-eight States of the American continent to tax the products of the others we should soon see the dissolution of the great Republic into thirty-eight warring factions. If any one doubts that free trade carries peace in its train let him study the internal free trade system of America.

The railway system, although an artificial creation, must rank as even more important than the great natural waterways, in its influence upon the unification of the people. A hundred and thirty thousand miles of railways—more than in the whole of Europe—traverse the country in all directions, and bind the nation together with bonds of steel. From the Atlantic to the Pacific, three thousand miles apart, or from New York to New Orleans, the traveller passes without change in the same moving hotel. In it he is fed and lodged, and has every want supplied.

Seven hundred and sixty thousand miles of telegraph, enough to put thirty girdles round the earth—the very nerves of the Republic—quiver night and day with social and commercial messages. The college-bred youth of Massachusetts is not separated from the paternal home and its associations when on his ranche in Colorado; nor is the Eastern young lady removed from the home influences of New York when she marries the Southern planter and goes forth to create a similar home in Texas. Constant communication between the families and frequent visits animate them with kindred ideas and keep them united. They carry the Stars and Stripes with them wherever they settle, and preserve the unity of the nation.

In the course of her short career the Republic has had to face and overcome two sources of great danger, either of which might have overtaxed the wisdom and courage of any political fabric, resting upon a less wide and indestructible base than the perfect equality of the citizen. The infant state was left with the viper, human slavery, gnawing at its vitals, and it grew and strengthened with the growth and strength of the Republic until sufficiently powerful to threaten its very life. Coiled round and into every joint and part of the body politic and sucking away the moral strength of the nation, the slave power, in an effort to extend its baneful influence, fortunately committed one morning what is, in the soul of every American, the one unpardonable sin. It fired upon the flag. Blessed shot! for it was required to bring home to the national conscience the knowledge that not only were freedom and slavery antagonistic social forces which never could be joined, but that slavery as a political institution was inconsistent with the republican idea. The shot fired that bright, sunny morning at the ensign, floating like a thing of joy over the ramparts of Fort Sumter, left the patriot no recourse. A thrill passed through the Free States, and once again for unity, as before for independence, men of all parties pledged their lives, their fortunes, and their sacred honour to uphold the Republic.

How nobly that pledge was redeemed is known to the world. Not only until every slave was free, but not until every slave was a citizen, with equal voice in the State, was the righteous sword of the Republic sheathed.

The second source of danger lay in the millions of foreigners who came from all lands to the hospitable shores of the nation, many of them ignorant of the English language, and all unaccustomed to the exercise of political duties. If so great a number stood aloof from the national life and formed circles of their own, or if they sought America for a period only, to earn money with which to return to their original homes, the injury to the State must inevitably be serious.

The generosity, shall I not say the incredible generosity, with which the

Republic has dealt with these people met its reward. They are won to her side by being offered for their *subject*ship the boon of citizenship. For denial of equal privileges at home, the new land meets them with perfect equality, saying, be not only with us, but be of us. They reach the shores of the Republic *subjects* (insulting word), and she makes them citizens; serfs, and she makes them men, and their children she takes gently by the hand and leads to the public schools which she has founded for her own children, and gives them, without money and without price, a good primary education as the most precious gift which she has, even in her bountiful hand, to bestow upon human beings. This is Democracy's "gift of welcome" to the new comer. The poor immigrant cannot help growing up passionately fond of his new home and, alas, with many bitter thoughts of the old land which has defrauded him of the rights of man, and thus the threatened danger is averted — the homogeneity of the people secured.

The unity of the American people is further powerfully promoted by the foundations upon which the political structure rests, the equality of the citizen. There is not one shred of privilege to be met with anywhere in all the laws. One man's right is every man's right. The flag is the guarantor and symbol of equality. The people are not emasculated by being made to feel that their own country decrees their inferiority, and holds them unworthy of privileges accorded to others. No ranks, no titles, no hereditary dignities, and therefore no classes. Suffrage is universal, and votes are of equal weight. Representatives are paid, and political life and usefulness thereby thrown open to all. Thus there is brought about a community of interests and aims which a Briton, accustomed to monarchical and aristocratic institutions, dividing the people into classes with separate interests, aims, thoughts, and feelings, can only with difficulty understand.

The free common school system of the land is probably, after all, the greatest single power in the unifying process which is producing the new American race. Through the crucible of a good common English education, furnished free by the State, pass the various racial elements — children of Irishmen, Germans, Italians, Spaniards, and Swedes, side by side with the native American, all to be fused into one, in language, in thought, in feeling, and in patriotism. The Irish boy loses his brogue, and the German child learns English. The sympathies suited to the feudal systems of Europe, which they inherit from their fathers, pass off as dross, leaving behind the pure gold of the only noble political creed: "All men are created free and equal." Taught now to live and work for the common weal, and not for the maintenance of a royal family or an overbearing aristocracy, not for the continuance of a social system which ranks them beneath an arrogant class of drones, children of Russian and German serfs, of Irish evicted tenants, Scotch crofters, and other victims of feudal tyranny, are transmuted into republican Americans, and are made one in love for a country which provides equal rights and privileges for all her children. There is no class so intensely patriotic, so wildly devoted to the Republic as the naturalized citizen and his child, for little does the native-born citizen know of the value of rights which have never been denied. Only the man born abroad, like myself, under institutions which insult him at his birth, can know the full meaning of Republicanism.

It follows, from the prevailing system of free education, that the Americans are a reading people. Arising out of this fact we find another powerful influence promoting unity of sentiment and purpose among the millions of the Republic — the influence of the American press. Eight thousand newspapers scattered throughout the land receive simultaneous reports. Everybody in America reads the same news the same morning, and discusses the same questions. The man of San Francisco is thus brought as near to a common centre with his fellow-citizen of St. Paul, New Orleans or New York, as is the man of London with him of Birmingham, Manchester, Liverpool, or Edinburgh, and infinitely nearer than the man of Belfast or Dublin. The bullet of the lunatic which killed President Garfield, could it have traveled so far, would have been outstripped by the lightning messengers which carried the sad news to the most distant hamlet upon the continent. The blow struck in the afternoon found a nation of fifty-six millions bowed with grief ere sunset. So, too, the quiet intimation conveyed one evening by Secretary Seward to the Minister of France, that he thought Mexico was a very healthy country for the French to migrate from, called forth at every breakfast table the next morning the emphatic response — "I rather guess that's so!" Fortunately, the Emperor was of the same opinion.

It is these causes which render possible the growth of a great homogeneous nation, alike in race, language, literature, interest, patriotism — an empire of such overwhelming power and proportions as to require neither army nor navy to ensure its safety, and a people so educated and advanced as to value the victories of peace.

The student of American affairs today sees no influences at work save those which make for closer and closer union. The Republic has solved the problem of governing large areas by adopting the federal, or home-rule system, and has proved to the world that the freest self-government of the parts produces the strongest government of the whole.

19
Capitalism:
"The Bugaboo of Trusts"

Andrew Carnegie had sought to prove in Triumphant Democracy *that the constitution written in Philadelphia in 1787 had been perfect in form and had been administered for the past century in so admirable a fashion as to produce the great material prosperity and progress the United States enjoyed in 1886. There had been, to be sure, a temporary and tragic breakdown in that system in 1861, but the Unions had been restored by force of arms, supported by the industries of the North. Now, twenty years after Appomattox, the United States had reached "the high noon" of industrial and agricultural preeminence in the western world.*

The fact that there were millions of his fellow Americans who did not feel they were standing in the warm prosperity of the sun at its zenith must have been apparent to Carnegie, however, even as he was boasting of his beloved Republic's "thundering past the old nations of the earth with the rush of an express." Since the 1870s, particularly among the farmers of the Midwest and South, there had been a growing criticism of the engineers who were driving this express train of rapid industrialization. These attacks had been manifested in the Granger movement and by a succession of third parties directed against monopolies. So far this activity had been kept on the fringe of American politics, and what electoral success these would-be levelers scored were only on the state level. Pressure was becoming ever more intense, however, for national legislation that would break up or at least restrict the existing monopolies. Here Carnegie unhappily saw a shadow, and it was being cast by that very system which he had so extravagantly extolled as being perfect. In a democracy, where in theory every man's vote was the equal of every other man's, the shadow could not be dispelled by mere fiat. The bright light of education was required.

Carnegie assumed for himself the responsibility of educating the public to a realization that its fear of trusts was groundless. In February 1889, he published in the North American Review *his celebrated article, "The Bugaboo of Trusts." As this journal had a circulation largely limited to the better educated and well-to-do, Carnegie at* his own expense produced thousands of reprints in pamphlet form which were distributed gratis to members of Congress and state legislatures and to political conventions throughout the nation.

In this article, Carnegie patiently explains that trusts are not the final triumph of a few evilly aggressive entrepreneurs, but rather they "are the products of weakness." Their triumph over competitors can only be temporary, for monopolies must automatically create a revived competition and they thus "write the charter of their own defeat." The only regulation needed is the immutable natural law of free competition, and the only ultimate victors are the consumers.

With this article hailing the efficacy of the free enterprise system, Carnegie may have succeeded in reassuring himself and his fellow capitalists. He was less successful in convincing the general public that trusts were a mere bugaboo of the imagination. The following year, Congress passed the Sherman Anti-Trust Act, hoping to quiet an angry public by giving free competition a helping hand in driving the bugaboo into oblivion.

We must all have our toys; the child his rattle, the adult his hobby, the man of pleasure the fashion, the man of art his Master; and mankind in its various divisions requires a change of toys at short intervals. The same rule holds good in the business world. We have had our age of "consolidations" and "watered stocks." Not long ago everything was a "syndicate"; the word is already becoming obsolete and the fashion is for "Trusts," which will in turn no doubt give place to some new panacea, that is in turn to be displaced by another, and so on without end. The great laws of the economic world, like all laws affecting society, being the genuine outgrowth of human nature, alone remain unchanged through all these changes. Whenever consolidations, or watered stocks, or syndicates, or Trusts endeavor to circumvent these, it always has been found that after the collision there is nothing left of the panaceas, while the great laws continue to grind out their irresistible consequences as before.

It is worthwhile to inquire into the appearance and growth of Trusts and learn what environments produce them. Their genesis is as follows: a demand exists for a certain article, beyond the capacity of existing works to supply it. Prices are high, and profits tempting. Every manufacturer of that article immediately proceeds to enlarge his works and increase their producing power.

In addition to this the unusual profits attract the attention of his principal managers or those who are interested to a greater or less degree in the factory. These communicate the knowledge of the prosperity of the works to others. New partnerships are formed, and new works are erected, and before long the demand for the article is fully satisfied, and prices do not advance. In a short time the supply becomes greater than the demand, there are a few tons or yards more in the market for sale than required, and prices begin to fall. They continue falling until the article is sold at cost to the less favorably situated or less ably managed factory; and even until the best managed and best equipped factory is not able to produce the article at the prices at which it can be sold. Political economy says that here the trouble will end. Goods will not be produced at less than cost. This was true when Adam Smith wrote, but it is not quite true today. When an article was produced by a small manufacturer, employing, probably at his own home, two or three journeymen and an apprentice or two, it was an easy matter for him to limit or even to stop production. As manufacturing is carried on today, in enormous establishments with five or ten millions of dollars of capital invested, and with thousands of workers, it costs the manufacturer much less to run at a loss per ton or per yard than to check his production. Stoppage would be serious indeed. The condition of cheap manufacture is running full. Twenty sources of expense are *fixed charges*, many of which stoppage would only increase. Therefore the article is produced for months, and in some cases that I have known for years, not only without profit or without interest upon capital, but to the impairment of the capital invested. Manufacturers have balanced their books year after year only to find their capital reduced at each successive balance. While continuing to produce may be costly, the manufacturer knows too well that stoppage would be ruin. His brother manufacturers are of course in the same situation. They see the savings of many years, as well perhaps as the capital they have succeeded in borrowing, becoming less and less, with no hope of a change in the situation. It is in soil thus prepared that anything promising relief is gladly welcomed. The manufacturers are in the position of patients that have tried in vain every doctor of the regular school for years, and are now liable to become the victims of any quack that appears. Combinations—syndicates—trusts—they are willing to try anything. A meeting is called, and in the presence of immediate danger they decide to take united action and form a trust. Each factory is rated as worth a certain amount. Officers are chosen, and through these the entire product of the article in question is to be distributed to the public, at remunerative prices.

Such is the genesis of "Trusts" in manufactured articles. In transportation the situation, while practically the same, differs in some particulars. Many small railway lines are built under separate charters. A genius in affairs sees that the eight or ten separate organizations, with as many different ideas of management, equipment, etc., are as useless as were the two hundred and fifty petty kings in Germany, and, Bismarck-like, he sweeps them out of existence, creates a great through line, doubles the securities or stock, the interest upon which is paid out of the saving effected by consolidation, and all is highly satisfactory, as in the case of the New York Central. Or a line is built and managed with such sagacity as distinguishes the Pennsylvania Railroad, and it succeeds in developing the resources of the State so extensively that upon a line of three hundred and fifty miles between Pittsburgh and Philadelphia it nets about thirteen millions of dollars per annum. Twelve millions of dollars of this it shows upon its books. From one to two millions extra are expended in making one of the best lines in the world out of a road which was originally designed as a horse-railroad. We do not call our railroad combinations Trusts, but they are substantially such, since they aim at raising and maintaining transportation rates in certain districts. They are "combinations" or "systems" which aim at monopolies within these districts.

During the recent Presidential campaign it suited the purpose of one of the parties to connect Trusts with the doctrine of protection. But Trusts are confined to no country, and are not in any way dependent upon fiscal regulations. The greatest Trust of all just now is the Copper Turst, which is French, and has its headquarters in Paris. The Salt Trust is English, with its headquarters in London. The Wire-rod Trust is German. The only Steel-rail Trust that ever existed was an international one which embraced all the works in Europe. Trusts, either in transportation or manufacturers, are the products of human weakness, and this weakness is co-extensive with the race.

There is one huge combination classed with Trusts which is so exceptional in its origin and history that it deserves a separate paragraph. I refer to the Standard Oil Company. So favorable an opportunity to control a product perhaps never arose as in the case of petroleum. At an early stage a few of the ablest business men that the world has ever seen realized the importance of the discovery, and invested largely in the purchase of property connected with it. The success of the petroleum business was phenomenal, and so was the success of these people. The profits they made, and, no doubt, as much capital as they could borrow, were fearlessly reinvested, and they soon became the principal owners, and finally, substantially the only owners of the territory which contained this great source of wealth. The Standard Oil Company would long ago have gone to pieces had it not been managed, upon the whole, in harmony with the laws which control business. It is generally admitted that the prices of oil to the consumer are as low today, and many think that they are even lower, than could have been attained had the business not been grouped and managed as one vast concern in the broad spirit for which the Standard Oil managers are famous. They are in the position somewhat of the Colemans, of Pennsylvania, who possess the chief source of the ore supply in the East. They own the Cornwall deposit of ore as the Standard Oil Company owns the source of the oil deposit. But as the company has continually to deal with the finding of oil in other localities, the price of its existence and success is the continuance of that exceptional ability in its councils and management displayed by its founders. Threatened opposition arises every now and then, and the chances are greatly in favor of the Standard Oil Company losing its practical monopoly, and going the way of all huge combinations. It is a hundred to one whether it will survive when the present men at the head retire; or perhaps I should say when the present man retires, for wonderful organizations imply a genius at the head, a commander-in-chief, with exceptionally able corps commanders no doubt, but still a Grant at the head. To those who quote the Standard Oil Company as an evidence that Trusts or combinations can be permanently successful, I say, wait and see. I have spoken thus freely of that company, because I am ignorant of its management, profits, and modes of action. I view it from the outside, as a student of political economy only, and as such have endeavored to apply to it the principles which I know *will* have their way, no matter how formidable the attempt made to defeat their operations.

We have given the genesis of trusts and combinations in their several forms. The question is, do they menace the permanent interest of the nation? Are they a source of serious danger? Or are they to prove, as many other similar forms have proved, mere passing phases of unrest and transition? To answer this question let us follow the operation of the manufacturing trust which we have in imagination created, salt or sugar, nails, beans, or lead or copper; it is all the same. The sugar refiners, let us say, have formed a Trust after competing one with another through years of disastrous business, and all the sugar manufactured in the country in existing factories is sold through one channel at advanced prices. Profits begin to grow. Dividends are paid, and those who before saw their property vanishing before their eyes are now made happy. The dividends from that part of a man's capital invested in the sugar business yield him profit far above the capital he has invested in various other affairs. The prices of sugar are such that the capital invested in a new factory would yield enormously. He is perhaps bound not to enlarge his factory or to enter into a new factory, but his relatives and acquaintances soon discover the fresh opportunity for gain. He can advise them to push the completion of a small factory, which, of course, must be taken into the Trust. Or, even if he does not give his friends this intimation, capital is always upon the alert, especially when it is bruited about that a Trust has been formed, as in the case of sugar, and immediately new sugar manufactories spring up, as if by magic. The more successful the Trust, the surer these off-shoots are to sprout. Every victory is a defeat. Every factory that the Trust buys is the sure creator of another, and so on *ad infinitum*, until the bubble bursts. The sugar refiners have tried to get more from capital in a special case than capital yields in general. They have endeavored to raise a part of the ocean of capital above the level of the surrounding waters, and over their bulwarks the floods have burst, and capital, like water, has again found its level. It is true that to regain this level a longer or a shorter period may be required, during which the article affected may be sold to the consumer in limited quantities at a higher rate than before existed. But for this the consumer is amply recompensed in the years that follow, during which the struggle detween the discordant and competitive factories becomes severer than it ever was before, and lasts till the great law of the survival of the fittest vindicates itself. Those factories and managers that can produce to the best advantage eventually close the less competent. Capital wisely managed yields its legitimate profit. After a time the growth of demand enables capital to receive an unusual profit. This in turn attracts fresh capital to the manufacture, and we have a renewal of the old struggle, the consumer reaping the benefit.

Such is the law, such has been the law, and such promises to be the law for the future; for, so far, no device has yet been devised that has permanently thwarted its operation. Given freedom of competition, and all combinations or trusts that attempt to exact from the consumer more than a legitimate return upon capital and services, write the charter of their own defeat. We have many proofs that this great law does not sleep, and that it will not be suppressed. Some time ago, as I have stated, the steel rail manufacturers of Europe formed a trust and advanced the price of rails to such an extent that American manufacturers were able for the first, and perhaps for the last time, to export steel rails to Canada in competition with the European. But the misunderstandings and quarrels, inseparable from these attempted unions of competitors, soon broke the Trust. With vindictive feelings, added to what was before business rivalry, the struggle was renewed, and the steel rail industry of Europe has never recovered. It was found that the advance in prices had only galvanized into life concerns which never should have attempted to manufacture rails; and so that Trust died a natural death.

During the great depression which existed for several years in this country in the steel rail trade many anxious meetings were held under circumstances described in the genesis of Trusts, and it was resolved that the plan of restricting production should be tried. Fortunately reaction soon came. A demand for rails set in before the plan went into operation, and, as a matter of fact, no restriction of product was ever attempted, and the steel rail industry was thus saved from a great error.

We have recently seen the lead industry of this country shattered and its chief owners bankrupted. The newspapers a few weeks ago were filled with accounts of the convention of the growers of cattle in St. Louis, resolved to break down the combination of slaughterers and shippers in Chicago and Kansas City. No business was poorer in this country for many years than the manufacture of nails. It was overdone. To remedy this the manufacturers did not form a Trust so far as the sale of product was concerned, but they restricted production. A certain percentage of their machines were kept idle. This percentage was increased from time to time, and only the quantity made that the market would take at a certain price. But the result was that there were soon more machines in America for the manufacture of iron nails added to the works than the demand for nails will require for many years to come, and this combination of nail manufacturers went the way of all Trusts, and left the business in a worse plight than it was in before.

The Sugar Trust has already a noted competitor at its heels. The Copper Trust is in danger. All stand prepared to attack a "trust" or "combine" if it proves itself worth attacking; in other words, if it succeeds in raising its profits above the natural level of profits throughout the country it is subject to competition from every quarter, and must finally break down. It is unnecessary to devote much attention to the numerous Trusts in minor articles which one reads of, a new one appearing every few days and others passing out of existence, because they are all subject to the great law. The newspapers charge that Trusts exist or have existed in wall paper, shoe laces, lumber, coal, coke, brick, screw, rope, glass, schoolbooks, insurance and hardware, and twenty more articles; but the fitting epitaph for these ephemeral creations is

> If I was so soon to be done for,
> I wonder what I was begun for!

We may exclaim with Macbeth, as he watched the shadowy descendants of Banquo filing past, "What, will the line stretch out to the crack of doom?" But as with Banquo's procession, so with Trusts, it is comforting to remember that as one approaches another disappears. They come like shadows, and so depart.

So much for Trusts in the manufacturing department. Let us now examine the railways, whose "pools" and "combinations" and "differentials" alarm some people. In all their various forms, these are the efforts of capital to protect itself from the play of economic forces, centered in free competition. In most cases the stocks of railways have been watered. Calculated upon the real capital invested the dividends of railway lines have been unusual, and much above the return which capital generally has yielded in other forms of investment. The entire capital stock of railways in the West as a rule has cost little or nothing, the proceeds of the bonds issued having been sufficient to build them. The efforts of railway managers today are therefore directed to obtain a return upon more capital than would be required to duplicate their respective properties. Their combinations and agreements of various kinds, which come to naught a few months after they are solemnly entered into, are evidences of this attempt. But, just as enormous profits on capital, received from the manufacture of any article, are sure to attract additional capital into the production of the article, so, in like manner, the unusual success of these railroads attracts new capital into their territory. New York Central paying dividends upon its eighty percent stock dividend culminates in the West Shore. The Pennsylvania Railroad, earning, as I have said, something like thirteen millions per annum upon its line in Pennsylvania, has its South Pennsylvania. One line between Chicago and Milwaukee being greatly profitable, fortunately brought into existence a parallel road. The two being unusually profitable, fortunately resulted in a third. There was one line between these points, and now there are six; and should the six combine tomorrow and exact from the public one percent more return upon capital than the average return, there would soon be seven, and very properly so.

This proves once more that there is no possibility of evading the great law, provided capital is free to embark in competing lines. In Great Britain and throughout Europe generally a different policy has been pursued in regard to railways from that of the free-to-all policy which we have followed. The railways and other transportation routes of Great Britain, in order to get permission to build, have cost nearly as much per mile as our cheapest Western lines have cost to build. Manchester, for instance, has recently decided to construct a canal, thirty miles long, to Liverpool, and the expense incurred in obtaining permission from Parliament to embark capital in this enterprise has cost nearly half a million of dollars up to this date. The Government, through a committee of Parliament, determines whether a proposed line is actually needed, and to settle this point everybody connected with existing transportation facilities in the neighborhood appears before the committee to prove that it is not needed, while the promoters of the scheme are at enormous expense to prove by hundreds of experts that it is. The empirical decision of the committee of the House of Commons on this question is not to be compared with the unerring decision of the capitalists interested. They know much better than any committee of the Legislature are likely to know whether the work in question will pay a fair dividend, and this is the best proof that it is required. The result of the American policy is seen in the fact that notwithstanding all the attempts upon the part of our railways to thwart the economic laws, nevertheless, the American people enjoy the cheapest transportation in the world. The railway rates upon freight in Europe, compared with those in America, show startling contrasts. The cost of freightage on English lines is upon the average more than double the American charge, and in many cases which I have examined it is three times as great. In not a few cases the British charge is far beyond three times the American.

A friend bought a cargo of grain at Leith, which had paid one dollar per ton freight from New York; it cost him ninety-six cents per ton to transport it thirty-five miles inland. Another purchased six hundred tons charcoal pig-iron upon Lake Superior, which cost four dollars per ton freight to Liverpool; he paid $2.87 per ton to carry it eighty miles inland by rail to his mills. For this amount our trunk lines carry rails five hundred and sixty miles, as against eighty miles in Britain. If Europe enjoyed our advantages of free competition in its transportation system, the development of its resources would be surprising, even at this late day in its history. There is, in my opinion, only cause for hearty congratulation as regards our railway policy. Its evils are trifling; its advantages over all other systems in the world enormous.

The people of America can smile at the efforts of all her railway magnates and of all her manufacturers to defeat the economic laws by Trusts or combinations, or pools, or "differentials," or anything of like character. Only let them hold firmly to the doctrine of free competition. Keep the field open. Freedom for all to engage in railroad building when and where capital desires, subject to conditions open to all. Freedom for all to engage in any branch of manufacturing under like conditions.

There can be no permanent extortion of profit beyond the average return from capital, nor any monopoly, either in transportation or manufacturing. Any attempt to maintain either must end in failure, and failure ultimately disastrous just in proportion to the temporary success of the foolish effort. It is simply ridiculous for a party of men to meet in a room and attempt by passing resolutions to change the great laws which govern human affairs in the business world, and this, whether they be railway presidents, bankers or manufacturers.

The fashion of trusts has but a short season longer to run, and then some other equally vain device may be expected to appear when the next period of depression arrives; but there is not the slightest danger that serious injury can result to the sound principles of business from any or all of these movements. The only people who have reason to fear Trusts are those foolish enough to enter into them. The Consumer and the Transporter, not the Manufacturer and the Railway owner, are to reap the harvest.

Even since the foregoing was written, a new form has appeared on the stage in the shape of "The President's Agreement—an agreement among gentlemen," in which the parties engage to control, strangle and restrict the future development of our magnificent railway system under the laws of natural growth, at a time when the country requires this development as much as it ever did. These gentlemen are not going to engage in building lines which will give the public the benefit of healthy competition, or permit such to be built hereafter. It is safe to say that very soon this toy will be discarded, like its predecessors, for another, and that the very men apparently most pleased with this new rattle will then regard it with the greatest contempt, and go forward in the good work, as hitherto, developing the railway system wherever and whenever they think they see a fair chance for profit. Whenever existing railways exact from the public more than a fair return upon the actual capital invested, or upon the capital which would be required to duplicate existing lines, competing lines will be built—fortunately for the interests of the country—which is much more concerned in getting cheap transportation than it is in insuring dividends for capitalists; and whenever a percentage is to be obtained by the negotiation of railway securities, bankers will be found—also, fortunately for the bests interests of the country—who will gladly find a market for them without stopping to inquire whether monopolies are to be overthrown by the new lines.

It is not in the power of man to exact for more than a brief season, and a very brief season indeed, unusual profit upon actual capital invested either in Transportation or Manufacture, so long as all are free to compete, and this freedom, it may safely be asserted, the American people are not likely to restrict.

20
Populism: "The A B C of Money"

During the 1880s, Andrew Carnegie had been so preoccupied with trying to bring democratic Chartist reform to Great Britain by his speeches and writings and through the medium of a chain of newspapers he had purchased in northern England that he had given little attention to American politics. He had dutifully contributed to the Republican party coffers, but a political system which he regarded as perfect did not need his guidance. Moreover, for a man of his active, restless temperament, the American political scene was dull—perfect but dull.

All this was to change abruptly in the 1890s with the rise of Populism. The Populist demand for the free, unlimited coinage of silver was the clanging siren of danger that would arouse Carnegie to political action on the home front. Since the days of the Greenback craze in the early 1870s, Carnegie had been an outspoken opponent of cheap currency. The Greenbackers, however, had been mild in their demands for an inflated currency compared to the silverites. Carnegie was particularly dismayed that it should be his own party that had opened the door to runaway inflation by passing the Sherman Silver Purchase Act in 1890 which required the U.S. Treasury to purchase 4,500,000 ounces of silver monthly. The Republican administration had done this in order to woo the newly admitted silver states of the West and to win their votes in Congress for a high protective tariff. Far better, in Carnegie's opinion, to have free trade than to accept free, unlimited coinage of silver. With a snort of anger, Carnegie sprang into action. He dashed off a long article entitled "The A B C of Money," which the North American Review *eagerly accepted and published in June 1891. With this article, Carnegie sought to give the American people a basic elementary course in economics by presenting a history of money which would point up the absurdity of bimetallism. Carnegie directed his arguments to every occupational group (except of course the silver-mine owners) and every social class in the country. As the title indicates, Carnegie spelled out for the illiterates in economics the monetary alphabet, preparatory to the establishment of his thesis, which was equally simplistic. Bimetallism was a delusion. No nation could keep gold and silver in balance in order* to maintain a bimetallic standard. The cheap, over-evaluated metal (silver) will always drive the under-evaluated, more valuable metal (gold) out of circulation. Silver will triumph, the dollar will be debased, and inflation will bring economic ruin to all.

Carnegie had hoped for "a vast audience" to attend his school in economics, but his article received little notice when it first appeared. It was Coin's Financial School, by the Populist propagandist, W. H. Harvey, that got the big enrollment from those suffering from the depression of 1893, particularly the farmers of the South and West, who blamed their plight on the lack of money in circulation. Only after the Populists captured the Democratic party at the national convention in Chicago in 1896 and found a powerful new voice in William Jennings Bryan was Carnegie's primer on fiscal conservatism resurrected from oblivion by the frightened Republican party stalwarts. They made it one of the most significant and certainly the most widely read article Carnegie ever wrote.

Mark Hanna, McKinley's campaign manager, wrote to Carnegie in the final days of the campaign: "It required but a moment for us to see that the leaflet was admirably calculated to make the money issue of this campaign clear to the simplest mind. We therefore printed and have circulated more than 5,000,000 copies of this leaflet, and the demand for it was as great as for that of any document we have issued. This of itself is evidence of its worth, but the scores of letters we have received commending the paper attest its value, and the powerful influence of good we feel it has exerted. . . . I want, in the name of and on behalf of the National Republican Committee, to thank you for your work, and assure you that we appreciate the service you have rendered the party and the country" (17 October 1896, Carnegie Papers, Library of Congress, vol. 39).

Carnegie took immense pride in this acknowledgment of his service to the Grand Old Party. He had given many thousands of dollars to help finance the Republican cause, but it was especially sweet for him to be told that his pen had contributed even more than his checkbook to effecting the defeat of Populism and its leader, whom Carnegie called "that light-headed, blathering demagogue" from Nebraska.

I suppose everyone who has spoken to or written for the public has wished at times that everybody would drop everything and just listen to him for a few minutes. I feel so this morning, for I believe that a grave injury threatens the people and the progress of our country simply because the masses — the farmers and the wage-earners — do not understand the question of money.

I wish therefore to explain "money" in so simple a way that all can understand it.

Perhaps someone in the vast audience which I have imagined I am about to hold spellbound cries out: "Who are you—a gold-bug, a millionnaire, an iron-baron, a beneficiary of the McKinley Bill?" Before beginning my address, let me therefore reply to that imaginary gentleman that I have not seen a thousand dollars in gold for many a year. So far as the McKinley Bill is concerned, I am perhaps the one man in the United States who has the best right to complain under it, for it has cut and slashed the duties upon iron and steel, reducing them 20, 25, and 30 percent; and if it will recommend me to my supposed interrupter, I beg to inform him that I do not greatly disapprove of these reductions, that as an American manufacturer I intend to struggle still against the foreigner for the home market, even with the lower duties fixed upon our product by that bill, and that I am not in favour of protection beyond the point necessary to allow Americans to retain their own market in a fair contest with the foreigner.

It does not matter who the man is, nor what he does—be he worker in the mine, factory, or field, farmer, labourer, merchant, manufacturer, or millionnaire—he is deeply interested in understanding this question of money, and in having the right policy adopted in regard to it. Therefore I ask all to hear what I have to say, because what is good for one worker must be good for all, and what injures one must injure all, poor or rich.

To get at the root of the subject, you must know, first, why money exists; secondly, what money really is. Let me try to tell you, taking a new district of our own modern country to illustrate how "money" comes. In times past, when the people only tilled the soil, and commerce and manufactures had not developed, men had few wants, and so they got along without "money" by exchanging the articles themselves when they needed something which they had not. The farmer who wanted a pair of shoes gave so many bushels of corn for them, and his wife bought her sun-bonnet by giving so many bushels of potatoes; thus all sales and purchases were made by exchanging articles—by barter.

As population grew and wants extended, this plan became very inconvenient. One man in the district then started a general store and kept on hand a great many of the things which were most wanted, and took for these any of the articles which the farmer had to give in exchange. This was a great step in advance, for the farmer who wanted half a dozen different things when he went to the village had then no longer to search for half a dozen different people who wanted one or more of the things he had to offer in exchange. He could now go directly to one man, the storekeeper, and for any of his agricultural products he could get most of the articles he desired. It did not matter to the storekeeper whether he gave the farmer tea or coffee, blankets or a hayrake; nor did it matter what articles he took from the farmer, wheat or corn or potatoes, so he could send them away to the city and get other articles for them which he wanted. The farmer could even pay the wages of his hired men by giving them orders for articles upon the store. No dollars appear here yet, you see; all is still barter—exchange of articles; very inconvenient and very costly, because the agricultural articles given in exchange had to be hauled about and were always changing their value.

One day the storekeeper would be willing to take, say, a bushel of wheat for so many pounds of sugar; but upon the next visit of the farmer it might be impossible for him to do so. He might require more wheat for the same amount of sugar. But if the market for wheat had risen and not fallen, you may be sure the storekeeper didn't take less wheat as promptly as he required more. Just the same with any of the articles which the farmer had to offer. These went up and down in value; so did the tea and the coffee, and the sugar and the clothing, and the boots and the shoes which the storekeeper had for exchange.

Now, it is needless to remark that in all these dealings the storekeeper had the advantage of the farmer. He knew the markets and their ups and downs long before the farmer did, and he knew the signs of the times better than the farmer or any of his customers could. The cute storekeeper had the inside track all the time. Just here I wish you to note particularly that the storekeeper liked to take one article from the farmer better than another; that article being always the one for which the storekeeper had the best customers—something that was most in demand. In Virginia that article came to be tobacco; over a great portion of our country it was wheat—whence comes the saying, "As good as wheat." It was taken everywhere, because it could be most easily disposed of for anything else desired. A curious illustration about wheat I find in the life of my friend, Judge Mellon, of Pittsburg, who has written one of the best biographies in the world because it is done so naturally. When the Judge's father bought his farm near Pittsburg, he agreed to pay, not in "dollars," but in "sacks of wheat"—so many sacks every year. This was not so very long ago.

What we now call "money" was not much used then in the West or South, but you see that in its absence experience had driven the people to select some one article to use for exchanging other articles, and that this was wheat in Pennsylvania and tobacco in Virginia. This was done, not through any legislation, but simply because experience had proved the necessity for making the one thing serve as "money" which had proved itself best as a basis in paying for a farm or for effecting any exchange of things; and, further, different articles were found best for the purpose in different regions. Wheat was "as good as wheat" for using as "money," independent of any law. The people had voted for wheat and made it their "money"; and because tobacco was the principal crop in Virginia, the people there found it the best for using as "money" in that State.

Please observe that in all cases human society chooses for that basis-article we call "money" that which fluctuates least in price, is the most generally used or desired, is in the greatest, most general, and most constant demand, and has value in itself. "Money" is only a word meaning the article used as the basis-article for exchanging all other articles. An article is not first made valuable by law and then elected to be "money." The article first proves itself valuable and best suited for the purpose, and so becomes of itself and in itself the basis-article — money. It elects itself. Wheat and tobacco were just as clearly "money" when used as the basis-article as gold and silver are "money" now.

We take one step further. The country becomes more and more populous, the wants of the people more and more numerous. The use of bulky products like wheat and tobacco, changeable in value, liable to decay, and of different grades, is soon found troublesome and unsuited for the growing business of exchange of articles, and they are therefore unfit to be longer used as "money." You see at once that we could not get along today with grain as "money." Then metals proved their superiority. These do not decay, do not change in value so rapidly, and they share with wheat and tobacco the one essential quality of also having value in themselves for other purposes than for the mere basis of exchange. People want them for personal adornment or in manufactures and the arts — for a thousand uses; and it is this very fact that makes them suitable for use as "money." Just try to count how many purposes gold is needed for, because it is best suited for those purposes. It meets us everywhere. We cannot even get married without the ring of gold.

Now, because metals have a value in the open market, being desired for other uses than for the one use as "money," and because the supply of these is limited and cannot be increased as easily as that of wheat or tobacco, these metals are less liable to fluctuate in value than any article previously used as "money." This is of vital importance, for the one essential quality that is needed in the article which we use as a basis for exchanging all other articles is fixity of value. The race has instinctively always sought for the one article in the world which most resembles the North Star among the other stars in the heavens, and used it as "money"—the article that changes least in value, as the North Star is the star which changes its position least in the heavens; and what the North Star is among stars the article people elect as "money" is among articles. All other articles revolve around it, as all other stars revolve around the North Star.

We have proceeded so far that we have now dropped all perishable articles and elected metals as our "money" or, rather, metals have proved themselves better than anything else for the standard of value, "money." But another great step had to be taken. When I was in China, I received as change shavings and chips cut off a bar of silver and weighed before my eyes in the scales of the merchant, for the Chinese have no "coined" money. In Siam "cowries" are used—pretty little shells which the natives use as ornaments. Twelve of these represent a cent in value. But you can well see how impossible it was for me to prevent the Chinese dealer from giving me less than the amount of silver to which I was entitled, or the Siam dealer from giving me poor shells, of the value of which I knew nothing. Civilized nations soon felt the necessity of having their governments take certain quantities of the metals and stamp upon them the evidence of their weight, purity, and real value. Thus came the "coinage" of metals into "money"—a great advance. People then knew at sight the exact value of each piece, and could no longer be cheated, no weighing or testing being necessary. Note that the government stamp did not add any value to the coin. The government did not attempt to "make money" out of nothing; it only told the people the market value of the metal in each coin, just what the metal—the raw material—could be sold for as metal and not as "money."

But even after this much swindling occurred. Rogues cut the edges and then beat the coins out, so that many of these became very light. A clever Frenchman invented the "milling" of the edges of the coins, whereby this robbery was stopped, and civilized nations had at last the coinage which still remains with us, the most perfect ever known, because it is of high value in itself and changes least. An ideally perfect article for use as "money" is one that never changes. This is essential for the protection of the workers—the farmers, mechanics, and all who labour; for nothing tends to make every exchange of articles a specualtion so much as "money" which changes in value, and in the game of speculation the masses of the people are always sure to be beaten by the few who deal in money and know most about it.

Nothing places the farmer, the wage-earner, and all those not closely connected with financial affairs at so great a disadvantage in disposing of their labour or products as changeable "money." All such are exactly in the position occupied by the farmer trading with the storekeeper as before described. You all know that fish will not rise to the fly in calm weather. It is when the wind blows and the surface is ruffled that the poor victim mistakes the lure for a genuine fly. So it is with the business affairs of the world. In stormy times, when prices are going up and down, when the value of the article used as money is dancing about—up today and down tomorrow—and the waters are troubled, the clever speculator catches the fish and fills his basket with the victims. Hence the farmer and the mechanic, and all people having crops to sell or receiving salaries or wages, are those most deeply interested in securing and maintaining fixity of value in the article they have to take as "money."

When the use of metals as money came, it was found that more than two metals were necessary to meet all requirements. It would not be wise to make a gold coin for any smaller sum than a dollar, for the coin would be too small; and we could not use a silver coin for more than one dollar, because the coin would be too large. So we had to use a less valuable metal for small sums, and we took silver; but it was soon found that we could not use silver for less than ten-cent coins, a dime being as small a coin as can be used in silver; and we were compelled to choose something else for smaller coins. We had to take a metal less valuable than silver, and we took a mixture of nickel and copper to make five-cent pieces; but even then we found that nickel was too valuable to make one- and two-cent pieces, and so we had to take copper alone for these—the effort in regard to every coin being to put metal in it as nearly as possible to the full amount of what the government stamp said the coin was worth.

Thus for one cent in copper we tried to put in a cent's worth of copper; in the "nickel" we tried to put in something like five cents' worth of nickel and copper; but because copper and nickel change in value from day to day, even more than silver, it is impossible to get in each coin the exact amount of value. If we put in what was one day the exact value, and copper and nickel rose in the market as metals, coins would be melted down by the dealers in these metals and a profit made by them, and we should have no coin left. Therefore we have to leave a margin and always put a little less metal in these coins than would sell for the full amount they represent. Hence all this small coinage is called in the history of money "token money." It is a "token" that it will bring so much in gold. Anybody who holds twenty "nickels" must be able to get as good as one gold dollar for them in order that these may safely serve their purpose as money. Nations generally fix a limit to the use of "token money," and make it legal tender to a small amount. For instance, in Britain no one can make another take "token money" for more than ten dollars, and all silver coins there are classed as "token money."

I cannot take you any more steps forward in the development of "money," because in the coined-milled metals we have the last step of all; but I have some things yet to tell you about it.

Although one would think that in coined metal pieces we had reached perfection, and that with these the masses of the people could not be cheated out of what is so essential to their well-being—"honest money"—yet one way was found to defraud the people even when such coin was used. The coins have sometimes been "debased" by needy governments after exhausting wars or pestilence, when countries were really too poor or too weak to recover from their misfortunes. A coin is called a "debased" coin when it does not possess metal enough to bring in the open market the sum stamped upon the coin by the government. There is nothing new about this practice which always cheats the masses. It is very, very old. Five hundred and seventy-four years before Christ the Greeks debased their coinage. The Roman emperors debased theirs often when in desperate straits. England debased hers in the year 1300. The Scotch coin was once so debased that one dollar was worth only twelve cents. The Irish, the French, German, and Spanish governments have all tried debased coin when they could wring no more taxes directly out of their people, and had therefore to get more money from them indirectly. It was always the last resort to "debase" the coinage. These instances happened long ago. Nations of the first rank in our day do not fall so low. I must pause to make one exception to this statement. I bow my head in shame as I write it—the republic of the United States. Every one of its silver dollars is a "debased coin." When a government issues "debased coin," it takes leave of all that experience has proved to be sound in regard to money. Sound finance requires the government only to certify to the real value possessed by each coin issued from its mints, so that the people may not be cheated. Every time the government stamps the words "One Dollar" upon 371¼ grains of silver, it stamps a lie; disgraceful, but, alas! too true, for the silver in it is worth today not a dollar, but only seventy-eight cents.

Another delusion about money has often led nations into trouble — the idea that a government could "make money" simply by stamping certain words upon pieces of paper, just as any of you can "make money" by writing a note promising to pay one hundred dollars on demand. But you know that when you do that, you are not "making money," but making "a debt": so is any government that issues its promise to pay. And there is this about both the individual and the government who take to issuing such notes upon a large scale: they seldom pay them. The French did this during their Revolution, and more recently the Confederate States "made money" at a great pace, and issued bonds which are now scarcely worth the paper they are printed upon. Every experiment of this kind has proved that there can be no money "made" where there is not value behind it. Our own country issued bonds, and the people of other nations bought them for forty cents upon the dollar, although they bore and paid interest at 6 percent in *gold*, so great was the fear that even the bonds of this country would not prove an exception to the usual fate of such securities issued during trying times. Only because the government kept strict faith and paid the interest and principal of these bonds in gold, and never in silver or in any depreciated currency, has the value of its bonds advanced, and the credit of the United States become the highest in the world, exceeding that even of Great Britain. There has never been a better illustration of the truth that in dealing with "money," as in everything else, "honesty is the best policy." Our government also issued some notes known as "greenbacks." But the wise men who did this took care to provide a fund of one hundred millions of dollars in gold to redeem them, so that any man having a greenback can march to the Treasury and receive for it one dollar in gold.

But I am now to tell you another quality which this basis-article of metal has proved itself to possess, which you will find it very difficult to believe. The whole world has such confidence in its fixity of value that there has been built upon it, as upon a sure foundation, a tower of "credit" so high, so vast, that all the silver and gold in the United States, and all the greenbacks and notes issued by the government, only perform 8 percent of the exchanges of the country. Go into any bank, trust company, mill, factory, store, or place of business, and you will find that for every one hundred thousand dollars of business transacted, only about eight thousand dollars of "money" is used, and this only for petty purchases and payments. Ninety-two percent of the business is done with little bits of paper—cheques, drafts. Upon this basis also rests all the government bonds, all State, county, and city bonds, and the thousands of millions of bonds the sale of which has enabled our great railway systems to be built, and also the thousands of millions of the earnings of the masses deposited in savings banks, which have been lent by these banks, to various parties, and which must be returned in "good money" or the poor depositor's savings will be partially or wholly lost.

The business and exchanges of the country, therefore, are not done now with "money"—with the article itself. Just as in former days the articles themselves ceased to be exchanged, and a metal called "money" was used to effect the exchanges, so today the metal itself—the "money"—is no longer used. The cheque or draft of the buyer of articles upon a store of gold deposited in a bank—a little bit of paper—is all that passes between the buyer and the seller. Why is this bit of paper taken by the seller or the one to whom there is a debt due? Because the taker is confident that if he really needed the article itself that it calls for—the gold—he could get it. He is confident also that he will not need the article itself, and why? Because for what he wishes to buy the seller or any man whom he owes will take his cheque, a similar little bit of paper, instead of gold itself; and then, most vital of all, every one is confident that the basis-article cannot change in value. For remember it would be almost as bad if it rose in value as if it fell; steadiness of value being one essential quality in "money" for the masses of the people.

When, therefore, people clamour for more "money" to be put in circulation—that is, for more of the article which we use to effect an exchange of articles—you see that more "money" is not so much what is needed. Nobody who has had wheat or tobacco or any article to sell has ever found any trouble for want of "money" in the hands of the buyer to effect the exchange. We had a very severe financial disturbance in this country only three months ago. "Money," it was said, could not be had for business purposes; but it was not the metal itself that was lacking, but "credit," confidence, for upon that, as you have seen, all business is done except small purchases and payments which can scarcely be called "business" at all. Today the businessman cannot walk the street without being approached by people begging him to take this "credit" at very low rates of interest: at 2 percent per annum "money" (credit) can be had day by day. There has been no considerable difference in the amount of "money" in existence during the ninety days. There was about as much money in the country in January as there is in March. It was not the want of money, then, that caused the trouble. The foundation had been shaken upon which stood the ninety-two thousand of every one hundred thousand dollars of business. The metal itself and notes—real "money," as we have seen—only apply to the eight thousand dollars. Here comes the gravest of all dangers in tampering with the basis. You shake directly the foundation upon which rests 92 percent of all the business exchanges of the country—confidence, credit—and indirectly the trifling 8 percent as well which is transacted by the exchange of the metal itself or by government notes; for the standard article is the foundation for every exchange, both the ninety-two thousand and the eight thousand dollars. So, you see, if that be undermined, the vast structure, comprising all business, built upon it, must totter.

I have finished telling you about "money." We come now to apply the facts to the present situation, and here we enter at once upon the silver question; and I am sure you are all attention, for it is the most pressing of all questions now before you. You see that the race, in its progress, has used various articles as "money," and discarded them when better articles were found, and that it has finally reached coined pieces of valuable metal as the most perfect article. Only two metals are used among civilized nations as the standard metal—gold in some countries, silver in others. No country can have two standards. Centuries ago silver was adopted as the standard in China, India, and Japan, and more recently in the South American republics; and it still is the standard in these countries. When adopted it was a wise choice; silver had nearly double its present value, and was then steady, and it answered all the needs of a rural people.

The principal nations of Europe and our own country, being further advanced and having much greater business transactions, found the necessity for using as a standard a more valuable metal than silver, and gold was adopted; but as silver was used as money in many parts of the world as the standard, and used in these gold-basis countries for "small change," it was advisable for these nations to agree upon the value in gold which would be accorded to silver, and this was fixed at fifteen and one-half ounces of silver to one of gold. Please note that this was then as nearly as possible the market value of silver as a metal compared with gold as a metal. The nations did not attempt to give to silver any fictitious value, but only its own inherent value. And, more than this, each of these nations agreed, when the agreement came to an end, to redeem all the silver coin it had issued in gold at the value fixed. Everything went well under this arrangement for a long time. The more advanced nations were upon a gold basis, the less advanced nations upon a silver basis, and both were equally well served.

What, then, has raised this *silver question* which everybody is discussing? Just this fact: that while the supply, and therefore the value, of gold remained about the same, great deposits of silver were discovered, wonderful improvements made in mining machinery, and still more wonderful in the machinery for refining silver ore; and as more and more silver was produced at less cost, its value naturally fell more and more; one ounce of it, worth $1.33 in 1872, being worth today only $1.04. It has fallen as low as 93 cents. It has danced up and down; it has lost fixity of value. To all countries upon a silver basis there have come confusion and disaster in consequence. The question in India, with its two hundred and eighty-five millions of people, is most serious; and you see how our South American republics are troubled from this fall in the value of their basis-article, by which all other articles are measured. Even the European nations which are upon a gold basis are troubled by this "silver question," for under the agreement to rate fifteen and half ounces of silver as worth an ounce of gold some of these nations have had enormous amounts of silver thrust upon them. Most of them saw what was coming many years ago, and ceased to increase their silver: some disposed of a great deal of what they had, and placed themselves strictly upon the gold basis; but there are still in European countries eleven hundred millions of dollars of silver legal-tender coins, not counting the amount of "token" silver money used for small change. It is now safe to say that less than twenty-five ounces of it would be found equal to one ounce of gold if put in the market instead of the fifteen-and-a-half-ounce basis upon which these countries have obtained it.

All European countries have been, and are still, trying hard to escape from silver. In 1878 those comprising the Latin Union, which fixed the price of silver— France, Belgium, Italy, Switzerland, and Greece—finally closed their mints to legal-tender silver. Norway, Sweden, and Denmark in 1873 and 1875 ran out from under the silver avalanche, and now stand firmly upon a gold basis. Holland also, in 1875, took its stand practically upon gold. Austria-Hungary has not coined silver since 1879, except a small amount of "Levant silver thalers" for a special trade purpose. Even half-civilized Russia took the alarm, and ran as fast as she could out of the silver danger, for in 1876 she shut her mints to the further coinage of the dangerous metal, except such small amount as China wished to take promptly from her. So you see that all those countries that have tried silver and found out the evils which it produces, and its dangers, have been, and are now, using every means to rid themselves of it. For thirteen years it has been cast out of their mints, for during this long period no full legal-tender silver coins have been issued in Europe. Only our republic, among nations, is boldly plunging deeper and deeper into the dangers of silver coinage. When we have had the experience of older nations as to its operations, we may and, I think, surely will wish, like them, to retrace our steps when it is too late. So, you see, there is trouble wherever there is silver. What to do with their silver, which has fallen so low in value, is a serious problem in all these countries. It hangs like a dark cloud over their future.

So much has silver fallen in all parts of the world and disturbed everything that several conferences have been called by the nations in recent years, to which the United States has sent delegates. The object of these was to see whether the chief commercial nations could not agree again upon a new gold value for silver. But the conclusion has always been that it was too dangerous to attempt to fix a new value for silver until it could be more clearly seen what the future was to show about its supply and value, for perhaps it might fall so low that twenty-five or thirty ounces of it would not be worth more than an ounce of gold; no one can tell. As our country has already gone so far into the danger as to have four hundred and eighty-two millions of dollars in depreciated silver, we had to confer with our neighbours in misfortune, and appear as creditors have to appear at meetings held to try to support the bad business of a failing debtor.

Perhaps you are asking yourselves why, when I spoke of all the European countries in relation to silver, I did not state the amount of silver held in reserve by our principal rival, Great Britain. Listen one moment, and then ponder over the reply. *Not one dollar.* France has no less than six hundred and fifty millions of dollars in silver in her bank; but every dollar of Britain's reserves is in the one steady, unchangeable basis-article—gold. Wise old bird, the dear motherland sits upon her perch, whistling away out of all danger from this silver trouble. She has made London the financial centre of the world. If anything be bought or sold in foreign lands, a draft upon London is demanded; because everyone knows that, come what may, it will be paid in the best article, which cannot fall in value—gold. No draft upon Paris or Vienna or New York for wise men. Why? Because the nations represented by these cities have become involved in great possible losses by their huge piles of silver, and may attempt by legislation to make drafts payable in that metal, which fluctuates so in value.

I wish the people of the United States would watch Britain carefully. She is keeping her own counsel; she is treating the silver-loaded nations with cool politeness in the conferences, which she graciously condescends to attend only because India, over which she rules, is unfortunately upon a silver basis; if it were not for that, she would probably politely decline. When they talk about fixing a gold value upon silver, she says that she really does not know what she will decide upon in the matter. What she is praying for is that the United States will continue to go deeper and deeper into silver until retreat is impossible, and she will keep her old policy, which has made her supreme in finance. Her only possible rival is not to be found in Europe, but here in the United States. What a grand thing for Britain if our country could be brought down to a silver basis—forced to relinquish the one standard which can alone give a nation front rank in the financial world! Silver for the republic, Gold for the monarchy: this is what Great Britain is hoping may come to pass, and what every American should resolve never shall. Governments may pass what laws they please about silver: the world heeds them not. Every business transaction between nations continues to be based on gold exclusively—nothing but gold— and will so continue. Britain knows this and acts accordingly.

I think I hear you ask indignantly: "How came our country to have three hundred and twelve millions of silver dollars in its vaults, like France, instead of having its reserves in the sure gold, like our rival, Britain, when, like Britain, we have gold as our basis?" That is a question every farmer and every toiler should ask, and demand an answer to, from his representative in Congress. The reason is easily given. Here is the history. Silver, as we have seen, had fallen in value, and was likely to fall still more. European nations were loaded down with many hundreds of millions of dollars, and all anxious to get rid of it; owners of silver and of silver mines were alarmed; what was to be done to prop the falling metal? Evidently the government was the only power which could undertake the task; and towards that end all the influence and resources of the silver power were bent—alas! with eminent success; for the masses of the people were represented as in favour of silver. If true, they were going with the speculators against their own interests, in the most direct way possible.

The first act which aimed to give by legislation a value to silver was passed in 1878. It required our government to buy at least two million ounces of silver every month, while all other governments had stopped coining it, because it had become dangerously erratic in value. The silver men insisted that these purchases would raise its value; but were they right? No. It did not advance in price. What was to be done then? "Ah!" said these silver-tongued speculators, "the trouble is, the government has not gone far enough; only increase the amount; let the government buy four and a half million ounces per month of our silver instead of two million per month, and this will take all that the country's mines yield, and more too, and so silver must advance in value." They were right in stating that four and a half millions per month are more than the total yield of the United States silver mines; and then eight to ten millions of silver are taken and used every year for other purposes than coining into "money," leaving not more than, say, four millions per month for coinage. Many people were persuaded that if the government bought so much silver per month the value of silver must advance. The price did advance, because many of these mistaken people bought it upon speculation before the bill passed. Silver rose from 96 to 121 — almost to its old rate in gold.

But what has been the result since the passage of the new bill? The answer is found in the quotation for silver today. It is back from 121 to 97, and here we are again. So, insted of being free from the silver trouble, as Britain is and we should have been, these men have succeeded in unloading upon the government already three hundred and ninety millions of dollars of their silver, and we are getting almost as badly off as France; but with this difference: France and other nations prudently stopped adding to their burdens of silver thirteen years ago, while our government is adding to its store four and one-half millions of ounces every month, costing a little more than that amount of dollars. The United States is trying to ignore the changed position of silver, and to make it equal to gold, against the judgment of all other first-class nations. To succeed, we shall have to buy not only what our own mines produce, but a great deal of what all other mines produce throughout the world, the total yield of silver being enough to make one hundred and sixty-eight millions of our silver dollars every year; and then we must, in addition, be prepared to buy the eleven hundred millions of dollars' worth with which European governments are now loaded down, and which they are anxious to sell.

So far from the government purchases of silver having raised its value, the government could not today sell the three hundred and thirteen millions of dollars' worth in its vaults without losing some millions upon the price it has paid the silver-owners for it. You will scarcely believe that the accounts of the treasury state that the government has made, so far, sixty-seven millions of profit upon its silver purchases. This is claimed because for the amount of silver put in a dollar it has paid only about eighty cents. All this "profit" is fictitious. You see, the nation has been led into very foolish purchases of silver. Four and a half millions of your earnings are taken through taxes every month, not for the constitutional purposes of government, but in an effort to bolster a metal by paying prices for it far higher than it otherwise would command. Your government is being used as a tool to enrich the owners of silver and silver mines. This is bad indeed, but hardly worth mentioning compared with the danger of panic and disaster it brings with it through the probable banishment of the steady gold basis and the introduction of the unsteady basis of silver.

The republic had the disgrace of slavery, and abolished it. Until this year it was disgraced in the eyes of the world because it had no law which secured to others than its own citizens the right to their literary productions. That disgrace has passed away also; but there has come upon it the disgrace of "debased coinage." The great republic issues dishonest coin, and it is the only nation in the world which does so, except Mexico, which still coins a little silver. But while the disgrace is upon us, the financial evils of "debased" coinage are yet to come; for, although the government issues debased coin, it agrees to receive it as worth a dollar in payment of duties and taxes, and makes it legal tender, and so it passes from hand to hand for the present as worth dollars. In this way the government has been able so far to prevent its depreciation. How long it can continue issuing four and a half millions more of these notes or coins every month and keep them equal to gold nobody can tell. But one thing is clear: ultimately the load must become too heavy, and, unless silver rises in value, or enough is put into the dollars to represent their value in gold, or the purchase of silver by the government is stopped, we must sooner or later fall from the gold basis to the condition of the Argentine and other South American republics.

This is how these silver dollars will act which have not metal enough to sell for dollars when the world begins to lose confidence in the ability of the government issuing them to pay gold for them when asked. Suppose a number of you had decided to carry a huge log from the woods, and you all got under, and, bending your necks, took its weight upon your shoulders, and then some doubted whether you really could stagger on under the load; and suppose two or three of you, after casting timid glances at each other, concluded you had better get from under: what would be the result? The lack of confidence would probably result in killing those who were foolish enough to remain. It is just so with this delicate question of the measure of values. A few speculators or "gold-bugs" will resolve that, come what may, they will make themselves safe and get from under.

Even in the mind of the most reckless there will be some doubt whether the United States alone can take the load of the world upon its shoulders and carry it, when all the other nations together are afraid to try it, and when no nation in the history of the world has ever succeeded in giving permanent value, as a standard for money, to a metal that did not in itself possess that value. Mark this: that our government has only succeeded so far in doing this with its silver dollars because it has issued only a limited quantity, and has been able to *redeem them in gold*—just as you could take a piece of paper and write on it, "This is good for one dollar, and I promise to pay it." That would be your "fiat" money. The question is, How long could you get people to take these slips for dollars? How soon would some suspicious man suggest that you were issuing too many? And then these slips would lose reputation; people would begin to doubt whether you could really pay all the dollars promised if called upon; and from that moment you could issue no more. Just so with governments: all can keep their small change afloat, although it may not contain metal equal to its face value; and it is a poor government which cannot go a little further and get the world to take something from it in the shape of "money" which is only partially so. But then, remember, any government will soon exhaust its credit if it continues to issue as "money" anything but what has intrinsic value as metal all the world over. Every nation has had eventually to recoin its "debased" coin or repudiate its obligations, and go through the perils and disgrace of loss of credit and position. In many instances the "debased" coin never was redeemed, the poor people who held it being compelled to stand the loss.

There is, however, one valuable feature of the present silver law which, if not changed, may stop the issue of many more "debased silver dollars." It requires that two millions of the four and a half millions of ounces of silver purchased each month shall be coined into money for one year. After that, only such amounts are to be coined as are found necessary to redeem the silver notes issued. As people prefer the notes to the silver, little or no coinage of silver dollars will be necessary, and only silver notes will be issued. When the government ceases to coin silver dollars, it will stand forth in its true character before the people—that of a huge speculator in silver, or, rather, as the tool of silver speculators, piling up in its vaults every month four and a half millions of ounces, not in the form of "money," but in bars. Surely this cannot fail to awaken the people to the true state of affairs, and cause them to demand that the reckless speculation shall cease.

It is in every respect much less dangerous, however, to keep the silver purchased in bullion than to coin it in "debased dollars," because it renders it easier at some future day to begin the coinage of honest silver dollars—that is, coins containing the amount of silver metal that commands a dollar as metal; instead of 371 grains of silver, 450, or 460, or more or less, should be used. This is just about the amount the government gets for each dollar. No possible act of legislation that I know of would produce such lasting benefit to the masses of the people of this country. But beyond material benefit something much higher is involved—the honour of the republic. The stamp of its government should certify only that which is true.

I do not suppose that there are many men in the United States, except owners of silver, who would vote that silver take the place of gold as the standard of value. If the people undersood that the question was whether the one metal or the other—silver or gold—should be elected as the standard, the vote would be almost unanimous for gold, its superiority is so manifest. Yet such is surely the issue, although the advocates of silver disclaim any intention to disturb the gold standard, saying they only desire to elevate silver and give it the position which gold has as money. But you might as well try to have two horses come in "first" in a race or to have two "best" of anything. You might as well argue for two national flags in one country. Just as surely as the citizen has to elect the banner under which he stands or falls, so surely must he elect gold or silver for his financial standard. The standard article cannot be made to share its throne with anything else, any more than the stars-and-stripes can be made to share its sovereignty with any other flag in its own country; for there is this law about "money": the worst drives the best from the field. The reason for this is very clear.

Suppose you get in change a five-dollar gold piece and five dollars in silver, and there is some doubt whether an act of Congress will really prove effective in keeping silver equal to gold in value forever: ninety-nine people out of a hundred may think that the law will give this permanent value to silver, which the article itself does not possess; but one man in a hundred may have doubts upon the subject. I think the more a man knows about "money," the more doubts he will have; and, although you may have no doubts, still the fact that I have doubts, for instance, will lead you to say: "Well, he may be right; it is possible I may be wrong. I guess I will give Smith this silver for my groceries tomorrow, and give the old lady this beautiful bright golden piece to put by; it needs no acts of Congress—all the acts of Congress in the world cannot lessen its value; the metal in it is worth five dollars anywhere in the world, independent of the government stamp; these five pieces of silver are worth only three dollars and seventy-five cents as metal. Yes, I shall let Smith have the silver—*gold is good enough for me.*"

And you may be sure Smith unloads the silver as soon as he can upon Jones. And many people will believe and act so, and the gold in the country will disappear from business, and silver alone will be seen and circulate; every man that gets it giving it to another as soon as he can, and so keeping it in active circulation; and every man that gets a bit of gold holding it, and thus keeping it out of circulation. So instead of having more money, if we go in for trying by law to force an artificial value upon silver in order to use it as money, we shall really soon have less money in circulation. The seven hundred millions of gold which is now in circulation, and which is the basis of everything, will speedily vanish, the vast structure of credit built upon it be shaken, and the masses of the people compelled to receive silver dollars worth only seventy-eight cents, instead of being, as now, redeemable in gold and always worth one hundred cents. For, remember, as I have told you, 92 percent of all operations conducted by "money" depends upon people having absolute confidence in the "money" being of unchangeable value.

Issue one hundred dollars of "debased" coin more than all men are sure can be kept of unchangeable value with gold—panic and financial revolution are upon you. More "money," you see, which could only be used in 8 percent of our smallest financial transactions, can easily be so issued as to overwhelm all the important business of the country by shaking "confidence," upon which 92 percent rests. To be always free from danger is to issue only such "money" as in itself has all the value certified by the stamp upon it. So jealously does Britain, our only rival, adhere to this that she is spending two millions of dollars just now to recoin gold coins which have lost a few cents of their value by wear. Her government stamp must always tell the truth. The republic should not be less jealous of its honor.

As you have seen, the silver-men were disappointed at the failure of acts of Congress to advance the value of their silver. Twice the government has been induced to do as they asked, under assurances that compliance would surely get the country out of its dangerous position as the owner of silver; twice it has been deceived. You would think the silver-owners would now admit their error and help the government to get back to safe ground with as little loss as possible. Far from it; instead of this they have taken the boldest step of all, and urged upon Congress what you have heard a great deal about—the "free coinage of silver." Now, what does that mean? It means that our government is to be compelled by law to open its mints and take all the silver with which European governments are loaded down, and part of all the silver mined in the world, and give for every seventy-eight cents' worth of it one of these coins, which you are compelled to take as a full dollar for your labour or products. It means that the European merchant will send silver over here, get it coined at our mints or get a silver-dollar note for it, and then buy a full dollar's worth of your wheat or corn, or anything he wants, for the silver he could get only seventy-eight cents for in Europe or anywhere else in the world. Europe is doing this every day just now with India, the Argentine Republic, and other countries upon a silver basis. The British merchant buys wheat in India upon the depreciated silver basis, takes it to Europe, and sells it upon the gold basis. He has thus to pay so little for Indian wheat that it has become a dangerous competitor to our own in Europe, which it could not be except that by the fall in silver the Indian farmer gets so little value for his products.

It is only a few months since the new Silver Bill was passed requiring the government to more than double its purchases, and already eight millions of dollars of silver more than we have exported has been sent into this country from abroad—something unknown for fifteen years, for we have always exported more silver than we have imported. Now we are buying all our own mines furnish, and being burdened with some from Europe, for which we should have received gold. In eighteen days of the month of April we have sent abroad nine millions of dollars in gold; so that under our present Silver Law you see Europe has already begun to send us her depreciated silver and rob us of our pure gold—a perilous exchange for our country and one which should fill our legislators with shame. Understand, please, that hitherto, under both bills compelling the government to buy silver, bad as these were, yet the government has got the metal at the market price, now about seventy-eight cents for 371¼ grains; and only this amount the government has put into the so-called dollar. Under "free coinage" all this will change. The owner of the silver will then get the dollar for seventy-eight cents' worth of silver. For pure, cool audacity I submit that this proposition beats the record; and yet when the Farmers' Alliance shouts for free coinage; this is exactly what it supports—a scheme to take from the people twenty-two cents upon each dollar and put it into the pockets of the owners of silver. Surely you will all agree that if seventy-eight cents' worth of silver is to be made a dollar by the government, then the government, and not the silver-owner, should get the extra twenty-two cents' profit on each coin, if it succeeds. The government needs it all; for, as I told you before, the silver bought by the government only at market value could not be sold today without a loss of millions.

If the free coinage of silver becomes law, our farmers will find themselves just in the position of the Indian farmer; and yet we are told that they are in favour of silver. If this be true, there can be only one reason for it — they do not understand their own interests. No class of our people is so deeply interested in the maintenance of the gold standard and the total sweeping away of silver purchases and debased coinage as the farmer, for many of his products are sold in countries that are upon the gold basis. If the American farmer agrees to take silver in lieu of gold, he will enable the Liverpool merchant to buy upon the lower silver basis, at present seventy-eight cents for the dollar; while for all the articles coming from abroad that the farmer buys he will have to pay upon the gold basis. He will thus have to sell cheap and buy dear. This is just what is troubling India and the South American republics. Prices for this season's crops promise to be higher than for years. *See that you get these upon the gold basis.*

Open our mints to the free coinage of silver, and thus offer every man in the world who has silver to sell a one-dollar coin stamped by the government, and taken by it for all dues, for which he gives only 371½ grains of silver, worth seventy-eight cents, and every silver mine in the world will be worked day and night and every pound of silver obtained hurried to our shores. The nations of Europe, with eleven hundred millions of depreciated silver already on hand, will promptly unload it upon us; they will demand gold from us for all that we buy from them, and thus rob us of our gold while we take their silver. With "free coinage" in sight, we shall fall from the gold to the silver basis before the bill is passed. The last words of the late lamented Secretary Windom will prove true:

Probably before the swiftest ocean greyhound could land its silver cargo in New York, the last gold dollar within reach would be safely hidden in private boxes and in the vaults of safe-deposit companies, to be brought out only by a high premium for exportation.

It is a dangerous sea upon which we have embarked. You should ask yourselves why you should endanger the gold basis for silver. Does any one assert that the silver basis would be better for you or for the country? Impossible. No one dares go so far as this. All that the wildest advocate of the change ventures to say is that he believes that silver could be made as good as gold. Everybody knows that nothing could be made better. Let us ask why any one but an owner of silver should wish silver to be made artificially anything else than it is intrinsically. What benefit to any one, except the owner of silver, that the metal silver should not remain where natural causes place it, like the metals copper and nickel? Why should it be credited with anything but its own merits? There was no prejudice in the mind of any one against it. It has had a fair race with gold; the field is always open for it, or for any metal, to prove itself better suited for the basis of value. If silver became more valuable in the market and steadier in value than gold, it would supplant gold. Why not give the position to the metal that wins in fair competition? Gold needs no bolstering by legislation; it speaks for itself. Every gold coin is worth just what it professes to be worth in any part of the world; no doubt about it; no possible loss; and what is equally important, no possible speculation; its value cannot be raised and cannot be depressed. The speculator, having no chance to gamble upon its ups and downs, does not favour it; but this is the very reason you should favour that which gives you absolute security of value all the time. Your interests and the interests of the speculator are not the same. Upon your losses he makes his gains.

One reason urged why silver should be purchased and coined is that the country has not enough "money," and that free coinage of silver will give it more. But if we need more "money," the only metal which it is wise to buy is gold. Why issue your notes for silver, which is falling in value and involves unknown dangers, when for these same notes you can get the solid, pure article itself, real money, *gold*, which cannot possibly entail a loss upon the country? But is it true that the country has not enough "money"?—that is, you remember, the coined article used for exchanging other articles. If so, it is a new discovery. We have not suffered for want of coined money in times past, and yet there is for each man, woman, and child five dollars more "money" in circulation than there ever was. We have more circulating medium—that is, "money"—per head than any country in Europe, with one exception, France, where the people do not use cheques and drafts as much as other similar countries—a fact which makes necessary many times more coined money than we require. Still there is little objection to having just as much coined money as is desired, provided it is not debased, but honest money; and the only way to be sure of that is to buy gold and coin it into "money"—not silver, the future value of which is so doubtful, and the purchases of which have so far been a losing speculation. Ask the advocate of more money why gold is not the best metal for the government to buy and coin into money for the people, and see what he has to say. Gold is as much an American product as silver; our mines furnish more than two millions of dollars of it every month. He could have no objection except that this would not tend to keep up the price of his own product, silver. He could not deny that it would give safer money for the people.

There is another plea urged on behalf of silver. Many public men tell us that silver coinage "is in the air," that people want it because they think that it will make money "cheap," and that, silver being less valuable than gold, the debts of people could be more easily paid. But let me call your attention to one point just here. The savings and the property of the people could only be thus reduced in value if the gold standard fell. As long as all government notes were kept equal to gold, as at present, no matter what amount of silver the government bought or coined, not the slightest change is possible. Only after the financial crisis had come, and the gold standard had gone down in the wreck, and every dollar of gold was withdrawn and held for high premiums, could any change occur to favour one class or another. If any man is vaguely imagining that he is to save or make in some way by the government becoming involved in trouble with its debased silver coin and silver purchases, let him remember that, in order that this vain expectation can be realized, there must first come to his government a loss of ability to make good its determination to keep its silver dollar equal to gold, when gold would at once vanish and command a premium. A wise Secretary of the Treasury has truly foretold the result:

This sudden retirement of $600,000,000 of gold, with the accompanying panic, would cause contraction and commercial disaster unparalleled in human experience, and our country would at once step down to the silver basis, when there would no longer be any inducement for coinage, and silver dollars would sink to their bullion value.

The man who tries to bring about this disaster in the hope to profit by it is twin brother to him who would wreck the express train for the chance of sharing its contents, or would drive the ship of state on the rocks for the chance of securing a part of the wrecked cargo. He is a wrecker and a speculator. His interests are opposed to the interests of the toiling masses.

Again, we are constantly told that the masses of the people favour "free silver coinage," or at least uphold the present silver laws, because they have received the impression, somehow or other, that the more silver there is coined the more money will come to them. Let us look into that. When the government buys silver bullion, it gives its own notes or silver dollars for it. Who gets these? The owners of the silver bullion. How can these be taken from their pockets and put into the pockets of the people? From what we know of the silver men, we cannot expect them to present many of their dollars to anybody; it will only be when they buy the labour or the products of the people that they will give these dollars at the value of a hundred cents which have cost them only seventy-eight. Will they give more of these seventy-eight-cent dollars than they would have to give of one-hundred-cent dollars for the same labour or products? No, not until or unless the effort of the government to give an artificial value to silver broke down, and our money lost value, when a dollar might not be worth half a dollar in purchasing power; calculated upon gold value, they would always give less value than before. How, then, can the working people or the farmers be benefited? It is the owners of the silver, who will give the government seventy-eight cents' worth of bullion and get for it a dollar, who will make the profit. Surely this is clear. Up to this time the dollar which the farmer or workingman receives is still worth a dollar because the government has been able, by trying hard, to keep it worth this; but when "free coinage of silver" comes, the silver dollar must fall to its real value—seventy-eight cents—and the farmer and workingman will be defrauded; so that the interests of the farmer, mechanic, labourer, and all who receive wages are that the "money" they get should be of the highest value, and not cheap—gold, and not silver.

Up to this time we have held fast to gold as the standard. Everything in the United States is based upon gold today, all silver notes or coins being kept equal to gold. Has that been a wise or an unwise policy? Would it now be best to let the gold standard go, to which the advanced nations cling, and especially Britain, and adopt the silver standard of our South American neighbours? Upon the solid rock of gold as our basis-article we have built up the wealthiest country in the world, and the greatest agricultural, manufacturing, and mining and commercial country ever known. We have prospered beyond any nation the sun ever shone upon. In no country are wages of labour so high or the masses of the people so well off. Shall we discard the gold basis, or even endanger it? This is the question before the people of the United States to-day.

The New York *Evening Post* is a free-trade organ, but it has recently said that it would rather be the party to pass ten McKinley Bills than one Silver Bill such as was urged; and I, a Republican and a believer in the wisdom of protection, tell you that I would rather give up the McKinley Bill and pass the Mills Bill, if for the exchange I could have the present Silver Bill repealed and silver treated like other metals. In the next presidential campaign, if I have to vote for a man in favour of silver and protection, or for a man in favour of the gold standard and free trade, I shall vote and work for the latter, because my judgment tells me that even the tariff is not half so important for the good of the country as the maintenance of the highest standard for the money of the people.

Would it not be well for you to listen to men who have your confidence, and who have been compelled by their official positions to investigate and study this silver question well? President Harrison is well known as a most conscientious man. He is not rich; he is poor. If he has anything at heart, it is the good of the plain working people of his country. He has had to study this subject, and he tells you that he finds that the first thing a debased silver dollar will do is to go forth and cheat some poor man who has to take it for his products or labour. Ex-President Cleveland, like President Harrison, is a poor man; his sympathies are with the plain working people—the masses. He had to study the question that he might act upon it; and although many of his party have been led away into the crusade for silver—temporarily, it is to be hoped (for to its credit, let me say, the Democratic party has hitherto been the staunch friend of the best money for the people)—Mr. Cleveland felt that he must tell the truth and denounce the free-silver-coinage idea, because he found that it must injure the workers of the nation. His recent letter gives another proof that he is a natural leader of men—a brave man and not a coward. His personal prospects he weighs not against the true welfare of the toilers who once made him President. In addition to these, no abler, purer, or grander Democrat ever managed the finances of this nation than Mr. Manning; no abler, purer, or grander Republican ever did so than Mr. Windom. These men were friends of the masses, if ever the masses had friends. Both had to investigate the silver question that they might learn what was best and act so as to promote the permanent welfare of the people. Both became deeply concerned about the impending danger of "debased money," and used all their powers to stop representatives in Congress from forcing the government to imperil the interests of the workingman, who must have the best money for his labour or products, or be the prey of speculators. These great men, two of them exalted to the highest political office upon the earth by your suffrages, had and have at heart only the good of the many as against the possible enrichment of the few. Political opponents as they were or are, that they should agree upon this question must surely give every farmer, mechanic, and workingman in the United States grave reason for believing that they, and not the advocates of silver, are his wisest counsellors.

I close with one word of advice to the people. Unless the government ceases to burden itself month by month with more silver, or if the free coinage of silver be seriously entertained, *avoid silver*; when you lay by anything, let it be in gold; when you deposit in the savings bank let it be a gold deposit—ask the bank to give you a gold receipt therefor. There is no use in the poor taking any risk. If you do not thus act promptly, you will find no gold left for you. The speculators and those closely identified with business will have it all. It is a fact full of warning that no bonds could be sold to advantage today which were not made specially payable in *gold.* There is danger ahead. Whatever happens, you can sleep soundly upon gold. Silver will bring bad dreams to wise men. Our government can do much; it is very strong; but there are two things which it cannot do: it cannot—by itself, against the world—permanently give to silver a higher value than it possesses throughout the world as metal, though this is what it is trying to do; and it cannot lessen the value of gold. Some day, perhaps, you may have reason to thank me for the advice I have given you, although I hope not.

Do not think, however, that I despair of the republic—never; even if dragged into the difficulties inseparable from silver, and matters become as bad with us as they are today in the Argentine Republic, where one gold dollar is worth two and a half currency dollars, there is no occasion to fear the final result. The good sense of the people will restore the gold basis after a time, and the republic will march on to the front rank among nations; but the silver experiment will cost much; and it is better that the direct loss should fall as much as possible upon the few of the moneyed class than upon the masses of the people. At best the latter must suffer most, for moneyed men know better than others can how to protect themselves. All this loss, I am sure, the people would prevent if they could only be made to understand the question; for their interests, far more than those of the rich, lie with honest money, and their wishes have only to be expressed to their representatives to prevent the threatened crisis.

Silver, owing to changes of value, has become the tool of the speculator.

Steady, pure, unchangeable gold has ever been, and never was so much as now, the best instrument for the protection of the masses of the people.

I have written in vain if this paper does not do something to explain why this is so, and to impel the people to let their representatives in Congress clearly understand that, come what may, the stamp of the republic must be made true, the money of the American people kept the highest and surest in value of all money in the world, above all doubt or suspicion, its standard in the future, as in the past, not fluctuating Silver, but unchanging Gold.

21
Progressivism: Trusts, the Bane of America

With the ascension of Vice-president Theodore Roosevelt to the White House following the assassination of President McKinley in September 1901, Andrew Carnegie, like millions of other Americans, had shifted over with surprising ease from complacent conservative Republicanism to enthusiastic Progressive reformism. In December 1901, Carnegie startled the business community by announcing that in his opinion, "the Tariff as a protective measure has lost much of its importance." Few believed, however, that he really meant this, especially in respect to the steel industry, and in 1908, he was subpoenaed to testify before the House Ways and Means Committee by its chairman, Sereno Payne, who looked to the man who had profited so handsomely from tariffs on steel to support once again the old order. To the distress of the chairman, Carnegie left no doubt as to where he stood on the tariff. "Can you arrive at any other conclusion than that the steel industry can stand on its own legs? . . . The time for free trade has come so far as steel is concerned."

Carnegie's attack upon protective tariffs was only one manifestation of his amazing metamorphosis from Conservative chrysalis to Progressive butterfly, alighting on every blossom of reform. He applauded Roosevelt's efforts to bring stricter regulation to the railroads and a closer supervision of the banking system and the stock exchange, as well as the conservation of natural resources. At a White House conference on the Conservation of Natural Resources, Carnegie presented a paper on "The Conservation of Ores and Related Minerals," which later was given wide distribution by the Government Printing Office. One can imagine the reaction of Charles Schwab and Henry Clay Frick to their former business associate's plea to the nation to use less steel and to find radically new sources of power, including solar power, in lieu of coal.

Some of his bewildered and angry fellow capitalists had little difficulty in explaining Carnegie's conversion to radical Progressive reform. Eugene Zimmerman, the Ohio railroad financier, called Carnegie "the most selfish man in the United States. Having made his own millions, he wants to prevent others doing likewise." Car-

negie, in Zimmerman's opinion, had with his retirement from business changed from aggressive industrialist to indolent philanthropist, from big manufacturer to big consumer.

For whatever might be his motivation, Carnegie was now to push as "inordinately" for governmental control as he had once pushed for unregulated laissez faire. By the end of Roosevelt's term of office, Carnegie was outdoing even his trust-busting, big-stick carrying mentor. With the following statement, which he submitted to the editors of American Industries *in February 1909, Carnegie went far beyond Theodore Roosevelt's Square Deal, Woodrow Wilson's New Freedom, and indeed the much later New Deal of another Roosevelt in advocating a "supreme industrial court" to regulate the nation's economy. Carnegie had moved far away from the time when he saw trusts as mere transitory bugaboo apparitions to be dismissed with a shrug of indifference. He was now convinced that the day of regulation by the natural law of free competition was over. The trusts had become a frightening reality, the bane of America, and they could only be exorcised by direct political action.*

You ask an amplification of my views in regard to the proposed Tariff Commission. The difficulty with Tariff Commissions composed of the members of Congress is that these men are necessarily uninformed upon the true conditions of the varied industries. Evidence given by interested parties cannot be depended upon as disinterested. Interested people form distorted views, colored as these are by their own interests.

... There should be a permanent staff of able, disinterested men, charged with studying the conditions in all manufacturing countries.

The industrial world is about to undergo the most momentous change known in its history, even more far-reaching than was the change from the individual domestic manufacturer, manufacturing at home, to the factory system and the huge establishments of today.

We are rapidly losing competition upon which nations have hitherto depended to ensure reasonable prices for the consumer. Some of our most important industries today are only nominally competitive and in reality are monopolies so far that an understanding is made as to prices that will prevail. We cannot, in my opinion, withstand this movement. It has to be received and tested, which means that these virtual monopolies must be controlled some way or another. The only force seems to be that of a national government. A supreme industrial court will have to be created and eventually it will have to pass upon prices—disguise this as we may.

To leave monopolists in control would not be tolerated by the people, therefore there must be control and that control, as far as one sees, must be in the hands of the general government.

This is even a larger question than the tariff, but our trouble with revisions of the tariff will be greatly overcome by a body of experts, keeping themselves fully informed of all matters pertaining to the question. . . .

There is nothing alarming in this changed condition, which requires changed regulations. Change is the necessary element in all progress and there should not be the slightest apprehension that the American people will not meet this new phase and adjust it for the best interests of the nation as a whole.

22
Socialism: "Individualism versus Socialism"

In 1908, Doubleday, Page and Company published ten essays on contemporary issues by Andrew Carnegie under the title Problems of To-Day: Wealth-Labor-Socialism. *Many of Carnegie's former business associates, having heard his pronouncements attacking protective tariffs and calling for "a supreme industrial court" to regulate the economy, were already convinced that Carnegie had forsworn his fealty to the free enterprise system and had joined the ranks of the Socialists, who by the first decade of the twentieth century were becoming a significant and alarming political force in both Great Britain and the United States.*

If Carnegie hoped that his essay on "Individualism versus Socialism" would correct this misconception, he was disappointed. For this essay, which he intended to be a reaffirmation of his allegiance to Individualism, was not the traditional attack upon Socialism expected of all good industrialists loyal to the American economic way of life. His metaphor of the fast but erratic hare (Socialism) who never gets underway in the race and the slow but steady tortoise (Individualism) who slowly plods his way toward the goal of a perfect society may have been amusing, but it was hardly what most capitalists wanted as a rebuttal to Socialism.

Carnegie in this essay never clearly defines what he means by the term Individualism, *and his attack upon the Socialists is not a flat rejection of their program, but rather the somewhat unusual argument that most of their objectives have already been, or are in the process of being, implemented by Individualism. The same sunshine optimism that had illuminated his* Triumphant Democracy *is shining even more brightly in this essay written a quarter of a century later. But now it is a Progressive Democracy of which he sings, and quite appropriately, Carnegie dedicates this book to:*

> *Theodore Roosevelt*
> *A Good and Great President . . .*
> *Foremost Apostle of the "Square Deal" for*
> *All Classes of Men; A True Man of the People.*

Socialism: "Individualism versus Socialism"

The alacrity displayed by Socialists in pasting their labels upon the products of Individualism is surprising, in view of the fact that many of the measures claimed as Socialistic have long been in operation in English-speaking lands.

Mr. Snowden,[1] for instance, gives what he claims to be the Socialist's ideas of taxation.

1. Both local and national taxation should aim, primarily, at securing for the communal benefit all "unearned" or "social" increment of wealth.

2. Taxation should aim, deliberately, at preventing the retention of large incomes and great fortunes in private hands, recognising that the few cannot be rich without making the many poor.

3. Taxation should be in proportion to ability to pay and to protection and benefit conferred by the State.

4. No taxation should be imposed which encroaches upon the individual's means to satisfy his physical needs.

He is quite entitled to Number One. No one but a Socialist would dream of taxing with a view of securing *all* "unearned" or "social" increment of wealth for Communism.

As to Number Two: Graduated taxation in Britain is an attempt to equalise the present unfair distribution of wealth, and is already at work in the death duties and in the difference in the income tax between earned and unearned wealth, both the work of Individualism. The strong and repeated recommendations of this policy by President Roosevelt are soon to bear fruit in the United States. He and his trusted advisers are Individualistic to the core.

Number Three is only Adam Smith's doctrine in different words. The nontaxation of imported food by Britain under Individualism as far as it has gone is in accordance therewith.

Number Four is another application of Adam Smith's doctrine. Until physical needs of individual and family are provided for, there is no "ability" to pay taxes.

Thus three of these ideas are the product of Individualism, and should bear its "hall mark," not the Socialist label.

Mr. Jowett[2] pastes the Socialistic label upon the "proper rating of site values,"

---

1. Snowden, Philip, 1st Viscount Snowden (1864–1937); chairman of the Independent Labor Party (1903–06, 1917–20); M.P. (1906–18, 1922–31); chancellor of the exchequer (1924, 1929–31); author of *Socialism and Syndicalism, The Living Wage, Labour and Finance, Labour and the New World.* [JFW]

2. Jowett, Frederick W. (1864–1944), English Labor party leader; M.P. (1906–18, 1922–24, 1929–31); commissioner of works in first Labor party cabinet (1924). [JFW]

as if this did not prevail under Individualism throughout our English-speaking race, except in the old home.

Mr. Macdonald,[3] regarded as the most philosophical of current Socialistic writers, while indulging in dreams of a far distant future, naturally restricts action in our day to practical measures. There is only to be "a steady readjustment of existing relations until the organic structure has been completely changed." He lays down as ripe for action the seven points in the Independent Labor Party programme, which he says is far and away the most representative Socialist body in Britain, thus stamping the Socialistic label upon all these points.

First in these comes an "Eight-hours Day." One naturally inquires under what system the hours of labor have been reduced from twelve and more to ten hours or less. Long before Socialism attracted the public, the reduction of the excessive hours of labor was the care of progressive men under the present Individualistic system in all English-speaking countries. Whether these can be wisely reduced still further is under consideration. To put the Socialistic label upon the policy of shortening the hours of labor is "as flat burglary as ever was committed."

Second comes "a workable Unemployed Act." Mark the adjective. The attention of the English Parliament was given last year to this very question. It is a difficult task to meet without doing more injury than good: when, or if, a *workable* Act is produced parties will then take their positions.

Third, "Old Age Pensions." Mr. Macdonald is here a day behind the fair. These have been established in Britain before this appears in print, both political parties being favorable. Socialism will have little right to label "Old Age Pensions" as its product. On the contrary, it is the product of the best elements of both political non-Socialistic parties.

Number Four is the "abolition of indirect taxation (and the gradual transference of all public burdens to unearned incomes)." Here we must read the bracketed words in the light of Mr. Macdonald's philosophy. This is a consummation which cannot be reached "until the organic structure has been completely changed." As far as the doctrine of lessening indirect taxation is concerned, it has been in practice since the repeal of the Corn Laws gave free food for the people. It is a wise policy. In America there are no duties of moment,

3. Macdonald, J. Ramsay (1866–1937), British Labor party statesman; secretary of the Labor party (1900–12); M.P. (1906–18); prime minister of Great Britain (1924, 1929–31, 1931–35); author of *Socialism and Society, Socialism and Government, The Social Unrest*. [JFW]

except such as bear upon the rich, who alone use imported articles; a protective tax recently imposed upon sugar, to test the ability of the country to produce its own supply, being the only exception.

Number Five is "a series of land acts (aimed at the ultimate nationalisation of the land)." See note to Number Four as to the words bracketed. Britain needs a series of land acts to bring her where all other English-speaking lands stand. None have primogeniture or settlements. All rate sites at market prices. Land is everywhere free except in Britain, and this has long been the case under Individualism. Socialism has no right to the label of Free Land, except as applicable to Britain, and even here a large number of non-Socialists have long urged the policy.

Sixth, "Nationalisation of Railways and Mines." As far as railways are concerned, Individualism has preceded Socialism in this department. Many countries own their railways. India under British control does, as also do some of the colonies. So do Austria, France, Germany, Switzerland, etc. Mines are precarious properties, and should be leased upon royalties when owned by the State. In some cases this is already done.

Seventh, "Democratic political reforms." This is so indefinite that nothing can be said upon the subject. The reforms are in supposition so far, and must be judged upon their merits when announced from time to time. In all English-speaking lands under Individualism, democratic reforms have long been the order of the day, never more so than now.

Mr. Hardie[4] claims there is perfect agreement among Socialists on two leading points, the first being "hostility to Militarism in all its forms, and to war as a method of settling disputes between nations."

Such of us as have inherited this doctrine under Individualism and proclaimed it all our lives rejoice that any body of men agree with us, but we of the Peace and Arbitration Societies in every English-speaking land who have upheld the doctrine, respectfully protest against the Socialists' use of a label to which the Individualistic men of peace have prior claim. Opposition of war and support of arbitration have developed under present conditions, and grow stronger with leaps and bounds these days, and are soon to triumph. One great victory is seen in Chile and Argentina ceasing to wage war and agreeing to settle disputed boundaries peacefully; they did so and both conquered. There now stands upon

---

4. Hardie, J. Keir (1856–1915), Scottish Socialist and labor leader; organized Scottish Miners' Federation (1886); chairman of the Scottish Labor party; founder and editor of *Labour Leader*; M.P. (1892–95, 1900–15); first leader of the Labor party in Parliament (1906–07). [JFW]

the highest peak of their boundary line a statue of Christ as Prince of Peace, cast from their discarded cannon. The pedestal bears this inscription: "Sooner shall these mountains crumble to dust than Chileans and Argentines shall break the peace, which at the foot of Christ the Redeember they have sworn to maintain." Socialism has no place in these lands.

Scarcely a week passes without one or more treaties of arbitration between nations being entered into.

All the nations assembled last year for the first time at The Hague Peace Conference and voted for obligatory arbitration, only eight dissenting, and these declaring they would make separate treaties with selected nations. Some such have already been made and others are now under consideration.

All this progress in the path of peace among nations has been made under our present system, and Socialism as such has no exclusive right to place its label upon the triumphs of peaceful arbitration. Members of all parties have cooperated in this, the most pressing duty of our day—the banishment from the civilised world of the crime of crimes, the killing of men by men in battle like wild beasts, as a mode of settling international disputes.

As we see, there is much that evolultionary Socialists advocate and claim to be Socialistic which we Progressives have long welcomed. The municipalisation of certain public utilities is undoubtedly a step in the right direction, but this had already been done under our present system before Socialism was much talked about. It has been proved that cities can advantageously own, in some cases operate, and in other cases lease for periods, their public utilities—water, gas and electric works, street railways, etc.—and that they can purchase and improve land to advantage in certain districts, and could do much more in that line in Britain were the laws like those of America and other English-speaking nations.

We have, perhaps, one of the best examples of this beneficent policy in the city of New York, now containing more than four millions of people. It never parted with its riparian rights, and owns these around the island, giving it more than twenty miles of waterfront. Some years ago it began building docks, issuing bonds thereof, with a sinking fund for their redemption. The rentals obtained for the docks meet the interest and sinking fund and leave a profit so great that it is estimated the city will possess the gigantic property free of cost before the bonds mature. The city is contracting for rapid transit subways, the building and operating contractors agreeing to pay the interest and sinking fund, and hand over the subways to the city free of cost at the end of fifty years.

No franchises will hereafter be bestowed by New York City except for stated periods. It is becoming the general policy of cities in America to avoid giving perpetual leases. Municipalisation to this extent is steadily winning its way. The water supply is another instance. The foresight of New York has secured at comparatively small cost, because taken in time, one hundred gallons per head daily for eight millions of people. The city owns all this supply, furnishing a great contrast to London. It also secured years ago, at small cost, seven thousand acres of land admirably adapted for city parks, which are now being rapidly utilised as population spreads around them.

The cooperative movement, wholesale and retail, in which manufacturing begins to make its appearance, is another development upon which the Socialistic label is often put, but cooperation was adopted many years ago. The members thus get control to some extent, in one branch, of the means of production and distribution. In this field there is desirable progress, but we note in all that has been done so far in this direction the parting of the ways between Individualism and Socialism. The latter has as its aim a State in which "every man renders service according to his ability and receives according to his needs." The needs of men in the main are common. Among a hundred men thrown upon an island, there would be found little difference. All could be treated alike. This would be pure Socialism; but in working municipal tramways, gas, and waterworks, and in the management of cooperative societies, the compensation paid has no reference to common needs. It is paid according to the value of service rendered, the essence of Individualism. The superintendent of the factory, the merchant in charge of the cooperative store, the employees down through the whole list, are paid exactly upon the same basis as in all private agencies of production. There is not a trace of Socialism here. In this vast field of progress all remains Individualistic.

Socialism versus Individualism is the race between the hare and the tortoise over again. Individualism—the tortoise—has found and kept the path upon which it has made and is making steady progress upward. Never has the tortoise had to stop long in its ascent, but, always carefully putting out its limbs, intuitively the steadily moving creature finds and treads the way onward and upward, moving neither to the right nor left until certain it is right, and then steadily pushing forward.

The hare had not yet made a start. It remains just where it was years ago, frisking round a circle. It knows where it wishes to end, tells us that clearly, but not how, when, or where it is to begin. One point it has settled, however.

It will not tread the tortoise path of Individualism, nor any path but that which our prehistoric ancestors trod many thousands of years ago, and which their progeny abandoned after years of trial and failure. The frisky hare today insists upon opening up again this abandoned path, and keeps scratching the earth and raising a dust as if it were preparing to start, but there is no saying whether it will do so in our generation. Meanwhile the tortoise, as we see, continues moving unceasingly upward, that which is, better than that which has been, and that which is to come, better than that which is. Lovers of progress cannot but hail its ascent as leading to the light. Foolish indeed would Labor be to retard this steady advance until the hare has given some evidence of ability at least to start, and demonstrate by experiment that it can overtake and distance its rival. President Lincoln, when asked where General Sherman was going with his army in the march through Georgia, replied, "I know where he went in, but I don't believe the General himself knows where he is going to come out." Socialism is in that position.

Let the Socialist produce one enterprise managed upon Socialistic principles as proclaimed. "To put an end forever to the wage system, to sweep away all distinctions of class" [Joint Manifesto, British Socialist Bodies]. "The complete emancipation of Labor from the domination of capitalism and landlordism, with the establishment of social and economic equality between the sexes" [Social Democratic Association].

So far as experiments with these doctrines have been attempted, as Hepworth Dixon informs us, they have failed. There have been some attempts to live together by small parties of mature age, seeking a retreat from active life. These ventures lay in the eddies out of the rushing current of human existence, their members striving to content themselves with the present, while the part which active men have to play on earth is that of improving conditions in every direction, making new discoveries, inventing new machines and processes, and extending the boundaries of knowledge. This is man's life work on earth, one of development toward the more perfect day: nothing yet finished, but all growing better through his strenuous exertions. "Rest and be thankful" is for another existence. Until Socialists can point to successful communities based upon their principles fulfilling this mission of progress, the Socialistic question is not within range of consideration—all is mere speculation, vain imaginings of a supposed heaven upon earth, as illusory as other dreams.

All that is desirable and even possible as man exists today is being accomplished—too slowly, we agree, much too slowly—but in no small measure realised from generation to generation under the present system, which always has been and is being now and always must be steadily modified and improved as man correspondingly advances and is himself modified and improved, but not otherwise. Man and his conditions must march abreast, acting and reacting upon each other, that improvement may be evolved. This is the law of his being.

In considering the wisdom of change from our present Individualistic to the proposed Socialistic system our first inquiry should be, How has the former resulted? Has the human race marched backward and deteriorated, or has it advanced and improved? If the former, we should welcome a promising change, and give it a trial tentatively upon a moderate scale. If the latter, common sense prompts us to refuse to make any revolutionary change, and to continue in the path upon which we have marched and are still marching steadily upward, always pushing hard that the pace may be hastened. We find that from the dawn of history until now man, overcoming temporary interruptions, has steadily developed, making great progress in every field. Contrast his condition at various periods in the past with the present and we have one unbroken record of improvement, morally, intellectually, and physically. Infant mortality is very much less, the death rate has fallen, the average of life has lengthened. Pestilences which swept away our progenitors are today unknown. Many diseases once uncontrollable are now conquered. The homes of the people have improved and the poor are now taken care of. The food and clothing of the people are better, hours of labor less, wages, much higher. Free education leaves no child in ignorance; illiteracy is almost unknown. Carlyle only ventured to imagine a future when every considerable town would have a collection of books; now they have free public libraries. Even the prisons have been improved. Sentences for crime have been lightened. Man has become more law-abiding and better behaved. There is less intemperance, and crime is less frequent. In every domain the comforts of life have been increased, its miseries mitigated. The masses of the people are better housed, better fed, better clothed, better educated and better paid than ever before, and the sums in the savings banks were never so great.

In the field of labor man has risen from serfdom and controls his labor as an equal with his employer, and in our own day is beginning to rise from workman to partner. Labor unions, cooperative stores, friendly societies and pension funds, have all been developed.

In all English-speaking lands the rule of the people prevails; only in Britain is hereditary privilege allowed to exist and obstruct their rule. Every public office is open to ability. Power is now in the hands of the masses wherever the English language is spoken. Never have the masses made such rapid and substantial progress as in recent years, and never were there within their reach in Britain so many far-reaching improvements in the laws, which, when adopted, will ensure to the masses the advantages already possessed by their own race in other English-speaking lands.

The various sections of progressive men have only to unite in the effort to free the old home from all in its laws that keeps it in contrast to Canada, Australasia, and America as governments of the people, for the people, and by the people.

It is under such encouraging conditions that the Socialist appears and distracts the masses, insisting upon discarding the system under which this triumphal march has been made—the only system in all the world's long history under which man has greatly advanced. That the organic structure can be completely altered in our day, even if desired, is impossible. That the alternative Socialistic scheme proposed can be established is equally so, because it first requires a change in human nature, a change quite as great as that involved in the evolution of the man-ape into the savage or the savage into civilised man.

It is not the success of the "presto, change" campaign, therefore, that is to be feared, nor even the attempt to establish the Socialistic state, because neither is possible as long as human nature remains what it is.

Mr. Ramsay Macdonald's warning before quoted, we hope, will sink deep into the minds of the earnest, sympathetic, able men who justly enjoy the confidence of the masses and are numbered among their leaders, but who at the present juncture are devoting their time and attention to the Socialistic system, which cannot be established except by "a steady readjustment of existing relations until the organic structure has been completely altered." To effect this change would be the work of centuries.

The Socialist should reflect it was under immutable law decreed that there should be evolved out of the burning mass of matter, the fair earth with all its charms; out of the beast, the higher organism—man with godlike powers; and that man should not eat the bread of idleness, but labor from morn till night in the noble task of making one small spot on earth, one small circle of his fellows, just a little better than he found it—a high mission—none too great, none too small to lose the privilege or to neglect the duty. Man does the latter at his peril, be he cottager or king.

So long as man on earth can aid in the smallest degree the progress of his race he should rejoice. How much fame or fortune he acquires, or how little, matters not, so long as he contributes by his labor and example to the general good. This is the true end, and should be the aim, of life.

Why should any man desirous of benefiting his fellows neglect the work of his own time which it is his duty to perform, and waste his abilities upon purely speculative ideas which it may or may not become the duty of future generations of men to adopt? Our duty of today is with today's problems. We have nothing to do with those of the distant future. We cannot legislate wisely for posterity. It is sad indeed to see able and good men, who could aid in improving the present, expending their talents upon a new system for a distant future, of which they can know nothing.

It is in this world that all our duties lie, and only our own generation can we know how to serve. Upon it our thoughts and efforts should therefore be concentrated. It is a serious waste of time to concern ourselves with any system which we know cannot be introduced until the organic relations of human society are altered. Upon the men of today only the work of today devolves.

Not "Heaven our Home" our motto, so much as "Home our Heaven." Franklin was right when he proclaimed that "The highest worship of God is service to man." Power to render service to the Unknown is not given us except by serving those of His creatures here with us in our own day and generation.

The man is not born who can legislate wisely for a future which has not been revealed to him, and of which, therefore, he can know nothing.

Sufficient unto our own day are the evils thereof. These we should endeavor to abolish or mitigate, leaving the future to our successors.

23
Race Relations: "The Negro in America"

In 1907, Carnegie was asked to deliver the opening address for the winter lecture series of the famed Edinburgh Philosophical Institution, an organization whose antecedents could be traced back to the eighteenth-century Scottish Enlightenment of David Hume, William Robertson, and Adam Smith. It was a signal honor being paid by the intellectual elite of Scotland to a native son who had only four years of formal schooling.

After much deliberation, Carnegie chose as his topic "The Negro in America," and he then went to work to collect information on a subject about which he actually knew very little. He hounded Booker T. Washington, the Tuskegee Institute faculty, and especially H. B. Frissell, the principal of Hampton Institute, for facts and figures on the economics and social conditions of African Americans in the South. What he ultimately produced was a black version of Triumphant Democracy. *It sounded the same hopeful note of progress, which he demonstrated by statistics on literacy, land holdings, and the accomplishments of African Americans as artists, poets, scientists, lawyers, teachers, doctors, and even capitalists. Only in the conclusion did he do an abrupt, realistic about-face by admitting that "the bright spots have been brought to your notice, but these are only small points surrounded by great areas of darkness." Not even Carnegie could claim for the black race in America that all was sunshine.*

What is remarkable is that Carnegie should have chosen this particular topic for his address. He had, to be sure, always evinced a sympathy for African Americans. As a newly arrived immigrant child, he had found slavery to be the one great, unforgivable blotch on what he otherwise regarded as the nearly perfect democracy in America. During the Civil War and Reconstruction, he had supported the Radical position on racial equality, and in the post-Reconstruction era, unlike most whites, he never entirely lost interest in this oppressed race. His most generous contributions to institutions of higher learning had gone to Tuskegee and Hampton, and the president of Tuskegee, Booker T. Washington, who had been a guest at Skibo Castle, was placed upon a private pension list reserved for Carnegie's closest friends and relatives.

Carnegie's choice of this topic for the Edinburgh Philosophical Institution, nevertheless, remains noteworthily curious. If the "Negro in America" had for many decades become Ralph Ellison's "Invisible Man" to most of his fellow white Americans, the "Negro in Scotland" was not only invisible, he was nonexistent. The reception that Carnegie received from his Edinburgh audience on 16 October 1907, was as chilly as the weather. Most of those in attendance had expected to hear a discourse on peace, or perhaps Carnegie's idiosyncratic interpretation of Herbert Spencer's philosophy. They were quite unprepared for and totally uninterested in the racial problem in America. It was not a successful evening. Never had Carnegie worked so hard for so little return in applause and commendation as in this instance. Yet the text of this address, more than anything else that Carnegie wrote in the Progressive era, gave to his liberalism a special distinction few others at that time could claim. In his concern for improved race relations, Carnegie had progressed far beyond white America's Progressivism.

The address was privately printed in pamphlet form in Inverness, 1907.

Ladies and gentlemen of the Philosophical Institution,

So many and varied have been the subjects treated by my predecessors in your long history, that one has some difficulty in selecting a theme. I escape this, however, by breaking fresh ground in bringing to your attention "The Negro in America."

No racial movement in the world today is more interesting; few, if any, are more important. We here deal with ten millions of people—double the population of Scotland—recently not men but slaves—the very last slaves held by a member of our English-speaking race—who were not only suddenly made freemen, but also entrusted with the ballot.

Proud is the boast,

> Slaves cannot breathe in Britain! If their lungs
> Receive our air, that moment they are free.
> They touch our country, and their shackles fall.

But where the poet-liberator stops, his part finisht, the stateman's work only begins. The shackles fall, but the citizen fails to emerge. How is the slave to gain self-control, wisdom's root, when all his days he has been controlled by others? "Arise and walk" was once said to the lame, but a miracle-worker was required to effect this instant cure. It is the necessarily slow development of the slave into the citizen which I propose to lay before you tonight.

In one respect the problem is unique. The Negro is called upon to rise in the scale from slavery to citizenship in the presence of a civilization representative of the highest—his shortcomings, backslidings, failures, cannot but be numerous and discouraging, and the contrasts between whites and blacks in many respects such as to produce the belief in the minds of their former masters that the end striven for is unattainable. Once a slave, always a slave, so far as the Negro race is concerned, is their natural conclusion.

The first cargo of slaves, twenty in number, was landed at Jamestown, Va., August 1619, only a few years after the original Colonists settled at Jamestown, and one year before the Pilgrims landed at Plymouth. When the Declaration of Independence was signed in 1776, there were already five hundred and two thousand slaves in the country. The Constitution, however, forbade their importation, and it was natural increase almost alone, therefore, which produced in the hundred years, 1790 to 1890, a ten-fold increase, to seven millions and a half. The last slaves were smuggled in against the law as late as 1858.

Boston had become the chief port for the slave trade, but experience proved that the warmer South, not the icy North, was to be the Negro's home. They rapidly gravitated southward, and found their place in the cotton fields. Virginia, under the influence of Jefferson, was the first to prohibit the importation of slaves. Slavery was abolisht by state after state in the North, and it became common for people of the best element in the border states, represented by Washington and his circle, to manumit their slaves. Needless to say, good men and women treated them well, and were often repaid by loyal and even intense devotion, but, if it were to continue, the relationship demanded that it be unlawful to teach slaves to read. Education is moral dynamite which invariably explodes into rebellion. This is one of the penalties that we of the English-speaking race have to pay for our well-meant attempts to govern what are called subject races. In teaching our history, we supply them with the most deadly explosives, sure some day to burst and rend the teacher. We "teach bloody instructions which return to plague the inventors," unless we be wise, and from time to time grant the liberties we ourselves extol and enjoy. Intelligence forces equal rights; hence the unrest in Egypt, India, the Philippines, and other countries under foreign tutelage is, in one sense, a wholesome sign as proving that the awakening masses are stirred to action and demand recognition as fellow-citizens, thus showing that our teaching, and especially our example, have had their inevitable and, let us never forget, their salutary effect. Let it never be said that our race teaches men how to remain slaves, but always how they can become freemen—not that they should forget their own country, but how they can repeat, like ourselves, with throbbing heart,

> Breathes there a man with soul so dead,
> Who never to himself hath said,
> "This is my own, my native land."

Only so can the mother of nations be proud of her children, or America some day be proud of the Philippines to which she has just given a legislature.

It is, at first thought, remarkable that the Negro in America has been so long-suffering. There never was a Negro conspiracy nor a united revolt. Never were national troops needed to repress serious outbreak. But let it be remembered that the Southerner, the master, knew better than to teach them as we now teach subject races. It was unlawful to teach the slave to read. Ignorance is the only possible foundation upon which dominion over others can rest. When I talked to the natives of India who had been educated in your schools there, and heard from them how Washington, Cromwell, Sidney, Pym, Hampden and others were revered, I was proud that our race develops men, not slaves. As Burke said—"We view the establishment of the colonies on principles of liberty, as that which is to render this kingdom venerable in future ages"—a nobler triumph than all Britain's armies and fleets ever give. This is true glory.

The North would probably have acquiesced in the constitutional recognition of slavery in the original slave states so long as each citizen felt that his own state was free from the guilt and curse, and it might have died peacefully as with you in the West Indies thru compensation.

You may remember that Lincoln earnestly favored this policy. When he met the Vice-President and other Confederate officials at City Point, he took a sheet of paper and said—"Gentlemen, let me write here at the top 'Emancipation,' and you may fill the rest of the sheet with your conditions." Imagine what would have been saved had the southern leaders been prepared to give up the accursed system—the hundreds of thousands of human lives sacrificed, the enmities aroused, thousands of millions of dollars wasted. So it is with brutal war which always decides, not who is right, but only who is strong.

Population from North and South began to pour into the western territories. Were these to be "slave" or "free?" This was the issue; hence sprang the irrepressible conflict. The South claimed the right to hold slaves anywhere upon common territory. The North determined that not one foot of territory beyond the old states, where the Constitution recognized slavery, should be trodden by a slave. The same spirit that stirred Britain and compelled the abolition of slavery in the West Indies animated the North. Slavery became the accursed thing, "the sum of all villainies," and, in addition to that, it was not good Americanism. Many runaway slaves crost the border, pursued by officers, who in some cases were accompanied by trained dogs. Slaves also past over the border rivers sometimes on the ice. The pursuers were not accorded enthusiastic welcome in the North, and little of the assistance which the law required was given in the chase. The South then forced a fugitive slave law thru Congress. The rival parties, Free-Soil Northerners and Slave-holding Southerners, encountered each other in the Territories, and very soon the whole country was at fever heat.

When the North was required by law to assist in capturing men flying from slavery and return them to it, there was an end to all discussion. Human slavery at last became a moral question. Was the Republic to be a Free or Slave Power? — an issue only to be decided by the most gigantic contest of modern times. Into this the slaves were drawn. Lincoln with a stroke of the pen emancipated them, and thus the last vestige of slavery vanisht from the civilized world. The rebellion was crusht, and so far all was well, but as the colored people were the only loyalists thruout the South (with certain notable white exceptions), and had served surprizingly well in the Army, the rash step was taken of instantly conferring the suffrage upon them. It was a choice of evils. Only thru Negroes was the general government enabled to maintain its sovereignty and ensure loyal congressional representatives, thus securing constitutional government over the South. The white people of the South, intensely loyal to their states as against the government, were infuriated by the ascendency of their former slaves. No situation could be imagined more certain than this to drive further apart the two races, and to embitter the feelings of the Southern whites against the colored allies of their conquerors. Such was the condition in America at the close of the war, some forty odd years ago.

Here we have between four and five millions of slaves, formerly held in dense ignorance, unable to read or write, without churches, schools, or property of any kind, and yet called upon to perform the duties of citizenship, their former masters surrounding them incensed at their elevation. How were the negroes recently slaves to be made fit as citizens? — a problem that might appal the bravest. Yet this was the one fundamental requirement, for without improvement of the black race no satisfactory solution was possible.

After a period of fifty years we are tonight to enquire whether the American Negro has proved his capacity to develop and improve: this I propose to answer by citing facts.

The first question the ethnologist will naturally ask is: Has he proved himself able to live in contact with civilization, and increase as a freeman, or does he slowly die out like the American Indian, Maori or Hawaiian? The census answers that the total number of Negroes in America in 1880 was 6,580,793; in 1900, 8,840,789. Increase in twenty years, 2,259,996, equal to 34.3 percent, almost double the rate of increase of the United Kingdom, and within three percent of the increase of America, white and black combined. The Negro race numbers today about ten millions. It does not increase as fast as the white in America because there is no black immigration; taking only native whites and blacks, their relative increase must be about equal. There is no trace of decline here, but a surprisingly rapid rate of increase, one of the surest proofs of a virile race calculated to survive in the struggle for existence. The first test, therefore, we may consider successfully met.

Now for the second: Scotland's proud position among nations rests chiefly upon the realization of the famous declaration of John Knox, "I will never rest until there is a Public School in every Parish in Scotland," which finally led to the noble enactment which proclaims that, "no father, of what estate or condition that ever he may be, use his children at his own fantasie, especially in their childhood, but all must be compelled to bring up their children in learning and virtue." You will agree with me, I am sure, that the second test of capacity to reach the standard of citizenship is the passion for education, the desire to be able to read, write and cypher. Before the war this broad avenue to all progress was closed to the slave. Let us see whether he has taken advantage of the door that opened after slavery was abolisht.

The censuses of 1870 and 1900, thirty years apart, compare as follows as to illiteracy of the Negro males of voting age:

	Total Number	Illiterate	Percent
1870	1,032,475	862,243	83.5
1900	2,060,302	976,610	47.4

Thus in thirty years illiteracy has fallen 43 percent [sic]. At the same rate of progress, it is today (1907) not one-half as great as in 1870.

Of the first 1,032,000 of people in 1870, 862,000 were illiterate. The second 1,028,000 of 1900 added only 114,000, nearly eight illiterates in the 1870 males of voting age to one illiterate in the second million increase up to 1900.

We have an instructive census table showing illiterates in the colored population of ten years of age and over for 1880 and 1900:

	Total	Illiterates	Percent
1880	4,601,207	3,220,878	70.0
1900	6,415,581[1]	2,853,194	44.5

a decrease of illiteracy of thirty-six percent in twenty years.

While illiteracy among the Negroes is being rapidly reduced, we must not forget an equally encouraging reduction among the poor whites, a class that was much to be pitied during the reign of slavery, with the contempt for honest labor that followed slavery as its shadow. The slave master performed no labor, and was as a rule above trade—a territorial magnate fashioned after that class in Britain. The poor white aimed at that standard and hence declined to learn handicrafts. A small piece of ground, usually rented, sufficed to keep him alive, and everything approaching manual labor was work for slaves. Illiteracy prevailed to an enormous extent. The census of 1900, however, showed that the South had reduced the percentage of native white males who could not read and write to sixteen percent.

In considering the Southern problem, we must never forget that the "poor whites" are an element complicating the situation, the attitude of this class to the black being intensely hostile—far beyond that of the educated whites.

There was no public school system in any Southern state before the war; now there is no state without one, embracing Negro as well as white schools.

Since 1880, Negro churches have contributed for Negro education $9,549,700, almost two millions sterling, to supplement deficiences of the state systems.

The colored church is chiefly composed of Methodists and Baptists, and is a great force among the Negroes, exercizing commanding influence. Let all doubters of the future of the Negro race remember that it has 23,462 church organisations and has built 23,770 churches, with a seating capacity of six millions eight hundred thousand. It has 2,673,977 communicants out of ten millions population; few adult Negroes are outside of the church. Their church property is valued at $26,626,448—over five and one-half millions sterling. It may be doubted whether even Scotland's percentage of communicants reaches that of the whole Negro race. Many of the foremost leaders of the Negro

---

1. Indians included, some 345,000.

people are to be found among their churchmen. They have been especially fortunate in their bishops who are elected, not appointed, and are active, progressive men.

In 1860, Negro schools were unknown, it being unlawful to teach the slave. In the year 1900, 1,096,734 colored youths attended public school, and 17,138 attended higher schools of learning. The warfare against ignorance goes on apace among both whites and blacks. For twenty years after the war progress in providing Negro schools by the states was very slow, but since 1880 there has been spent by the states in their support, $105,807,930 – about twenty-five millions sterling. In addition to this, all over the South the Negro is providing additional school buildings and extending the term for keeping them open each year beyond that fixt by the states, the additional cost thereof being defrayed by the Negroes.

The strong religious tendency which characterizes the Negro finds vent in Young Men's Christian Associations. Three men are employed by the National Committee, who devote themselves exclusively to their foundation and control. Thirty-seven associations already exist in the principal cities. Twenty-three paid secretaries give their entire time to the work, which is extending rapidly.

In seven states – Delaware, Arkansas, South Carolina, Georgia, Alabama, Mississippi and Louisiana – the cost of Negro common schools in 1900 was $1,345,859, whereas Negroes contributed $1,496,036. "Excepting a few city systems, it can be said that apparently Negroes in the South contributed to their schools in 1899, $3,762,617 out of a total cost of $4,675,504, leaving but $912,887 to be paid by the whites."

There are now in the country 136 colleges and "Industrial Schools" exclusively for the education of Negroes, apart from the public schools.

It will be many years before this immense and sparsely populated region known as The South can boast that Knox's scheme is completed; but at the present rate of progress this century apparently will not close upon a "Parish" minus its public school.

Such is the gratifying evidence that the Negro race shares with the Scotch the passion for education.

We now come to the third vital test of a race, only less important than the other two. We have seen that the Negro is rapidly becoming a reading and writing man; permit me to give some facts proving that he is also becoming a saving man.

Surely no better proof can be given of his desire and ability to rise and become a respectable member of society than the production of a bank book with a good balance, or, better still, the title to a farm or a home free of debt. The saving man is par excellence the model citizen — peaceable, sober, industrious and frugal. The magic of property works wonders indeed, and pray remember once more that only forty-three years ago he, a slave, the property of a master, found himself suddenly and without warning his own master, face to face with duties to which he was wholly a stranger — self-support, self-direction and self-control, the care of wife and children, wage-earning and the expenditure of wages, the duties of citizenship, including the right of voting, all thrust upon him who had been until that hour possest of nothing, not even of himself, without home, school, church, or any of the elements of civilized life. The horse or cow fed in its stall and worked on the estate had scarcely less to do with providing for itself than the general field slave. Only the few household servants and craftsmen were of a much higher class.

Has the Negro shown the ambition and the ability to save and own his home or his farm? Does he take to the land, and is he making a successful farmer and landlord? These are vital points bearing upon his future. Let us examine the record.

In 1900 no less than 746,717 farms, 38,233,933 acres, 59,741 square miles, just the area of England and Wales, or double that of Scotland, were owned or tenanted by Negroes, who forty years previously owned nothing. These embraced, in the Southern Central States, 27.2 percent of all the farms; in the South Atlantic States, 30 percent; in the Southern States — Florida 33 percent, Georgia 39.9 percent, Alabama 42 percent, Louisiana 50.2 percent, and Mississippi 55 percent. The negro has more farms than the whites in the last two states, but it must be remembered that the average size of Negro farms is very much less than those of the whites.

The figures just quoted include farms owned or tenanted by negroes, that is, they were either landlords or farmers. When we come to farms in the hands of owners we find that in the twelve Southern States Negro landlords in 1900 owned 173,352 farms, and the aggregate wealth of Negroes was estimated at $300,000,000.

The race that owned not an acre of land forty years ago is now possessor as landlords of an area larger than Belgium and Holland combined, and rapidly increasing. The Negroes have the land hunger, one of the best qualities, and they are entering freely into the landlord class, a statement which perhaps may be calculated to arouse your sympathy in Scotland, but when the owner is landlord, factor, farmer, and worker all combined, and really does a hard day's work, dividends appear.

The white American landlord, factor, farmer and worker, all in one, is the backbone of the body politic, always conservative as against revolutionary projects, but moving ahead with the times, intelligent, fair-minded, exceedingly well-behaved, a kindly neighbor and model citizen. They exceed five millions in number. The Negro landlord may be trusted to develop into the likeness of his white compeer and draw his race upward after him in due time.

Virginia is the foremost Southern State. She has one hundred counties. In thirty-three counties eighty percent of the Negro farmers own and manage their land; in fifty, seventy percent do so; and only nineteen counties have more white than Negro farmers.

In 1898, Negroes in Virginia owned 978,118 acres; in 1903, 1,304,471 acres, a gain by Negro landlords in five years of 326,353 acres.

The total business capital of Negroes in Virginia in 1889 was $5,691,137; in 1899, $8,784,637. Seventy-nine percent of them had less than $2500 each (£500), so that a great number use their own funds.

Georgia is one of the most prosperous of the Southern States.

Land owned by Negroes:

	Acres	Value
1900	1,075,073	$4,274,549
1901	1,141,135	4,656,042

showing 70,000 acres added in one year. The assest value (the actual value being double) of all property owned by Negroes in the state was:

In 1900	$14,118,720
1901	15,629,181

an increase of a million and a half of dollars, or nearly eleven percent, in one year.

The Negro has often been described as lazy and indolent, yet the census shows that in the South 84.1 percent of colored males and 40.7 percent of females over 10 years are engaged in gainful occupations, while of the white population of the country the percentage is 79.5, and only 16 percent of females. The Negro is chiefly employed in agriculture. The census of 1900 shows 1,344,125 agricultural laborers and 757,822 farmers, planters and overseers. The impression of laziness probably arises from climate. The Negro does not, nor does any race, work as hard in the sunny south as in colder climates. There is another point not to be lost sight of—how a man works as a slave or servant for a master does not prove how he will work as a freeman for himself.

The negro agriculturists, as has been seen, are rapidly becoming landlords. Those residing in cities show similar ambition to acquire real estate. Jackson, Mississippi, for instance, is owned to the extent of one-seventh by Negroes, who have two and a half millions of dollars worth of taxable property. A statement is given for Richmond, Va., showing that there as elsewhere Negroes are engaged in every occupation and profession—ten lawyers, thirty ministers, three dentists, ten physicians, two photographers, school masters, real estate dealers, merchant tailors, jewelers, thirty-five dressmakers, four savings banks, four newspapers (weekly), four restaurant-keepers, sixteen stenographers. Every field of human activity is represented. The first physician in Richmond to use a motorcar was a Negro. The resources of the First Colored People's Bank are reported at $555,288 (£115,000). There are thirty-two Negro banks in the country. Building and loan associations and insurance companies are not overlookt; several have been organized and are being successfully conducted by Negroes in various cities. There are in the United States 1734 Negro physicians and surgeons, and 125 drug stores owned by Negroes. Not only are all professions filled by Negroes; the Patent Office in Washington shows four hundred inventions patented by them.

The desire to own a home is one of the most encouraging of all traits in the masses of a nation. In 1865 the Negroes were without homes of their own. In 1900, thirty-five years later, there were 372,414 owners of homes, and of these 225,156 were free of encumbrance.

Home is the cradle of the virtues. Man is not quite up to the standard until he can say proudly to himself "This is my own, my precious home," and if he be able to add "and all paid for," so much the better. He has given the best proof possible of his good citizenship. This is our bulwark in America against revolutionary or socialistic ideas. So many millions own their homes that they control political action. The right of private property is sacred. Individualism rules in the Republic.

The Negro has not overlookt the press as an essential element of modern progress. Several attempts were made to establish newspapers previous to 1847. In later years, however, many have become successful. The newspaper directory for 1905 gives 140 publications of every class publisht by Negroes, but it is said to be incomplete. There are six Negro magazines, two of these quarterly, denominational publications, four being monthly and undenominational. Most of the newspapers are devoted to local affairs and of little general interest, but some twenty-five publisht by Negroes in different sections of the country are said to be really creditable to the profession of journalism.

The Negro has not failed to make his appearance in literature. Booker Washington's *Up from Slavery* needs no comment. Professor DuBois's *The Souls of Black Folk* has attracted much attention. Charles W. Chesnutt's several books, bearing upon the color line are notable. Dunday, the Negro poet, is extensively read. Thomas Fortune, editor of the *New York Age*, the most successful Negro editor, has written two interesting books, *The Negro in Politics*, and *Black and White*, has also published a volume of poems and has been prominent in all efforts to elevate his race. Dunbar, the poet, called the Burns of his race, who has recently passed away, was brought to the attention of the public by Howells. A new Negro poet who has recently claimed recognition is Mr. Braithwaite. Mr. Tanner, the Negro artist, has recently won the Gold Medal at Paris, and is now represented in the Luxembourg. A Negro student at Harvard University this year won the Rhodes Scholarship against fifty-six white competitors.

It is true that many of these and other conspicuous Negroes have white blood in their veins, but as they remain Negroes and labor for and with their people, this makes no difference whatever. We are ourselves fortunately a very mixed race. The point is not what the mixture but what the product is; and so in estimating the Negro race and its probable future we must take it as it is. The presence of white blood is one of the elements of the case.

Benjamin Banneker, the astronomer, and friend of Jefferson, was a pure Negro. So is J. G. Groves, the Negro "Potato King" of today, so-called from his having grown in the state of Kansas 72,150 bushels of that indispensable article, an average of 245 bushels to the acre, which is claimed to break all records. He is one of the coming Negro millionaires, and was born of Negro parents in slavery. He already owns five farms. Alfred Smith, the "Cotton King" of Georgia, is another typical instance of Negro ability; when Sherman marched thru Georgia he was a hotel porter, and had managed to save $2000 (£400). He emigrated early to Oklahoma and took up a "claim," and began taking premiums for the best cotton. In 1900 he received first prize at the World's Fair. Another millionaire in embryo.

Mr. Jackson is another. He has a reputation all over Georgia. He has for the past ten years brought the first bale of cotton to market, owns two thousand acres, employs one hundred men, and has forty-six mules and horses. Another Negro, Mr. Johnson, of Virginia, is one of the most successful exporters of walnut. At present he has three properties. He also is making a fortune rapidly. Mr. Montgomery, a slave until emancipated by Lincoln, was offered a bayou in Mississippi by the railroad company provided he succeeded in founding a Negro town, as white people could not live there. He succeeded, and is now at the head of about two thousand people, president of a bank, and his town is attracting attention. He is no ordinary man, having been elected to the State Constitutional Convention. (See *World's Work* for June.)

These and other examples show that, like other races that have risen, our own included, the Negro is capable of producing at intervals the exceptional man who stimulates his fellows. The race that produces leaders is safe and certain to develop. If a race bring forth at intervals a Wallace and a Bruce, a Knox and a Buchanan, a Burns and a Scott, a Hume and an Adam Smith, a Carlyle and a Mill, a Watt and a Nielson, the result must be an advanced people. Every leader compels a following, which improves his race. Even the humbler men in the South whom I have mentioned as developing natural resources, and making money in so doing, are in a sense also leaders among their people, and raise the standard of life in greater or less degree of those about them.

While the North has been for five years, and is still, enjoying the longest and greatest uninterrupted period of material prosperity ever known, and has had several shorter periods of similar character since the war, the South has only rallied from its lethargy within the past few years. It is now partaking of the boom, and prices of land, city lots, and all kinds of property have advanced; a scarcity of labor exists, and committees are being formed to induce organized immigration from Europe to Southern ports. Italian colonies are being planted in various localities.

Wealth is often underrated in both countries. It is upon the foundation of material prosperity that the South is now building more churches and schoolhouses, industrial and medical colleges, and the people spending more upon education. Without this new wealth there would be less surplus to apply to the higher ends. The dress of the people, and the homes and modes of life are changing rapidly for the better thru the entire South. Philanthropists laboring among the Negroes concur in testifying that nothing stirs their ambition and drives them to honest, unremitting labour, and to educate themselves, like the magical touch of property, something they can call their own. It may be doubted whether there be any guarantee for the production of desirable citizens, equal to the possession of their own sweet little homes. A man thus most surely gives a bond to fate, and makes assurance of good citizenship doubly sure.

Permit me to give you a few figures showing the rapid growth of the South. Before the war there was not a yard of cotton cloth manufactured there. Last year there were added 794,034 spindles and 9871 looms in her cotton factories. Most surprising fact of all, there were more yards of cloth woven in the South in 1906 than in the North, altho production in the North also slightly increased. This manufacture, hitherto mostly concentrated in the New England states, is being rapidly extended in the South where the cotton is grown. Now that labor is becoming honorable since slavery died, the poor whites are flocking to the cotton mills and various other factories now being establisht, and proving themselves capable operatives. Testimony has just been given that one-third more labor is required in the cotton mills, but the white element, partly immigrants, may be depended upon soon to supply this. Last year there were more than three thousand miles of railway built in the Southern States, and eighty-four million tons of coal mined. The yearly cotton crop exceeds eleven millions of bales. In 1850 it was only two and a quarter millions. It must be steadily increased to meet the world's needs. In short, the hitherto impoverisht South is sharing the unprecedented boom which has prevailed in the North for some years. The question used sometimes to be asked in former days—what could be done with the Negro? The question today is, how more of them and of other workers can be obtained. The Negro has become of immense economic value and is indispensable where he is.

Touching the good qualities of the Negro, he has much to his credit. During the civil war his devotion to good masters and mistresses was touching. They were left at home while their masters, almost to a man, joined the Southern army. It was the exception when slaves upon an estate were cruelly treated, and the relations between white and black were surprisingly free from bitterness. This does not mean that the slaves did not hail Lincoln's proclamation with joy, but it does prove that as a class the American Negro is of happy disposition, placable, affectionate, singularly free from promptings to commit secret crimes, most grateful and responsive to kindness. There is nothing of the plotting assassin in him.

We are staggered now and then by assaults of the lowest and most brutal Negroes upon white women in the less settled states. It is stated that in Virginia, Maryland, Kentucky and Missouri, which have large Negro populations, there are neither rapes nor lynchings. Every case of this kind is given widest publicity, and naturally arouses the strongest passions. These outrages are committed in lonely districts where policemen are unknown. There may be neither provost, judge, court, jail, nor officer of the law within a day's journey. The guilty fiend is captured by the residents, tried, and hung to the nearest tree. Every man and woman is aroused and mad for instant and sweeping punishment. Sometimes there are officials near who insist upon the wretch being imprisoned and duly tried months hence, but the maddened friends of the outraged victim are in no mood for parleying, and he is hung instanter. It is easy for those thousands of miles away, surrounded by all the machinery ready to punish crime, to preach patience with and obedience to all forms of the law's delay, but were we present, and the victim in the hands of the incensed neighbors, it may be doubted whether we could preserve the judicial spirit needed to preach patience. "Judge" Lynch is rarely, if ever, accused of punishing the innocent—undue haste or excessive "efficiency" is his fault. The number who suffer, not from injustice but undue haste, is not great. As the population becomes denser and the Negroes better educated, these brutal attacks may be expected to cease. They are steadily decreasing. In 1885, 181 assaults were made; in 1906 only 72, less than half, altho population had increased about one-third.

It is this crime only and the excessive publicity it invariably attracts that creates the false impression that the Negro as a class is lawless, while the contrary is true.

The remaining vital Negro political question is that of the suffrage. The national Constitution provides that no state shall discriminate on account of color. Many of the Southern States now require ability to read and write, which applies to whites as well as blacks. The best people, both North and South, approve this educational test. One good effect is that it gives illiterates, both white and black, a strong inducement to educate themselves. One cannot fail to sympathize with the educated element in communities mostly composed of illiterates, who outvote the intelligent. A few illiterates in an electoral district of the North, or here in Britain, matters little, but where these are in the majority it is an entirely different matter. The solution of the suffrage question probably lies thru this educational test. When Negroes generally are able to meet this, we may assume that their entrance into political life in due course will not be keenly resented. As Confucius long since told us—"There being education, there can be no distinction of classes."

Booker Washington's influence is powerfully exerted to keep the Negroes from placing suffrage in the front. He contends that good moral character and industrial efficiency, resulting in ownership of property, are the pressing needs and the sure and speedy path to recognition and enfranchisement. A few able Negroes are disposed to press for the free and unrestricted vote immediately. We cannot but hope that the wiser policy will prevail.

You may be wondering how this transformation from slave to citizen, so far as it has gone, has been accomplisht.

The education of the Negro began in earnest thru the Freedmen's Bureau, establisht by act of Congress in 1865, a few years after the war. General Howard, who was placed in command, proved most successful, head and heart being interested in the cause. At the end of five years, when it was thought no longer necessary because of the general interest awakened, its record showed that 4239 schools for colored pupils had been establisht in the South, with 9307 teachers and 247,333 pupils, the Bureau having taught nearly one million black children to read and write; the cost to the general government had been six and a half million dollars.

Upon the scene, now appeared one of those rare leaders who seem designed for new and difficult tasks, impossible for ordinary men — nothing short of an original holds the key. Such a man was revealed in a young enthusiast who, born of an American missionary family in Hawaii, became General Armstrong. Shortly after he graduated at Williams College in Massachusetts, came Lincoln's call for volunteers to save the Union. To this young Armstrong promptly responded. He put up a tent in the Public Park at Troy, and asked for recruits to form a company, who soon came to the bright, young would-be captain, and off he went to the front at their head. He writes to his mother — "The first day of January is at hand when the slaves shall be free; then I shall know that I am contending for freedom and for the oppressed. I shall then be willing and less grieved if I fall for such a cause." Here we have the spirit of the Crusader. He soon distinguisht himself, and was promoted to the rank of major. Tho his command had hitherto been over white troops, at his request he was made colonel of the first Negro regiment, and here his genius had scope. He wrote his mother upon taking command — "The star of Africa is rising. Her millions now for the first time catch glimpse of a glorious dawn, and their future, in my opinion, rests largely upon the success of the Negro troops in this war. Their honour and glory will insure the freedom of their race." The regiment soon made a mark for itself. One officer reported that "Armstrong's soldiers felt toward him a regard that amounted almost to deification." He was soon made a general. When the Freedman's Bureau was created at the close of the war, General Howard gave command of the Virginia District to Armstrong, who finally determined to devote his life to the elevation of the Negro race. He wrote to his mother—"Till now my future has been blind." He soon decided to establish a pioneer school to teach both sexes "manual labor as a moral force," and Hampton Institute appeared, pioneer of all succeeding Negro colleges. Under the slave regime, manual labor had been held as fit only for slaves, and naturally the enfranchised Negroes lookt upon idleness as the only real reward of life. They had now to learn that useful labor was the duty of man and his title to honor. Armstrong succeeded in interesting a number of excellent people in the North, and, after overcoming innumerable obstacles, he finally triumphed. He had rare power of attracting others and enthusing them with his own desire to labor for the Negro. Many New England teachers, especially women, went to Hampton and led lives of devotion to the holy cause of uplifting the former slave. No less than fifteen million of dollars (three millions sterling) have been contributed by Northern people for this purpose.

Among General Armstrong's private papers after his death this paragraph was found, giving what he "would wish known were he suddenly to die": "In the school the great thing is not to quarrel, and to get rid of workers whose temperaments are unfortunate no matter how much knowledge or culture they may have. Cantankerousness is worse than heterodoxy."

He wisht to be buried in the college graveyard among his colored students, "where one of them would have been had he died next. No monument or fuss whatever over my grave. I wish the simplest funeral service without sermon or attempt at oratory."

Booker Washington, who was a pupil under him and enjoyed his friendship thru life, says he was "the noblest, rarest human being that it has ever been my privilege to meet. I do not hesitate to say that I never met any great man who in my estimation was his equal. The first time I went into his presence as a student, he made the impression upon me as being a perfect man, and I felt there was something about him superhuman, and until he died the more I saw of him the greater he grew."

He is not alone in this estimate. Many who knew Armstrong endorse it. His life, recently publisht, reveals him to us. So far as we can judge, no nobler, more useful, or more self-sacrificing life was ever lived. I think his life would interest you deeply.

The students of Hampton, of both sexes, were first taught how to take care of their bodies and how to conduct themselves. A high standard of cleanliness and neatness was establisht and rigidly enforced. Then came instruction in some craft, the women being taught domestic duties. The making of useful saleable articles was the aim, and from these came the funds needed to pay a large part of the cost of education. All work was paid for.

Hampton traces twenty-five educational institutions as its outgrowths. Between six and seven thousand of her graduates and ex-students are scattered thruout the South teaching in various branches, 305 in business or clerical work, and 176 graduates pursuing higher courses. The high standard General Armstrong introduced is fully sustained by his worthy, self-sacrificing successor, Mr. Frissell, a Scottish Fraser, and his invaluable wife, equally devoted to the cause.

Josiah King, of Pittsburgh, as trustee of the fund of another citizen, Mr. Avery, who left his fortune for the benefit of the Negro race, gave the needed financial assistance which enabled General Armstrong to carry out his project of founding Hampton. I rejoice that Pittsburgh money found a mission so noble, and that I knew in my boyhood both testator and trustee. Strange to say, the small farm of 159 acres, bought for the Hampton Institute, bore the captivating name of "Little Scotland." Somewhere not far away there no doubt rests one unknown to fame of whom it can be said "A kindly Scot lies here."

Among the Hampton graduates the most distinguisht is Booker Washington, the founder of Tuskegee Institute, Alabama, which I had the pleasure of visiting last year for several days upon its quarter-centenary. I was never more deeply imprest. I saw the students of both sexes being taught the various occupations. Applicants must pass examination. The women are first shown their rooms, and instructed for a few days how scrupulously careful they must be to keep everything in perfect order, and in the performance of daily duties. Extreme attention is paid to personal habits, dress and deportment. Daily bathing and gymnastic exercizes are enforced. Each attends to her own room, and is taught cooking, baking, dressmaking, sewing and, generally speaking, all that becomes a young educated woman. The young men are governed with equal care. The result is an assembly of students, as at Hampton, that compare not unfavorably with white students in our northern universities.

I was escorted thru the industrial schools, where all the crafts are taught. Asking one who was learning to be a tinsmith how long he had been there, he replied, "Three years, sir." "How long have you yet to serve?" "Two more, sir." "You will soon be making your four dollars per day." "I expect to make more than that, sir," was the proud reply. The best tinsmiths make five dollars (£1 0s 10d) per day. He was ambitious, and expected to be first class.

Asking the superintendent if places could be found for all graduates in the crafts, he said that he had five applications for every graduate he could supply. Coachbuilders, masons, bricklayers, tinsmiths, blacksmiths and shoemakers are all there, soon to be earning wages very much higher than in Scotland. Plenty of work for them, for the Tuskegee and Hampton graduation certificate means not only a competent mechanic, seamstress or cook, but a self-respecting man or woman. There is no objection to Negroes being craftsmen thruout the South because under slavery the clever slaves did all such work, white craftsmen being few. Manual labor was only for slaves. Poor whites were above that degradation. They were poor, but gentlemen — at least they were white.

A traveling agricultural school, consisting of a large covered wagon, attracted my attention. Such wagons travel the region, giving Negroes needed lessons. Here were displayed large photographic specimens of the cotton plant and of maize grown upon soils plowed to different depths. The advantages of deep plowing were so clearly shown that the most inert farmer could not rest plowing as shallow as before. I was told that such lessons were promptly taken to heart, and that the old cry "thirty acres and a mule" as the height of the Negro's ambition is now "thirty acres and two mules," so that "plow deep" can be put in practice. Tuskegee takes deep interest in agriculture, and is rapidly raising standards, thru its experimental farm. Its students make great numbers of all kinds of agricultural implements and wagons. It is by these and kindred wise adaptations that Tuskegee has become a great educational force in many forms outside as inside her domain. Numerous are her off-shoots thruout the South — a fruitful brood.

Tuskegee has developed upon lines different from Hampton in one important feature. Here all is the work of Negroes, the principal and professors, and even the architects are colored. Hampton employs white professors, and has a white man in charge. The total number of scholars at Tuskegee, including classes outside, was last year 1948, 1621 being students regularly enrolled. All but about one hundred board and sleep in the grounds. Twenty-three hundred acres of land surrounding are owned by the Institute and cultivated by the students, part being an experimental farm.

The endowment fund amounts to $1,263,000, the largest by far of any colored institution. Mrs. Mary E. Shaw, a colored woman of New York, has just left all her money to it, $38,000, the largest gift ever made by a colored woman. Thirty-seven different occupations are taught in the "Schools of Agriculture," "Mechanical Industries," and "Industries for Girls"—each of these three departments has separate buildings. An annual Negro conference is held, and Negro farmers and others come from all parts of the South, so famous have these meetings become. Two days' sessions are now required, one for farmers and one for teachers.

The choir alone is worth traveling to Tuskegee to hear. The Main Hall is large and vaulted, the stage ample, acoustics fine. The great choir of more than five hundred students sat back of the speakers, who occupied the front of the stage. I was not prepared for such enchanting strains as burst upon us from unseen singers. The music was sacred, and some of the finest gems were sung. I have heard many of the fine choirs of the world, in the Crystal Palace, St. James's Hall, Rome, Dresden, Paris, New York, and elsewhere; seldom do I miss an oratorio if I can help it, but never in my life did choral music affect me as at Tuskegee. Even the Russian choir in St. Petersburg I must rank second. The pure Negro voice is unique. The organ fortunately was very small. One felt there was some ground for preferring the human voice for praise, for even the finest organ lacks something when Negro voices swell.

Booker Washington is the combined Moses and Joshua of his people. Not only has he led them to the promised land, but still lives to teach them by example and precept how properly to enjoy it. He is one of these extraordinary men who rise at rare intervals and work miracles. Born a slave, he is today the acknowledged leader of his race—a modest, gentlemanly man, of pure, simple life and engaging qualities, supremely wise, an orator, organiser and administrator combined. Considering what he was and what he is, and what he has already accomplisht, the point he started from and the commanding position attained, he certainly is one of the most wonderful men living or who has ever lived. History is to tell of two Washingtons, the white and the black, one the father of his country, the other the leader of his race. I commend to you his autobiography, *Up from Slavery*, as companion to *The Life of General Armstrong*.

"There were giants in those days," we are apt to exclaim, and lament their absence in our own age, but this arises from our failure to recognize the gigantic proportions of some of our contemporaries. Today is a king in disguise, Carlyle tells us. Hence our kings pass unnoticed until viewed in their proper perspective by one who has the gift to see and reveal the true heroes to the masses. Future ages are to recognize our contemporary, Booker Washington, the slave, as a giant, distinguishing the age he lived in, and General Armstrong, the pioneer, as another who can never be forgotten in the history of the Negro race. He will grow as he recedes. These men of our own day are hereafter to be canonized as true heroes of civilization, whose life-work was neither to kill nor maim, but to serve or save their fellows.

In the task of elevating the Negro, the part played by the Northern people, from the inception of the Hampton School idea to the present day, has been great. Not only have many millions of dollars been contributed, but many earnest men have given, and are still giving their personal services, giving not money only, but themselves to the cause. Among these there is one who deserves special recognition, Robert C. Ogden, of New York, than whom none was closer to General Armstrong from first to last, and who still serves as Chairman of the Southern Education Board. It is only just that the North should cooperate with the South in the great task, for it is equally responsible for slavery.

Lest you separate, holding the view that there remains little more to be accomplisht in the Negro problem, let me say that all that has been done, encouraging as it undoubtedly is, yet is trifling compared with what remains to be done.

The advanced few are only the leaders of the vast multitude that are still to be stimulated to move forward. Nor are the leaders themselves, with certain exceptions, all that it is hoped they are yet to become.

When you are told of the number owning land or attending schools, or of the millions of church members, and the amount of wealth and of land possest by the Negro, pray remember that they number ten millions, scattered over an area nearly half as great as Europe.

The bright spots have been brought to your notice, but these are only small points surrounded by great areas of darkness. True, the stars are shining in the sky thru the darkness, but the sun spreading light over all has not yet arisen, altho there are not wanting convincing proofs that her morning beams begin to gild the mountain tops.

All the signs are encouraging, never so much so as today. One is quite justified in being sanguine that the result is to be a respectable, educated, intelligent race of colored citizens, increasing in numbers, possest of all civil rights, and who in return will by honest labor remain notably the chief factor in giving the world among other things its indispensable supply of cotton and, to no inconsiderable extent, of the products of cotton, while individual members gifted beyond the mass will worthily fill places in all the professions. Nor will the race fail to be distinguisht from time to time in the future as in the past by the advent of great men, fit successors of Frederick Douglas [sic] and Booker Washington.

The Republic has its problems—fortunately so—without new problems there would be stagnation; but, as in the past, so in the future she will surmount all that now exist and any that may come. Our race has never failed so far. One of the most serious of the problems of the Republic in this generation has been that of the Negro, now, as I hope I have shown, slowly but surely marching to satisfactory solution.

What is to be the final result of the white and black races living together in centuries to come need not concern us. They may remain separate and apart as now or may intermingle. That lies upon the "lap of the gods." That they will henceforth dwell in peace, cooperating more and more as patriotic citizens of the Republic, is, I believe, already assured. I believe also that the Negro is to continue to ascend morally, educationally, and financially. I am quite resigned to our own and the Negro races occupying the South together, confident that as time passes the two will view each other with increasing regard, and more and more realize that, destined as they are to dwell together, it is advantageous for both that they live in harmony as good neighbors and labor for the best interests of their common country.

Meanwhile, my personal experience of the South, small as it is compared with that of many Northern men who have been from the first, and still are, leaders in the work of elevating the Negro, leads me to endorse the opinion of one of the best-known and foremost of these, the Rev. Lyman Abbott, editor of the *Outlook*, who has recently declared that "never in the history of man has a race made such educational and material progress in forty years as the American Negro."

24
Imperialism: "Distant Possessions: The Parting of the Ways"

Andrew Carnegie's strong support of the Monroe Doctrine gave a jingoistic aura to his public utterances on American foreign policy that often seemed at odds with his professed pacifism. He took as much delight in twisting the British lion's tail as did any Irish immigrant from the old sod of Erin. Grover Cleveland, even though a Democrat, became a hero in Carnegie's eyes when in 1895 he demanded that Great Britain either arbitrate the Venezuelan boundary dispute or expect military action from the United States. Like all good Americans, Carnegie subscribed to the adage that political partisanship stopped at the water's edge.

Carnegie was also one of the few major American industrialists in 1898 to urge a war with Spain over the issue of Cuba libre. Carnegie saw this as a just war in support of the Monroe Doctrine, fought to drive out one more vestige of European colonialism in the New World. The war, once underway, however, took on a momentum that went far beyond freeing Cuba. When Spain sued for peace after only four months of war and offered the United States the Philippine Islands halfway around the world, Carnegie belatedly realized that his beloved Republic was being tempted by the Satan of imperialism to bite into the apple of colonialism forbidden to innocent republics. If politics stopped at the water's edge, so also for Carnegie, the Monroe Doctrine stopped at the hemisphere's edge.

Carnegie threw himself into the battle to preserve what he regarded as the basic principles of American republicanism with a vigor he had never shown for any previous political issue, even the fight against silver in 1896. He rushed into print in the August 1898 issue of the North American Review with an article entitled "Distant Possessions: The Parting of the Ways." It was a bitter, unequivocal attack upon American imperialists. "Are we to exchange Triumphant Democracy for Triumphant Despotism?" he cried. He could not believe that was so.

Overnight, Carnegie the jingo had become the darling of the Anti-Imperialist League. So great an impact did his widely circulated article have that Senator Albert Beveridge *felt obliged to answer him on the floor of the Senate with a speech entitled "The March of the Flag." In this, the most memorable address the senator from Indiana ever uttered in Congress, Beveridge refuted Carnegie's thesis by pointing out that American had always moved westward from Jamestown and Plymouth Rock to California and Alaska. Imperialism was as American as Thomas Jefferson and Davy Crockett. To take the Philippines, Beveridge insisted, was no aberration in American republicanism. It was only one more step in following that destiny for America manifested by God.*

In his desperation to block the acquisition of distant possessions, Carnegie even offered to pay the $20 million Spain had asked for the Philippines in order that he himself could set the colony free — surely the only time in history that a private citizen sought to buy an empire from a sovereign nation. "I would gladly pay twenty millions today to restore our Republic to its first principles," he announced in the New York World.

It was Senator Beveridge, not Carnegie, who prevailed, however. McKinley wrestled with his doubts, and then in the name of God and civilization, he accepted Spain's generous offer.

Carnegie lost the political battle of 1898, but in the long run he won the judgment of history that this "splendid little war" did indeed prove to be a true "parting of the ways." With the entry of Commodore Dewey's fleet into Manila Bay, the United States had burst upon the world stage as a powerful new protagonist. For better or for worse, the road was now set for the next century, a road that would lead the United States from China to Chateau-Thierry, from Seoul to Saigon, from Berlin to Baghdad. America would move aggressively forward, motivated if not for distant possessions, most certainly by distant obsessions. The Monroe Doctrine had become global in its scope.

Twice only have the American people been called upon to decide a question of such vital import as that now before them.

Is the Republic, the apostle of Triumphant Democracy, of the rule of the people, to abandon her political creed and endeavor to establish in other lands the rule of the foreigner over the people, Triumphant Despotism?

Is the Republic to remain one homogeneous whole, one united people, or to become a scattered and disjointed aggregate of widely separated and alien races?

Is she to continue the task of developing her vast continent until it holds a population as great as that of Europe, all Americans, or to abandon that destiny to annex, and to attempt to govern, other far distant parts of the world as outlying possessions, which can never be integral parts of the Republic?

Is she to exchange internal growth and advancement for the development of external possessions which can never be really hers in any fuller sense than India is British or Cochin China French? Such is the portentous question of the day. Two equally important questions the American people have decided wisely, and their flag now waves over the greater portion of the English-speaking race; their country is the richest of all countries, first in manufactures, in mining, and in commerce (home and foreign), first this year also in exports. But, better than this, the average condition of its people in education and in living is the best. The luxuries of the masses in other lands are the necessaries of life in ours. The schoolhouse and the church are nowhere so widely distributed. Progress in the arts and sciences is surprising. In international affairs her influence grows so fast, and foreshadows so much, that one of the foremost statesmen has recently warned Europe that it must combine against her if it is to hold its own in the industrial world. The Republic remains one solid whole, its estate inclosed in a ring fence, united, impregnable, triumphant, clearly destined to become the foremost power of the world, if she continue to follow the true path. Such are the fruits of wise judgment in deciding the two great issues of the past, Independence and Union.

In considering the issue now before us, the agitator, the demagogue, has no part. Not feeling, not passion, but deliberate judgment alone, should have place. The question should be calmly weighed; it is not a matter of party, nor of class; for the fundamental interest of every citizen is a common interest, that which is best for the poorest being best for the richest. Let us, therefore, reason together, and be well assured, before we change our position, that we are making no plunge into an abyss. Happily, we have the experience of others to guide us, the most instructive being that of our own race in Great Britain.

There are two kinds of national possessions, one colonies, the other dependencies. In the former we establish and reproduce our own race. Thus Britain has peopled Canada and Australia with English-speaking people, who have naturally adopted our ideas of self-government. That the world has benefited thereby goes without saying; that Britain has done a great work as the mother of nations is becoming more and more appreciated the more the student learns of worldwide affairs. No nation that ever existed has done so much for the progress of the world as the little islands in the North Sea known as Britain.

With dependencies it is otherwise. The most grievous burden which Britain has upon her shoulders is that of India, for there it is impossible for our race to grow. The child of English-speaking parents must be removed and reared in Britain. The British Indian official must have long respites in his native land. India means death to our race. The characteristic feature of a dependency is that the acquiring power cannot reproduce its own race there.

Inasmuch as the territories outside our own continent which our country may be tempted to annex cannot be colonies, but only dependencies, we need not dwell particularly upon the advantages or disadvantages of the former, although the writer is in thorough accord with Disraeli, who said even of colonies: "Our colonies are millstones round the neck of Britain; they lean upon us while they are weak, and leave us when they become strong." This is just what our Republic did with Britain.

There was something to be said for colonies from the point of view of pecuniary gain in the olden days, when they were treated as the legitimate spoil of the conqueror. It is Spain's fatal mistake that she has never realized that it is impossible to follow this policy in our day. Britain is the only country which has realized this truth. British colonies have complete self-government; they even tax the products of their own motherland. That Britain possesses her colonies is a mere figure of speech; that her colonies possess her is nearer the truth. "Our Colonial Empire" seems a big phrase, but, as far as material benefits are concerned, the balance is the other way. Thus, even loyal Canada trades more with us than with Britain. She buys her Union Jacks in New York. Trade does not follow the flag in our day; it scents the lowest price current. There is no patriotism in exchanges.

Some of the organs of manufacturing interests, we observe, favor foreign possessions as necessary or helpful markets for our products. But the exports of the United States this year are greater than those of any other nation in the world. Even Britain's exports are less, yet Britain possesses, it is said, a hundred colonies and dependencies scattered all over the world. The fact that the United States has none does not prevent her products and manufactures from invading Japan, China, Australia, New Zealand, Canada, and all parts of the world in competition with those of Britain. Possession of colonies or dependencies is not necessary for trade reasons. What her colonies are valued for, and justly so, by Britain, is the happiness and pride which the mother feels in her children. The instinct of motherhood is gratified, and no one living places a higher estimate upon the sentiment than I do. Britain is the kindest of mothers, and well deserves the devotion of her children.

If we could establish colonies of Americans, and grow Americans in any part of the world now unpopulated and unclaimed by any of the great powers, and thus follow the example of Britain, heart and mind might tell us that we should have to think twice, yea, thrice, before deciding adversely. Even then our decision should be adverse; but there is at present no such question before us. What we have to face is the question whether we should embark upon the difficult and dangerous policy of undertaking the government of alien races in lands where it is impossible for our own race to be produced.

As long as we remain free from distant possessions we are impregnable against serious attack; yet, it is true, we have to consider what obligations may fall upon us of an international character requiring us to send our forces to points beyond our own territory. Up to this time we have disclaimed all intention to interfere with affairs beyond our own continent, and only claimed the right to watch over American interests according to the Monroe Doctrine, which is now firmly established. This carries with it serious responsibilities, no doubt, which we cannot escape. European nations must consult us upon territorial questions pertaining to our continent, but this makes no tremendous demand upon our military or naval forces. We are at home, as it were, near our base, and sure of the support of the power in whose behalf and on whose request we may act. If it be found essential to possess a coaling-station at Puerto Rico for future possible, though not probable, contingencies, there is no insuperable objection. Neither would the control of the West Indies be alarming if pressed upon us by Britain, since the islands are small and the populations must remain insignificant and without national aspirations. Besides, they are upon our own shores, American in every sense. Their defense by us would be easy. No protest need be entered against such legitimate and peaceful expansion in our own hemisphere, should events work in that direction. I am no "Little" American, afraid of growth, either in population or territory, provided always that the new territory be American, and that it will produce Americans, and not foreign races bound in time to be false to the Republic in order to be true to themselves.

As I write, the cable announces the annexation of Hawaii, which is more serious; but the argument for this has been the necessity for holding the only coaling-station in the Pacific so situated as to be essential to any power desirous of successfully attacking our Pacific coast. Until the Nicaragua Canal is made,

Imperialism: "Distant Possessions" 299

it is impossible to deny the cogency of this contention. We need not consider it a measure of offense or aggression, but as strictly defensive. The population of the islands is so small that national aspirations are not to be encountered, which is a great matter. Nor is it obtained by conquest. It is ours by a vote of its people, which robs its acquisition of many dangers. Let us hope that our far-outlying possessions may end with Hawaii.

To reduce it to the concrete, the question is: Shall we attempt to establish ourselves as a power in the far East and possess the Philippines for glory? The glory we already have, in Dewey's victory overcoming the power of Spain in a manner which adds one more to the many laurels of the American navy, which, from its infancy till now, has divided the laurels with Britain upon the sea. The Philippines have about seven and a half millions of people, composed of races bitterly hostile to one another, alien races, ignorant of our language and institutions. Americans cannot be grown there. The islands have been exploited for the benefit of Spain, against whom they have twice rebelled, like the Cubans. But even Spain has received little pecuniary benefit from them. The estimated revenue of the Philippines in 1894–95 was £2,715,980, the expenditure being £2,656,026, leaving a net result of about $300,000. The United States could obtain even this trifling sum from the inhabitants only by oppressing them as Spain has done. But, if we take the Philippines, we shall be forced to govern them as generously as Britain governs her dependencies, which means that they will yield us nothing, and probably be a source of annual expense. Certainly they will be a grievous drain upon revenue if we consider the enormous army and navy which we shall be forced to maintain upon their account.

There are many objections to our undertaking the government of dependencies; one I venture to submit as being peculiar to ourselves. We should be placed in a wrong position. Consider Great Britain in India today. She has established schools and taught the people our language. In the Philippines, we may assume that we should do the same, and with similar results. To travel through India as an American is a point of great advantage if one wishes to know the people of India and their aspirations. They unfold to Americans their inmost thoughts, which they very naturally withhold from their masters, the British. When in India, I talked with many who had received an English education in the British schools, and found that they had read and pondered most upon Cromwell and Hampden, Wallace and Bruce and Tell, upon Washington and Franklin. The Briton is sowing the seed of rebellion with one hand in his schools—for education makes rebels—while with the other he is oppressing patriots who desire the independence of their country. The national patriotism upon which a Briton plumes himself he must repress in India. It is only a matter of time when India, the so-called gem of the British crown, is to glitter red again. British control of India is rendered possible today only by the division of races, or rather of religions, there. The Hindus and Mohammedans still mistrust each other more than they do the British, but caste is rapidly passing away, and religious prejudices are softening. Whenever this distrust disappears, Britain is liable to be expelled, at a loss of life and treasure which cannot be computed. The aspirations of a people for independent existence are seldom repressed, nor, according to American ideas hitherto, should they be. If it be a noble aspiration for the Indian or the Cuban, as it was for the citizen of the United States himself, and for the various South American republics once under Spain, to have a country to live and, if necessary, to die for, why is not the revolt noble which the man of the Philippines has been making against Spain? Is it possible that the Republic is to be placed in the position of the suppressor of the Philippine struggle for independence? Surely, that is impossible. With what face shall we hang in the schoolhouses of the Philippines our own Declaration of Independence, and yet deny independence to them? What response will the heart of the Philippine Islander make as he reads of Lincoln's Emancipation Proclamation? Are we to practise independence and preach subordination, to teach rebellion in our books, yet to stamp it out with our swords, to sow the seed of revolt and expect the harvest of loyalty? President McKinley's call for volunteers to fight for Cuban independence against the cruel dominion of Spain meets with prompt response, but who would answer the call of the President of an "imperial" republic for free citizens to fight for Washington and slaughter the patriots of some distant dependency which struggles for independence?

It has hitherto been the glorious mission of the Republic to establish upon secure foundations Triumphant Democracy, and the world now understands government of the people, for the people, and by the people. Tires the Republic so soon of its mission, that it must, perforce, discard it to undertake the impossible task of establishing Triumphant Despotism, the rule of the foreigner over the people? and must the millions of the Philippines who have been asserting their God-given right to govern themselves be the first victims of Americans, whose proudest boast is that they conquered independence for themselves?

Let another phase of the question be carefully weighed. Europe is today an armed camp, not chiefly because the home territories of its various nations are threatened, but because of fear of aggressive action upon the part of other nations touching outlying "possessions." France resents British control of Egypt, and is fearful of its West African possessions; Russia seeks Chinese territory, with a view to expansion to the Pacific; Germany also seeks distant possessions; Britain, who has acquired so many dependencies, is so fearful of an attack upon them that this year she is spending nearly eighty millions of dollars upon additional warships, and Russia, Germany, and France follow suit. Japan is a new element of anxiety; and by the end of the year it is computed she will have sixty-seven formidable ships of war. The naval powers of Europe, and Japan also, are apparently determined to be prepared for a terrific struggle for possessions in the far East, close to the Philippines—and why not for these islands themselves? Into this vortex the Republic is cordially invited to enter by those powers who expect her policy to be of benefit to them. but her action is jealously watched by those who fear that her power might be used against them.

It has never been considered the part of wisdom to thrust one's hand into the hornet's nest, and it does seem as if the United States must lose all claim to ordinary prudence and good sense if she enter this arena and become involved in the intrigues and threats of war which make Europe an armed camp.

It is the parting of the ways. We have a continent to populate and develop; there are only twenty-three persons to the square mile in the United States. England has three hundred and seventy, Belgium five hundred and seventy-one, Germany two hundred and fifty. A tithe of the cost of maintaining our sway over the Philippines would improve our internal waterways; build the Nicaragua Canal; construct a waterway to the ocean from the Great Lakes, an inland canal along the Atlantic seaboard, and a canal across Florida, saving eight hundred miles' distance between New York and New Orleans; connect Lake Michigan with the Mississippi; deepen all the harbors upon the lakes; build a canal from Lake Erie to the Allegheny River; slack-water through movable dams the entire length of the Ohio River to Cairo; thoroughly improve the Lower and Upper Mississippi, and all our seaboard harbors. All these enterprises would be as nothing in cost in comparison with the sums required for the experiment of possessing the Philippine Islands, seven thousand miles from our shores. If the object be to render our Republic powerful among nations, can there be any doubt as to which policy is the better? To be more powerful at home is the surest way to be more powerful abroad. Today the Republic stands the friend of all nations, the ally of none; she has no ambitious designs upon the territory of any power upon another continent; she crosses none of their ambitious designs, evokes no jealousy of the bitter sort, inspires no fear; she is not one of them, scrambling for possessions; she stands apart, pursuing her own great mission, and teaching all nations by example. Let her become a power annexing foreign territory, and all is changed in a moment.

If we are to compete with other nations for foreign possessions, we must have a navy like theirs. It should be superior to any other navy, or we play a second part. It is not enough to have a navy equal to that of Russia or of France, for Russia and France may combine against us just as they may against Britain. We at once enter the field as a rival of Britain, the chief possessor of foreign possessions, and who can guarantee that we shall not even have to measure our power against her?

What it means to enter the list of military and naval powers having foreign possessions may be gathered from the following considerations. First, look at our future navy. If it is only to equal that of France it means fifty-one battleships; if of Russia, forty battleships. If we cannot play the game without being at least the equal of any of our rivals, then eighty battleships is the number Britain possesses. We now have only four, with five building. Cruisers, armed and unarmed, swell the number threefold, Britain having two hundred and seventy-three ships of the line built or ordered, with three hundred and eight torpedo boats in addition; France having one hundred and thirty-four ships of the line and two hundred and sixty-nine torpedo boats. All these nations are adding ships rapidly. Every armor- and gun-making plant in the world is busy night and day. Ships are indispensable, but recent experience shows that soldiers are equally so. While the immense armies of Europe need not be duplicated, yet we shall certainly be too weak unless our army is at least twenty times what it has been—say five hundred thousand men. Even then we shall be powerless as against any one of three of our rivals—Germany, France, and Russia.

This drain upon the resources of these countries has become a necessity from their respective positions, largely as graspers for foreign possessions. The United States today, happily, has no such necessity, her neighbors being powerless against her, since her possessions are concentrated and her power is one solid mass.

Today two great powers in the world are compact, developing themselves in peace throughout vast conterminous territories. When war threatens they have no outlying possessions which can never be really "possessed," but which they are called upon to defend. They fight upon the exposed edge only of their own soil in case of attack, and are not only invulnerable, but they could not be more than inconvenienced by the world in arms against them. These powers are Russia and the United States. The attempt of Britain to check Russia, if the wild counsels of Mr. Chamberlain were followed, could end in nothing but failure. With the irresistible force of the glacier, Russia moves upon the plains below. Well for Russia, and well for the world, is her advance over pagan China, better even for Britain from the standpoint of business, for every Russian today trades as much with Britain as do nine Chinamen. Britain, France, Germany, Belgium, Spain, are all vulnerable, having departed from the sagacious policy of keeping possessions and power concentrated. Should the United States depart from this policy, she also must be so weakened in consequence as never to be able to play the commanding part in the world, disjointed, that she can play whenever she desires if she remain compact.

Whether the United States maintain its present unique position of safety, or forfeit it through acquiring foreign possessions, is to be decided by its action in regard to the Philippines; for, fortunately, the independence of Cuba is assured; for this the Republic has proclaimed to the world that she has drawn the sword. But why should the less than two millions of Cuba receive national existence and the seven and a half millions of the Philippines be denied it? The United States, thus far in their history, have no page reciting self-sacrifice made for others; all their gains have been for themselves. This void is now to be grandly filled. The page which recites the resolve of the Republic to rid her neighbor, Cuba, from the foreign possessor will grow brighter with the passing centuries, which may dim many pages now deemed illustrious. Should the coming American be able to point to Cuba and the Philippines rescued from foreign domination and enjoying independence won for them by his country and given to them without money and without price, he will find no citizen of any other land able to claim for his country services so disinterested and so noble.

We repeat, there is no power in the world that could do more than inconvenience the United States by attacking its fringe, which is all that the world combined could do, so long as our country is not compelled to send its forces beyond its own compact shores to defend worthless possessions. If our country were blockaded by the united powers of the world for years, she would emerge from the embargo richer and stronger, and with her own resources more completely developed. We have little to fear from external attack. No thorough blockade of our enormous seaboard is possible; but even if it were, the few indispensable articles not produced by ourselves (if there were any such) would reach us by way of Mexico or Canada at slightly increased cost.

From every point of view we are forced to the conclusion that the past policy of the Republic is her true policy for the future; for safety, for peace, for happiness, for progress, for wealth, for power—for all that makes a nation blessed.

Not till the war-drum is silent, and the day of calm peace returns, can the issue be soberly considered.

Twice have the American people met crucial issues wisely, and in the third they are not to fail.

25
Pacifism: "'Honor' and International Arbitration"

Andrew Carnegie's crusade against imperialism in 1898 was to lead him directly into a much bigger crusade for the abolition of all wars, no matter for what cause they might be fought. Although in 1900 he wrote to W. T. Stead, the editor of Review of Reviews, *"I am not a 'peace at any price' man. . . . I believe it was my duty to be on the field at Bull Run" (4 October 1900, Carnegie Papers, Library of Congress, vol. 78), only seven years later he had found the concept of a "just" war to be nonsense. To Charles Eliot, the president of Harvard, he wrote in 1907, "just as when young I became a rabid anti-slavery zealot, so in regard to war—far more heinous than owning and selling men is killing men by men" (15 March 1907, Carnegie Papers, Library of Congress, vol. 140).*

In the quest for peace, Carnegie was willing to dispense funds extravagantly to build his "temples of peace" to house international organizations and to endow four major peace foundations. But he was not content to be simply a patron angel to finance the peace movement. He must also be the commanding general in this war against war. Much of his writing and most of his formal addresses after 1904 had but one theme, that of achieving international peace. He also eagerly assumed for himself the role of serving as the unofficial—and most often unwanted—chief counsel on foreign policy to the president of the United States. He was the self-appointed Secretary of Peace for every American president from 1901 to 1917, a minister extraordinary without portfolio and certainly without official recognition. His letters to Theodore Roosevelt, William Howard Taft, and Woodrow Wilson were frequent and insistent in the cause of peace. There were many other recipients of his unsolicited counsel as well—King Edward, Kaiser Wilhelm, and a motley collection of prime ministers, chancellors, foreign ministers, and ambassadors throughout the world. His counsel was not often welcome. Theodore Roosevelt wrote to a friend, "I have tried hard to like Carnegie, but it is pretty difficult. There is no type of man for whom I feel a more contemptuous abhorrence than for the one who makes a God of mere money-making and at the same time is always yelling out that kind of stupid condemnation of war which in almost every case springs from a combination of defective physical courage . . . and of hopelessly twisted ideals" (Roosevelt to Whitelaw Reid, 13 Nov. 1905, Reid Papers, vol. 105, no. 11147, Library of Congress). Even the mild-mannered Taft was driven in his exasperation to an unaccustomed use of sarcasm when he added as a postscript to one of Carnegie's letters before sending it on to Secretary of State Philander Knox, "Isn't it pleasant to be told how it could have been done. W. H. T." (note by Taft on a letter from Carnegie to Taft, 15 Dec. 1912, Philander C. Knox Papers, vol. 20, Library of Congress).

In 1910, however, Taft became Carnegie's newly found hero when the president quite abruptly announced that he would pursue the negotiations of treaties with Great Britain and France binding the United States and those nations to arbitrate peacefully all future disputes, even those involving questions of "national honor." Carnegie was ecstatic, for he had been a strong advocate of international arbitration dating back to the Alabama *claims controversy with Britain after the Civil War. With Taft's pronouncement, Carnegie could now feel that his persistent badgering of the White House had at last paid off. It was in this spirit of euphoria that Carnegie delivered the following address, "'Honor' and International Arbitration" to the annual meeting of the British Peace Society in the Guildhall of London, in June of that year (published in Burton J. Hendricks, ed.,* Miscellaneous Writings of Andrew Carnegie *[Garden City, N.Y.: Doubleday, Doran & Co., 1933], vol. 2, pp. 272–88).*

In this speech can be found references to all the major points in a program for world peace which Carnegie had vigorously promoted over the past decade: (1) holding frequent summit meetings of the heads of state of the great powers; (2) giving the same recognition to the Heroes of Peace who save lives that had historically been given to the Heroes of War who took lives; (3) submitting all disputes between nations to an international tribunal for adjudication; and (4) a League of Peace of the great powers to enforce the tribunal's decisions with economic sanctions, and that failing, with an international police force to bring an aggressor nation into line.

It is President Taft's proposal to submit all international disputes, not exempting questions involving national honor, that Carnegie develops most fully in this speech. Taft had gone further along the road that Carnegie saw as leading to world peace than had any previous head of state. At this moment, Carnegie had good reason to believe that "we are apparently on the eve of a decided step forward, soon the International Judicial Court is to appear, and the step from that to a League of Peace follows." "Be of good cheer, Brothers," he told the Peace Society. Certainly Carnegie was.

Pacifism: "International Arbitration"

I esteem it a privilege to address you in this memorable Guildhall. Let my first words be those of tribute to the great peacemaker we have just lost. We of the English-speaking race from across the Atlantic mingle our tears with yours, for King Edward, in his youth, captivated the American people.

Fortunately, there is every ground for belief that his successor will tread in his father's footsteps, and thus draw closer and closer together the two branches of our race.

Long and earnestly have the teachers of men sought relief from war, which has drawn from the most illustrious such fierce denunciations as no other crime has evoked—perhaps not all the other national crimes combined. Surely no civilized community in our day can resist the conclusion that the killing of man by man, as a means of settling international disputes, is the foulest blot upon human society, the greatest curse of human life, and that as long as men continue thus to kill one another they have slight claim to rank as civilized, since in this respect they remain savages. The crime of war is inherent, it awards victory not to the nation that is right, but to that which is strong. It knows nothing of righteous judgment.

In man's triumphant upward march he has outgrown many savage habits: he no longer eats his fellows, or buys and sells them, or sacrifices prisoners of war, or puts vanquished garrisons to the sword, or confiscates private property, or bombards unfortified ports, poisons wells, or sacks cities. No more

> the flesh'd soldier, rough and hard of heart,
> In liberty of bloody hand shall range
> With conscience wide as hell.

All these changes in the rules of war have been made from time to time, just as our race rose from the savage state toward civilization. They are chiefly the good fruits of the last century, for even Wellington sacked cities.

If all civilized people now regard these former atrocities of war as disgraceful to humanity, how soon must their successors regard the root of these barbarities, war itself, as unworthy of civilized men, and discard it as intolerable?

We are marching fast to that day, through the reign of law, under which civilized people are now compelled to live. No citizen of a civilized nation is permitted to wage war against his fellow-citizen or to redress his own wrongs, real or fancied. Even if assaulted he can legally use force only sufficient to protect himself; then the law steps in, and administers punishment to the aggressor based upon evidence. Hence, if a citizen attempts to sit as judge in his own cause or to redress his wrongs in case of dispute with another, he becomes a lawbreaker. Now, nations being only aggregations of individuals, why should they be permitted to wage war against other nations, when, if all were classed as citizens of one nation, they would be denied this right of war, and would have to subject themselves to the reign of law? Not long can this continue to commend itself to the judgment of intelligent men. Consider our own republic, with an area little smaller than that of Europe, within whose wide borders war is impossible, every citizen being honorably bound to keep the peace and submit to the courts of law, which alone administer judgment in cases of dispute, and contrast it with Europe, an armed camp—armed not against distant foreign enemies upon other continents, but against itself. Under present rules of war, there are in Europe as many possible centers of war as there are nations. We have forty-six nations in America, called states, yet there is not one center of war. Resort to force would be rebellion. This unity, which ensures freedom from danger of internal war and free exchange of products, is fast leading our Union to the front.

In considering the problem of war, let it be noted that it is no longer actual war itself which the world in our day has most to dread. This is not the greatest curse. It is the ever-present danger of war, which hangs over the world like a pall, which we have to dispel. Men are now born and die, their country's peace unbroken, but in scarcely a year of their lives it is not endangered, and not a day can pass which is not disturbed by the fearful note of "preparation for war" throughout the world, which some writers still venture to recommend even in editorial columns as the best preventative of war.

On the contrary, preparation by one nation compels rival preparation by others, each honestly protesting that only protection and not attack, is desired, the inevitable result being, however, that mutual suspicion is aroused, and as each vies with the other in fearful preparation national hatreds develop, and then only a spark is needed to kindle the torch of war.

Partial disarmament cannot remove this danger of war; it would only give quarreling neighbors two pistols instead of three, war continuing as probable as ever.

It is not what bearings a question at issue between nations may have upon the countries of the respective disputants which is of first importance in determining the result of peace or war; it is in what spirit, friendly or unfriendly, negotiations are entered upon. Disputes that would be easily settled between friendly nations become the basis of war when international jealousies exist. An illustration of this vital truth is the incident upon the Dogger Bank,[1] which recently excited Great Britain and Russia. It was promptly settled, but if the parties had been Great Britain and Germany it would in all probability have led to war, so readily does rival preparation provide the inflammable material upon which war feeds.

The insuperable objection to "preparation" is that it inevitably leads to the building of competing armaments by powers which otherwise would not have increased them, thus spreading the area of war and making more nations possible enemies. Hence the most prolific mother of war in our day is "preparation," as "territorial aggrandizement" has been until recently.

There is one important feature of our time which has to be most carefully considered—every ruler, statesman, and ambassador of every country repeatedly protests that their armaments are for protection only: that their country seeks not territorial addition: that its first and last desire is peace as the greatest blessing. In all this they are beyond question sincere, all really desire peace, and their armaments are intended to be protective instruments only. Why, then, is peace not secured? The answer is that the leaders of nations at their respective capitals are strangers to each other, and communicate only through their ambassadors; they do not trust each other; each suspects sinister designs in the other and, fearful of offending public opinion, so easily excited upon international issues, they hesitate to adopt broad peace measures of common justice or to agree to arbitration which might decide against their country. Under world conditions, if the makers of treaties knew and trusted each other war would soon become obsolete, for it is an indubitable fact that the reign of peace would be most advantageous for all nations. To every nation war would be a calamity. Let us rid ourselves of thinking that there are good nations who abhor war, and bad nations who lie in wait for an opportunity to attack the weak. In our day the peaceful development of nations is their most profitable policy.

Assuming that all civilized nations long for peace, if one or more of the chief powers were to approach the others in the proper spirit, a league of peace would seem highly probable.

---

1. On October 22, 1904, the Russian fleet, under Admiral Rozhdestvensky, on its way to far eastern waters, fired upon British trawlers in the North Sea under the impression that they were hostile torpedo boats, killing several British sailors. Tension was acute for a time, but the matter was settled by arbitration under the Hague Convention.

There is another point of view: the world, once so unknown, with ports so distant, has now shrunk into a neighborhood in constant and instantaneous communication, international exchanges reaching the enormous sum of £5,600,000,000 per year.

It stands to reason, therefore, that under these changed conditions no one or two nations should be permitted to disturb the world's peace, in which other nations have a common interest and upon which they are more or less dependent. Nations are partners today in this world-business, and have a right to be consulted in all matters pertaining to the world's peace. They are rapidly becoming interdependent, and international courts must of necessity soon be established. We have the germ of these already in the World Marine Court recently agreed upon in London by the delegates of the eight naval powers, Austria-Hungary, Great Britain, France, Germany, Russia, Japan, Italy, and the United States. This tribunal, composed of one judge from each land, is to pass final judgment upon all questions within its sphere. It is this which our Secretary of State, Mr. Knox, has wisely suggested should become an arbitral court, empowered to consider all disputes referred to it by the nations. If the powers agree to his admirable suggestion, which stamps him as a statesman, the world will soon have a permanent international court composed of the foremost of the world's jurists, ready to pass judgment upon any international dispute that may be submitted. Thus the world moves steadily toward peace and brotherhood.

Peaceful arbitration has so far been the chief agent of progress toward the reign of peace and can be credited with having already settled nearly six hundred international disputes. Secretary Root has broken all records by negotiating twenty-four arbitration treaties, and for this and other important services he deserves high place among the workers for international peace. Such treaties are not to be judged solely by their provisions. These to which we have referred are limited to certain subjects, exclusive of others, but the average citizen knows little of treaty contents, and hence the mere fact that his country has agreed with another to settle some issues peacefully, inspires friendly feelings which may some day count. Again, statesmen, knowing that their respective countries have agreed to settle some kinds of disputes peaceably, are predisposed to follow that mode for the settlement of others; therefore all treaties, whatever their limitations, make for peace.

But arbitration of international disputes has so far encountered a serious obstacle; nations have been and still are indisposed to submit all disputes to arbitration. Although Belgium and Holland, Chile and the Argentine, Norway and Sweden have done so, one or more exceptions are always made by the chief nations, and these are fatal to the one indispensable change required—the removal of the danger of war, without which nothing vital is gained.

Many devoted disciples of peace were seriously studying this feature of the problem when the solution came unexpectedly in a flash of inspiration from no less a ruler than President Taft that revealed the true path to the realization of peace on earth. Here is the deliverance before the Peace and Arbitration Society in New York on March 22, 1910, which we believe will remain memorable for untold ages, and give the author rank among the immortals as one of the foremost benefactors of his race:

> Personally I do not see any more reason why matters of national honour should not be referred to a court of arbitration than matters of property or of national proprietorship. I know that is going farther than most men are willing to go, but I do not see why questions of honour may not be submitted to a tribunal composed of men of honour who understand questions of national honour, to abide by their decision, as well as any other question of difference arising between nations.

In these few words President Taft becomes among rulers the leader of the holy crusade against man killing man in war, as Lincoln became the leader in the crusade against the selling of man by man. Much to the dismay of mere party politicians Lincoln went to the root of the curse of slavery, declaring that a nation could not endure permanently half slave and half free. Our leader of today declares it is the duty of nations to refer to a court of honor all questions thought to affect their honor as well as any other questions arising between them. Thus nations cannot sit as judges in their own causes, for this would violate the first principles of natural justice, as is shown by the fact that in our day a judge known to have sat in judgment in a cause in which he was even in the smallest degree personally interested would die in infamy. So will nations sink into infamy which insist much longer upon trampling under foot this benign rule of law. Courts of honor, such as suggested by the President, are rapidly coming into favor in countries which still tolerate the duel, which our race has discarded.

The German Emperor especially is reputed to have done much to introduce these, and hence to restrict duelling.

It is quite true that the President, as he says, "goes further than most men are willing to go," otherwise he would not be a leader; for a leader's place is in the front. But—and this is another characteristic of the truly great leader—

he goes no further than is absolutely necessary. Had he exempted any one subject, even that phantom called "honor," from arbitration—although no nation can dishonor another nation, and no man ever did or ever can dishonor another man, all honor's wounds being self-inflicted—he would have failed to bridge the chasm between peace and the danger of war, and little would have been gained. Armaments would continue to swell as at present, increasing suspicion, jealousy, and hatred between the powers until war broke forth as the natural result of mutual preparation, which from its very nature creates what it so vainly hopes to prevent.

When the final step is taken and the representatives of the nations assemble to organize the international court, to which they agree to submit all disputes, it may be assumed that they will specify as a fundamental principle that the independence of nations and their existing territorial rights shall be recognized and upheld as an integral part of the organization. Ex-President Roosevelt states this clearly in his recent Nobel Prize address at Stockholm. Hence no disputes could arise affecting either of these subjects. That the tenets of international law shall govern the action of the tribunal is also certain to be declared. Thus would be eliminated at the start the source of serious disputes affecting the honor or vital interests of nations.

Let all friends of peace hail President Taft as our leader, rejoicing that he has found the true solution of the problem.

The Peace Society of New York passed the following resolutions at its annual meeting in New York City on April 16th, a copy being sent to President Taft:

> Resolved, that the Peace Society of the City of New York hails the recent inspired utterance of President Taft in favour of the submission to Arbitration of all questions of difference among nations as the final stage in the long process of educating the world in the application of reason to international affairs as pointing the way of salvation to the bankrupt statesmanship of the nations, and as giving to our President a unique position of leadership among the rulers of the earth.
>
> Resolved further, that this Society invokes, in support of this wise and far-sighted policy, the fundamental principles of justice—as applicable to nations as to individuals—that no one shall be a judge in his own cause, a principle essential to the reign of law and the maintenance of Peace and order among men and nations.

Were this society to pass a similar vote, I am sure it would be appreciated and serve to draw our race closer together.

Dedicating the temple of the twenty-one American republics in Washington, last month, the President said:

It goes without saying that the foreign policy of the United States is for Peace among American Republics. We cannot afford to have any two or three of these quarrelling. We must not; but Mr. Carnegie and I will never be satisfied until nineteen of us can intervene by proper means to suppress a quarrel between any other two of us.

Gentlemen, this means a league of peace between our republics, to preserve the peace and uphold the reign of law. Never has ruler gone so far before. Would we had one or more of the rulers or governments of Europe to keep him company and make the league of peace worldwide.

You will have noticed that Mr. Roosevelt in his recent speech at Stockholm likewise advocated a supreme court for the world, after the pattern of the American Supreme Court, which lays down the law to the forty-six states of the Union, overruling all other courts, and even Congress and the President. He also says:

Finally, it would be a master stroke if those Great Powers honestly bent on peace would form a League of Peace, not only to keep the peace between themselves, but to prevent, by force if necessary, its being broken by others. The ruler or statesman who brings about such a combination would earn his place in history, and be entitled to the gratitude of all mankind for all time.

Upon the eve of the recent Hague Conference I asked your late Prime Minister[2] whether Britain would not welcome an invitation to join such a league. His reply was, "No party in Britain dare refuse." From what you have heard of our President's views you will probably infer the republic would not be backward. There would be tremendous strength in the united action of our English-speaking race, nor would we be left without associates. Our respective peace societies should confer freely with a view to united action. All we English-speakers are subjects of King Shakespeare, and so are we in some degree all subjects of President Washington, whose words were, "My first wish is to see this plague of mankind—war—banished from the face of the earth."

One of the most notable recent triumphs of peace is the prompt and complete exposure of the fallacy that war is the nursery of heroes. How often have we been told that

---

2. Sir Henry Campbell-Bannerman.

> When roll of drum and 'battle's roar
> Shall cease upon the earth, then no more
> The heroic deed, the race of heroes in the land.

Never was fallacy so rapidly dispelled. We all know that scarcely a day passes within the boundaries of our race in Canada, Newfoundland, America or Britain that does not reveal heroic acts in the realm of peaceful industrialism.

Let us not forget that His late Majesty was the first monarch to recognize such heroes of peace here in Britain. He recently summoned to Balmoral, and decorated with his own hand, five of these from the Orkneys, who, after two successful attempts, at risk of their own lives, had rescued a shipwrecked crew. He has done the same for heroic miners.

It was my privilege to shake hands with those heroes upon their return to the Orkneys, and to present to them the awards of the Hero Fund, assuring them that the victories of war which involved the death of men sank into insignificance compared with their victory of peace, saving men at the risk of their own lives. This is the difference between the hero of barbarism and the hero of civilization; one kills or maims his fellow men, the other saves or serves them.

Barbarism, which held that there was no career for gentlemen except that of man-killing, produced only brute courage, which in that day men shared with the brutes. Civilization developed moral courage which in turn led men to save or serve their fellows.

"I never wish to see a regiment of soldiers again," was General Grant's reply to the Duke of Cambridge, who offered him a military review.

"War is hell" was the verdict of General Sherman.

What need for wonder that in our day there is a growing scarcity of army officers in both Britain and America?

In conclusion, Mr. Chairman, surveying the past, what have we veterans of peace to point to as our greatest victory over war as a crime? It is the indisputable fact which cannot be gainsaid that in our time the killing of English-speaking men by English-speaking men as a means of settling international disputes has been banished for ever within the wide boundaries of our race. Never again is the world to witness the spectacle of English-speaking men destroying each other. If ever we have to protect the world's peace we shall be found standing side by side in that holy mission—this is certain. It was during the crucial test which led to this, the greatest of all victories, that your lamented King Edward first appeared in the role which he lived to make his own, that of the peacemaker. Many here will remember that President Cleveland demanded arbitration,[3] to which Mr. Gladstone had agreed, but which Lord Salisbury, who succeeded him, declined. The American people supported the President. Even so conservative a body as the New York Chamber of Commerce voted to do so by hundreds against a few scattered votes. The British people at first were not aware of the history of the question, but soon there began to come from across the Atlantic conciliatory indications. One morning the people rose to read a message from the most powerful of all voices which fell like grateful rain upon the parched earth. It was from one who had endeared himself to our people and had never failed to show his affection for us. It read thus, "I hope and believe that a peaceful solution will be found. (Signed) Albert Edward, Prince of Wales." The excited masses saw not only their friend, but Her Majesty, always a favorite, behind that message; the occupant of the throne, who with her own hand was reported to have modified a message to Washington during the Trent crisis. The Prince's prediction was soon verified, and peaceful arbitration triumphed, never again to be jeopardized. Hereafter no government on either side of the Atlantic would dare refuse peaceful settlement of any dispute between the old and the new homes of our race. If any government did, the people would not be slow to repeat the needed lesson that we of our race have government of the people, for the people, and by the people, and governments are only agents.

If the original message of the peacemaker can be found, it should be as carefully guarded as the Magna Charta, as being King Edward's first claim to the proudest of all his titles, a triumph which adds another to the many peaceful glories of the old home which has abolished private war between men, the duel; has established government by the people at home, and gives to all her colonies similar rights, which, in the words of Burke, is to make her venerated in after days.

We, the opponents of war, not only as being ruinously expensive, but as being criminally wrong, involving as it does the killing of our fellow-men, cannot be denied this, the greatest triumph of peace in our day, the banishment of war between members of our race. What is to be the next victory? For victories there are to be. You have heard the words of our able and zealous President, and of his marvelous predecessor, and of our Secretary of State, which incite to efforts for an extension of the area of peace beyond our race. Let

---

3. In the Venezuelan dispute.

us hope that there will arise in the old home successors to the great peacemaker, and that rulers in other lands may yet appear to follow his example. The rulers of the republic seem at present to be pioneers; we look to you of the army of peace here to emit no doubtful sound. It is not the enormous cost of war which will ever cause its abolition, it is its savagery that condemns it to extinction as true manhood develops.

Be of good cheer, Brothers, the good work goes steadily forward; nothing can prevent its triumph. We are apparently on the eve of a decided step forward, soon the International Judicial Court is to appear and the step from that to a League of Peace follows.

Civilized nations, as we have seen, have abolished many savage customs in obedience to the law that carries man ever upward and onward toward perfection. One savage custom still mars his existence and vetoes his claim to civilization, the killing of each other as a mode of settling their disputes. Only wild beasts are excusable for doing that, in this the twentieth century of the Christian era.

Part VI

Coda: The Undoing of the Self-Made Pacifist

Andrew Carnegie strongly advocated direct, face-to-face meetings between opposing parties in any dispute as the best means of achieving conflict resolution. He attributed much of what he regarded as his success in labor relations to his willingness to meet with his workers to discuss their grievances, and to the end of his life he clung to the belief that if only he had been on the scene in that fateful summer of 1892, the tragedy at Homestead would never have occurred.

This concept of the efficacy of personal contact was an essential component of his program for achieving harmonious relations among nations. In his article on "International Arbitration" (see #25), Carnegie made reference to the fact that "the leaders of nations at their respective capitals are strangers to each other, and communicate only through their ambassadors; they do not trust each other; . . . if the makers of treaties knew and trusted each other war would soon become obsolete."

Anticipating by half a century and more the great summit meetings which every American president has felt obliged to attend with his Soviet counterpart since Eisenhower met with Khrushchev in Geneva in 1955, Carnegie as early as 1908 was busily engaged in making summitry a reality. When he heard that Theodore Roosevelt planned to spend a year in Africa hunting big game as soon as he left the White House in 1909, Carnegie saw his opportunity. Roosevelt's grand safari would be financed by Carnegie and a few other men of wealth if the ex-president in turn, after bagging lions and rhinoceri in pursuit of the kill, would extend his travels to Europe in pursuit of peace. Roosevelt accepted the terms offered. He agreed to go to Berlin in the spring of 1910 to talk peace and naval disarmament with the kaiser and then conclude his travels with a visit to England to discuss the same subjects with the British cabinet.

This plan, to be sure, was not the great summit that Carnegie would have liked—a meeting in which the incumbent president of the United States, the British and French prime ministers, and especially the German kaiser would sit down together at the conference table. As an ex-president, Roosevelt would have no official status and would meet separately with the chief executives of the two great naval rivals, Britain and Germany, but under the circumstances, it was the best that could be arranged.

Roosevelt manfully carried out his end of the bargain. In attending the Nobel Peace Prize ceremony in Christiana, Norway, early in May 1910, he gave a splendid address on the necessity for a League of Peace in which he adhered closely to the script furnished him by Carnegie and Elihu Root. Following the ceremony, Roosevelt was scheduled to meet the kaiser in Potsdam and then on 20 May go on to the grand finale with the British cabinet at Wrest Park, outside London.

On 6 May, while Roosevelt was still in Norway, King Edward VII suddenly died of a heart attack. The nations of Europe immediately went into official mourning and all state affairs from London to St. Petersburg were cancelled. There would be no Wrest Park conference.

Roosevelt did meet briefly with the kaiser in Berlin, and, as it turned out, the kaiser would be traveling to London as well, but not to attend a summit meeting on peace—only to ride in King Edward's funeral procession. It was as if the gods of war were giving warning of what lay ahead.

Frustrated in this effort at international summitry but undaunted in his quest for peace, Carnegie in the same year 1910 established the Carnegie Endowment for International Peace, his most munificent gifts to the cause of peace. Four years later, largely at the insistence of his wife, he created the Church Peace Union, his last gesture in large-scale philanthropy for peace.

It was a cruel historical irony that Europe should seem so beautifully peaceful in the early summer of 1914. Nature itself contributed to this spirit of well-being, for throughout northern Europe from Scandinavia to Scotland there were long days of bright sunshine and short, white nights of gentle warmth. True, there were some dark

The Undoing of the Self-Made Pacifist 319

clouds on the international scene — the crown prince of Austria-Hungary was assassinated by a Serbian zealot in June, and the Irish patriots were making ominous sounds of rebellion against British rule; but Ireland and the Balkans, like the poor, Europe had with it always. Sarajevo was far away and there seemed little cause for concern.

Carnegie had promised Louise that this summer he would certainly finish the writing of his autobiography. The Carnegies were in their retreat at Aultnagar in early August 1914 and Carnegie was just finishing what was not intended but proved to be the last chapter of his memoirs. In this account of his meeting with the German emperor in 1907 and again in 1912, Carnegie was at his rollicking best in prose style. He had long considered Kaiser Wilhelm to be the key figure in securing peace among the great powers. He now recalled that in the 1912 meeting he had hailed the kaiser with the words, "And in this noblest of all missions you are our chief ally." Carnegie had just finished writing those words when the guns of August began to boom. Carnegie was forced to add a postscript to this chapter that he never imagined he would have to write: "[W]hat a change! Men slaying each other like wild beasts!" But even then Carnegie, ever the optimist, must also write, "I dare not relinquish all hope." Roosevelt had failed in his European tour, Taft had failed in getting his arbitration treaties through the Senate, the kaiser had ended his twenty-seven year "reign of peace" with a bang as his powerful Wehrmacht swept through neutral Belgium on its way to conquer Paris, but Carnegie already had found a new Hero of Peace in Woodrow Wilson: "Nothing is impossible to genius! Watch President Wilson!" And on that hopeful note written in a moment of deep anguish, as the editor of Carnegie's memoirs would later note, "Here the manuscript ends abruptly."

And so, in reality, did Carnegie's dream of "ever onward and upward to perfection." Louise Carnegie wrote in a preface to her husband's autobiography published one year after his death: "Optimist as he always was and tried to be, even in the failure of his hopes, the world disaster was too much. His heart was broken."

The Carnegies managed to get out of Britain in mid September. Andrew would never return to his beloved Skibo. On 11 August 1919, eleven months after the Great War had ended, Carnegie died at his newly acquired summer home in Lenox, Massachusetts. Three months after his death, the United States Senate, as it had done with President Taft's arbitration treaties, voted down "Mr. Wilson's Treaty," which had incorporated Wilson's — and Carnegie's — best hope for world peace, the League of Nations. Carnegie's last great hero had also failed. Carnegie was mercifully spared the knowledge of this, his final defeat as peacemaker.

26
Meeting the German Emperor

Chapter 29 of the Autobiography of Andrew Carnegie, *ed. John Van Dyke (Boston: Houghton Mifflin, 1920).*

My first Rectorial Address to the students of St. Andrews University attracted the attention of the German Emperor, who sent word to me in New York by Herr Ballin that he had read every word of it. He also sent me by him a copy of his address upon his eldest son's consecration. Invitations to meet him followed; but it was not until June, 1907, that I could leave, owing to other engagements. Mrs. Carnegie and I went to Kiel. Mr. Tower, our American Ambassador to Germany, and Mrs. Tower met us there and were very kind in their attentions. Through them we met many of the distinguished public men during our three days' stay there.

The first morning, Mr. Tower took me to register on the Emperor's yacht. I had no expectation of seeing the Emperor, but he happened to come on deck, and seeing Mr. Tower he asked what had brought him on the yacht so early. Mr. Tower explained he had brought me over to register, and that Mr. Carnegie was on board. He asked:

"Why not present him now? I wish to see him."

I was talking to the admirals who were assembling for a conference, and did not see Mr. Tower and the Emperor approaching from behind. A touch on my shoulder and I turned around.

"Mr. Carnegie, the Emperor."

It was a moment before I realized that the Emperor was before me. I raised both hands and exclaimed:

"This has happened just as I could have wished, with no ceremony, and the Man of Destiny dropped from the clouds."

Then I continued: "Your Majesty, I have traveled two nights to accept your generous invitation, and never did so before to meet a crowned head."

Then the Emperor, smiling—and such a captivating smile:

"Oh! yes, yes, I have read your books. You do not like kings."

"No, Your Majesty, I do not like kings, but I do like a man behind a king when I find him."

"Ah! there is one king you like, I know, a Scottish king, Robert the Bruce. He was my hero in my youth. I was brought up on him."

"Yes, Your Majesty, so was I, and he lies buried in Dunfermline Abbey, in my native town. When a boy, I used to walk often around the towering square monument on the Abbey—one word on each block in big stone letters 'King Robert the Bruce'—with all the fervor of a Catholic counting his beads. But Bruce was much more than a king, Your Majesty, he was the leader of his people. And not the first; Wallace the man of the people comes first. Your Majesty, I now own King Malcolm's tower in Dunfermline[1]—he from whom you derive your precious heritage of Scottish blood. Perhaps you know the fine old ballad, 'Sir Patrick Spens.'

> The King sits in Dunfermline tower
> Drinking the bluid red wine.

I should like to escort you some day to the tower of your Scottish ancestor, that you may do homage to his memory." He exclaimed:

"That would be very fine. The Scotch are much quicker and cleverer than the Germans. The Germans are too slow."

"Your Majesty, where anything Scotch is concerned, I must decline to accept you as an impartial judge."

He laughed and waved adieu, calling out:

"You are to dine with me this evening"—and excusing himself went to greet the arriving admirals.

About sixty were present at the dinner and we had a pleasant time, indeed. His Majesty, opposite whom I sat, was good enough to raise his glass and invite me to drink with him. After he had done so with Mr. Tower, our Ambassador, who sat at his right, he asked across the table—heard by those near—whether I had told Prince von Bülow, next whom I sat, that his (the Emperor's) hero, Bruce, rested in my native town of Dunfermline, and his ancestor's tower in Pittencrieff Glen, was in my possession.

---

1. In the deed of trust conveying Pittencrieff Park and Glen to Dunfermline an unspecified reservation of property was made. The "with certain exceptions" related to King Malcolm's Tower. For reasons best known to himself Mr. Carnegie retained the ownership of this relic of the past.

"No," I replied: "with Your Majesty I am led into such frivolities, but my intercourse with your Lord High Chancellor, I assure you, will always be of a serious import."

We dined with Mrs. Goelet upon her yacht, one evening, and His Majesty being present, I told him President Roosevelt had said recently to me that he wished custom permitted him to leave the country so he could run over and see him (the Emperor). He thought a substantial talk would result in something good being accomplished. I believed that also. The Emperor agreed and said he wished greatly to see him and hoped he would some day come to Germany. I suggested that he (the Emperor) was free from constitutional barriers and could sail over and see the President.

"Ah, but my country needs me here! How can I leave?"

I replied:

"Before leaving home one year, when I went to our mills to bid the officials good-bye and expressed regret at leaving them all hard at work, sweltering in the hot sun, but that I found I had now every year to rest and yet no matter how tired I might be one half-hour on the bow of the steamer, cutting the Atlantic waves, gave me perfect relief, my clever manager, Captain Jones, retorted: 'And, oh, Lord! think of the relief we all get.' It might be the same with your people, Your Majesty."

He laughed heartily over and over again. It opened a new train of thought. He repeated his desire to meet President Roosevelt, and I said:

"Well, Your Majesty, when you two do get together, I think I shall have to be with you. You and he, I fear, might get into mischief."

He laughed and said:

"Oh, I see! You wish to drive us together. Well, I agree if you make Roosevelt first horse, I shall follow."

"Ah, no, Your Majesty, I know horseflesh better than to attempt to drive two such gay colts tandem. You never get proper purchase on the first horse. I must yoke you both in the shafts, neck and neck, so I can hold you in."

I never met a man who enjoyed stories more keenly than the Emperor. He is fine company, and I believe an earnest man, anxious for the peace and progress of the world. Suffice it to say he insists that he is, and always had been, for peace. [1907.] He cherishes the fact that he has reigned for twenty-four years and has never shed human blood. He considers that the German navy is too small to affect the British and was never intended to be a rival. Nevertheless, it is in my opinion very unwise, because unnecessary, to enlarge it. Prince von Bülow holds these sentiments and I believe the peace of the world has little to fear from Germany. Her interests are all favorable to peace, industrial development being her aim; and in this desirable field she is certainly making great strides.

I sent the Emperor by his Ambassador, Baron von Sternberg, the book, *The Roosevelt Policy*,[2] to which I had written an introduction that pleased the President, and I rejoice in having received from him a fine bronze of himself with a valued letter. He is not only an Emperor, but something much higher — a man anxious to improve existing conditions, untiring in his efforts to promote temperance, prevent dueling, and, I believe, to secure International Peace.

I have for some time been haunted with the feeling that the Emperor was indeed a Man of Destiny. My interviews with him have strengthened that feeling. I have great hopes of him in the future doing something really great and good. He may yet have a part to play that will give him a place among the immortals. He has ruled Germany in peace for twenty-seven years, but something beyond even this record is due from one who has the power to establish peace among civilized nations through positive action. Maintaining peace in his own land is not sufficient from one whose invitation to other leading civilized nations to combine and establish arbitration of all international disputes would be gladly responded to. Whether he is to pass into history as only the preserver of internal peace at home or is to rise to his appointed mission as the Apostle of Peace among leading civilized nations, the future has still to reveal.

The year before last (1912) I stood before him in the grand palace in Berlin and presented the American address of congratulation upon his peaceful reign of twenty-five years, his hand unstained by human blood. As I approached to hand to him the casket containing the address, he recognized me and with outstretched arms, exclaimed:

"Carnegie, twenty-five years of peace, and we hope for many more."

I could not help responding:

"And in this noblest of all missions you are our chief ally."

He had hitherto sat silent and motionless, taking the successive addresses from one officer and handing them to another to be placed upon the table. The chief subject under discussion had been World Peace, which he could

---

2. *The Roosevelt Policy: Speeches, Letters and State Papers Relating to Corporate Wealth and Closely Allied Topics* (New York, 1908).

have, and in my opinion, would have secured, had he not been surrounded by the military caste which inevitably gathers about one born to the throne— a caste which usually becomes as permanent as the potentate himself, and which has so far in Germany proved its power of control whenever the war issue has been presented. Until militarism is subordinated, there can be no World Peace.

. . . .

As I read this today [1914], what a change! The world convulsed by war as never before! Men slaying each other like wild beasts! I dare not relinquish all hope. In recent days I see another ruler coming forward upon the world stage, who may prove himself the immortal one. The man who vindicated his country's honor in the Panama Canal toll dispute is now President. He has the indomitable will of genius, and true hope which we are told, "Kings it makes gods, and meaner creatures kings." Nothing is impossible to genius! Watch President Wilson! He has Scotch blood in his veins.

[Here the manuscript ends abruptly.]

Pittsburgh Series in Social and Labor History
Maurine Weiner Greenwald, Editor

And the Wolf Finally Came: The Decline of the American Steel Industry
John P. Hoerr

The Battle for Homestead, 1880–1892: Politics, Culture, and Steel
Paul Krause

City at the Point: Essays on the Social History of Pittsburgh
Samuel P. Hays, Editor

The Correspondence of Mother Jones
Edward M. Steel, Editor

Distribution of Wealth and Income in the United States in 1798
Lee Soltow

Don't Call Me Boss: David L. Lawrence, Pittsburgh's Renaissance Mayor
Michael P. Weber

The Inside History of the Carnegie Steel Company
James Howard Bridge

The Shadow of the Mills: Working-Class Families in Pittsburgh, 1870–1907
S. J. Kleinberg

The Speeches and Writings of Mother Jones
Edward M. Steel, Editor

The Steel Workers
John A. Fitch

Trade Unions and the New Industrialisation of the Third World
Roger Southall, Editor

The Transformation of Western Pennsylvania, 1770–1880
R. Eugene Harper

What's a Coal Miner to Do? The Mechanization of Coal Mining
Keith Dix

Women and the Trades
Elizabeth Beardsley Butler

Other titles in the series

The Emergence of a UAW Local, 1936–1939: A Study in Class and Culture
Peter Friedlander

Homestead: The Households of a Mill Town
Margaret F. Byington

The Homestead Strike of 1892
Arthur G. Burgoyne

Steelton: Immigration and Industrialization, 1870–1940
John Bodnar

Out of This Furnace
Thomas Bell

Steelmasters and Labor Reform, 1886–1923
Gerald G. Eggert

Steve Nelson, American Radical
Steve Nelson, James R. Barrett, and Rob Ruck

Working-Class Life: The "American Standard" in Comparative Perspective, 1899–1913
Peter R. Shergold

www.ingramcontent.com/pod-product-compliance
Lightning Source LLC
Chambersburg PA
CBHW031232290426
44109CB00012B/263